One People?
Tradition, Modernity, and Jewish Unity

MAGGID

THE RABBI SACKS LEGACY

Jonathan Sacks

ONE PEOPLE?

TRADITION, MODERNITY, AND JEWISH UNITY

The Rabbi Sacks Legacy
Maggid Books

One People?
Tradition, Modernity, and Jewish Unity

First edition, 1993
by the Littman Library of Jewish Civilization

First Maggid Books edition, 2024

Maggid Books
An imprint of Koren Publishers Jerusalem Ltd.

POB 8531, New Milford, CT 06776-8531, USA
& POB 4044, Jerusalem 9104001, Israel
www.korenpub.com

The publication of this book was made possible
through the generous support of *The Jewish Book Trust*.

ISBN 978-1-59264-626-5, *paperback*

Printed and bound in the United States

Mommy, for you, each and every Jewish person is holy.
You embrace people from all backgrounds unconditionally.
You are there for people, especially your family, when times
are tough. You are a role model for living a life with a deep
and steadfast commitment to Chesed, Torah, and Halacha.
Wishing you good health, happiness, Arichut Yamim,
Nachat, and Kol Tuv.

Daddy, a"h, you welcomed our extended family and friends
as if they were your own. You wanted nothing more
than to give to those around you and make them happy.
Others' joy was yours.
יְהִי זִכְרוֹ בָּרוּךְ

Thank you both for raising me in a home with these values.
We strive to follow in your footsteps of creating a home
and raising our children with a focus on
תּוֹרָה, עֲבוֹדָה וּגְמִילוּת חֲסָדִים

Love,
Becky and Avi Katz and Family

Author's Original Dedication

For Elaine

אֵשֶׁת־חַיִל מִי יִמְצָא וְרָחֹק מִפְּנִינִים מִכְרָהּ:
בָּטַח בָּהּ לֵב בַּעְלָהּ וְשָׁלָל לֹא יֶחְסָר:
גְּמָלַתְהוּ טוֹב וְלֹא־רָע כֹּל יְמֵי חַיֶּיהָ:

תְּנוּ־לָהּ מִפְּרִי יָדֶיהָ וִיהַלְלוּהָ בַשְּׁעָרִים מַעֲשֶׂיהָ:

THE RABBI SACKS LEGACY

The Rabbi Sacks Legacy perpetuates the timeless and universal wisdom of Rabbi Lord Jonathan Sacks as a teacher of Torah, a leader of leaders and a moral voice.

Explore the digital archive, containing much of Rabbi Sacks' writings, broadcasts and speeches, or support the Legacy's work, at www.rabbisacks.org, and follow The Rabbi Sacks Legacy on social media @RabbiSacks.

Contents

Publisher's Preface ....*xi*

Preface... *xiii*

Chapter 1. The Crisis of Contemporary Jewish Thought 1

Chapter 2. The Birth of the Adjectival Jew.....................21

Chapter 3. Orthodoxy, History, and Culture 51

Chapter 4. Orthodoxy and Jewish Peoplehood....................75

Chapter 5. Tradition and Diversity 101

Chapter 6. Inclusivism..133

Chapter 7. A Collision of Consciousness......................161

Chapter 8. Schism?...193

Chapter 9. The Future of a People 225

Bibliography 263

Index 283

About the Author 299

Publisher's Preface

Rabbi Lord Jonathan Sacks *zt"l* possessed and shared profound learning, moral depth, and sheer eloquence, expressed in his many published works. These made him a leading religious figure not only within contemporary Judaism but among people of all faiths (or none). Each meeting and conversation became a *shiur*, a lesson in how to look at the world and how to experience our relationship with the Creator.

It is a great privilege for us, paraphrasing the talmudic adage, "to return the crown to its former glory" by presenting these new editions of Rabbi Sacks' earliest publications. The earlier volumes were written by Rabbi Sacks as a professor of philosophy, as a thinker, rabbinic leader, and Principal of Jews' College, and are truly masterworks of exposition of contemporary Jewish thought. The later volumes represent Rabbi Sacks' thinking as he became Chief Rabbi, set out his perception of the challenges facing his community of Anglo-Jewry at that time, and articulated his vision for the path ahead. All of these works certainly stand on their own merit today and are as relevant now as they were when first written.

We wish to take this opportunity to express our appreciation to Becky and Avi Katz for their critical support of and partnership in this project. Becky and Avi are longtime communal leaders and supporters of Jewish education in North America and Israel, and on behalf of all of us at Koren, together with those who will cherish this new opportunity to be inspired by Rabbi Sacks' writings, thank you.

We wish to add our thanks to our colleagues at Koren who have worked on this series: Ita Olesker, Tani Bayer, Tomi Mager, Aryeh Grossman, and Rabbi Reuven Ziegler. The proofreading team included Debbie Ismailoff, Ruth Pepperman, Esther Shafier, and Nechama Unterman, and Marc Sherman updated the indexes of the volumes. We extend deep gratitude to our friends at The Rabbi Sacks Legacy for their continued partnership, together with Lady Elaine Sacks and the rest of the Sacks family for their continued support for our work.

May Rabbi Sacks' memory and Torah continue to be a blessing for future generations.

Matthew Miller
Koren Jerusalem

Preface

This book is about one of the most tantalizing and elusive ideas in contemporary Jewish thought: Jewish unity. The phrase is deceptively simple. It is easier to invoke than to understand, and is beset by irony. The idea that Jews are "one people" has emerged as a, perhaps the, dominant motif of post-Holocaust Jewish reflection. It is a constant presence in the public rhetoric of contemporary Jewry. It evokes passion and conviction, but seldom clarity. Set against the reality it seeks to describe, it is an aspiration, not an achievement; a myth rather than a reality. Not since the first and second centuries CE have Jews been less united. Rarely has it been harder to state what constitutes them as "one people." That, in itself, should not surprise us, because demands for unity surface only at times of great internal conflict. But it should at least suggest this: that the obstacles that stand in the way of its realization deserve the most careful analysis.

Words have hypnotic power. The existence of a concept leads us to believe that there is a reality that corresponds to it. Jewish unity exists as an *idea*. Why then should it not exist as a *fact*? Unity – at least in the minimalist sense of being able to live together, respect one another's integrity, and therefore act collectively towards shared objectives – tends to seem at the time, and all the more so in retrospect, to be so eminently achievable that we stand aghast at the failure of individuals to do just that. But to think this way is to fail to grasp the deep structures of division that lead human beings to conceive their destinies in incompatible ways. To believe, in particular, that Jewish unity is a simple idea in an age of unprecedented fragmentation is to have yielded to myth. Contrary to the conventional wisdom of a secular age, I do not believe that Jewish faith is the acceptance of myth. It is the constant battle *against* myth in the name of religiously conceived possibility. Faith does not ask us to see the world other than as it is. It does, however, ask us to imagine a world that *could be,* and to work, without illusions, for its realization. Intellectual honesty is a precondition of the religious life.

The reason why Jewish unity has come to seem so urgent and self-evident while at the same time so difficult to achieve is explored in detail in this book. To put it at its simplest, from the late eighteenth century onward, European emancipation presented Jewry with its most serious crisis of definition since the birth of rabbinic Judaism. Traditional Jewish belief and the mode of life it dictated were challenged at the most fundamental levels intellectually, socially, and politically. The nineteenth century was, for European Jewry, a time of momentous upheaval, against the backdrop of growing and racial antisemitism and vast Jewish migrations, mainly from the East to the West. A succession of revolutionary new interpretations of Jewish existence emerged, some predicating Jewish identity on a reformed version of Judaism as a religion, others on political autonomy, others again on culture and ethnicity, yet others on nationalism and a Zion reborn.

What separates contemporary Jewry from that age are the two framing events of the present century, the Holocaust and the birth of the State of Israel. The one represented the tragic end of European Jewry and the once bright hopes of emancipation. The other inaugurated the return of Jewry to the history of politics and power after an absence of almost two thousand years. No one could doubt that they were, respectively, the end of one chapter and the beginning of another in the long chronicles of the covenantal people. But, to a degree that is quite striking, Jews remain heirs to the nineteenth century. The disintegration that took place then still haunts Jewish existence today. The ideological battle-lines are the same. The same questions are asked and receive the same conflicting answers. Much has changed in the Jewish world, but our habits of thinking have not. The stage of world Jewry has moved from Central and Eastern Europe to Israel and America. What was, in the nineteenth century, a set of aspirations has today become a series of achievements: freedom, equality, and integration in the diaspora, and Jewish sovereignty in the land of Israel. But the fundamental divisions that were born in another age, another place, remain, though they are by now damaging and dysfunctional.

Recent history – the Holocaust, and the sense of involvement that most Jews throughout the world feel in the fate of Israel – has convinced us that the Jewish destiny is indivisible. We are implicated each in the fate of one another. That is the substantive content of our current sense of unity. But it is a unity imposed, as it were, from outside. Neither antisemitism nor anti-Zionism, we believe, makes distinctions between Jews. Hence our collective vigilance, activity, and concern. But from within, in terms of its own self-understanding, the Jewish people evinces no answering solidarity. External crisis unites Jews; internal belief divides. But that cannot be the basis of an enduring sense of peoplehood. Whether we understand Jewish existence as a religious or a secular phenomenon, if unity is to be a value it cannot be one that is sustained by the hostility of others alone. For a people as for an individual, authenticity requires that the terms of identity proceed from within, not from outside.

There are three primary fault-lines along which the Jewish people currently threatens to split apart: between secular and religious Jews, between Orthodoxy and liberal Judaisms, and between Israel and the diaspora. At times one, at times another, seems to be the most susceptible to seismic eruptions. In this book I have concentrated on one axis only, the religious divisions within Judaism, within Orthodoxy itself and between Orthodoxy and religious liberalism. That is not to say that I regard the others as of lesser importance; merely that I preferred to treat one subject in depth rather than several superficially.

But the analysis, if correct, has wider implications. For at its heart is what I have called a *collision of consciousness* between traditional and modern ways of understanding. The mutual incomprehensions to which this gives rise are not limited to this context. They are duplicated elsewhere. If we can understand this set of conflicts, I suspect we will better understand others as well, and not only within Jewry. The problem I explore is in its way a paradigm of what happens when any traditional religious culture enters the atmosphere of secular modernity and begins to fragment. The particular discovery to which the analysis leads is that both tradition and modernity have adequate ways of resolving conflict, but *that they systematically exclude one another.* This is the conceptual impasse that makes the very pursuit of unity inherently divisive. The more closely we pursue it, the further away it recedes. Finding a way out of this labyrinth is a primary task of Jewish thought in our time, and I have suggested ways in which it might be done.

Two points should be made clear at the outset if the book is not to be misunderstood. The first is that though the vantage-point from which I write is that of Orthodoxy, the argument of the book in no way depends on that fact. In the past two decades Orthodoxy has risen to great prominence within most Jewish communities throughout the world, most strikingly within Israel and the United States, two communities where it had previously seemed a marginal presence destined for eclipse. In part this has been due to demographic factors, in part to the clarity of Orthodoxy's beliefs and the high levels of commitment it evokes from its adherents.

Its influence has grown rapidly and is certain to increase yet further.

No analysis of the Jewish future can ignore it. Yet most do just that. Surveys of contemporary Jewry tend in the main to dismiss Orthodoxy in a throw-away sentence to the effect that it constitutes an exception to the trends under review, but one that affects only an insignificant minority of Jews. No one writing in Britain – where Orthodoxy is still the affiliation of three-quarters of the identifying Jewish community – could make that mistake. But no one writing elsewhere should make it either. A reading of the history of the Jews at times of crisis – the Babylonian exile, the Maccabean revolt, the destruction of the Second Temple, fifteenth-century Spain – suggests that the pattern of Jewry's continuity is determined at such moments by its most intensely religious members. I have devoted much of my analysis to Orthodoxy not because that is my own commitment, but quite simply because an honest confrontation

with the facts demands it. It is within Orthodoxy and between Orthodoxy and others that the clash of tradition and modernity – the *leitmotiv*
of modern Jewish life – is most starkly revealed.

At the same time, I have tried to do justice to non-Orthodox perspectives. This is not a polemical work. It is an honest attempt to step
back and view with detachment the processes that have shaped Jewish
responses to modernity. Jewish unity is a cause that is not advanced by
the advocacy of one point of view over another. It demands the difficult
but not impossible exercise of thinking *non-adjectivally* as a Jew: not as a
member of this or that group, but as a member of an indivisible people.
Since this is not often done, it is likely to be misunderstood. In writing
about Liberal, Reform, Conservative, and Reconstructionist Judaisms
I have tried to come to terms with positions that are fundamentally not
my own. If I have done them an injustice, I would accept that as a legitimate critique of my case.

Which brings me to the second point. For the most part I have
focused on American Reform rather than its British counterpart. The
reason is simple. The lines of the argument between Orthodoxy and
religious liberalism in the twentieth century have been determined in
America, much as they were in the nineteenth century in Germany. There
were and are other Jewries elsewhere where the conflict between tradition and modernity took quite different forms. But just as no one could
do justice to Jewish thought a century ago without referring to German
thinkers, so no one can do so today without reference to America. The
issues in Israel are different, and are of less relevance to the diaspora situation. Those in Britain are different again, but are subsumed within the
American case as the lesser problem is included in the greater.

British Reform is both smaller and more traditional than its
trans-Atlantic namesake. If anything, it is closer to American Conservative Judaism than to American Reform. It has rejected patrilineality as a
determinant of Jewish status. It insists on *milah* (circumcision), *tevilah*
(ritual immersion), and observance of at least some of the commandments as a precondition of conversion. It does not regard civil divorce
as adequate for the termination of a Jewish marriage. It gives less weight
to individual autonomy and more to the halakhic tradition than American Reform theologians would allow. The closest British counterpart to

American Reform is Liberal Judaism. These differences do not affect the substance of the argument, but it is important to spell them out.

I wrote this book in the closing months of 1988. At that time, the climate of Israeli politics seemed to herald a massive split within Jewry. The issue that then came to the fore was "Who is a Jew?" This single question – specifically, what constituted a valid conversion for the purposes of Israel's Law of Return – exposed some of the most sensitive tensions between Israel and the diaspora and between Orthodoxy and others. The book addresses that question only obliquely, because I believed then and still do that it is itself a symptom, not a cause, of the underlying problem, and that more fundamental analysis is necessary. For a variety of reasons, four years passed before I was able to make the final corrections before sending the book to the printers. But though that particular controversy has momentarily subsided, the issues discussed in the following pages are undiminished in their explosive potential and are likely to remain so for many years to come.

Confirmation of this belief came in the form of a recent book whose diagnosis neatly complemented my own: David Vital's *The Future of the Jews* (Harvard University Press, 1990). Our points of departure and working assumptions could not have been more different. Vital is a historian of Zionism, and a scholar who understands contemporary Jewry in secular and political terms. His concern in the book is the relationship between Israel and the diaspora. None the less, working independently along separate axes and from quite different intellectual perspectives, we had arrived at the same conclusion. "Today," he writes, "at the end of the unspeakable twentieth century, it is not too much to say that the survival of Jewry as a discrete people, its various branches bound to each other by common ties of culture, responsibility and loyalty, is entirely in doubt." The Jewish world "is now coming apart" and "the old unity of Israel...lies shattered today, almost beyond repair."

The difference between us is simply this: that where Vital's book ends, mine begins. Unlike him, I am not a pessimist. Pessimism is a prerogative denied to a religious believer, at least within Judaism. I believe that to make the effort to understand our conflicts is to take the first step to their resolution. More than this, I believe with the biblical prophets, the rabbinic sages, and the medieval philosophers that Jewish unity is in the end an irreducibly religious concept. There is no coherent secular equivalent. Indeed it is precisely the secularization of Jewish life that has made unity so problematic an idea. Nor do I believe that the continued secularization of Jewry is irreversible and inevitable. That thesis belongs to the now discredited sociological wisdom of the pre-1960s. Jewish unity, precisely because it is a religious idea, is a perennial possibility, however much history suggests otherwise. Too much of the Jewish story has been a sustained defiance of history for the Jewish people now to become its victims. The Torah which once shaped us into "one people" still and with undiminished force issues that challenge. To that vision this book is dedicated.

Many people helped me with the final drafting of the text, and to them I owe my thanks. They were drawn from the entire range of the religious spectrum, and what most heartened me was that each commented favourably on the work, including those whose positions were furthest from my own. In particular I would like to thank Professor J. David Bleich, Professor Judith Bleich, Dayan Chanokh Ehrentreu, Judge Israel Finestein, and the editors of the Littman Library for their detailed comments, and Lord Jakobovits and Rabbi Nachum Rabinovitch for their encouragement.

I cannot, though, avoid a note of profound sadness that three of the people to whom the work owes its genesis have since died: Dr. David Goldstein and Dr. Vivian Lipman, two editors of the Littman Library, and Mr. Louis Littman, its founder and benefactor. David and Vivian graced Anglo-Jewry by their scholarship, and Louis by his sustained and sustaining support. These were men who in their lives earned a special kind of immortality, and Jewry is bereaved by their loss. Each held the belief that scholarship has the power to bring together minds that would otherwise be divided, and I offer this book as my personal tribute to their memory.

J. S.
London
1992

Chapter 1

The Crisis of Contemporary Jewish Thought

Alasdair MacIntyre begins his revolutionary diagnosis of contemporary moral theory, *After Virtue*,[1] with a chilling parable. Imagine, he says, that there is a widespread revolution against science. There is a series of ecological disasters. Science and technology are blamed. There is public panic. There are riots. Laboratories are burned down. A new political party comes to power on a wave of anti-scientific feeling and eliminates all science teaching and scientific activity. A century later, the mood subsides. People begin to try to reconstruct what was destroyed. But all they have is fragments of what was once a coherent scientific culture: odd pages from old books, scientific instruments whose use has been forgotten, bits and pieces of information about theories and experiments without the background knowledge of their context.

---

1. Alasdair MacIntyre, *After Virtue: A Study in Moral Theory* (London: Duckworth, 1981).

1

These pieces are reassembled into a discipline called science. Its terminology and some of its practices resemble science. But the systematic corpus of beliefs which once underlay them has gone. There would be no unitary conception of what science was about, what its practices were for, or what its key terms signified. The illusion would persist that science had been recovered; but it would have been lost, and there would be no way of discovering that it had been lost.

What is conjectured in this parable is, MacIntyre argues, what has actually happened to moral thinking. The Enlightenment and the social processes which accompanied it succeeded in destroying the traditions to which the key terms of morality belonged and within which they had lucidity and coherence. The words survived – good, right, duty, obligation, virtue – but were now severed from the context which gave them sense. For they had belonged to coherent social orders in which people were shaped by a collective vision, in which there were social roles not chosen but given by birth and tradition, and in which there was a narrative continuity between generations and within individual lives. Those socially given shared meanings have now gone, to be replaced by a Kantian conception of morality as autonomous choice or a Nietzschean world constructed by individual will. The language of morality survives, but without the systematic corpus of beliefs which underlay them. "What we possess," says MacIntyre, "are the fragments of a conceptual scheme, parts of which now lack those contexts from which their significance derived. We possess indeed simulacra of morality, we continue to use many of the key expressions. But we have – very largely, if not entirely – lost our comprehension, both theoretical and practical, of morality."[2]

For morality, read Judaism, and we have before us a precise description of the problem confronting contemporary Jewish thought. The momentous dislocations of modernity – social, intellectual, and geographical – have proved in retrospect and were indeed recognized at the time to be as disruptive of Jewish continuity as the series of catastrophes that forced rabbinic Judaism into being: the cessation of prophecy, the collapse of national autonomy, the destruction of the Second Temple,

---

2. Ibid., 2.

the end of the sacrificial system, the loss of priesthood, the termination of collective national history, and the beginning of a long, seemingly open-ended exile; in short, the "hiding of the face" of God.

The processes that have shaken Jewry from the late eighteenth to the late twentieth centuries have been no less revolutionary: emancipation, the belated confrontation with enlightenment, acculturation, assimilation, the metamorphosis of religious anti-Judaism into racial antisemitism, the transformation of Jewish existence into "the Jewish problem," and the attendant crises of Jewish self-definition. From these traumas emerged a bewildering variety of ideologies: religious reform, from Conservative to Liberal to Reconstructionist; Zionism in its various constructions, secular, religious, utopian, pragmatic, restorative, or revolutionary, each with its own inner diversity of shadings; secular Jewish identities, intellectually, culturally, politically, or ethnically conceived; and the various Jewish exorcisms of Judaism, neo-Spinozist, Marxist, or Freudian.

It is neither necessary nor appropriate to wax nostalgic about the premodern Jewish past, with its partially enclosed culture, autonomous community governance, its ghettos and *Gemeinschaft*. None the less, and without yearning for *temps perdu*, we recognize to our disquiet that questions that have become unanswerable now were unaskable then. Who and what is a Jew? What is Torah? What is *galut* (exile), and what is the Jewish hope that lies beyond exile? The substantive daily content, metaphysical significance, and historical context of a Jewish life were bedrock data. They were given, not chosen. They were part of the world into which one was born. They carried meanings which every social interaction, whether with Jews or non-Jews, tended to confirm. There may have been fierce argument over the details of Jewish life but not over the framing fundamentals. Within this context the language of Judaism was coherent, consistent, and designated a palpable objective reality.

The language has survived but its context has not. The key words remain – terms such as *Torah, mitzvah* (commandment), *galut* (exile), *ge'ulah* (redemption), *am Yisrael* (the people of Israel), *eretz Yisrael* (the land of Israel). But the meanings attached to them differ systematically from group to group within the Jewish world. What is a *mitzvah*? Is it an act performed in response to the divine command? Or from loyalty to historical tradition? Or as an act of group participation? Or as a blend of ethnicity and nostalgia? Or as a freely chosen act of autonomous Jewish self-expression? What is *galut?* Is it a geographical term meaning "outside Israel"? Or a cultural term meaning "a sense of not-at-homeness"? Or a religious term meaning "a time not yet redeemed"? Is America *galut?* Is Israel?

BABEL INVERTED

The problem that threatens to render all contemporary Jewish thought systematically divisive is not the *absence,* but paradoxically the *presence,* of a shared language. Jews use the same words but mean profoundly different things by them. The point was dramatically illustrated by an utterance delivered at a, perhaps the, key moment in modern Jewish history.

The issue was the State of Israel's Declaration of Independence. The moment was fraught with meaning. But which meaning? Conceived *religiously,* the people of Israel were returning to their land after an exile of almost two thousand years. The hand of God was once again manifest in history. The period of the "hiding of the face" of God was, said Rabbi Joseph Soloveitchik,[3] at an end. The biblical resonance of the ingathering of exiles was unmistakable. "Even if you have been banished to the most distant land under the heavens, from there the Lord your God will gather you and bring you back. He will bring you to the land that belonged to your fathers, and you will take possession of it."[4] It was the fulfilment of a prophecy, the consummation of an ancient religious hope.

Even that father of modern Jewish heresies, Baruch Spinoza, had predicated his abandonment of Judaism on the fact of exile, and had envisaged a possibility that would overturn his analysis. "I would go so far as to believe," he wrote of the Jews, "that if the foundations of their religion have not so emasculated their minds they may even, if occasion offers, so changeable are human affairs, raise up their empire afresh, and that God may a second time elect them."[5] Even for Spinoza, then,

---

3. Abraham R. Besdin, *Reflections of the Rav: Lessons in Jewish Thought Adapted from the Lectures of R. Joseph B. Soloveitchik* (Jerusalem: WZO, 1979), 34–39.
4. Deut. 30:4–5.
5. Baruch Spinoza, *Tractatus Theologico-Politicus* [1670], trans. R. H. M. Elwes (New York: Dover, 1951), 56.

the rebirth of a Jewish state in Israel would have vindicated a religious interpretation of history.

But Spinoza had added a rider: "if the foundations of their religion have not so emasculated their minds." Here was the crux. The Zionist movement involved a radical *secularization* of Jewish history. Redemption was to come by human efforts. The return to Zion was to be brought about not by a submission to Providence but by a determined effort to take active control of the Jewish destiny. The first formulations of Zionism in the 1860s tried to avoid the split between faith and action. The religious thinkers Zvi Hirsch Kalischer and Yehudah Alkalai argued that the process of redemption began by human initiative. The secular thinker Moses Hess was inspired by the religious roots of Jewish nationalism. But by half a century later, the intellectual schism was almost complete. The religious thinkers of Agudat Yisrael were by now arguing that political Zionism was an attempt to "force the end" by pre-empting divine deliverance and thus usurping the role of Providence in history. The secularists were beginning to see religion as their primary obstacle, a sustained tutorial in passivity, an emasculation of the mind.

The point was made with passion by Joseph Chayyim Brenner. "In their prayers, their liturgy, and sacred books the Jews complained to God for not redeeming them, for not restoring them forever to their homeland.... At the same time, however, they were always quite content to remain where they were, among the wicked gentiles, so long as the latter allowed them to remain."[6] Nachman Syrkin, the theorist of Zionist socialism, described religion as "the major impediment confronting the Jewish nation on the road to culture, science, freedom." Ber Borochov chose to identify with the "wicked son" of the Passover text, the Haggadah, because he refused to accept a freedom given by God but instead insisted on creating it for himself. For Borochov, it was the "wicked sons" of the present generation who were creating "the foundation for the construction of new Jewish life."[7]

---

6. In Arthur Hertzberg (ed.), *The Zionist Idea* (New York: Atheneum, 1981), 310.

7. Quoted in Charles Liebman and Eliezer Don-Yehiya, *Civil Religion in Israel: Traditional Judaism and Political Culture in the Jewish State* (Berkeley: University of California Press, 1983), 36–37.

How then was the culminating moment of these conflicting visions – Israel's Declaration of Independence – to be described? Religious groups were insistent that the declaration should contain a reference to God. The secularist groups were equally insistent that it should not. The final draft read: "Placing our trust in the Rock of Israel [*tzur Yisrael*], we set our hand and testimony to this Declaration, here on the soil of the Homeland, in the city of Tel Aviv, on this day, the eve of the Sabbath, 5 Iyar 5708, 14 May 1948." To the religious, the phrase "Rock of Israel" signified God. It was to the "Rock of Israel" that they daily prayed for deliverance and salvation. To the secular it meant not God but the Jewish people and its indomitable national will.

Nor was this all. Translated into religious and secular frames of reference, the whole sentence reverberated with multiple evocations and associations. Did "Homeland" signify the Holy Land of the covenantal promise to the patriarchs, or was it merely the geographical-historical locus of the Jewish people that Spinoza described as "a certain strip of territory"?[8] Was "the eve of the Sabbath" to be understood in its secular, modern sense, as Friday? Or was it meant in its religious usage as the threshold of the day of rest, the gateway to Israel's sanctuary in time, the Sabbath? Beyond this, did the phrase "the eve of the Sabbath" carry its traditional metaphorical significance as the period penultimate to the messianic age? If so, was this the religious-redemptive vision of the Bible or the secular utopia of Zionist socialism? And in which framework of time was the declaration signed? In religious time – Iyar 5708 – or in the secular twentieth century – May 1948?[9]

The sentence, a triumph of diplomatic ambiguity, is a paradigm of the fate of the contemporary vocabulary of Judaism. Jews are, to use Bernard Shaw's phrase, divided by a common language. Our condition

---

8. Spinoza, *Tractatus Theologico-Politicus*, 46. See Arnold Eisen, *Galut: Modern Jewish Reflection on Homelessness and Homecoming* (Bloomington, IN: Indiana University Press, 1986), 59–90; Arnold Eisen, "Off Center: The Concept of the Land of Israel in Modern Jewish Thought," in Lawrence A. Hoffman (ed.), *The Land of Israel* (Notre Dame, IN: University of Notre Dame Press, 1986), 263–96.

9. See Harold Fisch, *The Zionist Revolution: A New Perspective* (New York: St. Martin's Press, 1978), 79–96; Charles Liebman and Eliezer Don-Yehiya, *Religion and Politics in Israel* (Bloomington, IN: Indiana University Press, 1984), 17–18.

is an ironic inversion of Babel. "Behold, here is one people speaking the same language." Yet despite this, "they cannot understand one another's speech."[10]

INTERPRETING THE HOLOCAUST

This helps to explain the extraordinary history of the impact on Jewish consciousness of the two decisive events of the present century: the Holocaust and the birth of the State of Israel. No event in Jewish history since biblical times has so nakedly disclosed the shared fate of Jews as Hitler's Final Solution. The gas chambers at Auschwitz made no distinction between assimilators and traditionalists, believers and heretics, atheists and Jews of faith. Every Jew after the Holocaust knows that he or she is in some sense a survivor – in Emil Fackenheim's phrase, part of an accidental remnant.[11] We have become acutely conscious, to use Rabbi Soloveitchik's terminology, of the *berit goral*, the "covenant of fate," that unites all Jews, willingly or against their will.[12]

Yet, though the Holocaust has made its impact on every group within the Jewish world, it has pointed, like a compass gone wild, in all directions sequentially.[13] For some, like the late Rabbi Joel Teitelbaum, the leader of the Satmar group of Hasidim, it represented the God of history taking retribution for the sin of Zionism. The Zionist movement was an unprecedented rebellion against the terms of Jewish history in exile. As a result, the nations into which Jews had been exiled rose as terrible instruments of divine vengeance. For others the Holocaust represented the God of history taking retribution for the sin of *anti*-Zionism. Since emancipation, for the first time in eighteen hundred years of exile, Jews had ceased to wish for a return to their land and had instead sought to make their permanent home in Europe. The Holocaust was the hand of Heaven signalling that exile is not home. For both these schools of thought there was, in the catastrophe, a divinely ordained punishment.

---

10. Gen. 11:6–7.
11. Emil Fackenheim, *To Mend the World: Foundations of Future Jewish Thought* (New York: Schocken, 1982), 308.
12. Joseph Soloveitchik, *Divrei Hagut Veha'arakhah* (Jerusalem: WZO, 1981), 32–48.
13. See "The Holocaust in Jewish Theology," in Jonathan Sacks, *Tradition in an Untraditional Age* (London: Vallentine, Mitchell, 1990), 139–60.

But for which of two contradictory sins? A third school, equally Ortho-dox, rejected this approach and instead saw the Holocaust as the ultimate "hiding of the face" of God. A fourth, throwing off religious categories altogether, saw it as the decisive refutation of the God of history.

For some Israeli thinkers, the Holocaust refutes diaspora exis-tence and delivers the imperative of living in Israel. For some diaspora intellectuals it argues against the geographical concentration of Jews and demonstrates the necessity of dispersion. For some, the Final Solution proves the impossibility of escaping from Jewish identity. For others it proves the urgency of so doing.

Why is the Holocaust so given to multiple explanations or to the insistence that there can be none? The answer is not to be found – and here I differ from most interpreters – in features of the Holocaust itself, its uniqueness, inexplicability, or over-explicability. It lies elsewhere. Manifestly, we have not yet learned how to integrate the Holocaust into Jewish consciousness as we once integrated the exodus or the destruction of the Temples. The reason is not to be sought in the Holocaust itself but in something that preceded and still survives it. Namely, that since emancipation, there is no such thing as a common Jewish conscious-ness for any Jewish experience to be integrated into. Each of us relates to the Holocaust in our own way; but there is no longer a collective way, as there was when the Ninth of Av, the day of mourning for the loss of the Temples, was instituted. We are no less fragmented after Auschwitz than we were before it.[14]

THE SIGNIFICANCE OF ISRAEL

The same applies to the State of Israel. Not only has identification with Israel become a primary axis of Jewish identity in the diaspora,[15] but the events surrounding the 1967 Six Day War catalysed a revolution in Jewish sensibilities the like of which had not been seen since the beginnings of

---

14. For these last few sentences see ibid. 153–54.
15. See Jonathan Woocher, *Sacred Survival: The Civil Religion of American Jews* (Bloom-ington IN: Indiana University Press, 1986); Calvin Goldscheider, *Jewish Continuity and Change: Emerging Patterns in America* (Bloomington IN: Indiana University Press, 1986).

emancipation. For many Jews, Israel represented a defiant "Never Again" to the Holocaust. It transformed the tragic sense of *kiddush hashem*, sanctification by martyrdom, into an affirmative *kiddush hachayim*, sanctification by refusing to suffer martyrdom.[16] It stood, as Irving Greenberg diagnosed, for the Jewish emergence from powerlessness into an ethic of power. It embodied, as Emil Fackenheim argued, a determination to survive, experienced as a religious imperative, a "614th commandment." It symbolized what the Christian theologian A. Roy Eckardt has called "the new Jewish stand."[17] Israel more than any other component of contemporary Jewish life evokes the recognition that "We are one."

But Israel, the concept, is a concatenation of ambiguities. What does "Israel" represent to the contemporary Jewish imagination? Does it signify the land, the nation, the people, the state, or the government? Is it, in Eliezer Schweid's open question, a homeland or the land of destiny?[18] Does Israel support or refute the diaspora? Is it the culmination or the conscious rejection of Jewish history in exile? Is it the normalization of Jewish existence or a breathtaking demonstration that Jewish existence cannot be normalized? Is it a Jewish state or merely a state populated by Jews? Does it have religious significance, and if so, how? What is the implication of Israel's existence for the present connotation of the word *galut*, exile? And where, above all, does Israel stand on the road to the messianic age, secularly or religiously conceived?

---

16. This transformation was born earlier, in the Warsaw Ghetto uprising, when Rabbi Isaac Nissenbaum declared: "This is a time for *kiddush hachayim*, the sanctification of life, and not for *kiddush hashem*, the holiness of martyrdom. Previously the Jew's enemy sought his soul and the Jew sanctified his body in martyrdom; now the oppressor demands the Jew's body, and the Jew is obliged therefore to defend it, to preserve his life." Quoted in Shaul Esh, "The Dignity of the Destroyed," in Y. Gutman and L. Rothkirchen (eds.), *The Catastrophe of European Jewry* (Jerusalem: Yad Vashem, 1976), 355.

17. A. Roy Eckardt, *Jews and Christians: The Contemporary Meeting* (Bloomington, IN: Indiana University Press, 1986), 37–61.

18. Eliezer Schweid, *The Land of Israel: National Home or Land of Destiny* (London: Associated University Presses, 1985); see also his *Israel at the Crossroads* (Philadelphia: JPS, 1973).

To these questions every conceivable combination of answers is possible and actual. Israel's centrality in current Jewish self-definition rests precisely on its conceptual ambiguity and on a tacit agreement, pragmatically justified, not to push clarification too far. As David Vital put it recently, writing about the terms in which Israel is discussed by Jews, "Obfuscation, hidden agenda, double-talk and, commonest of all, double-think are still very much the order of the day."[19] What contemporary sociologists term "civil Judaism," the new public consensus of Jews, rests on a subtle investiture of the traditional language of Jewish destiny with secular meanings and the tolerance of a high level of indeterminacy with regard to all the potentially divisive issues of Israel's relationship with the diaspora.[20]

The fate of Israel in current Jewish philosophy is the reverse of that of the Holocaust. While the latter has been subjected to massive and conflicting theological treatment, the former has been largely neglected. Yet Zionism had been the concept into which thinkers of all kinds, from the most avowedly secular to the most incandescently spiritual, had poured their visions of the Jewish vocation from the late nineteenth century up until the creation of the state. As Steven Katz notes, "It is all the more remarkable given the richness of pre-state Zionist literature that there is not even one major post-1948 work emanating either from the diaspora or Israel, which offers a satisfying Jewish philosophical account of Zionism and Jewish nationalism."[21] Or as Jacob Neusner put it, rather more acerbically, "The creation of the first Jewish state in two thousand years yielded nothing more interesting than a flag and a rather domestic politics, not a world view and a way of life.... The rise of the State of Israel destroyed a system, the Zionist one, but replaced it with nothing pertinent to Jewry at large."[22]

---

19. David Vital, *The Future of the Jews* (Cambridge, MA: Harvard University Press, 1990), viii.
20. Liebman and Don-Yehiya, *Civil Religion in Israel*; Woocher, *Sacred Survival*.
21. Steven T. Katz, "An Agenda for Jewish Philosophy in the 1980s," in Norbert M. Samuelson (ed.), *Studies in Jewish Philosophy* (Lanham, MD: University Press of America, 1987), 94.
22. Jacob Neusner, *Understanding Seeking Faith* (Atlanta: Scholars' Press, 1986), 101–2.

UNDERSTANDING PEOPLEHOOD

The same phenomenon has afflicted the third component of contemporary Jewish thought, the concept of *peoplehood*. Enlightenment thought had stressed the idea of universal humanity on the one hand, and the abstract individual on the other, freed from the constraints of tradition to make his own world of meanings through his choices.[23] This was a language into which traditional Jewish identity could not be translated, and the sense of Jewish peoplehood suffered accordingly, especially in Western Europe. The terms of emancipation liberated Jews as individuals, not as a collectivity. John Murray Cuddihy has defined "assimilation in the diaspora" as "seeking status-enhancement for yourself alone, not for your group."[24] Social advancement at the price of denying, disguising, or diluting Jewish origins was, in Norman Podhoretz's phrase, the "brutal bargain" of emancipation.[25]

The new Jewish political-ethnic assertiveness since the 1960s has therefore been a stunning transformation. In part it belongs to the impact of the Holocaust on Jewish consciousness, an awareness of the "singled-out" condition of the Jew. In part it emerged in response to the sense of Israel's vulnerability in the weeks preceding the 1967 war and its subsequent international isolation. Jews in Israel and the diaspora had, it seemed, only one another. In part, too, it is a symptom of the general revival of ethnicity since the early 1960s. The modern state turned out to be less of a melting-pot than nineteenth-century thinkers had envisaged. Rather than a single overarching culture into which minorities assimilated, it has evolved into an arena in which ethnic variety and pluralism flourish.

Jewish peoplehood emerged as a key component of identity. Daniel Elazar has called this a "neo-Sadducean Judaism." Its adherents are "Jews who seek to be Jewish through identification with the Jewish people as a corporate entity, its history, culture and tradition, but without

---

23. See Jonathan Sacks, *The Persistence of Faith* (London: Weidenfeld and Nicolson, 1991).

24. John Murray Cuddihy, "Introduction," in *The Ordeal of Civility: Freud, Marx, Levi-Strauss and the Jewish Struggle with Modernity*, 2nd ed. (Boston: Beacon Press, 1987), x.

25. Norman Podhoretz, *Making It* (New York: Random House, 1967).

necessarily accepting the authoritative character of halakhah [Jewish law] or the centrality of halakhah in defining their Jewishness."[26] The most potent phrases of American civil Judaism and its fund-raising rhetoric are "We are One" and *am echad*, "One people." Jonathan Woocher has described Jewish unity as the primary article of the civil Jewish faith.[27]

Solidarity between the Jews of the West, Israel, the Soviet Union, and threatened diaspora communities has become more than the object of activism. It has become a carrier of identity. "At the very heart of the mystery of Jewish survival throughout the ages, in magnificent denial of the normal laws of history that decree the death sentence on peoples that lose their homeland, is the idea of community...the sense of a profoundly shared destiny, a shared purpose, a shared history and customs, a shared responsibility."[28] Thus declared one American lay leader, articulating the new consciousness. Twentieth-century Jewish history seemed conclusively to refute the universalism of the Enlightenment. Particularism has returned to Jewish thought.

But though the idea of a single Jewish people dominates contemporary Jewish awareness, it has never been more problematic ideologically, halakhically, and existentially. *Ideologically*, the issue is most acute in terms of the conflicting modes of Israel's and the diaspora's definition of Jewishness. Though the sharp conflicts between diasporists and Zionists in the nineteenth and early twentieth centuries have softened, the abyss remains between those who see Jewish identity in geographical, political, and national terms, and those who see it as an essentially religious construct.[29] Living testimony to the conceptual impasse is the unprecedented phenomenon of *yoredim*, Jews who have left Israel for the diaspora, of whom there are an estimated three hundred thousand in the United States. Alienated from the diaspora's religious institutions of Jewish continuity, regarded as betrayers of Zionism by Israel itself, they are Jews whose identity is wholly defined in terms of living in a land from which they are absent. They appear to be almost

---

26. Daniel J. Elazar, "The New Sadducees," *Midstream* (Aug.–Sept. 1978), 20–25.
27. Woocher, *Sacred Survival*, 67–71.
28. Ibid., 70.
29. See, e.g., Eisen, *Galut*.

the first group since the lost ten tribes to have no theoretical basis for their Jewish survival.[30]

Halakhically the problem is dramatized in the political-religious battles over the question "Who is a Jew?" Orthodoxy had long refused to grant halakhic validity to conversions performed by Reform and Conservative rabbis. Some or all of the requisites were lacking: acceptance of the commandments, circumcision in the case of males, and immersion in a *mikveh* (ritual bath). But the issue has been heightened by two factors. First was the official acceptance, in 1983, by the American Reform movement of the "patrilineal principle" which accords Jewish status to a child either of whose parents is Jewish, on the basis of "appropriate and timely acts of identification with the Jewish faith and people." Jewish law, by contrast, recognizes only the child of a Jewish mother as a born Jew. Second has been Orthodoxy's unexpected return to demographic and political power, and hence the increased likelihood of confrontation. Some writers have warned of an impending schism that would resemble the rift between Judaism and Christianity and divide Jews irreparably into two peoples.[31]

Existentially the issue is best seen through an argument currently raging among American Jewish sociologists and demographers. The question is neatly posed in the title of a book by Steven Cohen, *American Assimilation or Jewish Revival?*[32] Judged by traditional indices of Jewish continuity, the American Jewish community – along with other diaspora populations – is undergoing rapid disintegration and decline. The rate of increase of intermarriage and divorce, which accelerated sharply in the 1960s, has slowed, but it continues on its upward path. Jews are marrying later than other ethnic and religious groups and having fewer children. The doom-laden prediction of the 1970s, that American Jewry would be reduced within a century from six million to one hundred

---

30. See Moshe Shokeid, *Children of Circumstances: Israeli Emigrants in New York* (Ithaca, NY: Cornell University Press, 1988).

31. Reuven P. Bulka, *The Coming Cataclysm* (Oakville, Ontario: Mosaic Press, 1984); Irving Greenberg, *Will There Be One Jewish People by the Year 2000?* (New York: National Jewish Center for Learning and Leadership, 1986).

32. Steven M. Cohen, *American Assimilation or Jewish Revival?* (Bloomington, IN: Indiana University Press, 1988).

thousand, is being revised, but no one disputes that the community is shrinking. Religious behaviour, hitherto the one vehicle of diaspora continuity, continues its downward trend. Increasing numbers neither attend nor affiliate with a synagogue and receive no form of Jewish education.

On the other hand, a number of observers – most notably Charles Silberman[33] and Calvin Goldscheider[34] – have recently argued to the contrary, that the American Jewish community is undergoing unprecedented revival. Against expectation, Jews are not disappearing as an identifiable ethnic group. Jews remain Jewish in their social reference groups and political affiliations, most notably in their support for Israel. Their peculiar modes of educational and career mobility have, in the very course of their integration into American society, tended to make them more like one another and less like other Americans. More than any other religious or ethnic grouping, they go to university and pursue academic, managerial, or other professional careers. Work, neighbourhood, cultural background, and economic status tend to reinforce intra-Jewish interaction. Even intermarriage might not be seen as a net loss to the Jewish community, since those who have married out no longer wish to be dissociated from the community, and a proportion wish to raise their children as Jews. Increasingly they are being accommodated, especially by the Reform movement.

At stake in this argument is the very definition of what it is to be a Jew and how Jewishness is to be measured. Goldscheider has argued that "the definition of the Jewishness of the family in terms of biology (or halakhah) is becoming less important for American Jews than it was in the past and less relevant to Jewish communal continuity than how people define themselves behaviourally, communally, and culturally, and how the community defines them."[35] Needless to say, others have argued that predicating Jewish revival on criteria that have no basis in halakhah, tradition, or commitment is both complacent and methodologically

---

33. Charles Silberman, *A Certain People: American Jews and Their Lives Today* (New York: Summit Books, 1985).

34. Calvin Goldscheider and Alan Zuckerman, *The Transformation of the Jews* (Chicago: University of Chicago Press, 1984); Goldscheider, *Jewish Continuity and Change*; id., *The American Jewish Community* (Providence, RI: Brown University Press, 1986).

35. Goldscheider, *The American Jewish Community*, 19.

unsound. Arthur Hertzberg has argued that mere ethnic difference "hardly seems worth suffering for," and that Judaism cannot be semantically reduced to "no more than a triumph of adjustment to suburban life."[36] Charles Liebman has put the problem well. "The major categories for the expression of and determination of Jewish authenticity have always been legalistic, but the primary modes of Jewish expression today simply do not fit these categories."[37]

Again, a shared language divides. Almost all Jewish groups in Israel and the diaspora express a commitment to Jewish survival, peoplehood, and unity. But the interpretation of those concepts differs systematically from group to group. Along religious, ethnic, cultural, and national axes, there coexist two deepening senses, of kinship with, and estrangement from, other Jews. Ideology conflicts with empirical reality, and the global vision of peoplehood fragments as soon as the attempt is made to specify it with any precision.

STRATEGIES OF JEWISH THOUGHT

The language of contemporary Judaism, in other words, bears all the signs of collapse that Alasdair MacIntyre diagnosed in post-Enlightenment moral discourse. The vocabulary has persisted while the universe of shared meanings has collapsed. Communication between Jews. When it attempts to cross the boundaries of subcommunities and address the Jewish condition as a whole, depends on the tolerance of a high level of ambiguity and the prior knowledge that key words and sentences will convey different and incompatible meanings to different groups of listeners. At the very moment, therefore, when the Holocaust, Israel, and peoplehood stand at the forefront of Jewish identity, they do so in bewilderingly multiple ways. The same is true of the central terms of traditional Jewish self-understanding. Each has been appropriated by the various segments of the Jewish world and given new and revisionary senses.

It is hardly surprising, given the impact of enlightenment and emancipation on Jewish thought, that much of the most powerful work of nineteenth-century Jewish self-definition was explicitly confrontational

---

36. Quoted in Steven M. Cohen, *American Assimilation or Jewish Revival?*, 118.
37. Charles Liebman, *The Ambivalent American Jew* (Philadelphia: JPS, 1973), 182.

and built on negation. Reform thought was constructed in terms of liberation from an antiquated and dysfunctional tradition, redolent of the ghetto, still embodied in the few vivid outposts of anachronistic Orthodoxy which would be swept away on the tide of modernization. Orthodox traditionalism for its part sustained a fierce rhetoric against Reform, as it did against the entire secularization of contemporary culture. Samson Raphael Hirsch, architect of Neo-Orthodoxy, waged a battle on both fronts – against traditionalists who bore Judaism in their hands "as a sacred relic, as a revered mummy, and fear to awaken its spirit," and against Reformers who saw Judaism "as a lifeless framework, as something which should be interred in the grave of a past long since dead and buried."[38] The same affirmation-through-negation marked the Zionist and anti-Zionist polemics of the half century prior to Jewish statehood, the former seeing diaspora Judaism as lifeless, equivocating, and doomed to extinction, the latter seeing Zionism as a secularization of Jewish history and a route to collective assimilation.

Nor is it surprising that in an effort to heal the wounds caused by this divisive cast of thought, some of the most resonant Jewish thinkers of the twentieth century – Martin Buber, A. J. Heschel, and Rabbi Avraham Hacohen Kook among them – wrote in poetic, enigmatic, and aphoristic prose whose precise meaning is almost impossible to determine. Their language is a curious hybrid of theology and diplomacy, hovering above the inevitably fragmenting ground of referential precision. Nor, in this context, is it hard to understand why another central thinker, Rabbi Joseph Soloveitchik, forswore any aspiration to universality in his most famous essay, "The Lonely Man of Faith," and chose instead the route of philosophy as conceptualized autobiography. "My interpretive gesture," he writes, in a remarkable abdication of authority, "is completely subjective and lays no claim to representing a definite halakhic philosophy.... I shall not feel hurt if my thoughts will find no response in the hearts of my listeners."[39] Jewish thought, it

---

38. Samson Raphael Hirsch, *The Nineteen Letters on Judaism* [1836], trans. Bernard Drachman (New York: Feldheim, 1960), 126–27.
39. Joseph Soloveitchik, "The Lonely Man of Faith," *Tradition*, 7:2 (1965), 10.

seems, is caught between being denominational and divisive, or global and ambiguous, or determinate and private.

There is a pragmatic issue here, and an intellectual one. The intellectual one was put fairly by Menachem Kellner in an essay in which he argued that contemporary Jewish philosophy has now become impossible. "The first task of the thinker seeking to recreate Jewish philosophy as it is classically understood is the examination of Judaism: What is unhyphenated Judaism? Since I personally believe that what holds Jews together in the modern world is a kind of un-reflective nationalism and not shared theology, I am not too optimistic about this project. But it ought to be undertaken, even if only to show that it cannot succeed."[40] There is, for Kellner, no longer any substantive single entity described by the words Judaism, Jewish identity, or Jewish peoplehood. The philosophical enterprise, which was to give systematic and rigorous content to these ideas and their interrelationships, can therefore not be undertaken except, perhaps, from a partial and denominational perspective.

The pragmatic point is that not only is Jewish thought impossible; it is undesirable. The very attempt to press into precision the loose congeries of ideas that frame contemporary Jewish life is likely to prove splintering. A semblance of Jewish unity is necessary to the various practical projects that bring Jews together in collaborative undertakings. Diplomatic silence on the key questions of meaning and identity is preferable to divisive articulation. Jonathan Woocher's recent study of the civil religion of American Jews contains this telling passage:

> For the civil religion, Judaism is very much a matter of concern; God is not. This does not, however, imply that civil Judaism is atheistic. The existence of God is never questioned, much less denied.... Rather, the civil religion is by and large simply silent on the matter.... The watchword of civil Judaism is unity. Theology, except at the most rudimentary formulaic level...is inherently divisive in contemporary Jewish life.... By remaining silent on the nature or role of God in human life and Jewish destiny... it also

---

40. Menachem Kellner, "Is Contemporary Jewish Philosophy Possible? – No," in Samuelson (ed.), *Studies in Jewish Philosophy*, 20.

avoids having to deal with potentially difficult, even embarrassing theological issues.... Such assertions, vital, we have seen, to the civil religion, are perhaps better left as incoherent statements of faith rather than being subject to theological examination. It is then not so much God who is missing from civil Judaism as it is any serious theological discussion.[41]

The civil Jewish consensus rests on a tacit agreement not to try to shape into coherence a substantive vision of Jewish purpose or belief.

BEYOND PESSIMISM AND OPTIMISM

The starting assumption of this essay is that these diagnoses are simultaneously too pessimistic and too optimistic. They are too optimistic in assuming that halakhic or theological debate can be endlessly deferred. To be sure, diplomacy is always to be preferred to war, actual or ideological. But it is not always robust enough to resist it. It is difficult to predict where, and on what issue, the next schismatic confrontation will take place, whether between Israel and the diaspora, Orthodoxy and Reform, or different groups within Orthodoxy itself. But the levels of tension within world Jewry have been perceptibly rising in the last decade, and the task of reconciliation cannot be forever delegated to a messianic tomorrow.

But it is a pessimistic fallacy to infer that, because a unified presentation of Jewish belief is at present impossible, a first step cannot be taken in that direction. The following chapters aspire to neither a practical nor a philosophical programme for Jewish unity. Instead they attempt to address two questions. Firstly, how did our contemporary fragmentation arise? Secondly, does the Jewish tradition itself contain resources for handling diversity without disunity? Jewish thought can at least undertake to ask how we arrived where we are, and where we might go from here. If this is not Jewish philosophy in any traditional sense, it is none the less a prolegomenon to it.

Though neither a historian nor a sociologist, I have been driven to these disciplines in an attempt to delineate the problems under review.

---

41. Woocher, *Sacred Survival*, 91–92.

Alasdair MacIntyre conjectured the possibility that a traditional mode of thought might be lost even while its vocabulary remained. The argument of this chapter has been that this accurately describes the condition of contemporary Jewish thought. The loss of traditional meanings is rendered invisible by the persistence of traditional terminologies. The attempt therefore has to be made to get behind the languages of theology and halakhah, and this can only be done through the use of alternative disciplines.

The subject before us, then, is the effect of modern consciousness on Jewish self-definition. How did a coherent tradition come to be fragmented, presenting Jews with radically incompatible ways of conceiving themselves, their faith, and their people?

Chapter 2

The Birth of the Adjectival Jew

The word "Jew" testifies to conflict. Before there were Jews, there was Israel, the people chosen by God to be the bearer of His covenant. After the death of Solomon the people split in two, into a northern kingdom of ten tribes called Israel, and a southern kingdom called Judah, though it comprised the tribe of Benjamin as well. In the eighth century BCE the northern kingdom was conquered by the Assyrians and its population deported. Rapidly they merged with the surrounding peoples, losing their language, their distinctive faith, and their identity. They assimilated and disappeared from the pages of history, to be remembered as the lost ten tribes. Those who remained were *yehudim,* Judeans, or, as the word gradually evolved from Greek to Latin to English, Jews. The history of the word takes us inexorably back to the first great division in Israel's memory. It was not the last.

The idea of Jewish unity is not marginal to Jewish self-understanding. Its appearance in the early rabbinic literature is evidence of a long and disastrous series of internal conflicts which at times threatened the integrity and survival of the Jewish people. To take a single example: an early rabbinic commentary contains a remark that sheds light on the rabbis' understanding of their people's past. The subject under discussion is the moment when the Israelites prepared to accept the Torah at Sinai, their constitution as a holy people. The biblical verse reads: "They departed from Refidim and arrived at the Sinai Desert and camped in the wilderness; *and Israel camped there* opposite the mountain" (Ex. 19:2). In the Hebrew, the first three verbs are in the plural, the last in the singular. The plural "they" had become, momentarily, a single "Israel." The rabbis, sensitive to the nuance and sensing that form mirrored content, understood this to mean that it was at this point that a fissiparous collection of individuals was fused into a single nation. Rashi cites the traditional comment thus: "And Israel camped there – *as one person with one heart.* But all their other encampments were marked by dissension and argument."[1]

The interpretation is drawn from the *Mekhilta,* an early rabbinic commentary on the book of Exodus. We cannot date its origin with precision, but we can be reasonably certain of the context in which it was made. Jews in the first and second centuries CE had suffered a series of internal tensions, religious, cultural, and political, which led to and left them unprepared for the two great catastrophes that were to determine the course of Jewish history for centuries to come. There were two ill-conceived rebellions against Rome: in 66 CE and again sixty-five years later under Bar Kochba. As a result of the first, the Temple was destroyed. As a result of the second, all immediate hope of the recovery of autonomous Jewish life in the land of Israel was effectively buried, and remained so for eighteen hundred years. Tradition has handed down to us the memory of rabbinic voices raised at that time in favour of caution, coexistence, and moderation. It seems they were ignored. The Jewish people had proved, not for the first time in its history and not for the last, to be its own worst enemy.

Trying to understand the events that had overtaken them, the rabbis passed a significant judgement. The first Temple had been destroyed, they said, because Jews had been guilty of cardinal sins: idolatry, murder, and sexual immorality. But the second had been destroyed for no other reason than what the sages termed *sinat chinam,* baseless mutual hatred,

---

1. Rashi on Ex. 19:2. Rashi is paraphrasing the *Mekhilta* of Rabbi Yishmael ad loc.

the simple inability of Jews to live together.[2] The most searing indict-
ment of those times is contained in the statement of Rabbi Chanina, the
prefect of the priests: "Pray for the welfare of the state, for were it not for
the fear of it, we[3] would have swallowed each other up alive." Better, suggests Rabbi Chanina, the rule of a tyrannical Rome than Jewish civil war.

The desire for unity comes to the fore at times of conflict. The
midrashic comment on the Israelites at Sinai is a telling indication of
how seriously the sages took the challenge of unity, and how difficult
they knew it was. At critical moments in its history the Jewish people
has a tendency to split apart and inflict on itself grievous wounds.
Rabbinic consciousness had been forged in an era which had begun
with one war of Jew against Jew, Maccabeans against Hellenizers, and
had ended with another, the innumerable militant factions who strove
with one another as the Romans were besieging Jerusalem. The sages
saw internecine friction as a persisting theme of Jewish history, one
that could be traced back to the murmurings in the wilderness. But it
was not inevitable. When the Israelites agreed to receive the Torah,
the disputes that had surrounded them throughout the years of wan-
dering fell away and they became "one person with one heart." The
implication was clear. Were Jews prepared *now* to live by the Torah,
unity would once again prevail.

But the rabbinic idea of unity is evidence of more than a divided
past. It suggests well-grounded fears of a divided future. The sages of the
second century CE were aware that the geographical and political bases
of peoplehood had disappeared and were unlikely soon to return. The
unity of a people that shares a land and governs its own affairs does not
need to be provided with a theoretical base. Manifestly, its members
share a fate. But the unity of a people contemplating its own exile and
dispersion is far from self-evident. What in the future would link Jews to
one another, now that hopes of Jewish sovereignty had been abandoned
to a metaphysical end of days; now that Jerusalem, the spiritual centre

---

2. Yoma 9b.
3. Mish. Avot 3:2. Thus the reading in the Kaufman manuscript. Printed editions,
   however, have the verb in the third-person plural, "men would swallow each other
   up alive." The phrase is probably a reference to Ps. 124:3.

from which all else radiated, had been reduced to ruins and the Roman city of Aelia Capitolina built in its place? The idea of Jewish nationhood had lost its "plausibility structure," its concrete embodiment in institutions and palpable reality.

It is at this stage that the concept of Jewish peoplehood began to take on a moral-mystical dimension that was to exercise a hold over the Jewish imagination for sixteen centuries. A striking early expression occurs in the *Mekhilta Derabbi Shimon bar Yochai*. On the biblical phrase "And you shall be to me a kingdom of priests and a holy nation" the midrash supplies the following interpretation: "'A nation' – this teaches that they are like a single body and a single soul, and thus it says, 'And who is like your people Israel, a nation one on earth' [II Sam. 7:23]. If one of them sins, they are all punished, as it is said, 'When Achan the son of Zerach acted unfaithfully regarding the devoted things, did not wrath come upon the whole community of Israel?' [Josh. 22:20]. If one of them is smitten, they all feel pain."[4] Texts here are martialled to prove what could no longer be taken for granted: the collective responsibility and indivisible destiny of Israel. A holy nation, even exiled and dispersed, remains a single entity. The covenant binding Jews, not only to God but to one another, remains in force. No longer a political fact, Jewish unity persists as a religious reality.

It was a mystical vision. But in retrospect it proved to be a surprisingly accurate one. Writing in the tenth century CE, the rabbi-philosopher Rav Sa'adia Gaon pondered the question of what constituted the Jews as a nation. That they *were* still a nation, "one people," no one doubted, at least not until the late eighteenth century, when the French Revolution redefined the terms of the nation-state and raised intractable questions about the character of Jews as a group. Until then, Jews saw themselves and were seen by others as a single, scattered people. But in what sense? They were dispersed across the world. They had neither land nor political sovereignty. Taken collectively, they spoke a multiplicity of languages, possessed a diversity of cultures, and had none of the conventional bases of nationhood.

---

4. In *Mekhilta Derabbi Shimon bar Yochai* on Ex. 19:6.

Sa'adia's answer was simple and at the time incontestable. "Our nation, the children of Israel, is a nation only in virtue of its religious laws."[5] Jews were a single religious-political entity because they shared the same laws and constitution: the Torah. To be sure, there were different groupings, Ashkenazim and Sephardim, rationalists and mystics, and a host of regional differences in customs and manners. There were periodic serious divisions, the Maimonidean controversy of the twelfth to fourteenth centuries and the collisions between Hasidim and their opponents in the eighteenth among them. But they were a single entity, united by Torah and its practical expression, *halakhah* (Jewish law), the architecture of Jewish life.

The story of modern Jewry can be told in terms of the collapse of this idea. Modernity – which here means the two hundred years since the beginning of European Jewish emancipation – has transformed the Jewish world from the outside through a series of epic processes: secularization, assimilation, racial antisemitism, the Holocaust, and the birth of the State of Israel. But it has transformed the Jewish world no less deeply from within.

The most striking manifestation of what has changed is that it is no longer possible to be a Jew *tout court*. The noun, to convey anything at all, now needs to be qualified by an adjective, perhaps several. There are Orthodox, Reform, Conservative, Liberal, Reconstructionist, and secular Jews. There are Israeli and diaspora Jews, Zionists and non-Zionists. Each label is further subdivided. Zionists are religious or secular. Religious Zionists are messianic or pragmatic. And so on. Jewish existence has become adjectival existence. There is no longer a common content to being a Jew as such, whether in behaviour or belief. Jews have begun to search, as they did in the second century CE, for an affirmation of Jewish unity. The search itself is evidence, as it was then, of a crisis in the definition of the Jewish people. It signals fission and disintegration. How did it occur? Through two processes, one general, another which had a particular impact on Jews. The first was secularization; the second, emancipation.

---

5.   Sa'adia Gaon, *Emunot Vede'ot*, iii. 7.

SECULARIZATION AND THE PERSISTENCE OF RELIGION

In the nineteenth and early twentieth centuries, virtually every social theorist foresaw the demise of religion in the civilized world.[6] Under the impact of industrialization, *Gemeinschaft* was giving way to *Gesellschaft:* the small traditional community to urban anonymity. Science was displacing theology as the means of explaining the world. The key factor in decision making was no longer tradition but rationality. Bureaucracy was displacing personal authority. The calculation of consequences was replacing the ethics of obligation. Objects no longer had an essence but a function, and persons no longer a substantive identity given by birth, but instead a set of roles. The social universe was rapidly becoming, in Max Weber's word, "disenchanted," stripped of supernaturalism. Religion was in the process of being marginalized and would eventually be eclipsed.

The transformation of society was profound and irreversible. It was taking place in several dimensions: through industrialization, economically; urbanization, geographically; the rise of the nation-state, politically; and the philosophy of the Enlightenment, intellectually. Modernization meant secularization, which meant "the process by which sectors of society and culture are removed from the domination of religious institutions and symbols."[7] Twentieth-century humanity was succeeding where the men on the plain of Shinar, after the Flood, had failed: in building a tower of Babel. Nietzsche drew the inevitable conclusion. Man was supplanting God.

The prediction proved false. In the late twentieth century, religious life is strong and growing stronger – especially, and paradoxically,

---

6. For the argument of this section see Bryan Wilson, *Religion in Secular Society* (London: Pelican, 1969); id., *Religion in a Sociological Perspective* (Oxford: Oxford University Press, 1982); Peter L. Berger, *The Sacred Canopy: Elements of a Sociological Theory of Religion* (New York: Doubleday, 1967); id., *Facing up to Modernity* (New York: Basic Books, 1977); id., *A Rumour of Angels* (London: Allen Lane, 1970); Peter L. Berger, Brigitte Berger, and Hansfried Kellner, *The Homeless Mind: Modernization and Consciousness* (London: Pelican, 1974); Michael Hill, *A Sociology of Religion* (London: Heinemann, 1973); Charles Glock and Rodney Stark, *Religion and Society in Tension* (Chicago: Rand McNally, 1965); Phillip E. Hammond (ed.), *The Sacred in a Secular Age* (Berkeley: University of California Press, 1985); Sacks, *The Persistence of Faith.*

7. Berger, *The Sacred Canopy,* 107.

those strands in Judaism and Christianity which are generically described by their opponents as "fundamentalism," and which are most antithetical to modernity. The "secularization thesis" has had to be rewritten. The processes of modernity have not dethroned religion. But they have profoundly transformed it. How so?

The liberal democratic state transfers tradition, morality, and meaning from the public to the private domain. It substantively separates church from state, though a nominal connection may remain. The state itself is no longer conceived as the embodiment of a collective morality, which it enforces by law. Instead it becomes the arena of competing interests and makes decisions on the basis of a rational computation of consequences. Individuals – on John Stuart Mill's influential account of liberty[8] – are afforded the maximum freedom to pursue their own choices consistent with the avoidance of harm to others.

Though the modern state vastly increases the scope of individual rights and freedoms, it is not without its discontents. In particular, the absence of a shared moral culture is experienced as a loss of personal meaning: anomie, as Durkheim called it. Instead of experiencing identity as something given by birth, tradition, and community, individuals are thrown in upon themselves, facing a vast choice of educational, career, and relationship patterns. "On the one hand, modern identity is open-ended, transitory, liable to ongoing change. On the other hand, a subjective realm of identity is the individual's main foothold in reality. Something that is constantly changing is supposed to be the *ens realissimum*. Consequently it should not be a surprise that modern man is afflicted with a *permanent identity crisis.*"[9]

It is here that religion re-enters contemporary society. For its great strength is that it offers a content to personal identity. It provides a mode of belonging. It anchors life-cycle events in a scheme of traditional meanings. It offers community in place of the often functional and faceless structures of the state. It is a sheltered space of order away from the open plains of choice. Despite the massive secularization of

---

8. John Stuart Mill, *On Liberty*, repr. in H. B. Acton (ed.), *Utilitarianism, Liberty, Representative Government* (London: Dent, 1987).

9. Berger, Berger, and Kellner, *The Homeless Mind*, 74.

contemporary Britain or America, a significant majority of the population still declares a belief in God and an interest in religion.

But though religion has not been eclipsed, it has moved from the public to the private domain. Its new setting is the individual, the family, and the local congregation. The distinguishing feature of modern religious affiliation is that it is voluntary: a matter of personal choice rather than external authority. In the traditional community a single vision united its members. In the modern conurbation a vast variety of creeds, ideologies, and lifestyles is on offer. The religious situation becomes a marketplace of competing choices. For the first time, religions are offered not as truth and command but as satisfying the psychological needs of the individual. This, as Peter Berger notes, "represents a severe rupture of the traditional task of religion, which was precisely the establishment of an integrated set of definitions of reality that could serve as a common universe of meanings for the members of a society."[10] Faith is privatized, pluralized, and subjectivized.

ACCOMMODATION OR RESISTANCE?

Two broad strategies are available to religious leadership in the secular situation: accommodation and resistance. Accommodation, going with society's flow, means a substantial sacrifice of the certainties of the past. It means, among other things, de-emphasizing authority, objective truth, and the value of obedience, and stressing instead "relevance," personal autonomy, and self-fulfilment. Liberal theologies translate religious terms from the language of the external world into that of the self. "History becomes biography," and religion becomes a phenomenon of consciousness. Religious groups that accommodate to modernity recognize that "secularization brings about a demonopolization of religious traditions and thus, *ipso facto,* leads to a pluralistic situation."[11] The characteristic mode of religious organization that emerges is the *denomination,* which has been defined as a body that has had to come to terms with the permanent presence and competition of other religious groups within its

---

10. Berger, *The Sacred Canopy,* 133.
11. Ibid., 134.

own territory.[12] Reform and Conservative Judaism are the results of two such accommodating strategies.

But those whose primary concern is with the conservation and preservation of religion's traditional contents must opt to resist secularization. This necessarily involves a measure of withdrawal from society. Pluralism, relativism, and individualism run deep in contemporary culture. Since these are incompatible with traditional religion, traditionalists must, as far as possible, exclude that culture and its manifestations. They must construct an enclosed and enclosing alternative culture of their own. This, again to quote Berger, "entails the maintenance of *sectarian* forms of socio-religious organization."[13]

The sociological analysis of sects, which we owe to such scholars as Troeltsch, Weber, and H. Richard Niebuhr, is largely confined to the study of Christianity. But some features, as outlined by Bryan Wilson,[14] are of general relevance. The sect is marked by its condemnation of or distance from secular society. It is exclusive. It tends to see itself as a small group of the elect. It demands a higher level of commitment from its members than do other forms of religious organization. "The sect provides a total reference group for the individual who belongs, rather as the ghetto community provided such a group for eighteenth-century European Jews."[15]

THE JEWISH EXPERIENCE OF MODERNITY

Thus far we have spoken of the effects of secularization on religion as a generalized process that has been experienced by all societies that have undergone industrialization and urbanization. The dynamic of Jewry over the last two centuries has conformed to this pattern. But its experience of modernity has been particularly acute – traumatic might be a better word – and the key factors can be identified more precisely. For secularization was not experienced by Jews as a broad and gradual

---

12. Ibid., 136; see Hill, *A Sociology of Religion*, 71–97.
13. Berger, *The Sacred Canopy*, 163.
14. Bryan Wilson, "An Analysis of Sect Development," *American Sociological Review*, 24:1 (Feb. 1959), 3–15; id., *Sects and Society* (London: Heinemann, 1961); id., *Religion in Secular Society*, 207–49.
15. Id., *Religion in Secular Society*, 211.

process, but as an exact and sudden change of their position in society, namely, emancipation.

Emancipation promised Jews for the first time an equal place in European society. It heralded the end of the ghetto and Jewish exclusion from the universities, professions, and the instrumentalities of government. It meant, in effect, the end of the self-governing Jewish community, with its limited but real autonomous powers, that had been a characteristic of diaspora Jewish life since the fall of the Second Temple. But the prize of civil equality had a price. It involved the end of Jewry as a separate realm within the state, governing itself through the sanctions of fines and excommunication.

This was what the Count of Clermont-Tonerre meant when he delivered his speech in the French National Assembly in 1789 on the eligibility of Jews for citizenship in the new democratic state. "Jews must be citizens," he said. "It is intolerable that the Jews should become a separate political formation or class in the country. Every one of them must individually become a citizen; if they do not want this, they must inform us and we shall be compelled to expel them." The terms of emancipation were made brutally clear, and they were to determine the shape of the debate for the next century. "The Jews should be denied everything as a nation, but granted everything as individuals."[16]

The transfer of religion from the public to the private domain, which for other religions took place slowly and imperceptibly over an extended period, was demanded of Judaism almost overnight. It was a fateful and in a sense impossible request. Judaism is not a religion in the Protestant sense, the personal religious persuasion of choosing individuals. It is the faith of a people with its own distinctive culture, history, and destiny. This was how Jews saw themselves; more significantly, it was how they were seen by others. The abstract rationalism of the Enlightenment, with its image of universal humanity and its neat dichotomization of public and private spheres, failed to take account of powerful forces of feeling. Max Nordau, speaking a century later at the first Zionist Congress, said in retrospect, "The emancipation of the

---

16. Paul Mendes-Flohr and Jehuda Reinharz (eds.), *The Jew in the Modern World: A Documentary History* (New York: Oxford University Press, 1980), 103–5.

Jews was an example of the automatic application of the rationalistic method...the emancipation of the Jews was proclaimed in France, not out of fraternal feeling for the Jews, but because logic demanded it."[17] By then the Dreyfus affair had exposed a deep current of antisemitism in France and had radicalized Theodor Herzl into Zionism.

But the demand of Clermont-Tonerre met with compliance. Already in his Preface (1782) to Menasseh ben Israel's *Vindiciae Judaeorum, a*nd his great defence of religious liberty, *Jerusalem* (1783), Moses Mendelssohn had argued that the Jewish community should relinquish its internal ecclesiastical powers, in particular the right to excommunicate. "Excommunication and the right to banish...are diametrically opposed to the spirit of religion."[18] Over the next century, and with surprisingly little protest or debate, Jewish communities ceded the right. The way was open to the collapse of the traditional *kehillah*, the vehicle of Jewish social and political autonomy. Though Jewish law itself remained unchanged, its authority was now to be voluntary. The Jewish public domain had been secularized. The consequences were dramatic.

THE ADJECTIVAL JEW

In 1806 Napoleon convened a group of French Jewish "Notables" to elicit their answers to a series of questions designed to test whether Judaism was compatible with citizenship and civic morality. A year later he summoned Jewish religious leaders to constitute a "Sanhedrin" to give these answers the force of halakhah, binding law. It was during the discussions of the "Sanhedrin" that Abraham Furtado (1756–1817), an advocate of emancipation and enlightenment, described the more conservative rabbis as "Orthodox Jews." The phrase itself had probably been in circulation for some years, but this is its first recorded use.[19] The disjunction, proposed by Clermont-Tonerre, between the Jew as member of a people

---

17. In Hertzberg (ed.), *The Zionist Idea*, 236.
18. Moses Mendelssohn, *Jerusalem*, trans. Allan Arkush (Hanover, NH: University Press of New England, 1983), 73.
19. See Samuel C. Heilman, "The Many Faces of Orthodoxy," *Modern Judaism*, 2:1 (1982), 25–26.

and Judaism as a religion of individuals, had entered Jewish consciousness. The adjectival Jew was born.

The primary change, of course, was that Jewishness itself had been transformed from noun to adjective. The French Jew had been turned into a Jewish Frenchman. For the first time, Jewishness was no longer the primary mode of identity. Where once there had been Jews who happened to live in England, France, or Germany, there were now Englishmen, Frenchmen, and Germans who happened to be Jews. But though the "Sanhedrin" concluded, as had Mendelssohn before, that the transformation could be achieved without substantive halakhic change, it was not long before the call was heard for reform.

The reason was this. Jewish law imposes a code of difference. Jews are not to be "like all the nations." Internally, this was a source of pride, expressed in Balaam's blessing, "It is a people that dwells apart, not reckoned among the nations."[20] Externally it was a source of resentment, caught in Haman's complaint to Ahasuerus, "There is a certain people, scattered and dispersed among the other peoples in all the provinces of your realm, whose laws are different from those of any other people."[21] This discipline of difference, as even a secularist critic like Spinoza had seen, had been a key to Jewish survival. But for the enthusiasts of emancipation it was now dysfunctional. It was an obstacle to integration.

Non-Jewish opponents of emancipation had argued that the Jewish hope for a return to Zion meant that Jews could not be true European citizens. Their loyalties would be divided. They still had aspirations to independent nationhood.[22] When the Reform temple opened in Hamburg in 1817, it diluted those passages in the liturgy referring to the return to Zion.[23] Its designation as a "temple" was itself a symbolic gesture. Its members no longer mourned the ruined Temple in Jerusalem. Judaism was henceforth to be seen as a purely religious confession,

---

20. Num. 23:9.

21. Esther 3:8.

22. See Jacob Katz, *Out of the Ghetto: The Social Background of Jewish Emancipation 1770–1870* (Cambridge, MA: Harvard University Press, 1973).

23. For a recent history see Michael A. Meyer, *Response to Modernity: A History of the Reform Movement in Judaism* (New York: Oxford University Press, 1988), 53–61. Meyer writes, "Without question the omission and alteration of certain liturgical

without ethnic, national, or geographic particularity. A temple could be built in Hamburg no less than in Israel.[24]

The traditional rabbinate, quick to see the implications, responded with a condemnation: "They have perpetrated a sore evil by removing all references to the Ingathering of the Exiles.... This belief is one of the major tenets of our holy Torah."[25] But the dynamic of reform could not rest here. Not only Jewish belief but Jewish law stood in the way of acculturation. The dietary laws impeded social mixing. The laws of the Sabbath hindered Jewish entry into certain occupations, and were proving difficult for Jewish pupils at non-Jewish schools. The Jewish laws of divorce seemed to indicate a reluctance to accept civil law and a maintenance of rabbinic authority.

German Reform, by midway through the nineteenth century, was to abandon all these areas of halakhah to a greater or lesser extent. The most cogent rationale was given by one of its more radical thinkers, Samuel Holdheim, who argued, as Spinoza had done, that Jewish law had been the constitution of a nation. Now that Jews no longer saw themselves as a nation, all laws that had the effect of segregating Jews were null and void, and were to be replaced by a dramatic extension of the rabbinic rule *dina demalkhuta dina,* "the law of the land is law."[26]

Reform thus became a radical movement of accommodation.[27] To be sure, its early founders had counter-assimilatory as well as assimilatory

---

passages dealing with the messianic return to Zion was the most audacious innovation of the Hamburg reformers. It cast doubt on a central principle of Jewish faith firmly grounded in all layers of Jewish tradition."

24. See W. Gunther Plaut, *The Rise of Reform Judaism: A Sourcebook of its European Origins* (New York: World Union for Progressive Judaism, 1963).

25. *Eleh Divrei Haberit* [Altona, 1819]; trans. in Mendes-Flohr and Reinharz (eds.), *The Jew in the Modern World,* 150–56.

26. See Gil Graff, *Separation of Church and State: "Dina de-Mmalkhuta Dina" in Jewish Law, 1750–1848* (Tuscaloosa, AL: University of Alabama Press, 1985), 110–32.

27. Sociologically, the Reform movement is unusual in that it was a schismatic movement that moved from a higher to a lower state of tension with its sociocultural environment. Most schisms produce sects, groups that break away from religious establishments that they see as having accommodated too far to society. Reform Judaism was the opposite. See Stephen Steinberg, "Reform Judaism: The Origin and Evolution of a Church Movement," *Journal for the Scientific Study of Religion,* 5

motives. They sought to recast Judaism in a form that would retain the loyalties of rapidly Germanizing Jews. They hoped to stem the tide of conversion and defection. They believed that a Judaism purged of much of its ritual would not only be less restrictive of social integration, but it would recover, too, some of its pristine spiritual force. None the less, in effect if not in intention, it provided religious legitimation for the acculturating processes Jews were undergoing in early nineteenth-century Germany and subsequently in America. It did so by substituting for halakhah a conception of Judaism as ethics, and later as personal autonomy. It transposed the key term, *exile,* from a word that signified not-at-homeness into one that meant the mission to the gentiles. Exile was turned from dislocation into vocation.

There were other accommodationist movements, some that saw Reform as having gone too far, others that believed it had not gone far enough. Zechariah Frankel, in the mid-nineteenth century, argued for a greater emphasis on tradition. He believed in change, but felt that it should take place slowly and imperceptibly. Reform, he felt, should be so gradual that, in his words, "the forward progress will seem inconsequential to the average eye." He called his approach "positive-historical," and it took institutional shape in the form of American Conservative Judaism.

The Conservative rabbinical school in New York, the Jewish Theological Seminary, had on its faculty in the 1920s a radical thinker, Mordecai Kaplan, who had been deeply influenced by Emil Durkheim's sociology and Achad Ha'am's cultural Zionism. Durkheim had seen religion not as an expression of the transcendental but as performing the social function of maintaining group identity. Achad Ha'am had seen Judaism not as the word of God but as the embodiment of the Jewish people's creative genius. Kaplan called his philosophy, and the movement that later emerged from it, Reconstructionism, best summed up in the title of his most influential book, *Judaism as a Civilization.*[28] This was a Judaism without supernaturalism, which celebrated Jewish culture while

---

(1965), 117–29; Rodney Stark, "Church and Sect," in *Hammond* (ed.), *The Sacred in a Secular Age,* 139–49. See also Norman L. Friedman, "Boundary Issues for Liberal Judaism," *Midstream,* 19:9 (1973), 47–52.

28. Mordecai M. Kaplan, *Judaism as a Civilization* [1934] (Philadelphia: JPS, 1981).

eliminating its belief in a personal God. It was an ideological statement of what might best be called religion as ethnicity.

JUDAISM AND DENOMINATION

Reconstructionism, Reform, and Conservatism were all responses not to secularization as such but to the particular form in which it confronted Jews: economic and cultural integration into newly open societies. Each of them was, relative to tradition, liberal and accommodationist. Each involved a substantive break from traditional Jewish belief and authority, though each argued its continuity with the past. And each was, in the sense described above, a *denomination*. None, that is to say, maintained that it held a monopoly of Jewish truth. Each eventually, if not initially, accepted the *de facto* legitimacy of the others, including Orthodoxy itself.

Which brings us to a central point about the contemporary Jewish situation. The accommodationist strategy, as we have seen, accepts one of the most striking features of modernity, what sociologists have described as the "plurality of life worlds."[29] The "urbanization of consciousness" involves the individual in constant awareness that he is surrounded by others whose lifestyles and beliefs are vastly different from his own. They are accessible to him if he chooses to adopt them. He may choose not to; but then his own lifestyle is the result not of necessity but of choice. The denomination is the institutional equivalent of this consciousness. It announces itself as one way, but not the only way, of being religious; in this case, of being Jewish.

As Will Herberg pointed out in the 1950s, being Protestant or Catholic or Jewish is no longer regarded as making a personal statement about ultimate reality; rather, these are three alternative modes of being American.[30] Within Judaism itself, Orthodoxy, Conservatism, Reform, and Reconstructionism are regularly portrayed as the four Jewish denominations. Those who think in these terms see such a description as just that: neutrally descriptive. But it contains a momentous hidden premiss. It imports *pluralism* into Judaism. And this itself is an accommodation to secularization.

---

29. See Berger, Berger, and Kellner, *The Homeless Mind*, 62–77.
30. Will Herberg, *Protestant-Catholic-Jew* (Garden City, NY: Doubleday, 1956).

Orthodoxy does not, and cannot, make this accommodation. It recognizes pluralism along many axes. It recognizes at least some other faiths as valid religious options for non-Jews. It recognizes, within Judaism itself, different halakhic traditions: Ashkenazi and Sephardi, for example, or Hasidic and Mitnagdic. Beyond halakhah, it legitimates a vast variety of religious approaches: rationalist and mystical, intellectual and emotional, nationalist and universalist, pietist and pragmatic. But it does not recognize the legitimacy of interpretations of Judaism that abandon fundamental beliefs or halakhic authority. It does not validate, in the modern sense, a plurality of denominations. It does not see itself as one version of Judaism among others.

DENOMINATION AND MUTUAL MISUNDERSTANDING

There is therefore a systematic mutual misunderstanding between Orthodox and non-Orthodox Jews about the nature of Orthodoxy. Those outside Orthodoxy allocate it to a category that, within Orthodoxy, does not exist: the denomination. This category-error is embedded in the language of contemporary Judaism, for "Orthodox" is an adjective linguistically on a par with "Reconstructionist," "Reform," and "Conservative." It was just this that led Samson Raphael Hirsch to object to the term "Orthodox." It was, he wrote, "not the so-called orthodox Jews who introduced the name orthodoxy into the Jewish sphere." Reform Jews had coined the word as a term of abuse. Against this, Hirsch insisted that "Judaism does not recognise any variants. It knows of no mosaic, prophetic or rabbinic, and of no orthodox or progressive Judaism. It either is Judaism or it is not."[31] But the term persisted, giving rise to conflicts of understanding.

Non-Orthodox Jews often expect, and feel frustrated by the lack of, Orthodox legitimation. For if Orthodoxy is perceived as a denomination then it must be neither wholly inclusive nor wholly exclusive. A denomination is, by definition, a religious group that accepts the coexistence and legitimacy of alternatives. But Orthodoxy involves, among other things, the denial that denominations exist within Judaism. It is

---

31. Quoted in Hermann Schwab, *The History of Orthodox Jewry in Germany* (London: Mitre Press, 1950), 9.

exclusive of other Judaisms and inclusive of all Jews. The expectation that it should recognize other movements as valid interpretations of Judaism is one that in principle cannot be met. For Jewish Orthodoxy to be pluralist in the requisite sense, it would have to accept a degree of tacit secularization incompatible with its most basic beliefs. It would cease, in short, to be Orthodoxy.

So Orthodoxy is fated to be misunderstood by those who stand outside it. But this misunderstanding works in the opposite direction also. Orthodoxy has an inbuilt tendency to misconstrue non-Orthodoxy. It arises for the following reason. Orthodoxy is committed to a strong conception of Jewish unity. The halakhic system embraces all Jews, not only those who have chosen voluntarily to accept it. For Judaism – though European emancipation sought to deny it – is collective as well as individual. It is the religion of a people. Obligation flows from a fact of birth. To be born Jewish is to be born into the commandments. There is no act for a Jew that corresponds to the act of a convert: a moment of free acceptance of Jewish law. Orthodoxy thus sees itself as the faith not of Orthodox Jews only, but of all Jews.

From this premiss follow a number of consequences relating to Jewish unity. The subject of the covenantal promises is not the sub-community of pious Jews but *keneset Yisrael*, the collective entity of the people of Israel. All Jews are responsible for one another.[32] Israel, as we have seen, was for the rabbis a single body. When one sins, all suffer. When one is injured, all feel pain. The power of the sages to legislate was circumscribed by the need to unite, not divide, the community. No decree may be enacted, they ruled, to which the majority of the community is unable to adhere.[33] These propositions follow from the fact that, classically, Judaism is neither a denomination nor a sect, but what sociologists call a "church" – in Jewish terms, *keneset Yisrael* – namely a body that claims both unique legitimacy and total inclusivity.

Rabbinic Judaism contains no terminology that would sustain the existence of denominational alternatives. Jews were either Jews or

---

32. Sanhedrin 27b; Shevuot 39a.
33. Avodah Zarah 36a; Maimonides' *Mishneh Torah, Yad Chazakah* (henceforth, Yad), *Mamrim* 2:5.

apostates. True, the either-or was not absolute. There was considerable debate as to whether an apostate still retained his Jewish status. How far, in other words, did the principle that "Although he has sinned, he remains a Jew" extend?[34] There was the question of the halakhic status of *conversos* or *marranos,* Jews who had ostensibly converted to Christianity or Islam but maintained their Judaism in secret.[35] There was the significant category of the *tinok shenishbah,* the "child raised among gentiles," to which could be assigned groups whose apostasy was considered not to be deliberate.[36] But the existence of these grey areas and borderline cases cannot conceal the fact that to be a Jew and to be a member of the halakhic community were coextensive. There was no third alternative: a Jew whose Jewishness was positive but not halakhic.

The absence of this intermediate category can be seen most clearly in a famous ruling of Maimonides. Jewish law had recognized certain circumstances in which a husband could be forced by a *beit din* (rabbinical court) to grant his wife a divorce. This raised an obvious question. A divorce must be freely given to be valid. A divorce given under pressure of a Jewish court of law seemed, therefore, to be a contradiction in terms. Maimonides explains as follows. The concept of coercion applies when a person is forced to do something he is not obliged to do in Jewish law. But when he is forced to do something he is already legally obliged to do, he is not being coerced against his will. For ultimately he wishes to do it. His apparent reluctance is merely the prompting of his "evil inclination," not an index of his true desires. "Since he wishes to be a Jew [*rotzeh liheyot miYisrael*], and wishes to fulfil all the commandments and avoid transgressions," his true desire is to abide by the decision of the court and the law on which it was based. The court's coercion liberates rather than frustrates his will.[37]

---

34. See Jacob Katz, *Exclusiveness and Tolerance* (Oxford: Oxford University Press, 1961), 67–76; Gerald Blidstein, "Who Is Not a Jew? The Medieval Discussion," *Israel Law Review,* II (1976), 369–90.

35. See, e.g., Maimonides, *The Epistle on Martyrdom,* trans. Abraham Halkin, *Crisis and Leadership: Epistles of Maimonides* (Philadelphia: JPS, 1985), 13–90.

36. See, e.g., Yad, *Mamrim* 3:3.

37. Ibid., *Gerushin* 2:20.

Such a view of coercion is possible only when a profound coincidence can be assumed between Jewish identity and the acceptance of Jewish law. Maimonides' transitional "and" is natural and unselfconscious: "Since he wishes to be a Jew *and* wishes to fulfil all the commandments." It was just this "and" that was called into question by modernity: by the existence of Jews – Reconstructionist, Reform, and Conservative – who wished to be Jews, indeed religious Jews, without accepting the totality of Jewish law.

Orthodoxy, confronting this phenomenon, is faced with a conflict. On the one hand it recognizes a kinship with and responsibility for all Jews, Jewishness here being defined in terms of birth, not faith. On the other hand, it cannot recognize as legitimate any other interpretation of Judaism that secularizes halakhah into "civilization," "personal autonomy," or "historical process." Charles Liebman has put the dilemma well: "If non-Orthodox Jews were unorganized, the consequences of Orthodoxy's doctrinal position would not be contradictory. It could simply undertake missions to the non-Orthodox. But when, in fact, about half of the non-Orthodox [in America] are organized in the Conservative and Reform movements, and the remainder are almost beyond reach of any religious group in Jewish life, then Orthodoxy is confronted with two mutually exclusive mandates – to promote faith and observance among non-Orthodox Jews, while giving no recognition and comfort to the only existing institutions which can reach those Jews."[38]

Liebman errs in calling this a contradiction. Orthodoxy resolves it thus: Reform Jews are Jews, but Reform Judaism is not Judaism. This is not a contradiction but a statement of the fact that tradition is constructed in terms of a *keneset Yisrael* – the totality of Jews – united by halakhah. From this vantage point it is not Orthodoxy but the existence of non-Orthodox Jewish denominations that is a contradiction in terms. But Liebman is right in identifying it as an irresolvable tension.

For Orthodoxy is faced with two alternatives. It can take Reform Judaism seriously as heresy, or it can regard Reform Jews as *tinokot shenishbu,* Jews whose dissenting views are to be attributed to cultural and

---

38. Charles Liebman, "Orthodoxy in American Jewish Life," in Reuven P. Bulka (ed.), *Dimensions of Orthodox Judaism* (New York: Ktav, 1983), 48–49.

parental influence but not to personal conviction. The former strategy writes them out of the fold, the latter embraces them but at the cost of refusing to take seriously the way Reform Jews define themselves. This is a dilemma for Reform Jews too, for they cannot but come to the conclusion that it is those within Orthodoxy who best understand them that most oppose them. The most lenient halakhic rulings *vis-à-vis* Reform are based on a systematic denial of Reform rabbinic legitimacy. Those halakhic authorities who take seriously Reform Judaism's self-definition as a distinct religious alternative are necessarily those most disposed to rule that it is an alien religion, having the same status in Jewish law as Christianity or Islam.

THE SECULARIZATION OF UNITY

Division and systematic mutual misunderstanding are therefore the results of secularization as it has affected Judaism in the past two centuries. Modernity confronted Jews as the sudden, stark demand of emancipation. The pressures of acculturation could not be contained, so it was believed, within traditional parameters of belief and practice. Movements arose to give Jewish legitimation to social change. These were, of necessity, both accommodationist and schismatic. They gave rise to the denomination and to the adjectival Jew. But denominationalism creates expectations of coexistence and mutual legitimacy that cannot be satisfied within the traditional terms of Jewish self-definition. For to be a Jew, traditionally, is to be a Jew without adjectives.

What does this mean for our understanding of Jewish unity? Sa'adia Gaon, we recall, predicated the oneness of Israel as a nation on halakhah. Jews were a people bound together and constituted as such by their shared acceptance of Jewish law. No one from the second to the eighteenth centuries would have contested this definition. Even those, such as Spinoza, who abandoned Jewish law understood that this meant abandoning membership of the Jewish people. The birth of liberal Judaisms thus represented a phenomenon for which there was no precedent in rabbinic tradition: namely, Jews who wished to be Jews without being bound by halakhah. That was the first stage in the birth of a crisis.

But only the first. For at this point the problem was not yet acute. The radical reformers of the mid-nineteenth century, especially

Holdheim, willingly accepted the consequence of their position. Jews were indeed not a nation at all, as they had once thought themselves to be. Instead, for them, Judaism was a religion in the Protestant sense, which is to say the private confession of individuals rather than the constitution of a people. Jewish unity was not a value; to think otherwise was to misunderstand what it was to be a Jew in post-Enlightenment Europe. If the loss of halakhah meant the dissolution of Jewish peoplehood, so be it. The new political dispensation demanded nothing less.

The precondition of the problem was created in the nineteenth century, but the problem itself was not. It has been only in recent decades that the idea of Jewish unity has resurfaced with compelling urgency. As we saw in the last chapter, both the Holocaust and the State of Israel have, in their different ways, powerfully suggested to Jews the indivisibility of their fate. The ancient rabbinic texts have recovered their salience. Jews see themselves interconnected as if into a single body. So, at any rate, the logic of modern antisemitism and anti-Zionism implied. The idea that Jews might simply dissolve into a nation-state in Israel and a series of diaspora denominations with no collective bond between them has not materialized. There is a profound desire for unity, but an equally profound uncertainty as to what such unity represents. This, then, is the problem. Sa'adia Gaon had stated that only halakhah, Jewish law, joined Jews together into a people. What then becomes of peoplehood once the majority of Jews worldwide – some 80 per cent, according to Daniel Elazar[39] – no longer see themselves as bound by halakhah?

For at least eighteen hundred years, from the destruction of the Second Temple to European emancipation, Jewish unity was conceived in religious terms. The idea itself was a religious construct, part ethical, part legal, part mystical. Today such an interpretation seems unavailable. Not all Jews understand their identity in religious terms. Even those who do are split in their understanding of Judaism as a religion. The strongest contemporary pressures towards unity are distinctly secular. They come from the arenas of fund-raising, political and financial support for the State of Israel, and the lay leadership of Jewish communal organizations. Halakhah, far from uniting Jews, is now a shibboleth dividing them. The

---

39. Daniel J. Elazar, *People and Polity* (Detroit: Wayne State University Press, 1989), 153.

pragmatic consensus called "civil Judaism" – tradition translated into the language of secular Jewish institutions – rests on a deliberate sidestepping of theological issues.

One serious attempt to give Jewish unity a theological basis in a secular age deserves, in this context, careful consideration. It comes from the American thinker Irving Greenberg. It provides a vivid demonstration of the extent to which the idea of unity becomes de-traditionalized when applied to the contemporary Jewish situation. Greenberg's position, in outline, is this.[40] The key categories of Judaism – exodus and redemption – are historical. Judaism itself is thus a phenomenon of history. That history can be divided into three great epochs.

The first, the biblical era, was marked by the immediacy of God, intervening in the human situation through miracles and prophetic revelation. In the second, the rabbinic era, God was more hidden. He was found not in prophecy but through study, and not in the Temple but through prayer. The divine presence was less directly but more widely accessible. The prophets were rare individuals; the Temple was a specific place. But in rabbinic Judaism, through study, prayer, and the life of the commandments, every individual and place became open to the divine encounter. With the destruction of the Second Temple and the transition from biblical to rabbinic Judaism, God was experienced less *in*tensively but more *ex*tensively.

The third era, that of modern Judaism, was born in the Holocaust. The Holocaust marked a yet deeper "hiding of the face" of God, so much so that it has become impossible to have any theological certainties any more. But just as had happened in the rabbinic era, this hiddenness meant that the scope of religiously significant activity became wider still. The birth of the State of Israel meant that political action, the

---

40. Irving Greenberg, "Cloud of Smoke, Pillar of Fire: Judaism, Christianity and Modernity after the Holocaust," in Eva Fleischner (ed.), *Auschwitz: Beginning of a New Era?* (New York: Ktav, 1977), 7–56; id., *On the Third Era in Jewish History: Power and Politics* (New York: National Jewish Resource Center, 1980); id., *The Third Great Cycle in Jewish History* (New York: National Jewish Resource Center, 1981); id., *Voluntary Covenant* (New York: National Jewish Resource Center, 1982); id., *The Ethics of Jewish Power* (New York: National Jewish Resource Center, n.d.); id., *Toward a Principled Pluralism* (New York: National Jewish Center for Learning and Leadership, 1986).

building of a society, an economy, and an army, the handling of power, even philanthropic and political support for Israel in the diaspora, have been endowed with religious meaning. To put it more precisely: the meaning of what is "religious" has changed.

We have entered a period of what Greenberg calls "holy secularity." In the passage from biblical to rabbinic Judaism, sanctity was transferred from holy people and places to every Jew and everywhere. Halakhah created an environment of holy acts. Now, in the passage from rabbinic to modern Judaism, halakhah itself must broaden to embrace what have hitherto been seen as secular activities. "Every act of social justice, every humane or productive factory, every sport contest in community centers, every act of human socializing and dignity will become a secularized halakhah as Jewish religious insight deepens and the sacred dimensions of the profane are uncovered."[41]

Greenberg's thought involves a radical secularization of the key terms of Judaism. The idea of a covenant between God and Israel remains, but it has been transposed into a new key. In the first era, God was the senior partner in the covenant. In the second, man and God were more equal. In the third, man has emerged as the dominant voice. Judaism's key institutional expressions, too, have changed. In the first era, they were the Temple, priests, and prophets; in the second, the synagogue, the house of study, and rabbis; in the third they are the Knesset, Israel's defence forces, Holocaust memorial centres, politicians, lay leaders, and academics.

Religious pluralism necessarily follows. As long as one could speak of theological certainties, there could be Orthodoxy on the one hand, heresy on the other. But after the Holocaust there are no certainties. The very basis of covenant has become voluntary. Any Jew who chooses to associate with his people demonstrates faith, however that faith is expressed. The traditional opposition of Orthodoxy and Reform must be replaced by a vision which sees both as "aligned along a continuum of attempts to live by the covenant."[42]

---

41. In Greenberg, *The Third Great Cycle*, 20–21.
42. Id., *Voluntary Covenant*, 23.

This analysis is an attempt to give theological justification to secular Judaism's refusal to discuss theology. Its revolutionary thrust is unmistakable. It is far more radical than, for example, Reform or Conservative Judaism. For while they concede that Orthodoxy is a viable contemporary option, it follows from Greenberg's premisses that Orthodoxy is strictly speaking impossible in a post-Holocaust world. Religious *certainty* and halakhic *authority*, the key categories of rabbinic Judaism, are cognitively and socially unavailable to the modern Jew.

Greenberg's analysis, a strenuous attempt to arrive at a pluralistic understanding of Jewish unity, is a vivid demonstration of how far the contemporary search for unity takes us from tradition. The premiss on which all else rests is that "we are entering a period of silence in theology."[43] We can now no longer make statements about God; we can make statements only about the image of God that is man. Were we able to make statements about God, Orthodoxy would be possible. Were Orthodoxy possible, pluralism would be impossible. Here then is the irony. Once the presence of God was believed to make peace between Jews. Now peace is believed to require his absence.

ORTHODOXY AND JEWISH UNITY

What then follows for those who believe that religious certainty and halakhic authority remain available even after Auschwitz; that so long as there is a Jewish people the terms of the covenant have not changed? For some Orthodox thinkers, the division of the Jewish people into Orthodoxy and others, deeply tragic though it is, does not sanction the pursuit of unity at the cost of other values. Creating unity in the short term, if it involved abandoning covenantal imperatives that traditionally constituted Jewish peoplehood, would be both impossible and undesirable: impossible because it would mean abandoning values that are non-negotiable, undesirable because pluralism might result in greater disunity in the long term.

There are precedents. Moses, Elijah, and Nehemiah were willing to engage in confrontation and opposition with a people they believed were abandoning the terms of Jewish destiny. They would have preferred

---

43. Id., *The Third Great Cycle*, 16.

not to. At one point Moses says, "I cannot carry all these people by myself; the burden is too heavy for me," and he prayed to die.[44] Divisive confrontation is undertaken not out of desire but necessity. If Orthodoxy believes that the Jewish world is, for the most part, engaged in an ultimately destructive process of secularization, it might come to the conclusion that it is commanded to take a confrontational stance against the Jewish attitudes of the age. This would be a tragedy, but it would be right, it could be argued, to risk it to pre-empt a greater tragedy.

This is an important line of argument whose roots in tradition need to be taken seriously by any Jewish thinker. There were schisms in the Jewish past which led to irreparable breaches within the Jewish people: between Hellenizers and zealots, Samaritans and Pharisees, Jews and Christians, Rabbanites and Karaites. Unity is undeniably a Jewish value, but not necessarily and in all circumstances a supreme and overriding one.

One central question of modernity is therefore whether the divisions between Orthodoxy and non-Orthodoxy are inherently schismatic. Does Jewish tradition contain the resources to interpret them otherwise? Are there alternative halakhic strategies that stop short of confrontation and irreparable breach? Is disunity, especially from the perspective of Orthodoxy, an unavoidable tragedy?

But there is a second tragedy in the contemporary Jewish world that cannot be thought unavoidable. That is the fragmentation within Orthodoxy itself. If all Orthodox Jews hold in common the traditional commitment to God, Torah, and halakhic authority, then division between them cannot be justified on the basis of defence of a principle sufficiently crucial to warrant division. Those values that would justify confrontation, they already hold in common.

Orthodoxy *is* divided, and the tensions between its component groups have escalated in recent years. There is a fundamental disagreement between those who take a positive view of secular culture and those who see it as subversive of Jewish values. There is conflict between those who see the State of Israel as part of the process of redemption, those who regard it as religiously neutral, and those who view it negatively

---

44. Num. 11:14–15.

as a secularization of Jewish identity. There is dissension between the advocates of tolerance towards non-Orthodox and secular Jews and those who favour a more exclusive and segregated Orthodoxy. There are disputes concerning the degree to which halakhah can be responsive to social change, in particular the transformation of the social situation of women. Old arguments once thought to have expired, like those between Hasidim and their opponents, have flared into new life. Orthodoxy itself is no longer a single entity, but a congeries of communities often denying one another's religious credentials.

Not only, then, has modernity turned "Orthodox" into an adjective descriptive of some, not all, Jews. More than this: Orthodoxy itself must now be qualified by secondary adjectives – modern and ultra-, left, centrist, and right-wing, Zionist, non-Zionist, and anti-Zionist, *dati* (religious) and *charedi* (pietistic). Rabbi Louis Bernstein, honorary president of the Rabbinical Council of America, epitomized the condition of Orthodoxy in America as "flourishing but divided." He drew this picture. "The yeshiva world...flares into verbal conflagration with the chassidic elements.... On occasion (far too frequent) verbal differences are translated to violence." Concerted action is impossible. "Orthodoxy's major problem...is itself."[45]

In fact, the divisive issues of recent decades have usually been trivial when weighed against the transcending value of unity. Rabbi Aharon Lichtenstein, surveying American Jewish Orthodoxy, was moved to write of being "overwhelmed by the impression that the major challenges confronting American Orthodoxy were neither demographic nor ideological, not how to deepen Jewish identity and weld the community, and not how to come to grips boldly with the social and intellectual impact of secular culture. These were, rather, determining the status of metropolitan *eiruvin* [devices to allow carrying on the Sabbath] and finding the right tuna fish."[46] Issues of halakhic disagreement, instead of being subjects for debate and resolution by consensus, become emblems of factional division and mutual delegitimation. Halakhah itself, once the basis of a community of action, is drawn into the vortex of strife and

---

45. Louis Bernstein, "Orthodoxy: Flourishing but Divided," *Judaism*, 36:2 (1987), 174–78.
46. Aharon Lichtenstein, "The State of Orthodoxy: A Symposium," *Tradition*, 20:1 (1982), 50.

adds to its momentum. Faced with such a situation, one must seriously question the current power of Torah to unite.

The question is not addressed to Torah itself, but to the fate of Torah in a secular society. For we are confronted here with a phenomenon that has less to do with the inner logic of Judaism than with the culturally fragmenting force of secularization. A second key question of Jewish modernity is, therefore: Does rabbinic tradition possess the resources to prevent the splintering of Orthodoxy? Are its current divisions and the way these are handled consistent with or antithetical to tradition?

A RELIGIOUS IDEA IN A SECULAR AGE

These are questions that go to the heart of Jewry and Judaism. The mystical tradition spoke of three interconnected unities. "The Holy One, blessed be he, the Torah, and Israel are one."[47] That is a mystical doctrine, but it can be unravelled into its non-mystical components. Judaism is monotheism. The rabbis, no less than the prophets, fought against the concept of *shetei reshuyot*, "dualism," or the idea that there is more than one ultimate cosmic power. Fundamental to Jewish belief is the unity of God.

But if there is one God, then there may only be one Torah. One of the formative crises of rabbinic Judaism came "when the disciples of Shammai and Hillel multiplied, who had not served [their teachers] sufficiently." As a result, "disputes multiplied, and the Torah became like *shetei torot*, two Torahs."[48] Such division had to be resolved if the integrity of the Torah was to be preserved.

The rabbis fought equally against the idea – though they did not use the phrase – of *shetei umot*, two nations. In one dazzling image they said that just as Jews bind themselves to God by wearing tefillin (phylacteries), so God binds himself to Israel. Our tefillin, containing the verse "Hear O Israel, the Lord our God, the Lord is one," assert the unity of God. God's tefillin, containing the verse "Who is like your

---

47. This particular formulation may be relatively late. For an early version of it see Zohar, *Acharei Mot*, 73a.
48. Sotah 47b, Sanhedrin 88b.

people Israel, a nation one on earth?" assert the unity of Israel.[49] The early rabbinic literature is set against the backdrop of a people divided politically, culturally, and religiously. Its insistence on "one people" is therefore a theological affirmation in the face of crisis. The unity of the Jews, like that of Torah, is the counterpart, as it were, of the unity of God. To destroy one is to compromise the others. Rabbinic Judaism rests on these three unities – Israel, the Holy One, blessed be he, and the Torah – themselves united by the covenant at Sinai.

Daniel Elazar is surely correct when he writes: "The Jewish people today are in the process of millennial change, the kind of change that has not taken place since the triumph of Pharisaic Judaism eighteen hundred years ago or the emergence of the diaspora nine hundred years before that."[50] But do Jews hold enough in common for their shared nationhood to persist through such change? Can we still speak of the Jewish people?

Jewish unity was, traditionally, a religious idea. My assumption throughout this study is that it remains so. In the past two centuries alternative definitions have been offered: territorial, political, ethnic, and cultural. None of these, I believe, has even the most remote chance of uniting a world Jewry divided between Israel and the diaspora and split into a vast multiplicity of cultures and ethnicities. Only a religious idea can span these divergences of interest and identity. But it is precisely the religious idea of Jews as one people that has become uniquely problematic in modern times. The fragmentation has taken place along two axes: between Orthodoxy and others, and within Orthodoxy itself.

The question before us, then, is this. Does the rabbinic tradition, which once forged unity out of disintegration, have the resources to do so again? In later chapters we shall consider the relationship between Orthodoxy and others. But first we must consider the divisions within

---

49. I Chr. 17:21 and II Sam. 7:23; Berakhot 6a. The biblical phrase *goy echad ba'aretz* might be translated as either "a nation one on earth" or "a nation unique on earth." In choosing to understand it in the first sense, the rabbis were undoubtedly influenced by Ezek. 37:22 ("I will make them a single nation in the land...never again shall they be two nations, and never again shall they be divided into two kingdoms"), where it clearly bears this meaning. The sages were concerned to stress the *unity* as well as the *uniqueness* of the Jewish people.

50. Elazar, *People and Polity*, 475.

Orthodoxy itself. How did they arise? Are they insuperable? Is Ortho-doxy, with its deep religious commitment to Jewish unity, condemned to inflict a defeat on one of its own key values? Is adjectival Orthodoxy unavoidable?

Chapter 3

Orthodoxy, History, and Culture

Secularization, as we have seen, does not eclipse religion, but it transforms it. Faced with social processes that threaten to undermine their values, religions must choose between accommodation and resistance. In the case of Judaism, the Reform, and later Conservative and Reconstructionist movements, emerged as modes of accommodation. Each was schismatic in the sense that it involved changes that went beyond the traditional parameters of Jewish belief and practice. But none announced itself as revolutionary. On the contrary, each sought to identify itself as heir to the Jewish past. Each saw itself as a Jewish denomination. The paradox is that Judaism traditionally had no place for the concept of a denomination. Orthodoxy maintains that belief. The result is that liberal Judaisms and Orthodoxy are condemned to systematic mutual misunderstanding, a situation that leads to division without providing any shared language through which division might be transcended. Secularization proved destructive of Jewish unity while giving disunity a compelling momentum of its own.

What happened to Orthodoxy in the process? Thus far we have spoken of the various liberal non-Orthodoxies as accommodationist, perhaps seeming to imply that Orthodoxy, for its part, adopted a strategy of resistance. In fact, though, it was not uniformly so. There were a great variety of Orthodox responses. Some groups were opposed to and resisted the changes emancipation heralded. But others developed positive ideologies celebrating the new era. Yet others responded pragmatically, seeing no need to develop any ideological response to social change. Others again, while welcoming modernity, felt that the particular form it had taken in Europe would prove fatal for Jewish continuity and looked instead to a movement of renewal in Zion.

There was thus no single Orthodox strategy for confronting modernity. Instead there were strategies of every kind. This too is testimony to the fact that Orthodoxy is not a movement or denomination but a set of boundary principles within which lie a vast variety of culturally, intellectually, and spiritually distinguishable tendencies. In this chapter we consider Orthodox responses to emancipation and the collapse of the traditional structures of Jewish community. How did such a highly elaborated body of law and doctrine give rise to so diverse a range of reactions? Why did there emerge not one Orthodoxy but many?

CONSERVING THE COVENANT

Traditionally, Judaism comprises laws and beliefs. All Orthodox responses to change hold one premiss in common: any social process that involved abandoning either an extant law or a central belief would have to be resisted. It was this that distinguished Orthodoxy from the other movements we have considered and led to its image as a mode of resistance.

This was Orthodoxy's non-negotiable axiom. It was not a response to modernity as such, but instead a principled continuity that can be traced back to the origins of rabbinic Judaism and beyond. The covenant between God and Israel, of which the Mosaic books were the record and constitution, embodied a way of life represented by the commandments, along with a framework for the understanding of Jewish history. One of the central elements of the covenant was its own eternity, and the corresponding promise of the eternity of the people of Israel. Envisaging catastrophe and exile, Moses had communicated the divine promise, "Yet, even then, when they are in the land of their enemies, I will not reject them or spurn them so as to destroy them, annulling my covenant with them, for I am the Lord their God."[1]

The eternity of the covenant was the eternity of the people. This gave Judaism its peculiar combination of resistance and impetus to change. The developments that took place in the transition from biblical to rabbinic Judaism, for example, were radical. The moves from Temple to synagogue, from sacrifice to prayer, from prophecy to the study of the Torah, from the rule of kings to that of sages, and other changes no less fundamental, transformed the character of Jewish life from one predicated on national institutions into one capable of survival in exile. But the logic of these changes was consistently *to preserve the covenant* in situations where some of its major institutions had been destroyed. The heirs to tradition in the nineteenth century inherited this combination of flexibility of form, conservatism of content. The image of Orthodoxy as resistant to change, an image it itself sometimes encourages, is true at one level, false at another. Its primary concern is to conserve the covenant, keeping faith with the past and discharging its duty to the future. Within this overall objective, institutional change is permitted; covenantal change is not.

This made some aspects of modern consciousness wholly unacceptable to Orthodoxy. Reform's abandonment of the binding authority of halakhah was one. Conservative Judaism's historicization[2] of the halakhic process was another. Reconstructionism's removal of the category of revelation was a third. Each of these was a significant secularization of the concept of covenant, and none could be contemplated by even the most liberal of Orthodox thinkers. The notion of historical progress which so dominated the nineteenth century was profoundly at odds with the traditional Jewish idea of revelation, in which the past addressed the present and could not be superseded by it. Even the most enthusiastic of all Orthodox advocates of modernity, Samson Raphael Hirsch, made this principle clear. "We declare before heaven and earth," he wrote in 1854, "that if our religion demanded that we should renounce what is

---

1. Lev. 26:44.
2. On this see Jonathan Sacks, *Crisis and Covenant: Jewish Thought after the Holocaust* (Manchester: Manchester University Press, 1992).

called civilisation and progress we would obey unquestioningly, because our religion is for us truly religion, the word of God before which every other consideration has to give way."[3]

INTERPRETING CHANGE

But not all issues were so straightforward, for two reasons. First, it was not always clear what constituted a continuation of the covenant. Were historical processes leading towards or away from a fulfilment of Jewish destiny? Second, what *was* the covenantal way of life? Was it that area bounded by halakhah, or did it extend beyond? Was Torah all-embracing, or were there areas of human experience that were religiously neutral? Since there was more than one possible answer to these questions, there was more than one possible Orthodox response to modernity.

Taking the first point first: social change required evaluation from the point of view of Jewish values. Was a new development in the situation of Jews covenantally sanctioned or not? An answer involved sophisticated historical judgement. It lay in the nature of the question that not all Orthodox thinkers concurred at any given moment, and there were times when a previous consensus was reversed.

The point is exemplified in the shifting history of Orthodox responses to the return to Zion. The Hamburg rabbinical court, as noted in the previous chapter, was severely critical of the programme of the reformers who had built the Hamburg temple. Among other innovations, they had deleted from the prayer book certain references to the ingathering of exiles and the restoration of Jewish life in Israel. The Orthodox response, published in 1819, condemned this as the abandonment of one of the fundamentals of Jewish faith. The return to Zion was affirmed by the traditional rabbinate as central to Jewish hope. One of the contributors to the volume, Rabbi Moses Sofer (1762–1839; known as the Chatam Sofer), was an enthusiastic supporter of Jewish settlement in Israel and was seen by some, in retrospect, as one of the early inspirations of the Zionist movement.[4]

---

3. Samson Raphael Hirsch, "Religion Allied to Progress," in *Judaism Eternal*, trans. I. Grunfeld (2 vols.; London: Soncino, 1959), ii. 234–35.
4. See D. Zahavi, *Mehachatam Sofer ad Herzl* (Jerusalem: Hasifriya Hatzionit, 1966),

In his reply to the reformers, Sofer had written dismissively of the benefits of European emancipation and longingly of his feelings for the land of Israel. "We do not need to eat the fruits and be sated with the goodness [of an easy and tranquil life among the nations. Were this so] one could then make the blasphemous claim, "Have we not found tranquillity and goodness among the Gentiles, so what need have we for the land of Israel?" Heaven forbid! We do not pour out our hearts and wait in anticipation all our days for an illusory material tranquillity. Rather our hope is to dwell in the presence of God there [in the land of Israel], the place designated for His service and for the observance of His Torah."[5] There is the same mood here of yearning for Israel that we find in the writings of Judah Halevi and Nachmanides in the Middle Ages. Sofer was a passionate particularist, who saw the cultural force of Enlightenment universalism as antithetical to Jewish sensibilities and ultimately destructive of them. Far from heralding a new golden age for Jews, emancipation was a trial, tempting Jews through integration into assimilation.

But a quite different attitude was possible within the same framework of Jewish values. In 1836, the young Samson Raphael Hirsch (1808–88) published, under a pseudonym, an enthusiastic Orthodox response to emancipation. The *Nineteen Letters* were a guide to the perplexed of his time, and they argued that the new social and intellectual avenues open to Jews held the possibility of a renewal of Judaism. The impact of the work was dramatic. A young intellectual, Heinrich Graetz (1817–91), later to become nineteenth-century Jewry's greatest historian, wrote on first reading it, "With avidity I devoured every word. Disloyal though I had been to the Talmud, this book reconciled me with it."[6] He went to stay with Hirsch and studied under him for three years.

In the *Nineteen Letters*, Hirsch de-emphasized the Zionist dimension of Judaism. First, it was only a means, not an end. "The independent

---

364; S. Ehrmann, "Moses Sofer," in Leo Jung (ed.), *Jewish Leaders* (New York: Bloch, 1953), 117–38.

5. *Eleh Divrei Haberit*, 154–55.

6. Quoted in Noah Rosenbloom, *Tradition in an Age of Reform* (Philadelphia: JPS, 1976), 71.

national life of Israel was never the essence or the purpose of our existence as a nation, but only a means of fulfilling our spiritual mission."[7] Second, the ingathering of exiles was part of metaphysical, not political, history. "We hope and pray" for the messianic ingathering, "but actively to accelerate its coming is prohibited to us."[8] Third, even the rebirth of Israel will not be primarily a revival of Jewish nationhood, but the inauguration of an era of universal humanity when "hand in hand with us, the entire [human] race will be joined in universal brotherhood through the recognition of God."[9]

These propositions are impeccably consistent with the same constellation of values which gave rise to Rabbi Sofer's rejection of emancipation. But they point in a different direction. An open European society was for Hirsch not a temptation to be avoided but a challenge to be embraced. "It is our duty to join ourselves as closely as possible to the state which receives us into its midst, to promote its welfare and not to consider our own well-being as in any way separate from that of the state to which we belong."[10] Hirsch here means more than active citizenship and civic responsibility. He goes on to develop his own statement of the thesis that so dominated non-Orthodox Jewish thought of the early nineteenth century: the mission to the gentiles. "Picture every son of Israel a respected and influential priest of righteousness and love, disseminating among the nations not specific Judaism – for proselytism is forbidden – but pure humanity."[11] Hitherto, their segregation and civil disabilities had prevented Jews from exercising this exemplary role. Emancipation now accorded Judaism "a greater opportunity for the fulfilment of its task, the realization of a noble and ideal life."[12]

Were these two approaches, Hirsch's and Sofer's, incompatible? No more and no less than those of Jeremiah and Ezekiel some two and a half thousand years earlier. Jeremiah had sent a letter to the exiles in Babylon advising them to "Build houses and settle down; plant gardens

7. Hirsch, *Nineteen Letters*, 107.
8. Ibid., 108.
9. Ibid.
10. Ibid., 107.
11. Ibid., 108.
12. Ibid., 111.

and eat their produce.... Seek the peace of the city to which I have exiled you. Pray to the Lord for it: for in its peace you will find peace."[13] Ezekiel had delivered a prophecy denouncing the exiles. "You say, 'We want to be like the nations, like the peoples of the world, who serve wood and stone.' But what you have in mind will never happen.... I will bring you from the nations and gather you from the countries where you have been scattered, with a mighty hand and an outstretched arm and with outpoured wrath."[14] Jeremiah insists that exile must be endured; Ezekiel issues the reminder that exile is still exile, not home. Jeremiah warns against a premature forcing of history. Ezekiel warns against assimilation. Each was to be a significant proof-text in the history of Orthodox responses to Zionism. They are part of the same vision. They differ in what they judge to be the imperative of the hour.

DEVELOPMENTS AND VARIATIONS

It would be anachronistic to describe Sofer as a Zionist, Hirsch as a non-Zionist. At that time, in the early nineteenth century, the Zionist movement existed neither in fact nor in imagination. A massive leap of thought had to take place before the traditional Jewish longing for a return to the land could be translated from prayer to political programme. At most there was a difference of emphasis between the two men. Sofer, like many other rabbis of the eighteenth and nineteenth centuries,[15] expressed his love of the land of Israel in terms of support for Orthodox Jewish settlements there. Hirsch, as a defender of Orthodoxy in a rapidly acculturating German Jewry, stressed diaspora Jewish patriotism and universality. There is in his writings a barely veiled apologetic motif. But as the century progressed, what had been no more than a mild difference became markedly more pronounced.

The particularism implicit in Rabbi Moses Sofer was taken further by Zvi Hirsch Kalischer (1795–1874) and Yehudah Alkalai (1798–1878),

---

13. Jer. 29:5.
14. Ezek. 20:32, 34.
15. In the 18th cent. these included Elijah the Gaon of Vilna, and various Hasidic leaders, including Menachem Mendel of Vitebsk, Abraham of Kalisk, and Nachman of Bratslav. In the 19th cent. they included Rabbis Elijah Guttmacher, Azriel Hildesheimer, and Jacob Ettlinger.

two Orthodox rabbis who argued that the process of redemption must begin with human efforts to resettle the land of Israel.[16] The work of Kalischer in particular struck a chord with a secularist Jew and one-time colleague of Karl Marx, Moses Hess. Hess's *Rome and Jerusalem* (1862) laid the basis for secular Zionism, and was an attack on emancipation and Reform as powerful as any delivered by Orthodoxy. Where Clermont-Tonerre had argued that Jews should be emancipated individually, not nationally, Hess argued that only national, not individual, emancipation was possible. He was savage in his critique of Jews who had "religion-ized" Judaism and de-emphasized its national component. The Jew who denies Jewish nationalism, he wrote, is "a traitor to his people and to his family."[17] He was particularly critical of those who welcomed integration into European society and spoke as if "the *dispersion* of the Jews were the *Mission* of Judaism."[18]

In the opposite direction, German Reform and Orthodox rab-bis – the so-called *Protestrabbiner* – were to come together in a rare dem-onstration of solidarity to denounce the first Zionist Congress (1897) and to assert: "The efforts of the so-called Zionists to create a Jewish National State in Palestine are antagonistic to the messianic promises of Judaism."[19] The rabbis hinted ominously that political Zionism con-flicted with the loyalty of German Jews to their country. Herzl, under pressure, had to transfer the congress from Munich to Basle.

Zionism had thus brought one group of Orthodox Jews – mainly East European – into a temporary kinship with secularists, and another – mostly from Western Europe – into a momentary alliance with Reform. The shifts and ironies were to continue. Almost all the children and grandchildren of the anti-Zionist *Protestrabbiner* even-tually settled in Israel.[20] East and West European Orthodoxy, divided between the influences of Sofer and Hirsch, eventually converged in the

16. On Alkalai and Kalischer see Hertzberg (ed.), *The Zionist Idea*, 101–14; Jacob Katz, *Jewish Emancipation and Self-Emancipation* (Philadelphia: JPS, 1986), 89–115, 153–66.

17. Moses Hess, *Rome and Jerusalem* [1862], trans. Maurice J. Bloom (New York: Philo-sophical Library, 1958), 27.

18. Ibid., 58.

19. In Mendes-Flohr and Reinharz (eds.), *The Jew in the Modern World*, 427–29.

20. See "Protestrabbiner," *Encyclopaedia Judaica* (Jerusalem: Keter, 1972), xiii. 1255.

non-Zionist Agudat Yisrael (1912). Rabbi Solomon Breuer, a student of Moses Sofer's son, Abraham, and son-in-law and successor of Hirsch,[21] symbolized this new consensus, and took an active part in Agudat Yisrael. Zionism was variously to be conceived by Orthodoxy as satanic (Rabbi Joel Teitelbaum), messianic (Rabbi Abraham Isaac Kook), a pragmatic solution to persecution (Rabbi Isaac Reines), and the context of Judaic renewal (Isaac Breuer).

Each of these attitudes was possible within the same highly articulated rabbinic tradition. All parties agreed, in other words, that the present condition of Jews was to be characterized as *galut,* exile; that their desire was for the messianic age; and that the messianic age would witness a return of Jews to Zion. All agreed that neither Jewish dispersion nor Jewish nationhood was an end in itself. All, too, agreed that Jewish history was not secular, made entirely by man. It was providential, shaped by God. All Orthodox thinkers therefore parted company with the most basic premises of Reform on the one hand and secular Zionism on the other. But despite this considerable area of substantive agreement, incompatible positions and sometimes violent conflict were possible. Every shade and nuance of diversity to be found outside Orthodoxy was mirrored within Orthodoxy itself, translated, to be sure, into different frames of reference.

The example of Zionism illustrates a fundamental point about Orthodoxy, or more precisely, about Torah. The application of Torah to new social, historical, or political circumstance always involves a social or historical or political judgement. The covenantal imperative is never self-evident, never the direct application of text to situation. Before a situation can be judged, it must first be characterized. Which of two alternative futures – individual emancipation in Europe or collective emancipation in Israel – was the next step in history to which Jews were being called? Which was more threatening to Jewish integrity: assimilation into non-Jewish society or the secularization of a Jewish state? How was one to view political action to bring about Jewish sovereignty in Israel? Pragmatically or theologically? If pragmatically, would it

---

21. Schwab, *The History of Orthodox Jewry in Germany,* 115–26.

worsen or improve the situation of Europe's Jews? If theologically, was it a response to Providence or an attempt to frustrate it?

Orthodoxy acts to conserve the covenant, to write the next chapter in a continuous narrative whose beginning and end are both revealed in the Torah. But what that next chapter is involves sensitive judgement, both of Torah and of the contemporary situation. Judgement is not the deductive inference of conclusions from premises, but the weighing of alternatives and a search for analogies, none of which is precise. It admits of more than one right answer. This is the first reason for Orthodox diversity.

TORAH AS CODE OR CULTURE

One question which modernity posed was thus the direction of covenantal history. A second was the scope of covenantal existence.

As noted in the previous chapter, secularization involves the transference of religious values from the public to the private domain. In the case of Judaism, the change involved was sudden and substantial. Prior to emancipation, Jews had lived within an integrated and enveloping Jewish culture. To be sure, trade and geographical proximity brought them into contact with non-Jews. At no stage were Jewish ideas and practice hermetically sealed from the surrounding popular or high culture. But education, adult study, and the economic, welfare, and judicial institutions of communal life were administered by the Jewish community itself. Jews lived together and formed an autonomous reference-group with its own distinctive values. To be a Jew was to be born into a coherent culture which embraced far more than religious law and teaching. Jewish identity was for the most part unproblematic: we find no soul-searching on this point prior to modernity. Jewish selfhood was essential, not adjectival.

The transition from Jew to Jewish German, Frenchman, or Englishman was profound. Jews in Germany were called on, and summoned themselves, to drop Yiddish or *Judendeutsch* and learn pure German. Jewish children were to be given a secular education. A common assumption of Jewish and non-Jewish liberals of the Enlightenment was that the culture of the ghetto was anachronistic and unrefined. It stood in the way of social acceptance. Great emphasis was placed on new kinds of school that would provide Jews with *Bildung* and *Sittlichkeit*, education in character and respectability. Jewish periodicals like *Sulamith* and *Hame'asef* delivered homilies on the need for culture and rectitude.[22] Jews passed through the trauma of what John Murray Cuddihy has called "the ordeal of civility."[23]

Culturally, intellectually, and socially, the Jewish reference-group was, for the first time, the majority non-Jewish society. This was made possible by the secularization of the public domain. No longer did Jews confront a Christian or Islamic state. It was a neutral, or, as Jacob Katz has termed it, a semi-neutral society, for old hostilities remained. Some Jews converted, especially among the higher economic and intellectual strata. Heinrich Heine called the baptismal certificate "the ticket of admission to Western culture." But for the most part Jews pursued, in the public arena, a religionless universality. Indeed, Jewish intellectuals displayed an almost religious fervour for secularism. Thinkers of Jewish ancestry were some of the most powerful iconoclasts of the modern world, among them Marx, Durkheim, and Freud.

What, then, remained of Judaism? Precisely that: Judaism. The word itself is a symptom of modernity, no less than the word "Orthodox." "Judaism" signifies a religion in the peculiarly modern sense, a personal set of convictions acted out for the most part in private contexts. "The conception of Judaism as an organized body of doctrine...derives from an age in which people had determined that Judaism belonged to the category of *religion*.... The source of the categorical power of "Judaism" derives from the Protestant philosophical heritage that has defined scholarship, including category-formation, from the time of Kant onward."[24] The environing culture of traditional Jewish societies could not be expressed by a word as narrow in its compass as "Judaism." The question

---

22. See Katz, *Out of the Ghetto*; George L. Mosse, "Jewish Emancipation: Between Bildung and Respectability," in Jehuda Reinharz and Walter Schatzberg (eds.), *The Jewish Response to German Culture* (Hanover, NH: University Press of New England, 1985), 1–16.

23. Cuddihy, *The Ordeal of Civility*.

24. Jacob Neusner, *From "Judaism" to "Torah": An Essay in Inductive Category Formation* (New York: Hunter College, 1986), 4–5.

was therefore: Could Torah as hitherto conceived survive within this circumscribed space, *as* Judaism?

The early reformers answered the question in the negative. Only an abridged Torah could survive, one that had been pruned of its segregating beliefs and prohibitions. It was Samson Raphael Hirsch's genius to see that an affirmative answer could be given. Precisely because Jewish entry into German society was a question, not of religion but of culture – *derekh eretz,* as he called it – emancipation was religiously neutral and could be undergone without a single compromise of halakhah. Hirsch called his symbiosis of secular culture and Jewish religiosity *Mensch-Jissroel,* or Man-Israel. Adopting a phrase from the Mishnah which had originally meant "Torah combined with a worldly occupation," he called his programme *torah im derekh eretz.*[25] In Hirsch's usage the phrase now evoked a rich set of associations: Torah together with civility, secular culture, and exemplary citizenship.

In his early career, as a young rabbi in Oldenburg, Hirsch was something of a radical, preaching sermons in high literary German, wearing canonicals, introducing a choir into the synagogue, and abolishing the *Kol Nidrei* prayer on Yom Kippur. These were all innovations later to be regarded, especially by the Hungarian Orthodox rabbinate, as symptoms of Reform. Hirsch, of course, was in no way a reformer: of his generation, he was the most ardent and successful polemicist against Reform. His importation into the synagogue of non-Jewish models of decorum had already become the norm in the Orthodox establishments of countries such as England and France, where the process of emancipation was more advanced.[26] Hirsch was merely demonstrating that the "ordeal of civility" required only cosmetic changes. It was a matter

---

25. Mish. Avot 2:2. Hirsch was not the first to use the phrase *torah im derekh eretz* in this context. That had been done earlier by Naftali Herz Wessely in his tract on enlightened Jewish education, *Divrei Shalom Ve'emet* (Berlin, 1782).

26. For comparisons between the English and French Jewish adjustment to modernity and the German experience see Michael Graetz, "The History of an Estrangement between Two Jewish Communities: German and French Jewry during the Nineteenth Century," and Todd Endelman, "The Englishness of Jewish Modernity in England," both in Jacob Katz (ed.), *Toward Modernity: The European Jewish Model* (Oxford: Transaction Books, 1987), 159–70, 225–46.

not of substance but of style. Reform could be successfully confronted on its own ground – cultural accommodation – without any sacrifice of principle or practice.

DUAL SENSIBILITIES

But Hirsch's substantive achievement did not so much lie in synagogue life as in education. It was here that *torah im derekh eretz* offered the possibility of a genuinely creative synthesis. It brought together two strong currents: the traditional Jewish reverence for study, and the early nineteenth-century German preoccupation with educational philosophy. Hirsch was deeply critical of the Jewish education of his day, divided as it was between highly secularized schools such as the Philantropin in Frankfurt, and the traditional *chadarim* (Hebrew schools) which had offered no response to new economic and cultural challenges. The former were technically proficient in training young people for careers but were cursory in their treatment of Judaism and in what Hirsch called "the education of the heart."[27] The latter taught "uncomprehended Judaism as a mechanical habit... without its spirit."[28] Evidently Hirsch's parents took the same view, for they sent their son to the local non-Jewish grammar school in Hamburg in preference to the several available Jewish schools.[29] The way was open for a new kind of Jewish day school, one that would combine secular excellence with rigorous Torah study; and in 1853, as the newly appointed rabbi in Frankfurt, Hirsch created it.

Hirsch's educational philosophy has been characterized as one of compartmentalization. The "with" of "Torah with *derekh eretz*" suggested dualism rather than dialogue. Torah and secular knowledge, on this view, "can co-operate, even as the limbs of a body co-operate and co-ordinate; but they cannot interact and speak to each other, even as a sane and balanced person does not talk to himself."[30] Hirsch himself certainly aspired to something larger. He believed that Jewish spirituality

27. Hirsch, *Nineteen Letters*, 115
28. Ibid., 126.
29. See Rosenbloom, *Tradition in an Age of Reform*, 53–56.
30. Norman Lamm, "Two Versions of Synthesis," in *Faith and Doubt* (New York: Ktav, 1971), 71.

had atrophied in the ghetto. Cut off from general culture, "every mind that felt the desire for independent activity was obliged to forsake the paths of study and research open in general to the human intellect and to take recourse in dialectical subtleties and hair-splittings."[31] Hirsch felt that the emancipation of Jews would be the emancipation of Torah and its re-engagement with the real world. This would in turn inform the way a Jew studied secular disciplines. "Nature should be contemplated with the spirit of David; history should be perceived with the ear of an Isaiah."[32] Hirsch believed in synthesis and in the essential harmony of all knowledge. "It is the Jewish view that truth, like God its source, is one and indivisible, and that therefore knowledge of it can be only one and indivisible."[33] History reveals Providence; science discloses Creation. Secular education, quite apart from training for a career and livelihood, "contributes greatly at the same time to deepening and broadening Jewish religious education."[34]

By and large, the synthesis did not happen. The fault lay in neither Hirsch nor his ideals, but in the social context.[35] The very secularization of European culture, which allowed Jews to participate in it, frustrated attempts to Judaize it. If the products of Hirsch's school were compartmentalized, it was because the wider society of which they were a part produced compartmentalized identities. In response to the large, faceless, and value-neutral structures of corporate and bureaucratic life has come "the creation of the private sphere as a distinctive and largely segregated sector of social life, along with the dichotomization of the individual's societal involvements between the private and public spheres.... A specific private identity provides shelter from the threats of anonymity."[36]

---

31. Hirsch, *Nineteen Letters*, 121.
32. Ibid., 127–28.
33. Hirsch, *Judaism Eternal*, i. 207–8.
34. Ibid., 209.
35. To my sociological interpretation, Professor Judith Bleich adds another explanation: "One of the major deficiencies of Hirsch's school system appears to have been the lack of an intensive higher-level Judaic Studies curriculum. Had this been instituted, the question 'Can a *torah im derekh eretz* synthesis be achieved?' might have had a different answer" (Judith Bleich, personal communication).
36. Berger, Berger, and Kellner, *The Homeless Mind*, 166–67.

The nineteenth-century aphorism that one should be "A man in the street and a Jew at home" deserves to be seen as part of a universal process – the disjunction between private identities and public roles – and not a specifically Jewish one.

It may therefore be that what Hirsch might have regarded as his greatest failure was, in fact, his greatest success: the creation of the compartmentalized Jew. Charles Liebman has pointed out that while compartmentalization is philosophically unsatisfying and possibly indefensible, it is an extraordinarily successful survival strategy. He argues that "most Orthodox Jews have retained their ritual tradition and belief system virtually intact and at the same time have acculturated in language, dress and education to American styles because they have been able to separate these two aspects of life so that they impinge on one another as little as possible."[37]

In his reflections on Hirsch's school, Jacob Rosenheim noted that its success in producing religious commitment was not due to the school itself, its curriculum, or its methodology, but to its close links with Hirsch's synagogue and the Frankfurt community. Those who remained within the community stayed Orthodox; those who left Frankfurt tended not to. A recent study of Frankfurt Jewry concluded that "the long-term effectiveness of the school in educating its pupils depended on the success and strength of the community itself."[38]

Hirsch had thus found one way of solving the dilemma of modern Jewish identity. It lay not so much in his philosophy as in its institutional and social reality. There were two domains: the secular, public world and the private, Jewish world. The former, being secularized, was halakhically neutral. It was the territory of neither the commanded nor the prohibited, but of the permitted. In this area, Jews might pursue careers, acquire cultural depth, and be active shapers of society while at the same time meticulously avoiding transgression of Jewish law. The latter was where a Jew became and remained a Jew. To maintain an identity on so

---

37. Charles Liebman, "Orthodox Judaism Today," 116.
38. Robert Liberles, *Religious Conflict in Social Context: The Resurgence of Orthodox Judaism in Frankfurt am Main 1838–1877* (Westport, CT: Greenwood Press, 1985), 154.

slender a base required a strong and disciplined community in which synagogue, school, and adult study all reinforced one another. The two worlds did not connect. Hirsch wished they would. Sociological reality dictated otherwise. But the strength of the Frankfurt community meant that Hirsch's most basic concern was met: Torah would have priority over *derekh eretz* – or as we might otherwise put it, secular activity was what one *did*, Jewishness was what one *was*.

Hirsch's solution came to be known as Neo-Orthodoxy. The description is not altogether apt. It was not Modern Orthodoxy in the sense which came to be attached to the phrase in America in the 1960s. Hirsch was and saw himself as a traditionalist rather than a modernist. His enthusiasm for emancipation lay in the fact that he saw in it the opportunity for a return to a richer version of tradition than had been possible in the narrow centuries following the Spanish expulsion. But he was, none the less, conscious of living at a time of massive social change, and believed that Judaism should meet the challenge directly rather than cling to the manners and mores of the ghetto. He recognized, *de facto*, that Jewish institutions and culture no longer comprised the totality of life for the modern Jew. Jewish juridical autonomy had ceased. Much of Judaism's civil law had become inoperative. Jews were part of a wider culture. The few specifically Jewish contexts that remained were the "four cubits" of family, synagogue, school, and the fellowship of study. Jewish experience had contracted to fit the space available for it. It had become "Judaism."[39]

DEREKH ERETZ: JEWISH OR SECULAR?

It was here that a critical argument emerged over the phrase *derekh eretz*. At all periods, rabbinic Judaism had recognized a domain outside Torah but essential to it. In the Mishnah in which the phrase *torah im derekh eretz* originally appeared, it meant an occupation, a means of earning a living. Elsewhere it carried a spectrum of senses: good manners and etiquette, practical wisdom, or civilized or socially constructive

---

39. See Charles Liebman, "Religion and the Chaos of Modernity: The Case of Contemporary Judaism," in Jacob Neusner (ed.), *Take Judaism, for Example* (Chicago: University of Chicago Press, 1983), 147–64.

behaviour.[40] *Derekh eretz* bore roughly the same relationship to rabbinic Judaism as did the Wisdom literature, such as the book of Proverbs, to biblical Judaism.

Hirsch saw that whereas Torah was constitutive of Judaism, *derekh eretz* – "the way of the world" – was not. The particular social, economic, and cultural forms of the ghetto belonged to one phase of Jewish history. They did not belong to the core of Jewish identity. Hirsch drew a clear distinction between matters of halakhah – the commanded and forbidden – and matters of custom, habit, folklore, and convention. *Torah im derekh eretz* meant that Torah could be combined with selective elements of any culture in which Jews were located, provided that it involved no breach of a command or prohibition. Just as Jews dressed differently in different times and places and spoke different languages, so they could now acquire European mores while leaving the essential core of Torah untouched.

Others, though, saw emancipation quite differently. In the Mishnah and Talmud, Jewish-gentile relationships had been subsumed under the tractate Avodah Zarah, the tractate dealing with idolatry. Throughout the Middle Ages, Jews for the most part confronted a Christian or Islamic society. A vast ideological chasm, in other words, separated them from their neighbours. To identify fully with the host culture meant apostasy. That which flowed from the outside as *derekh eretz* was necessarily marginal. With emancipation, the scope and impact of *derekh eretz* were dramatically increased, and threatened instead to marginalize Judaism. Samuel Heilman has gone so far as to suggest that the new social order was "a new version of the age-old Christian efforts to convert Jews. Now instead of demanding a conversion to Christianity, the Christians were demanding a Jewish conversion to secular citizenship."[41]

There were those who concluded that Torah, though it was still to be accompanied by *derekh eretz*, needed a specifically Jewish *derekh eretz*. The culture of the ghetto might have been, in its time, halakhically neutral, but it now took on a new significance. It was an essential bearer of tradition and continuity. No change could be regarded as merely

---

40. "Derekh Eretz," in *Entziklopediah Talmudit* (Jerusalem, 1947–), vii. 672–706.
41. Heilman, "The Many Faces of Orthodoxy," 23–24.

cosmetic. The abandonment of Yiddish in favour of the vernacular, the application to the synagogue of non-Jewish models of decorum and refinement, and the pursuit of a general education were concessions to an intrusive secularity. Hirsch's programme was a Trojan horse. The point was made in the twentieth century by a Jewish secularist, Gershom Scholem. *Torah im derekh eretz*, he argued, became "a vehicle of a kind of assimilation whose demonic triumphs in the Orthodox camp would require a Jewish Balzac to describe them in their full extent." It was intended "to strengthen the Jewish backbone of the pious." Instead it "has done more than anything else to break it."[42] This perception had been registered at the very beginning of the nineteenth century. Its chief proponent was Rabbi Moses Sofer.

Sofer, the architect of Hungarian Orthodoxy, applied to every accommodation to modernity the maxim *chadash asur min hatorah*, "the new is biblically forbidden." This was a pun based on a statement in the Mishnah[43] relating to the prohibition against eating produce from the new harvest prior to the bringing of the Omer offering. In Sofer's homiletical usage it now expressed an opposition to any innovation in Jewish life, especially within the twin sanctuaries of the synagogue and school.

In retrospect we can understand the logic of this position. The rabbis of the mishnaic and talmudic periods had seen as part of their mandate not merely the direct enforcement of biblical law but also its indirect protection. According to the Mishnah at the beginning of tractate Avot, the Men of the Great Assembly had formulated the principle "Make a fence for the Torah."[44] The sages were accordingly empowered to enact decrees forbidding what was otherwise permitted on the grounds that certain acts, in themselves neutral, might eventually lead to transgressions of biblical law or other forms of social disintegration.[45] This power had lapsed in the post-talmudic, or at least post-gaonic, period. None the less, the perception which underlay it was still germane. Not

---

42. Quoted in Rosenbloom, *Tradition in an Age of Reform*, 354–55.
43. Mish. Orlah 3:9.
44. Mish. Avot 1:1.
45. For a survey of the nature and scope of such decrees see *Entziklopediah Talmudit*, v. 529–40.

everything that was halakhically permissible was neutral from the broad perspective of halakhic continuity. On the contrary, minor aesthetic or educational changes today might lead tomorrow to substantive and unacceptable reforms. So the prehistory of the Reform movement showed.

Rabbi Sofer's perception seems to have been that in an age marked by flight from tradition, small deviations heralded major breaches. The new, if not in itself forbidden, would in the end lead to acts that were. It was a position taken further by the next generation of Hungarian halakhists, among them his son Rabbi Abraham Sofer, Moses Schick, and Judah Aszod. An ultra-traditionalism developed in Hungarian Orthodoxy which invested custom with emblematic significance as a fence around Jewish law. Continuity demanded not a new *derekh eretz* but the vigilant maintenance of the old. Judaism was a total way of life and therefore nothing – certainly not secular culture – could escape categorization into that which enhanced and that which endangered religious observance in the long run. The doors that Hirsch opened, Sofer and his disciples closed. Their objective was the same: the defence of Orthodoxy as a way of life. But their strategies were opposed. What was seen in Germany as a possible synthesis was seen in Hungary as an inescapable antithesis.

Sofer's followers took a markedly negative view of secular culture. They therefore needed an institutional base quite different from Hirsch's Frankfurt model of the *torah im derekh eretz* day school. It came in the form of the yeshiva. Rabbi Sofer founded his yeshiva in Pressburg and it quickly became the largest in Europe.[46] Its significance was immediately grasped by the Hungarian reformers, one of whom, Wolf Breisach, made a determined attempt to have it closed.[47] Others flourished throughout Austro-Hungary, among them Eisenstadt, Huszt, and Satmar. They were particularly effective in training dedicated and learned alumni, many of whom subsequently occupied rabbinic positions. But the true home of

---

46. See Jacob Katz, "Contribution towards a Biography of R. Moses Sofer," in *Studies in Mysticism and Religion Presented to Gershom Scholem* (Jerusalem: Magnes Press, 1967), 115–48.

47. See Michael Silber, "The Historical Experience of German Jewry and Its Impact on the Haskalah and Reform in Hungary," in Jacob Katz (ed.), *Toward Modernity*, 107–58.

the modern yeshiva proved to be Lithuania, where Volozhin, founded in 1803 by Rabbi Chayyim Volozhiner (1749–1821), quickly became the model which others sought to emulate.

The Lithuanian-style yeshiva differed from its predecessors in a number of ways. It was independent of the local community, both in its funding and in its student body. Students often came from a distance. During their stay, the yeshiva became a home and its head a figure of quasi-parental authority. No longer simply a place of Jewish instruction, the yeshiva became a bulwark against secularization. It was a total environment, the locus of a spiritual elite who would remain faithful to tradition while around them the Jewish world crumbled.

Throughout Eastern Europe during the nineteenth century, new yeshivot emerged. Mir, Slobodka, Telz, Kovno, and Ponevezh developed into leading centres. As in Pressburg, they faced fierce opposition from *maskilim,* enthusiasts of the Enlightenment, who described them as "nurseries of fanatical rabbis." Determined attempts were made within the yeshivot to counteract the corrosive effects of secular culture, to which the students were not immune. A decision was taken, in 1892, to let Volozhin yeshiva be closed rather than accede to government insistence that it teach the Russian language and elementary general knowledge.[48] Some believed that traditional textual learning was no longer enough. Rabbi Israel Salanter developed a vigorous system of personal ethical discipline, *musar,* which eventually gained ground in the Lithuanian yeshivot. The yeshiva became the locus of a Jewish counter-culture. It was perceived by supporters and opponents alike as the last refuge of tradition as a total and indivisible way of life.

PRINCIPLE AND POLICY

As in the case of Zionism, the issue of Torah and secular culture was to undergo evolutions and ironies. Rabbi Abraham Isaac Kook developed a mystical synthesis that attempted to transcend the dichotomy as set out by the Hirsch and Sofer schools. Like Hirsch he believed that Judaism could and should embrace secular culture. Like the Chatam Sofer

---

48. See Jacob J. Schachter, "Haskalah, Secular Studies and the Close of the Yeshiva in Volozhin in 1892," *The Torah U-Madda Journal,* 2 (1990), 76–133.

he believed that Judaism demanded a distinctively Jewish culture. The two propositions were incompatible only because of the terms of Jewish existence in an emancipating diaspora. Their resolution was to be found in Jewish national rebirth in the land of Israel. There, Jewish spirituality would undergo a renaissance, led by a new type of yeshiva that would combine Talmud with Jewish poetry, philosophy, and mysticism. Jewish culture as a whole would be transfigured and sanctified. Rabbi Kook celebrated the founding of the Bezalel Academy of Arts and delivered a warm address at the opening of the Hebrew University on Mount Scopus. That which seemed secular was only apparently so. Once Torah radiated through Israel, it would reveal the essential harmony and holiness of all branches of human endeavour. He saw secular culture not as something to be studied, or avoided, but as something to be transformed.[49]

Meanwhile, Hirsch's programme was in retreat among his own followers. His son-in-law, Solomon Breuer, student of Abraham Sofer, instituted a yeshiva on the Pressburg model in Frankfurt. Hirsch's daughter intimated that her father had intended *torah im derekh eretz* as a model for German Jewry only.[50] Thus began a sustained revisionist reading of Hirsch which maintained that he had permitted secular studies only as a means to earning a livelihood or as a temporary concession to social crisis.[51] There was an equally dramatic move in the opposite direction. Rabbi Chayyim Soloveichik (of Brisk, 1853–1918) had been one of the great intellectual influences of East European traditionalism, as teacher and animating genius of the Volozhin yeshiva. His grandson, Rabbi Joseph Soloveitchik, became the dominant influence of American Modern Orthodoxy. Volozhin had rigorously excluded all secular disciplines. Two generations later, Joseph Soloveitchik brought to his expositions of Judaism an encyclopaedic mastery of Western philosophy, hermeneutics, theology, and theoretical physics. In his essay *The Lonely Man of Faith* (1965) he was to develop the most complete, if ultimately tragic,

---

49. On Kook and secular culture see Zvi Yaron, *Mishnato shel Harav Kook* (Jerusalem: WZO, 1974), 189–230; Eliezer Schweid, "Two Neo-Orthodox Responses to Secularisation," *Immanuel*, 20 (1986), 107–17.
50. See Heilman, "The Many Faces of Orthodoxy," 42–51, and the sources cited there.
51. See I. Grunfeld, *Three Generations* (London: Jewish Post Publications, 1958); Immanuel Jakobovits, *"Torah im Derekh Eretz* Today," *L'Eylah*, 20 (1985), 36–41.

exposition of the modern Jew as a man divided between two sensibilities, the secular and the religious.

With Zionism, the question had been the evaluation of history. With *torah im derekh eretz* the question was the evaluation of culture. As before, there was much common ground. All agreed that Torah was primary, that its authority was non-negotiable, and that its lines traced the contours of Jewish identity. But how far did Torah extend? Did the "four cubits of halakhah" include, as Maimonides had said, all natural and human sciences,[52] or did they exclude them? How far was secular culture neutral, or a positive aid to the understanding of Torah, or a negative force undermining it?[53] How far was the traditional Jewish culture of the ghetto and *shtetl* accidental or essential to Jewish self-definition? These questions could not be answered by reference to Torah alone, for it was precisely the definition of Torah that was at stake. The key sources – which until now had been unproblematic – were revealed, on application to the new cultural circumstances, to be systematically ambiguous. The principle of *torah im derekh eretz*, if not the phrase itself, was subscribed to by all parties but given a different interpretation by each.

The issue was not only one of principle but also of policy. Which strategy would best conserve the covenant? As we have seen, shrewd sociological insight lay behind the success of Neo-Orthodoxy's compartmentalization. Secularization is not a linear process. The tide of modernity does not sweep away every vestige of tradition in its path. Religious institutions can thrive in the semi-private spaces of synagogue, school, and family life; and it is here that identity is formed.

But behind the Chatam Sofer's resistance to modernity lay an opposite but no less profound sociological assessment. Marion J. Levy has drawn attention to a general feature of the encounter between traditional societies and the modernization process. The acculturating

---

52. Berakhot 8a: "From the day the Temple was destroyed, the Holy One, blessed be He, has had nothing in His world except the four cubits of halakhah alone." See Maimonides, *Commentary on the Mishnah*, Intro.

53. The argument is explored in detail in Norman Lamm, *Torah Umadda* (Northvale, NJ: Jason Aronson, 1990).

avant-garde "see before them many and various results of the process" on which they are to embark, some benign, others destructive. They "are obsessed with the belief that they can take what they please and leave the rest." This selective accommodation lies at the heart of the Neo-Orthodox strategy. Levy, however, concludes that "the myth of easy independent selectivity from among the social structures of highly modernized societies must be recognized for what it is and has always been – a hybrid of wishful thinking and sentimental piety." Modernity exercises an "explosive subversion" of tradition.[54] Those who chose to avoid any accommodation to secular society had an alternative logic on their side. The strategic issue that divided followers of Samson Raphael Hirsch from those of Rabbi Sofer still divides sociologists.

We have seen how two issues – history and culture, or the direction and scope of covenantal continuity – led to deep differences of opinion within the Orthodox world. Lines were drawn and redrawn. Positions held by one group were sometimes reversed by its own next generation. Orthodoxy was highly reactive to the movements of modern Jewish history, but in each case a delicate issue of judgement was involved. Did the process enhance or threaten the life of Torah? An unequivocal answer was rarely available, for it depended on historical assessment, sociological insight, and a bold interpretation of the rabbinic heritage.

But differences of opinion are not new to Judaism. The Mishnah celebrated what it called "argument for the sake of heaven."[55] One impact of modernity on Orthodoxy therefore remains to be considered. What led from difference and division to fragmentation? What led from a tradition that embraced internal dialogue and argument to one that has come to be characterized by fission and mutual delegitimation? What led, in short, to adjectival Orthodoxy?

---

54. Marion J. Levy, *Modernization and the Structures of Societies* (Princeton, NJ: Princeton University Press, 1965), cited in Cuddihy, *The Ordeal of Civility*, 180–81.

55. Mish. Avot 5:20.

Chapter 4

Orthodoxy and Jewish Peoplehood

Two issues, the historical and cultural dimensions of emancipation, divided Orthodoxy. But have they fragmented it? To answer this we must confront a third dilemma of modernity. It concerns the concept of the covenantal community. In traditional Jewish thought, the bearer of the covenant was *keneset Yisrael,* the Jewish people in its totality – past, present, and future. The Jewish community was linked not merely by faith but also by birth. It was a biological family.[1] The commands of the Torah were not addressed universally to mankind, nor restrictively to Jews who voluntarily chose the life of faith, but to a particular people. Judaism was therefore particularist in its concept of a chosen people,[2] and at the same time inclusivist in its attitudes towards the members of that people. The Jew who sins remains a Jew.

---

1. On this concept see Michael Wyschogrod, *The Body of Faith: Judaism as Corporeal Election* (Minneapolis, MN: Seabury Press, 1983).
2. On the stresses to which this concept has been subject in modernity see Arnold Eisen, *The Chosen People in America: A Study in Jewish Religious Ideology* (Bloomington, IN: Indiana University Press, 1983).

What was the fate of Jewish peoplehood in modernity? On the one hand Judaism is too deeply predicated on such an idea for it to have been jettisoned by any Orthodox thinker. On the other, the Jewish people was itself disintegrating at an alarming pace, divided into non-Orthodox readings of Judaism as religion, and secular interpretations of Judaism as a national, ethnic, cultural, or political entity. How did Orthodoxy respond to this process? On the first two issues, as we have seen, the great figures of Hungarian and German Orthodoxy, Moses Sofer and Samson Raphael Hirsch, adopted different approaches. On this third issue they took the same approach, while Orthodoxy elsewhere took other directions.

ENGLISH AND FRENCH MODELS OF EMANCIPATION

It is striking, in retrospect, how the great arguments over Orthodoxy were shaped in Germany and Hungary, two communities that were in many respects atypical. It was there, and subsequently in America, that Orthodoxy was forced into self-definition by the presence of a powerful and aggressive Reform movement, whereas Reform made no headway in Eastern Europe and was a relatively marginal factor in the Jewish communities of nineteenth-century France, Italy, and England.

In England, emancipation took place both earlier and more smoothly than in Germany.[3] As early as the end of the eighteenth century, Jews had become considerably integrated into English society. At the top end of the social scale, wealthy Jewish bankers and businessmen had made their entry into London social life and had acquired the dress and manners of their non-Jewish peers. In the summer of 1755 the famous Rabbi Chayyim Yosef Azulai visited London to collect funds for his

---

3. For useful studies of Anglo-Jewish history see Eugene C. Black, *The Social Politics of Anglo-Jewry, 1880–1920* (Oxford: Blackwell, 1988); David Cesarani (ed.), *The Making of Modern Anglo-Jewry* (Oxford: Blackwell, 1990); Anne and Roger Cowen, *Victorian Jews through British Eyes* (Oxford: Oxford University Press for the Littman Library, 1987); Todd M. Endelman, *The Jews of Georgian England* (Philadelphia: JPS, 1979); id., *Radical Assimilation in English Jewish History, 1656–1945* (Bloomington, IN: Indiana University Press, 1990); Vivian Lipman, *A History of the Jews in Britain since 1858* (Leicester: Leicester University Press, 1990); Bill Williams, *The Making of Manchester Jewry, 1740–1875* (Manchester: Manchester University Press, 1976).

yeshiva in Hebron. He found that the leading Jews were not there: they had left for their country houses. Jews had been admitted to Masonic lodges and elected as Fellows of the Royal Society. At the lower levels, too, the Jewish street-traders became part of their urban environment and quickly adopted its way of life.[4]

The result was that there was little pressure for reform of Jewish faith or practice. England was altogether a less intellectual and ideological society than Germany. Jews themselves quickly acquired this trait. Their route to social acceptance did not lie through education and ideas, but through trade, finance, wealth, and the accoutrements of rank and civic responsibility. Political life, too, was free of the sharp demands made on Jews in some other European countries. "Emancipation in England was unique in modern Jewish history: it was not conditional. Parliament did not expect Jews to reform any of their beliefs or practices as a prerequisite to full political equality; in fact Parliament had little interest in what Jews thought or prayed or how they acted in their shops and synagogues."[5] English society also lacked a focused and politically powerful strand of antisemitism of the kind that periodically surfaced in Germany.

There was, notwithstanding, a discreet social pressure for religious life to be more decorous and to divest itself of those traditional customs that sat awkwardly with English notions of ecclesiastical etiquette. But these were cosmetic changes, and were undertaken by the Orthodox congregations themselves. In the mid-eighteenth century, the Great Synagogue introduced the wearing of canonicals – gown and bands – by the *chazan*. In the 1840s Chief Rabbi Nathan Marcus Adler (1803–90) banned conversation during services, forbade very young children to attend synagogue, ended the sale of synagogue honours, and encouraged the creation of all-male choirs.

As a result, until the 1930s there was no serious movement of Reform. A Reform congregation, the West London synagogue, had been founded in 1840, but it lacked the radical thrust of its counterparts in Germany and Hungary. Only two others were created in the nineteenth century. The necessary accommodations had already been

---

4. See Endelman, "The Englishness of Jewish Modernity in England."
5. Ibid., 242.

made by Orthodoxy, which became overwhelmingly the voice of the religious establishment.

In France, the Jewish experience was altogether different.[6] The issue of emancipation had been raised by the Revolution, and Jews became citizens of the new state in 1790–1. Napoleon, however, had a clearly articulated programme for the integration and assimilation of Jews into French life. This proceeded through a series of highly formal stages: the Assembly of Jewish Notables in 1806, the convening of a "Sanhedrin" in 1807, and the establishment of a consistorial system for the governance of Jewish life in 1808. The rabbinate and the direction of Judaism itself were thus brought into the ambit of the state.

Undoubtedly the consistorial structure had the effect of hastening the process of assimilation, with occasionally tragic results. Both the son and son-in-law of Rabbi Emanuel Deutz (1763–1842), *grand rabbin de France*, converted to Christianity. But it also, paradoxically, restored to French Jewry a rough equivalent of the *kehillah* or community-wide government that had been lost in other countries. French Jewry remained unified and, as in England, Reform made no headway during the nineteenth century. To be sure, there were periodic attempts to make the synagogue conform more closely to non-Jewish models. In 1856 the accommodationists succeeded in establishing a number of reforms. The number of *piyutim* (liturgical poems) was to be reduced. Greater use was to be made of the sermon as a vehicle of edification. Clerical robes were to be worn. The length of services was to be reduced, and services themselves were to be conducted with greater decorum. But the instigator of these changes, *grand rabbin* Ullmann, whom Michael Graetz describes as "the most progressive and most inclined towards reform of the rabbis to have entered the Central Consistory,"[7] was none

---

6. For recent studies see Ilan Greilshammer, "Challenges to the Institutions of the Jewish Community of France during the Nineteenth and Twentieth Centuries," in Stuart Cohen and Eliezer Don-Yehiya (eds.), *Conflict and Consensus in Jewish Political Life* (Ramat Gan: Bar-Ilan University Press, 1986), 31–60; Dominique Schnapper, "The Jews and Political Modernity in France," in S. N. Eisenstadt (ed.), *Patterns of Modernity*, vol. i: *The West* (London: Frances Pinter, 1987), 157–71; Graetz, "The History of an Estrangement."

7. Graetz, "The History of an Estrangement," 165.

the less emphatic that no change was to be contemplated that could not be justified by halakhah.

English and French Jewry, in their different ways, thus succeeded in confronting modernity without the sharp ideological wars that marked the communities of Germany and Hungary in the nineteenth century. This is not to deny that there was a continuing Anglo-Jewish debate during the nineteenth century about the demands and price of emancipation, that non-Jews occasionally questioned whether Jews could ever become fully integrated, and that Jews questioned whether they wished to be. But for the most part the debate was mild, and most Anglo-Jews were untouched by it.[8] The Orthodox programme of aesthetic modifications alongside a loyal adherence to halakhah – innovation in style but not in substance – was strikingly similar to that undertaken by Samson Raphael Hirsch in his early years. Hirsch himself had been a candidate for the English chief rabbinate in 1844, and the man who was appointed, Nathan Marcus Adler, had been his predecessor at Oldenburg. But the social environment was different. In England and France, Jewish institutions were not fragmented by the struggle for emancipation. The pressures which in Germany gave birth to radical Reform were here less sharp and less disruptive of religious continuity.

Adjectival Judaism, the division of the community into denominations, was for the most part avoided. The necessary adjustments could be made within the boundaries of halakhah by Orthodoxy itself. As Robert Liberles summarizes it, "the Jewish establishment responded to emancipation in time to avoid a serious religious schism. This meant that until the arrival of East European immigrants around the turn of the century, the religious institutions of England and France represented neither Neo-Orthodoxy nor old Orthodoxy, but simply Jews and Judaism."[9]

---

8.   See Israel Finestein, "Anglo-Jewish Opinion during the Struggle for Emancipation," *Transactions of the Jewish Historical Society of England*, 20 (1964), 113–43; id., *Post-Emancipation Jewry: The Anglo-Jewish Experience*, The Seventh Sacks Lecture (Oxford: Oxford Centre for Postgraduate Hebrew Studies, 1980).

9.   Liberles, *Religious Conflict in Social Context*, 230.

EASTERN EUROPE

In Eastern Europe Reform made no significant progress, but for quite different reasons. The processes of enlightenment and emancipation were there much slower in making their mark. More importantly, the East European intellectual climate was more collectivist in character. West European liberalism envisaged the modern state as the neutral arena of competing interests, and saw religion as a function of private life. The central thrust of early Reform was the transformation of Judaism into a religion in this narrow sense, by eliminating its collectivist, national dimension. This held no resonance for the Jews of Eastern Europe, whose revolutionary modernity took the form of secularism – cultural, socialist, or Zionist – which stressed the national at the expense of the religious.

Ironically, it was the German socialist Moses Hess who, in the 1860s, gave the earliest formulation of this Eastern orientation.[10] He was deeply critical of Western Reform as the attempt to deny Judaism's national component. It sought "to separate the political from the religious element in Judaism."[11] In so doing it hoped to reduce antisemitism and provide a religious basis for social integration. But it was based on several miscalculations. First, it underestimated the deep roots of German antisemitism. "Because of the Jew-hatred which surrounds him, the German Jew is only too eager to cast aside everything Jewish and to deny his race." But "even baptism itself does not save him from the nightmare of German Jew-hatred."[12] Second, it was a self-deception which robbed Jews of national pride and was seen as such by non-Jews. "It is not the old Orthodox Jew, who would rather have his tongue cut out than betray his nationality – but the modern Jew, who denies his nationality, who is being despised."[13] Third, it misconceived the very basis of Jewish identity. Judaism is a matter of birth more than faith. The apostate Jew remains a Jew. When Jews pray they do so collectively, on behalf of the entire

10. For a recent study see Shlomo Avineri, *Moses Hess: Prophet of Communism and Zionism* (New York: New York University Press, 1985).
11. In Hess, *Rome and Jerusalem*, trans. Bloom, Foreword.
12. Ibid., 25.
13. Hess, *Rome and Jerusalem*, trans. from Avineri, *Moses Hess*, 194.

people. Jewish law functioned to preserve the identity of the people in its dispersions. "First and foremost, Judaism is a nationality."

This cluster of ideas – later to become the basis of much collectivist Jewish thought, from Achad Ha'am's secular Zionism to Mordecai Kaplan's Reconstructionism – was revolutionary for its day. It led to clear conclusions that ran directly counter to the assumptions of the West. Judaism as religion without peoplehood held no future. "The Jew who does not believe in the national rebirth of his people can only work for the liquidation of his religion."[14] Precisely because of its national dimension, however, Judaism had a future to which even Christianity could not aspire. The prevailing Christian wisdom was that Judaism was an anachronism, long since superseded by Christianity. Hess argued the opposite: that because Christianity was purely a faith while Judaism was the code of a people, the former was threatened by secularization while the latter was not. Faith might be in danger, but peoples survived.

Hess's analysis led directly to Zionism. But he was also acute enough to see that the real roots of collective Jewish sentiment lay in the East, not the West to which he belonged. In Russia, Poland, Prussia, Galicia, and Turkey, the mass of Jews "devoutly pray day and night to the God of their ancestors for the restoration of the Jewish realm. They have preserved the living kernel of Judaism – I mean Jewish nationality – in much more authentic fashion than their Western brethren, who wanted to revive everything in the beliefs of our ancestors – except the hope for the re-establishment of the Jewish nation." He added, "Our cultured Western Jews, living in opulent luxury, have no idea with what deep longing the great Jewish popular masses of the East await their final deliverance from an exile lasting two thousand years."[15]

Hess was ahead of his time. It was not until the Russian pogroms of 1881–3 and the Dreyfus case of the mid-1890s had energized Pinsker and Herzl into formulating their programmes that the Zionist movement gained critical momentum. In the previous chapter we considered the complex pattern of Orthodox responses to Zionism. But Hess spoke to something more profound than the specifics of the Jewish return

14. Ibid., 58.
15. Ibid., 186.

to the land. He identified a component of peoplehood that lay at the heart of Jewish religiosity. It was precisely this that was most at risk in West European Jewish accommodations to emancipation. Hess singled out for praise the group of Jews most derided by the enlightened: the Hasidim. It was they, he argued, not Reform, who had managed the transition to modernity without losing "the living Jewish spirit." They retained Jewish collectivism (or as Hess put it, the "socialist life") as against the individualism of Western Jews which was so damaging to the deep structures of Judaism.

In one sense, of course, Hess's hope was unfulfilled. The secularizing ambitions of the post-Herzl Zionists led to the estrangement of most of Eastern Europe's religious leaders from the cause, Hasidim among them. But the collectivist strand remained prominent in their thought, despite their often bitter battles with the *maskilim*, proponents of Enlightenment. The great Naftali Zvi Yehuda Berlin (1817–93; known as the Netziv), for example, head of the Volozhin yeshiva, was an active supporter of the Chibbat Zion movement in its early years and urged Orthodox Jews to support settlement in Israel despite the fact that many of the settlers were irreligious Jews.[16] His conception of the Jewish people as "one union" also led him strongly to oppose setting up separatist Orthodox communities – a tendency which he considered "as painful as a dagger in the body of the nation."[17]

Two alumni of the Volozhin yeshiva, Rabbi Isaac Reines and Rabbi Abraham Hacohen Kook, went on to develop the implications of peoplehood in different directions. Reines saw the emergent Zionist movement as a practical solution to several of the most pressing Jewish needs.[18] In the light of the Russian persecutions of the 1880s it was clear that Jews needed a safe haven away from Europe. A Jewish settlement in Eretz Israel would also be the most effective safeguard against assimilation. And the Zionist movement itself both encouraged and expressed

---

16. Rabbi Barukh Halevi Epstein's biography (1928) has been translated into English by Moshe Dombey, *My Uncle, the Netziv* (Jerusalem: Artscroll, 1988).

17. *Meshiv Davar*, i. 42.

18. For a recent study of Reines, see Geulah Bat-Yehudah, *Ish Hame'orot* (Jerusalem: Mosad Harav Kook, 1985). See also Hayyim Z. Reines, "Isaac Jacob Reines," in Leo Jung (ed.), *Jewish Leaders (1750–1940)* (New York: Bloch, 1953), 275–93.

national identity. Peoplehood and Judaism, he argued, were inseparable. "Peoplehood is the main foundation of the faith of Israel. Even when they were dispersed among the nations, Jews were identified as a specific people because of their hope to return to their land. The combination of a specific people with a specific religion is conceivable only when it has a land or the hope of a return to it."[19]

Reines radically distinguished the Zionist programme from the metahistorical religious framework of redemption and the messianic age. For that reason, Orthodoxy could have no ground for opposing it as an attempt to bring redemption by human activity, a secularization of the messianic idea. On the contrary, he argued, it was a pragmatic solution to a practical problem. For that reason he was deeply supportive of Herzl's political Zionism and critical of the attempt to give Zionism a cultural dimension. He went so far as to support Herzl's abortive "Uganda scheme," a plan to establish a Jewish colony in British East Africa as an immediate place of refuge. Nor could the movement be delegitimized on the grounds that it was led by secular Jews. Religious intention, he argued, is necessary for commandments between man and God. But Zionism was about the saving of Jewish lives – a commandment between man and man, to be measured by its results, not its motivation.

Reines was also one of the few Eastern Europeans to attempt an educational synthesis along the lines of Samson Raphael Hirsch's *torah im derekh eretz*. He opened a yeshiva in Sventsyany which combined secular with talmudic studies. The project aroused fierce local opposition and had to be abandoned. Twenty years later he revived it in the form of the Torah Veda'at yeshiva in Lida (1905). It was aimed at producing two groups of alumni: rabbis and educated laymen. The former needed sufficient secular education and training in the art of homiletics to command respect in congregations. The latter needed basic secular skills to be qualified for a livelihood, together with deep talmudic grounding. It was an effort to heal the growing rift between the *maskilim* (Jewish advocates of enlightenment) and the religious, and it eventually succeeded in attracting a large student body and a distinguished reputation.[20]

---

19. Isaac Reines, *Or Chadash*, v. 9; quoted in Bat-Yehudah, *Ish Hame'orot*, 87.
20. On this project see Lamm, *Torah Umadda*, 25–28.

Reines was a pragmatist; Kook was a mystic.[21] For him, Jewish
unity was more than an ethical commitment and a practical concern. It
lay at the heart of his vision of the universe. All things radiated a divine
light. Existence in its totality is holy. Evil and error arise only when a
part is detached from the whole. All secularly proceeds from the idea
of independence; all holiness discloses the sense of interdependence.
For a Jew, to be united with God is to be united with the Jewish people.
When the Jewish people is united with God, humanity itself is united.
The concepts of unity and harmony are thus the axes on which his whole
philosophy turns.

For Kook, secularization and the divisions within the Jewish
world were intimately related. Both stemmed from exile, and both would
be cured by a return of Jews to their land. If there was something profoundly wrong about secular Zionism, for Kook it was the error of taking
the part for the whole, in this case seeing nationalism as an end in itself.
But there was also a saving dimension. The Zionist movement was an
expression of collective as opposed to individual Jewish identity. And
this for Kook was a constitutive element of Jewish spirituality. Criticiz-
ing secular Zionism, he added: "Nevertheless it cannot be denied that,
with all this, we have here also a great positive force, a deep love for our
people, a firm dedication to extend the practical work of rebuilding Eretz
Yisrael, to direct the spirit of our generation to draw closer to the land
and the nation, in keeping with the historic character of our people."[22]

A central theme in the work of Rabbi Kook is that of *teshuvah,*
return, understood in its full range of biblical and rabbinic resonances:
spiritual return to Torah, geographical return to Eretz Yisrael, and affec-
tive return to the Jewish people. "The basic step in *teshuvah* is to attach
oneself again to the soul of the people."[23] In this remark of Kook there
is something evocative of the sentence with which Moses Hess began
his *Rome and Jerusalem,* the work which marked his conversion from
communism to Zionism: "Here I stand again in the midst of my people,

21. On Kook see Yaron, *Mishnato shel Harav Kook.*
22. Abraham Isaac Kook, *Igerot Harayah* (3 vols.; Jerusalem: Mosad Harav Kook, 1962),
    ii, no. 427, 79–80.
23. Id., *Orot Hateshuvah* (Jerusalem: Yeshivat Or Etzion, 1966), iv, no. 7.

after being estranged from it for twenty years, and actively participate in its feasts and fasts, in its memories and hopes, in its inner spiritual struggles and its contacts with the civilized nations of the world."[24] The awakening sense of identification with peoplehood seemed, to Kook, to presage not only a return to the land but ultimately a return to Jewish spirituality.

The prevailing attitudes of secularism and atheism were, he argued, a natural reaction against a Judaism that had become overly spiritualized by prolonged exile. They were part of a dialectical process that would eventually restore to the Jewish soul a plenitude it had lost. In exile Judaism had gradually become confined to the study of texts and the observance of prescribed religious acts. It had lost its contact with nature, work, society, and culture, with the fullness of human experience. Secular Zionism, socialism, and even atheism were not to be understood simply as destructive forces, but as protests against the atrophy of Judaism. Zionism would restore to Judaism its link with peoplehood and land, socialism its dimension of social justice, and atheism its realization that the divine cannot be compassed by concepts or finite human understanding.

These were more positive evaluations of Jewish rebellion than had ever been seen before in the rabbinic literature, and could be justified only by Kook's mysticism and his sense of the dynamic of modern Jewish history. Rebellion was a passing phenomenon, part of the "pangs of cleansing"[25] that must precede redemption. Eventually it would be absorbed into the renaissance of religious creativity that a return to the holy land would set in motion. "The sounds of song, the majesty of the holy tongue, the beauty of our precious land, which was chosen by God, the ecstasy of heroism and holiness, will return to the mountains of Zion."[26]

EAST EUROPEAN ECHOES

For Reines and Kook, the theme of peoplehood was primarily linked to the efforts of Jews to re-establish a Jewish settlement in Zion. But it

---

24. Hess, *Rome and Jerusalem*, 13.
25. Abraham Isaac Kook, *Orot* (Jerusalem: Mosad Harav Kook, 1963), 124.
26. Ibid., 134.

had other dimensions and could be taken in different directions. One of these lay in the mysticism of the group of Hasidim known as Lubavitch or Chabad. Its first leader or *rebbe,* Rabbi Shneur Zalman of Lyady (1745–1813), had developed the mystical implications of the command "You shall love your neighbour as yourself." In the physical domain there was division; in the spirit there was unity. Jews were distinct as bodies, but they had a collective soul. "Your neighbour" *was,* in this sense, "yourself." Jews were therefore bound by a mutual love that underlay the apparently confrontational commands to rebuke the wrongdoer and hate evil. Jewish unity was a counterpart of, and embraced by, the unity of God.[27]

These themes were developed by the *rebbe* of Chabad, Rabbi Menachem Mendel Schneerson, into a practical programme of worldwide outreach to alienated Jews.[28] Jews are, for Chabad as for Judah Halevi in the Middle Ages, qualitatively different from non-Jews.[29] The difference lies not so much in what Jews do, or what they are called on to do, as in what they are. Their souls have a different structure. This has immediate practical implications. Even the most estranged Jew possesses an intrinsic holiness. The Jewish imperative is to disclose this holiness by removing the "husks" which conceal it. Chabad can therefore regard the non- or anti-religious lifestyle of alienated Jews as a superficial phenomenon, unrelated to the essence of character. Using the early Hasidic metaphor that the souls of Jews are like the letters of a Torah scroll (and a Torah scroll which has a letter missing or erased is invalid), it sees its task as restoring all Jews to their religious heritage so that the congregation of Israel once again regains its essential completeness.

This is an apolitical religious programme[30] which has made Chabad unique in the modern Jewish world in the intensity and scope of its efforts to bring about religious return. The State of Israel as such does not figure centrally in its thought, which explains the apparent

---

27. *Tanya,* i. 32.
28. For a study of Lubavitch's work among one particular group of estranged Jews – Israeli emigrants living in New York – see Shokeid, *Children of Circumstances,* 139–60.
29. *Tanya,* i. I; Judah Halevi, *Kuzari,* i. 103, 115.
30. To be sure, in recent years the Lubavitch movement has been actively and controversially involved in Israeli politics. This involvement dismayed many of its supporters, and has been followed by the more usual pattern of detachment.

contradiction between its positive commitment to Israel as a Jewish home – something that has aroused the violent opposition of the anti-Zionist Hasidic group, Satmar – and its denial of redemptive significance to the state. At one time, indeed, Chabad – in the form of its fifth *rebbe*, Rabbi Shalom Baer Schneersohn (1866–1920) – expressed strong opposition to the secularizing aims of the Zionist movement, a critique shared by most of the East European Torah leadership of the early twentieth century.[31] Chabad shares with Rabbi Reines the clear distinction between the political and pragmatic forces that shape the Jewish presence in Israel and the quite different spiritual forces that govern the dynamic from exile to redemption. Unlike Reines, its primary concern is with the latter.

A quite different approach to peoplehood characterized the thought of Rabbi Chaim Hirschensohn (1857–1935).[32] Hirschensohn was the son of an East European rabbi who had been, with Rabbi Zvi Hirsch Kalischer and Rabbi Elijah Guttmacher, one of the early supporters of the movement for Jewish settlement in Eretz Israel. He had moved to Safed in 1848, where Chaim was born. Chaim's sympathetic involvement with secular aspects of Zionist renewal brought him – as it did his contemporary, Rabbi Kook – into conflict with the traditionalists of the old *yishuv,* and in 1904 he left for America, where he served as a rabbi.

Initially he had shared the assumption of both Reines and Kook that the secular rebellion was a passing phase in Jewish history. On arrival in America he discovered that the abandonment of Judaism had gone further and deeper than he had suspected, and the situation was not about to be reversed. More than any other Orthodox thinker of his time, he confronted the implications of secularization for Judaism generally and halakhah specifically.

He noted a fundamental asymmetry between the outlook of the religious and non-religious Jew. For the former, he argued, religion was inseparable from peoplehood. But for the latter, peoplehood was separable from religion. The religious must therefore work for the promotion

---

31. See I. Domb, *The Transformation: The Case of the Neturei Karta* (London: Hamadfis, 1958), 179–244.

32. On Hirschensohn see Eliezer Schweid, *Demokratiah Vehalakhah* (Jerusalem: Magnes Press, 1978).

of Torah within the Jewish people, but they must recognize that the sense of peoplehood itself – even secularized – was a positive value. That sense persisted in all Jews who had not deliberately abandoned their identity or totally assimilated. "The religion of Israel is national, but the nationality of Israel is not exclusively religious."[33] Rabbi Hirschensohn draws from the prophetic literature, in the spirit of Maimonides' moving *Epistle on Martyrdom,* to argue that even when the majority of Israel were idolaters, they were still called "the people of God": a sinning nation, but a nation none the less. The Jewish people without Judaism was impoverished, living a spiritual death, but it remained the Jewish people. And since Judaism was essentially national, religion must drive the Jew to identify with his people, even if identifying with his people did not drive the Jew to Judaism.

Central to his thought is the idea of the covenant at Sinai as the voluntary undertaking of mutual obligations by God and Israel. Halakhah must once again be sovereign among the Jewish people, but this could not be achieved by coercion. Jewish law in the present must be informed by a clear sense of history and of the profound differences between the traditional and modern situation of the Jew in society. Hirschensohn was not a Conservative thinker, admitting historical development in the halakhah. Halakhah, as he put it once, is not to be judged by history; history is to be judged by halakhah.[34] But this halakhic view of history would immediately reveal that whereas in pre-modern times rabbis had the power to enforce adherence by restrictive legislation, *gezerot,* a similar approach today would have the opposite result and increase defections. Utterly opposed to Reform, which he saw as the abandonment of halakhah, he believed that Jewish law itself contained both the resources and the imperative to confront changing social circumstance.[35] No Orthodox thinker so stressed the values of democracy, individual freedom, and the need of halakhah to reckon with the reality of a non-religious Jewish majority.

---

33. Chayyim Hirschensohn, *Malki Bakodesh.* (6 vols.; St. Louis, MO: Moirester Printing Co., 1919–28), iv. 244.
34. Ibid., 196.
35. Ibid., ii. 7–8.

Rabbi Hirschensohn, who died in the same year as Rabbi Kook, did not live to see the creation of a secular Jewish state. The half-century since their death has vastly deepened the historical consciousness of peoplehood through two momentous events. The Holocaust was not only the most grievous human tragedy in the long Jewish scroll of tears. It was also the intended destruction of a people considered as such. Jews were to be extinguished not for what they believed or did, but for what they were. The State of Israel, too, has become a focus of Jewish identity, transcending religious divisions, not so much through its inception in 1948 as by its isolation prior to the 1967 Six Day War and since. Jews in Israel and outside shared the feeling that they were each other's only support.

The clearest theological definition of this mood was given by Rabbi Joseph Baer Soloveitchik in his essay "Kol Dodi Dofek."[36] Jews are, he argues, united by two covenants, the *berit goral* and the *berit ye'ud,* respectively the covenants of history and of destiny. The former was born in the shared historical experience of the exodus from Egypt. The latter was forged in the revelation of Torah at Sinai. The *berit goral* has four components: the sense Jews have of sharing a history; their collective emotional involvement in Jewish suffering; their mutual responsibility; and their collective action to improve the material situation of Jews. The concept of a *berit goral,* which has some affinities with Rabbi Hirschensohn's idea of a national covenant, is an attempt to give religious dignity to the secular fact of peoplehood as it has emerged in twentieth-century Jewish history.

Joseph Soloveitchik is, in this respect, a distinctively East European figure, drawing both on his memories of his grandfather, Rabbi Chayyim Soloveichik of Brisk,[37] and on ideas borrowed from Chabad mysticism. Like Kook and Hirschensohn before him, Soloveitchik is pained by the phenomenon of an Orthodoxy in which the idea of kinship with all Jews is in eclipse. He tells of the moment in his youth when he first became aware of it, when "a famous German rabbi, fully observant, let slip the remark...that he had more in common with a German than

---

36. Soloveitchik, *Divrei Hagut Veha'arakhah,* 9–56.

37. See id., *Halakhic Man,* trans. Lawrence Kaplan (Philadelphia: JPS, 1983), 90.

he had with an irreligious Polish Jew."[38] Such an attitude, he argues, at its most basic level is contradicted by history. What the rabbi and the irreligious Polish Jew had in common was Hitler's hatred. But it is not history alone that enforces the *berit goral*. Faith in *keneset Yisrael*, the collective entity of Israel, is an essential component of Jewish belief, dramatically symbolized in Jewish law by the sacrifice brought by the High Priest on the Day of Atonement which atones collectively for the whole people. Accordingly, "a Jew who has lost faith in *keneset Yisrael*, even though he may personally sanctify and purify himself by being strict in his observance of the precepts and by assuming prohibitions upon himself – such a Jew is incorrigible and is totally unfit to join in the Day of Atonement which encompasses the whole of *keneset Yisrael*, in all its components and all its generations."[39]

THE HUNGARIAN AND GERMAN EXPERIENCE

So while English and French Jewry preserved a framework of unity institutionally, East European Jewry – or at least many of its key think-ers – did so ideologically. The contrast between them was great. England and France had strong Jewish institutions, but no explicit ideology. No major thinkers emerged from either community during the nineteenth century. Eastern Europe had strong ideologies, but no institutional base into which they were translated. The yeshiva was, of course, the institu-tional home of Orthodoxy, but not of a collective Jewish voice.

Initially the Zionist movement seemed the appropriate vehicle. Rabbi Hirschensohn, Rabbi Soloveitchik, and Rabbi Naftali Berlin's son, Meir Bar-Ilan, found a home in the Mizrachi movement, which had been founded by Rabbi Reines in 1902. The name Mizrachi stood for *merkaz ruchani*, Israel as the "spiritual centre" of the Jewish people. But Zionism itself, as we have seen, soon became a major source of dissension. At the tenth Zionist Congress (1911) the secularists insisted on including cultural as well as political objectives within the movement. A year later, Orthodox leaders from East and West joined to create Agudat Israel, as

---

38. Id., *Chamesh Derashot* (Jerusalem: Tal Orot, 1974), 94.
39. Id., *Al Hateshuvah*, ed. P. Peli (Jerusalem: WZO, 1974), 98.

a secession from secular Zionism. Mizrachi was left to fight an increasingly difficult battle to maintain dialogue with both sides.

What the two Jewries had in common was the absence of a strong movement of Reform. It was in Hungary and Germany that the Reform movement made its greatest initial impact. Accordingly, it was in those two communities that a quite different ideology and strategy emerged: Orthodox secession.

The movement for Reform – or Neology, as it was then called – was initially less radical in Hungary than in Germany, but it precipitated an earlier crisis. Slow to make a substantive break with halakhah, the pace of reform accelerated rapidly at the time of the Hungarian revolution in 1848. In 1868 the government convened a General Jewish Congress to determine the basis of Jewish communal organization. The Neologists by then were in a majority: 126 to the 94 Orthodox representatives. They refused to accept the binding force of the *Shulchan Arukh* in determining the parameters of community regulation, at which point a section of the Orthodox group left the Congress. It petitioned parliament for the right to be exempt from the regulations, and in 1870 it succeeded. Hungarian Orthodoxy was thereafter divided into three groups: those who remained within the Congress; those who availed themselves of the 1870 law and organized themselves into separate communities; and the so-called "status quo" congregations, who allied themselves to neither Congress nor the separatists but retained their traditional regulations.

A similar process occurred throughout Germany.[40] As in Hungary, the initial impetus for Jewish communal unity came from outside, as a governmental administrative convenience. In Frankfurt, for example, the senate passed a law in 1864 removing all extant limitations on the political rights of its Jewish citizens, with one exception: that Jews were still required to hold membership in the Jewish community, which bore the responsibility for providing for their health-care, education, and religious facilities. The problem arose where Reform was in a majority on the community council and insisted on imposing halakhically unacceptable innovations on the Orthodox minority.

---

40. On secession in German Jewry see Liberles, *Religious Conflict in Social Context*; Schwab, *The History of Orthodox Jewry in Germany*.

In 1869, twenty-five Orthodox members of the Baden community broke away from the community board, the Oberrat, after the majority had voted to introduce organ music into the Sabbath services. The government upheld the legality of the action. Samson Raphael Hirsch, in Frankfurt, was quick to defend the secessionists against the charge of divisiveness. "Religious unity," he wrote, "has not existed for some time and wherever it is missing, the enforced unity of the community... is nothing but an empty, meaningless form."[41] It was clear that he was preparing to take similar action himself in Frankfurt.

Actual secession often proved unnecessary. In a number of German communities, Orthodoxy effectively used the threat of seceding to secure provisions in keeping with their requirements. But Hirsch was determined to make the break regardless. In 1876, the Prussian parliament passed a law of secession, after some years of struggle led by Hirsch. He now asked the members of his congregation to join him in withdrawing from the Frankfurt community. In fact only a small minority – some 80 of the 360 members – did so. A more traditional rabbi in Frankfurt, Moses Mainz, opposed the breach and negotiated an arrangement whereby Orthodox members would be exempt from contributing to the Reform school and synagogue, and Orthodox institutions, including a new synagogue and *mikveh*, would be supported by communal funds.

Hirsch remained implacable, and Germany's leading talmudist, Rabbi Seligmann Baer Bamberger (the Würzburger Rav, 1807–78), was invited to give his opinion. Initially Bamberger had been inclined to support Hirsch, but on visiting the community was satisfied with the compromise solution and ruled that if the necessary guarantees were given, "it could no longer be deemed necessary to secede from the Reform community." Hirsch rejected Bamberger's verdict in two fierce open letters.

Frankfurt, like Hungarian Orthodoxy, was now divided in two. The rabbi of the new non-separatist Orthodox community was a distinguished talmudist, Rabbi Marcus Horovitz (1844–1910).[42] Hirsch's own position, initially opposed to that of Rabbi Sofer in Hungary, was

---

41. Liberles, *Religious Conflict in Social Context*, 202.
42. On Horovitz see Isaac Heinemann, "Marcus Horovitz," in Jung (ed.), *Jewish Leaders*, 261–72.

now launched on a path of convergence. As we saw in the last chapter, this occurred in the next generation in the person of Rabbi Solomon Breuer, Hirsch's son-in-law and successor and a student of Rabbi Abraham Sofer. Breuer was a participant in the formation of Agudat Yisrael, which in bringing together Orthodox rabbinic leadership from across Europe sought at the same time to exclude non-secessionist (*Gemeinde*) rabbis and those associated with Mizrachi.

The issue of secession had been, except for Samson Raphael Hirsch, a matter not of principle but of practical politics. Seligmann Bamberger, who opposed secession in Frankfurt, supported it in Karlsruhe, Vienna, and Wiesbaden. Another leader of German Orthodoxy, Rabbi Azriel Hildesheimer, said of it, "It has caused me many sleepless nights in which I have shed many tears."[43] It arose when two factors were present: a government attempt to impose a unified Jewish communal structure, and an intransigent Reform majority. For the most part, Orthodox leaders of the nineteenth century in principle preferred communal unity, and abandoned it only when halakhic integrity made it impossible in practice. But a half-century later, largely through the efforts of Isaac Breuer, Solomon's son, it had been elevated to the status of a fundamental shibboleth. Orthodoxy was now divided between those for whom concerted action sanctioned working with Jews who did not share their views, and those for whom such joint efforts represented a fundamental compromise of halakhic integrity.

As with the debates over Zionism and *torah im derekh eretz*, the ground shared by all sides of the argument was substantial. All agreed on the non-negotiability of halakhah in any collective undertaking. All agreed that Reform on the one hand, secular Zionism on the other, were categorical breaches with traditional Judaism on which no legitimation could be conferred. The pain we discern in the writings of Kook at the conduct of the rebels he undertook to defend is no less than that of Moses Sofer or Samson Raphael Hirsch, who chose the path of disassociation. Nor was there, among the secessionists, a retreat from the principle of Jewish unity. The question was in part strategic, in part empirical, in

---

43. I. Unna, "Esriel Hildesheimer," in Leo Jung (ed.), *Guardians of our Faith* (New York: Bloch, 1958), 227.

part a matter of priority. Did isolation or communal involvement better promise the achievement of Torah goals? Was Jewish unity obtainable or irretrievably lost? And which took priority: the strengthening of Orthodoxy as a group or the Jewish people as a whole? In part, too, one can sense a difference of temperaments between Rabbi Kook, the poet and peacemaker, and Samson Raphael Hirsch, who had identified, as a child, with the figures of Pinchas and Elijah, the two biblical zealots who had fought to defend the faith.[44]

CONSEQUENCES OF SECESSION

Secession revealed, in paradoxical ways, the impact of secularization on Orthodoxy. The opening shot in the Jewish campaign for emancipation had been fired by Moses Mendelssohn. In his *Jerusalem* (1783) he had argued for freedom of religious conscience as the hallmark of the liberal state. Religious affiliation should be the private and voluntary choice of the individual. Mendelssohn's two severest critics had been Rabbi Moses Sofer and Samson Raphael Hirsch. Sofer had carried on an unceasing battle against the Mendelssohnian projects of translating the Torah into German and developing a philosophical understanding of Judaism.[45] Hirsch, in the *Nineteen Letters*, had accused Mendelssohn of approaching Judaism from outside, through metaphysics and aesthetics, rather than from within its own categories.[46] Yet both Hirsch and the followers of Sofer relied on the Mendelssohnian argument of freedom of conscience in proposing secession. To be forced to associate with a non-traditional Jewish community, they contended, infringed the very liberties on which the modern state was based. Hirsch entitled one of his secessionist pamphlets "The Principle of Freedom of Conscience."[47]

The privatization of religion and its voluntariness, the two hallmarks of modernity, were seen by Hirsch and Sofer in their different ways as offering a genuine opportunity to safeguard tradition. Orthodoxy

---

44. See Liberles, *Religious Conflict in Social Context*, 124–33.

45. Moses Sofer, *Derashot*, ed. J. N. Stern (Klausenberg: Friedman and Weinstein, 1929), i. 81a, 113b, 142b.

46. Hirsch, *Nineteen Letters*, 123–25.

47. See Schwab, *The History of Orthodox Jewry in Germany*, 68.

could now be detached from the constraints of communal unity and flourish on its own. Within the enclosure of the Pressburg yeshiva or the Frankfurt school and synagogue, a subcommunity of like-minded individuals could develop an environment in which Jewish values took on an intensity sufficient to counteract any cultural influences from outside. Hitherto Judaism had been marked by its inclusivity: it represented *keneset Yisrael*, the organic body of all Jews. Now Orthodoxy, both Hirsch's and Sofer's, was to be marked by its exclusivity. It was an elite. To be sure, it understood itself essentially as a defence of tradition. But it was tradition in a form unknown for eighteen hundred years, namely, tradition as maintained by a self-conscious, defiant minority within Jewry.

In an earlier chapter we spoke of two broad patterns of response to secularization: accommodation and resistance. Accommodation generally leads to pluralism and the denomination. Resistance leads, so Peter Berger has argued, to sectarian forms of religious organization, marked by their exclusivity and strong internal authority. The sect demands higher standards of behaviour and belief from its members than is the norm outside. It sees itself as a religious elite, often in a confrontational stance towards contemporary culture and less strenuous forms of religiosity. In applying this terminology to Judaism we must be careful to distinguish ideology from organization. Ideologically, Judaism does not sanction sectarianism. The ideas of inclusivity, the unity of the Jewish people, and the collective entity of Israel are deeply embedded in its beliefs, liturgy, and practice. But organizationally, sectarianism was always a possibility, though the communal structure of *kehillah* militated against it. This then was the significance of secession, and why Isaac Breuer was not wrong to see it as a fundamental principle. It meant the clear identification of tradition-in-modernity as a movement of resistance. Organizationally, it meant the sectarianization of Orthodoxy.

Sectarianism has consequences. We have already traced them. The two secessionist Orthodoxies, of Sofer and Hirsch, initially at variance on Zionism and secular culture, began to converge. *Torah im derekh eretz*, once seen as a principle to be embraced, rapidly came to be seen as a temporary concession of no lasting validity. The ardent longing of Rabbi Moses Sofer for a return to Israel was neutralized by Agudat Yisrael's disengagement from the Zionist movement. Why was it that a negative view of Zionism and secular culture prevailed, rather than the reverse? The reason is that both, by the beginning of the twentieth century, had become stances of resistance. The alternatives – participation in secular culture and secular Zionism – involved accommodation. The debate over Jewish peoplehood and unity was thus the most profound of the three we have considered, for it had consequences for the other two. Those who emphasized peoplehood were driven towards a positive evaluation of *derekh eretz* and Zionism. Those who preferred Orthodox separatism were ineluctably driven to take a neutral and sceptical view of both.

But though sectarianism tends to produce a convergence of attitudes, it does not militate in favour of co-operation. Over the course of the twentieth century, a striking similarity developed between three kinds of Orthodoxy that had initially been vastly different: German Neo-Orthodoxy, Hungarian and East European traditionalism, and the various Hasidic groups. Most developed a preference for the Lithuanian yeshiva as the educational model. Most evolved a structure of authority on the Hasidic paradigm, with the *rosh yeshivah* (yeshiva head) emerging as a figure of comparable charisma to the *rebbe* in Hasidic life, and with a corresponding loss of authority to the congregational rabbinate. Most borrowed from German Orthodoxy its political activism. But the conflicts and clashes between them remain as heated as ever and show no signs of diminution. Sectarianism encourages a worldview which does not allow room for rival interpretations or pragmatic compromise. The difficulty encountered by separatist groups in agreeing on joint action is a direct result of separatism itself. In the modern situation, the price of intensity is disunity.

But secularization presses remorselessly towards the sect as the vehicle of religious continuity. The history of the great inclusivist visions of Orthodoxy in the twentieth century has been one of disillusionment. Secular culture, the Reform movement, and secular Zionism turned out to be less hospitable to tradition than the optimists had hoped. One of the seminal documents of modern Orthodoxy, Rabbi Soloveitchik's "The Lonely Man of Faith," is written out of the depths of this tragic awareness. It begins by describing the double nature of the religious personality. On the one hand he is active, majestic, mastering creation;

on the other he is passive, covenantal, serving creation. The two aspects are brought together in Judaism: both are part of the divine mandate to mankind. But in the closing pages of the essay this unity is suddenly split asunder. All this was in the past; in contemporary culture, Soloveitchik argues, majestic man has tried to absorb covenantal man. Secularity has invaded the sanctuary. The implication is clear, and is an exact reversal of Rabbi Kook's. For Kook the holy would absorb and transform the secular. For Soloveitchik, it is the secular that threatens to absorb and profane the holy. The essay ends with the man of faith retreating into solitude. It is the psychological equivalent of the social processes that led Hirsch into secession.

Increasingly, then, the secessionist pattern that emerged in Hungary and Germany as a response to immediate political crisis has come to dominate Orthodoxy in Israel and America. Separatism was Orthodoxy's reaction of self-preservation in a situation where it was a minority. As the Jewish world continues to secularize, Orthodoxy's sense of minority standing deepens. As religion and society drift apart, the projects of *torah im derekh eretz*, religious Zionism, and communally involved Orthodoxy – all three of them efforts to hold religion and society together – come to seem less and less plausible. Secessionist Orthodoxy tacitly accedes to the secularization of the public domain and builds its strongholds elsewhere.

Thus is Orthodoxy not merely divided but fragmented. Secessionist Orthodoxy, miraculously rebuilding itself after the ravages of the Holocaust, has proved the power of separatism as a survival strategy in a deeply secularized pluralist society. Pluralism acts to its advantage, shifting the weight of identity-shaping culture to the "intermediate structures" – in this case, the Jewish day school, yeshiva, synagogue, and family – that are its particular strength. After the Holocaust, accommodation has ceased to be a self-conscious Jewish ideology. Indeed pluralization has meant that it is no longer a necessary strategy. Less and less is there a common public culture to accommodate to. Increasingly, even Jewish groups far removed from Orthodoxy are embracing its sociological insights and turning towards particularism, community, tradition, and authority and away from universalism, social action, liberalism, and autonomy.

In this environment, the three programmes through which Orthodoxy sought to bring together what social forces were driving apart – Torah and secular culture, Judaism and Zionism, and the Jewish people as a collective entity – run directly against the sociological tide. Charting the history of each of these three tendencies, we witness the dream of synthesis giving way to the reality of disintegration. Thus, with the exception of those Jewries that still maintain the English or French model of establishment Orthodoxy, they are presently in retreat.

CONTRARY FORCES

The analysis would end there were it not for three powerful forces operating in the opposite direction. The first is the deep contradiction between contemporary social reality and Jewish belief. Ideologically, Judaism recognizes neither denominations nor sects. Sociologically, it is currently organized into just those forms. Ideologically, Judaism is inclusive of all Jews. Sociologically, exclusivist attitudes prevail in just those sectors of Orthodoxy that most strive to maintain continuity with the past. Jewish unity and peoplehood are too constitutive of Judaism to be abandoned. They are endorsed as values by almost every sector of the Jewish world. The fragmentation of peoplehood, brought about by modernity, cannot simply be acceded to without deep conflict with inescapable Jewish values.

Secondly, the Holocaust and the State of Israel have immeasurably deepened the sense of *berit goral*, the shared Jewish covenant of history. The ideological divisions of the nineteenth century were intense and substantive. They involved fundamental differences of opinion as to whether the Jewish future lay in European integration, enclosed Jewish communities, or a new settlement in Eretz Israel. The events of the twentieth century have greatly closed the gap between these alternatives. They have taught that Jewish destinies are interlinked. The institutional forms of the nineteenth century have persisted, but are now acutely dysfunctional. They prevent inter-Jewish reconciliation at the very time when it is sensed to be most necessary.

Thirdly, Jewish destiny is a sustained defiance of history. Nietzsche, a fierce and fateful critic of Judaism, saw the point clearly: "The Jews are the most remarkable nation of world history because, faced with the question of being or not being, they preferred, with a perfectly uncanny conviction, being at any price.... They defined themselves counter to all those conditions under which a nation was previously able to live, was permitted to live – they made of themselves an antithesis to natural conditions."[48] A century later, having witnessed the consequences of a Nietzschean ethos that placed nature above morality, that Jewish vision remains undimmed. Judaism does not lightly resign itself to historical processes. But the fragmentation of Jewish peoplehood is the result of just such a resignation. It grew out of a shared conviction that in the modern world, Jewish tradition would survive only among a minority of Jews. The non-Orthodox preferred the path of the majority. Orthodoxy chose the way of the minority. But a resignation towards the future is profoundly out of key with traditional Jewish attitudes. Judaism radically distinguishes between fact and value. That secularization is a fact does not entail that it is to be embraced as a value. If it leads to denominationalism and sectarianism, that may itself be a reason to resist the process.

So we must reopen the question that history seemed to have closed. Is the recovery of Jewish peoplehood a possibility? Can we begin to undo the impact of secularization on Jewish consciousness? Can we learn to think of ourselves again as non-adjectival Jews?

---

48. Friedrich Nietzsche, *Twilight of the Idols* and *The Anti-Christ*, trans. R. J. Hollingxdale (London: Penguin, 1968), 134.

Chapter 5

Tradition and Diversity

The argument of the preceding chapters can now be summarized. Enlightenment and emancipation set in motion deeply fragmenting forces within the Jewish world, forces whose full disintegrative potential is as yet unexhausted. It set before Jews the question asked with brutal clarity some two hundred years ago by the Count of Clermont-Tonerre. Are Jews individuals who have in common no more than a private religious belief, or are they a people, a nation? The question, of course, could not be answered, for both were true. Judaism was the religion of a people, and Jews were a people constituted by a religion. Judaism essentially contradicted the terms of the either-or. But the question could not be evaded, not only because it formed the political choice Jews were called on to make in the nineteenth century, but because at a deeper level it is the choice posed to all religions by secularization. As the institutions of the public domain are progressively removed from ecclesiastical power, society itself becomes differentiated into a secular state and an increasingly private religiosity. In which category, therefore, did Jewish identity belong?

Either answer involved a revolution. Secular Zionism predicated Jewish identity on secular nationhood and the state to be formed by the return of Jews to their land. Liberal, Reform, and to a lesser extent

Conservative theologians saw Jewish identity as essentially religious, not national. But the accommodations they felt were necessary to ensure Jewish integration within a non-Jewish society led to either a formal break with halakhah or a radical reinterpretation of the halakhic process. Orthodoxy, bound by the covenantal tradition, resisted the terms of the question. Judaism was both religious and national. A non-religious nationalism and a non-national religion both misrepresented Judaism's historic character. But by the end of the nineteenth century Reform and secular Zionism were powerful forces, and Orthodoxy was bound to part company with both.

But there were profound divisions within Orthodoxy itself. There were movements to hold together what secularization was driving apart: Torah and secular culture, Judaism and Zionism, and the Jewish people. Paradoxically these three movements – *torah im derekh eretz*, religious Zionism, and communally involved (*Gemeinde*) Orthodoxy – have often been grouped together under the name "Modern Orthodoxy." Strictly speaking, however, they were the opposite, for they were an attempt to go against the grain of modernity. Contemporary culture replaces the traditional "and" with a disjunctive "or": Torah *or* secular culture, Judaism *or* Zionism, Orthodoxy *or* the Jewish people as a whole. In each case religious principle suggested that the former must take precedence over the latter. So modernity favoured those branches of Orthodoxy that made the choice, rather than those that resisted it. While in principle they retained their commitment to *derekh eretz*, the return to Zion, and Jewish unity, in practice the full implications of these tenets were neutralized. So the cluster of attitudes associated with secessionist Orthodoxy – rejection of secular culture, an attitude of detachment towards the State of Israel, and a refusal to engage in joint action with the non-Orthodox – has prevailed. Modernity has been hostile to "Modern Orthodoxy."

The past two centuries have therefore been profoundly destructive of the coherence and integrity of Jewish peoplehood. We have analysed the processes historically and sociologically, since it is only from these perspectives that the phenomenon is fully visible. From the vantage-point of philosophy, theology, or ideology it tends to be hidden. Thus, for example, there is hardly a contemporary version of Judaism or Jewish identity which does not stress the central value of Jewish unity.

From this one might conclude that unity was either actual or possible, since all sides desire it. In fact, though, what we possess is a series of radically incompatible conceptions of unity which could not, in principle, be simultaneously realized. Religious unity as conceived outside Orthodoxy, for example, depends on a pluralism which cannot be stated within the terms of Orthodoxy. The tragic impasse to which this leads is that the pursuit of Jewish unity is inherently divisive, and the faster we move towards it, the further it recedes.

I have had recourse to terminology drawn from the sociology of religion. That terminology sounds strange and not a little alien in a Jewish context, developed as it was from the study of Christianity. But it helps in stating the dilemma with some precision. The key terms have been "church" (for which we used the phrase *keneset Yisrael*), "denomination," and "sect." Using Roland Robertson's cogent analysis, we can see these terms as lying along two axes. The first is the principle of *inclusivity* or *exclusivity.* Does the religious body under review aim to embrace as many members as possible within its ranks, or does it propose high standards of admission, necessarily excluding many? The second is the principle of *unique* or *pluralistic* legitimacy. Does it hold itself to be the only legitimate interpretation of the faith, or merely one of several acceptable options? A "church" is uniquely legitimate and inclusive. A "sect" is uniquely legitimate and exclusive. A "denomination" is pluralistically legitimate and inclusive.[1]

The dilemma of Jewish modernity is this. Jewish tradition is predicated on the idea of "church," which is to say, *keneset Yisrael.* It is inclusive of all Jews. To be sure, it was possible to leave Judaism by apostasy, or to join it by conversion. There were exits and entrances, but these were the exceptions, not the rule. There is a line of thought that runs through the Middle Ages which seeks to include even the Jewish apostate within the rule that "though he sins, he remains a Jew."[2] What is more, even Isaac Arama (1420–94), living in Spain at a time of unprecedented Jewish

1. Roland Robertson, *The Sociological Interpretation of Religion* (Oxford: Blackwell, 1970). See also John Milton Yinger, *The Scientific Study of Religion* (London: Collier-Macmillan, 1970); Hill, *A Sociology of Religion.*

2. Sanhedrin 44a; Jacob Katz, "Af Al Pi Shechata, Yisrael Hu," *Tarbitz,* 28 (1958), 84–85;

conversions to Christianity, was able to take it as axiomatic that the majority of Jews will remain faithful to their tradition. This for him had the status of natural law. As natural as it is for living things to desire life, so it is for the Jew to desire Judaism.[3] Though it is normal for Jewish writers in the Middle Ages to bemoan the "many sins" of their generation, none prior to modernity conceives the possibility that Jewish tradition might be adhered to by only a minority of Jews. Sa'adia Gaon's axiom, that "Israel is a people only in virtue of its religious laws," held true.[4] The laws of Torah might occasionally be as honoured in the breach as in the observance, but there was no doubt that they constituted the basis of peoplehood. Tradition was thus inclusive and uniquely legitimate. It embraced all Jews, and denied the possibility of any alternative basis of identity. Torah was essentially linked to the idea of *keneset Yisrael.*

Judaism cannot be translated without remainder into the language of denominations or sects. It cannot be translated into denominations because, however loosely interpreted, it has dogmas or constitutive beliefs. There were many arguments over Maimonides' specific formulation of the "Thirteen Principles" of faith, but all parties agreed that there were principles of faith.[5] It was precisely over such principles that the great schisms were formed between Pharisees and Sadducees, Jews and Christians, Rabbanites and Karaites. Judaism is not pluralist as between acceptance and non-acceptance of its fundamentals. It cannot accord legitimacy to movements that deny revelation, the binding force of the commandments, or the authority of rabbinic interpretation. It cannot, consistently with its beliefs, accept the validity of Reform and

---

id., *Exclusiveness and Tolerance*, 67–81; Aharon Lichtenstein, "Brother Daniel and the Jewish Fraternity," *Judaism*, 12:3 (1963), 260–80; Blidstein, "Who Is Not a Jew? The Medieval Discussion."

3. *Akedat Yitzchak* (Salonika, 1522) s.v. "Nitzavim." Arama calls the internalized imperative of the covenant a *chok mutba*, a "natural law" of Jewish character. On Arama and the conversos of Spain see Paul Johnson, *A History of the Jews* (London: Weidenfeld and Nicolson, 1987), 224.

4. Sa'adia Gaon, *Emunot Vede'ot*, 3:7. For an English version see S. Rosenblatt's translation, *The Book of Beliefs and Opinions* (New Haven, CT: Yale University Press, 1948).

5. See Menachem Kellner, *Dogma in Medieval Jewish Thought* (Oxford: Oxford University Press for the Littman Library, 1986).

Conservative Judaisms as alternative readings of Torah. Pluralism here founders on the rock of Orthodoxy.

Nor can Judaism be translated into sects. To be sure, its history is punctuated with elite forms of spirituality – sometimes philosophical, sometimes mystical, sometimes pietistic. The most common was the elite of learning, which set the *talmid chakham* (disciple of the wise) against the *am ha'aretz* (common man).[6] But there were always countervailing tendencies, aimed at preserving the dignity of the non-elite and the integrity of the people as a whole. Jewish law recognized a distinction between *din* and *lifnim mishurat hadin*, "law" and "beyond the letter of the law," and Jewish life generalized it. The saint, the mystic, or the philosopher represented exceptional piety, to be admired but not to be prescribed as a universal norm. The Torah was "not given to the ministering angels."[7] It was necessarily within the reach of the ordinary Jew. There were exclusive circles of elite piety, but they were not constitutive of Judaism. Rather, they were heroic deviations from the norm. The primary bearer of Jewish identity – halakhah – was addressed to the "majority of the community."[8] It was *law*, which is to say – as Maimonides noted – the constitution of a people.[9] One might go beyond the letter of the law, but one might not confuse supererogation with the law itself. Halakhah was inclusive as Judaism itself was inclusive. The exclusivism of secessionist Orthodoxy therefore, though it commends itself as a survival strategy, runs counter to a – perhaps the – basic Jewish value. Sectarianism here founders on the rock of *keneset Yisrael*.

The paradox of Jewish modernity, then, is that Jewish religious life is organized into structures into which tradition does not fit. This is an outcome willed by no one, which emerged from the varied responses to social, political, and cultural challenges that seemed to threaten Jewish continuity at its foundations. That past cannot be unwritten, nor is it profitable to engage in counter-factual speculation as to whether it might

---

6. See E. E. Urbach, *The Sages: Their Concepts and Beliefs* (Jerusalem: Magnes Press, 1975), 630–48.
7. Berakhot 25b.
8. Avodah Zarah 36a; Yad, *Mamrim* 2:5.
9. See *Guide of the Perplexed*, ii. 40; iii. 34.

have happened otherwise. "What was, was," as the rabbis said. The only meaningful question concerns the future. Does the tradition itself contain the resources to handle diversity without disunity? My argument in this and the next chapter is that it does. It rests on three phenomena which we must now explore: aggadic pluralism, halakhic universalism, and Jewish inclusivity.

AGGADIC PLURALISM

Orthodoxy is not a denomination. It encompasses astonishing variations. Partly, these are geographical: Russian, Polish, British, French, Italian, Yemenite, and American Jews all evolved their own syntheses of Jewish tradition and local culture. Partly, they are institutional: from the eighteenth to the twentieth centuries, each of the many Hasidic groups and each, too, of the major yeshivot developed its distinctive and indigenous style, from manners of dress to ways of analysing biblical and talmudic texts. Partly they are temperamental: the rational confidence of Samson Raphael Hirsch, the urgent mysticism of Abraham Isaac Kook, and the introspective conflicts of Joseph Soloveitchik could not be less alike. And partly, as we have seen, they are ideological, for different groups evolved widely different responses to modernity.

Orthodoxy, then, is diverse. While it does not recognize the existence of alternative denominations, it does embrace a wide variety of different constructions. To what might we compare it? Perhaps the best analogy is a language. A language is determined by rules of syntax and semantics. But within that language an infinite number of sentences can be uttered or books written. Within it, too, there can be regional accents and dialects. Orthodoxy is determined by beliefs and commandments. These are its rules of syntax and semantics. But within that framework lies an open-ended multiplicity of cognitive, emotional, spiritual, and cultural styles.

The community of faith shares a language. Because it shares a language, it can have conversations and arguments. This, at any rate, was the traditional pattern. A sharp distinction was made between the rules that determine the language and the many different sentences that can be spoken within the language. The rules that determine the language of Judaism are fundamental beliefs on the one hand, halakhah on the other. Of course, there was some latitude for disagreement on both. There were differing interpretations of some of the principles of Jewish faith, and differences as to what was a principle of faith. There were different halakhic schools, most noticeably between Ashkenazim and Sephardim, but also to some extent between Hasidim and their opponents. But these disagreements, of necessity, were marginal. They split the language into several dialects. Had they been other than marginal they would have split it into several languages.

Because there was essential agreement on the rules that constituted the language of faith, conversation and argument were not only possible; they celebrated the fact of shared language. The Christian spokesmen at the Barcelona Disputation of 1263 were frankly astonished at the ease with which Nachmanides, the Jewish representative, took issue with some of the classic rabbinic texts on the subject of the messianic age. Nachmanides patiently explained to them the difference between *halakhah* and *aggadah*, law and exegesis. Law was binding. So too was belief in the fundamentals. But there were areas of interpretation where argument was open-ended.[10] That the messiah would come, all Jews believed. But as to how and when, there was no normative Jewish view.[11]

In terms of the analogy I have been drawing, belief in the messianic age was one of the ground-rules of the language; but detailed explication of the messianic age belonged to a range of many sentences possible within the language. This was not because the subject was trivial or marginal. On the contrary: the messianic age is the end-point to which all Jewish history is a journey. The distinction between halakhah and aggadah is not between the major and the minor or the central and the marginal. It is the distinction between those things on which it is

---

10. *Kitvei Ramban*, vol. i, ed. C. D. Chavel (Jerusalem: Mosad Harav Kook, 1964), 308. An English version can be found in Hyam Maccoby, *Judaism on Trial: Jewish-Christian Disputations in the Middle Ages* (London: Associated Universities Presses for the Littman Library, 1982), 115–16. See the notes of Chavel and Maccoby, ad loc. See also in this context Marvin Fox, "Nahmanides on the Status of Aggadot: Perspectives on the Disputation at Barcelona, 1263," *Journal of Jewish Studies*, II:I (1989), 95–109.

11. So Maimonides rules in Yad, *Melakhim* 12:2.

necessary to agree for there to be a community of faith, and those things on which it is not necessary to agree.

This distinction was not unique to Nachmanides. In one form or another it was shared by all the medieval thinkers. Maimonides, both in his law-code and in his philosophical writings, feels free to provide explanations of Jewish law other than those expounded in the classic rabbinic texts.[12] Rashbam and Ibn Ezra were the most conspicuous examples of a general tendency among the biblical commentators to give interpretations which conflicted with midrashic tradition.[13] Rashi, perhaps the most traditional of the medieval commentators, does likewise at a number of points. There are, he says, midrashic interpretations, but the plain sense of the text is otherwise.[14] Nachmanides' own work in this respect is stunning in its sophistication. In his Bible commentary he will cite the rabbinic tradition, together with Rashi's understanding of it, defend it, provide alternative interpretations at the level of plain sense, and then allude to mystical dimensions of the same words. Reading Nachmanides is an object-lesson in seeing a text from multiple perspectives – first traditionally, then historically, then mystically.

In short, the post-talmudic tradition recognized that there were matters on which a normative consensus was crucial, and others on which many different stances could be taken, and from many points of view. Maimonides formulated the general rule that any issue of attitude or interpretation that did not have direct legal consequences did

---

12. See Malakhi Hacohen, *Yad Malakhi* [1767] (New York: Bet Hasefer, 1974), 182 (*Kelalei Harambam*, rule 4).

13. For a general survey see Ezra Zion Melammed, *Mefarshei Hamikra* (Jerusalem: Magnes Press, 1975). See also the speculation of David Weiss Halivni, *Midrash, Mishnah, and Gemara* (Cambridge, MA: Harvard University Press, 1986), 105–16, who suggests that "medieval exegesis is...another manifestation of an abiding concern for explaining and justifying the law." Commentators such as Rashbam, Halivni argues, believed that studying the plain sense of the text was part of the command of Torah study, even where it conflicted with the accepted halakhic interpretation. The explanation is intriguing, but it is more likely that this kind of exegesis grew out of the challenge of Karaite and Christian polemics against rabbinic readings of the text.

14. See, e.g., Rashi on Gen. 3:8, 23; 35:16; Ex. 6:3.

not call for a definitive resolution.[15] For the sake of clarity let us give this territory a name, *aggadah*, and define it negatively as that which is not halakhah.[16] Traditionally, aggadah referred to non-legal parts of the early rabbinic literature: homiletical or ethical interpretations of biblical narrative. For our purposes I shall use the term "aggadah" more widely to include also the areas of philosophy and mysticism, and historical or ethical evaluation. But the essential quality of aggadah, however understood, is that it is not halakhah. It designates, in other words, the domain where rabbinic tradition refrained from issuing authoritative rulings applicable to all Jews at all times. When two halakhic opinions conflict, we must decide between them. When two aggadic opinions conflict, we need not.[17]

The distinction becomes clear when we consider two apparently parallel talmudic passages. In the first we read that for three years there was a dispute between the schools of Shammai and Hillel. Each claimed that the halakhah was in accordance with its views. "A heavenly voice was heard, announcing: These and those are the words of the living

---

15. Maimonides, *Commentary on the Mishnah*, Sanhedrin 10:3. The point is frequently made in the rabbinic literature. The Talmud interprets Jeremiah's phrase "Is not my word like fire and like the hammer that breaks the rock in pieces?" (Jer. 23:29) to mean that every word of Torah split into seventy languages or interpretations (Shabbat 88b, Sanhedrin 34a). Aggadah represents speculative possibility rather than received and normative tradition; see Hai Gaon, *Otzar Hageonim*, Chagigah 67 (vol. iv, ed. B. M. Lewin [Jerusalem: Hebrew University Press, 1931], pp. 59–60, paras. 67–68). It is open-ended (Sherirah Gaon, ibid. 68). There are "seventy faces to the Torah": *Radbaz*, iii. 643 and see Nachmanides on Gen. 8:4. Accordingly, *ein meshivin al haderush* ("One does not attempt to refute a midrashic exegesis"): Isaac b. Judah Halevi, *Pane'ach Raza* [1607] (Warsaw, 1860), ch. 7:1.

16. See Shmuel Hanaggid, *Mavo Hatalmud*, printed at the end of the Vilna ed. of tractate Berakhot. See also *Entziklopediah Talmudit*, i. 60–62.

17. Hyam Maccoby, writing in the context of Nachmanides' remarks at the Barcelona Disputation, puts the matter finely when he says: "In Judaism, the centre is occupied by the Law, which regulates the behaviour of the community and the individual. It is in the sphere of law that the serious effort towards definition and precision occurs. Here it was that methods of formal logic and dialectic were developed in order to arrive at hard-and-fast solutions of any problems that arose. But there was no such logic or dialectic for dealing with matters which Christians would have called 'theological'... There was no real argument on such matters, for in this area contradictory propositions could both be true": Maccoby, *Judaism on Trial*, 48.

God, but the halakhah is in agreement with the school of Hillel."[18] In the second, Rabbi Abiatar and Rabbi Jonathan disagree as to the interpretation of a biblical passage. Rabbi Abiatar is then graced by a revelation of the prophet Elijah, who tells him that the Holy One, blessed be he, is presently studying that very text. The Talmud then records the following dialogue. "Abiatar: 'How does he interpret the passage?' Elijah: 'He says, my son Abiatar says this and my son Jonathan says that.' Abiatar: 'Can there be doubt in Heaven?' Elijah: 'These and those are the words of the living God.'"[19]

Both passages assume that two conflicting positions can both be the words of the living God, which is to say, legitimate interpretations of Torah. This is itself a sublime vindication of the ethic of argument. Disagreement need not always be between truth and falsehood. It may be between truth and truth. But at this point, the two passages diverge. The first concerns halakhah. The second concerns aggadah, a point of biblical interpretation that does not have direct legal consequences. When the conflict concerns halakhah, there must be a normative resolution, in this case in favour of the school of Hillel.[20] But when no issue of halakhah is directly at stake, there need be no resolution. Both Rabbi Abiatar and Rabbi Jonathan are right, each in his own way.[21]

The rabbinic literature, early and medieval, is full of instances of arguments left open-ended, as if to say that each position is warranted within the tradition. Was the education a parent must give his son vocational or purely religious? Rabbi Meir and Rabbi Nehorai disagreed.[22] Was the Roman empire to be admired for its technological prowess or shunned for its ethical shortcomings? Rabbi Judah bar Ilai and Rabbi Shimon bar Yochai disagreed.[23] Should an accommodation be reached with a repressive Roman regime, or should one choose to die rather than cease teaching Torah in public? Rabbi Jose ben Kisma

---

18. Eiruvin 13b.
19. Gittin 6b.
20. Later rabbinic terminology was to distinguish between *halakhah* and *halakhah lema'aseh*, respectively a defensible halakhic opinion and a binding halakhic ruling.
21. See the comments of Chanokh Zundel in *Etz Yosef*, on *Ein Ya'akov*, Gittin 6b.
22. Mish. Kiddushin 4:14.
23. Shabbat 33b.

and Rabbi Chaninah ben Teradion disagreed.[24] Was the messianic age an event within natural history or a supernatural break with history? Rabbi Jochanan and Shmuel disagreed.[25] These arguments call for, and receive, no final resolution. That is not because they are of secondary significance. On the contrary, they concern ultimate issues of evaluation and ideal. None the less they belong within the broad category of aggadah, which is to say, matters on which the rabbinic tradition did not find it necessary to issue a definitive ruling.

Why? Several answers are possible. It may be that some disagreements concern matters where religious truth is not monolithic, where its fullness is perceived only through a multiplicity of perspectives.[26] Some may involve judgements that are specific to the place and time: now one, now the other is appropriate.[27] Some may represent an ongoing tension between the demands of realism and pursuit of the ideal.[28] Some may involve differing evaluations of history or society, such that only the passage of time will vindicate one view against another.[29] The fact remains, however, that within the rabbinic tradition not every question of religious import called for a single normative answer. Some did, and thus became halakhah. Others did not, and thus by definition remained within the category of aggadah.

Aggadah, then, is rabbinic Judaism's domain of pluralism, the realm in which the truth of one side of the argument does not entail the falsity of the other. It too may be true: in a different sense, or from another perspective, or at another time, or for another kind of person.

---

24. Avodah Zarah 18a.

25. Berakhot 34b.

26. Kook, *Olat Rayah* (2 vols.; Jerusalem: Mosad Harav Kook, 1962), i. 330–31.

27. "It was not appropriate in all this [the domain of ethics] to command details, for the commandments of the Torah are obligatory for every period and all time and in every circumstance, but the virtues of man and his conduct vary according to the time and the people"(*Magid Mishneh* on Yad, *Shekhenim* 14:4).

28. On the argument between Rabbi Shimon bar Yochai and Rabbi Ishmael, for example, as to whether one should study all the time or engage in a worldly occupation also, the Talmud (Berakhot 35a) records the pragmatic judgement, "Many acted in accordance with the view of Rabbi Ishmael and succeeded. Some acted in accordance with Rabbi Shimon and did not succeed."

29. See *Magid Mishneh* on Yad, *Megillah* 2:18.

The existence of such a domain points to a fundamental distinction between halakhah and the fundamentals of faith on the one hand, and matters of attitude and evaluation on the other. The former are normative for all Jews at all times, the latter are not. Halakhah constitutes the rules of the language of Judaism. Aggadah represents the many different statements possible within it.

Peter Strawson has proposed a general philosophical analysis that illuminates this distinction.[30] He differentiates between "social morality" and "individual ideal." Social morality refers to the "rules or principles governing human behaviour which apply universally within a community or class." This, in Judaism, is the domain of halakhah. Individual ideal refers to the "region of diverse, certainly incompatible and possibly practically conflicting ideal images or pictures of a human life, or of human life." It is, he says, the region in which "there are truths but no [single] truth." This is the domain of aggadah. True, the two are not watertight categories. There is a rich and complex interplay between them. But the basic distinction is clear. Halakhah constitutes the Jewish people as a community of faith and action. Aggadah provides it with a vocabulary of diverse and sometimes conflicting ideals. Halakhah is the domain of consensus and norm. Aggadah is the territory of legitimate difference.

ALTERNATIVE INTERPRETATIONS

To which category, then, are we to assign the conflicts we have studied in the previous two chapters, over Orthodoxy's response to Zionism, secular culture, and Jewish peoplehood? There can be no doubt that they belonged to aggadah, or as it has more recently come to be called, *hashkafah* (worldview, outlook). They involved attitude and interpretation. They concerned philosophical orientation and sociological strategy. They were, in their way, paradigms of those issues of evaluation and ideal that in Judaism lend themselves to multiple readings. As we saw, all parties to the disputes agreed on the fundamentals of faith and the inviolability of halakhah. They differed in their interpretation of social processes and priorities. These are not differences that call for definitive resolution.

---

30. P. F. Strawson, "Social Morality and Individual Ideal," in his *Freedom and Resentment* (London: Methuen, 1974), 26–44.

The point was made early on in the debate over Samson Raphael Hirsch's programme of *torah im derekh eretz*. It was, claimed the revisionists – among them, as we have seen, Hirsch's own daughter – merely a *hora'at sha'ah*, a temporary ruling, a concession to time and place. Hirsch himself certainly believed otherwise. But the revisionists were correct. Where they erred was in seeing the alternative – Torah without *derekh eretz* – as a permanent ideal. As we have seen, it was not. The rejection of secular education was equally a response to the times. The argument over whether Torah was to be combined with *derekh eretz* – variously conceived as secular knowledge, vocational training, or a worldly occupation – has persisted since the earliest rabbinic literature and continued unabated through the Middle Ages. It was debated by Rabbi Ishmael and Rabbi Shimon bar Yochai in the second century CE,[31] by Maimonides and Rabbi Shimon ben Zemach Duran in medieval times,[32] and by Rabbi Moses Isserles and Rabbi Shlomo Luria in the sixteenth century.[33] Which side prevailed depended on cultural circumstance and evaluation. The debate was left open-ended. Rulings on both sides were invariably *hora'ot sha'ah*, specific to their time and place.

One twentieth-century authority, Rabbi Abraham Isaac Bloch, head of the yeshiva in Telshe, stated the point explicitly. In 1934 he, along with three other leading halakhists, had been asked by Rabbi Simon Schwab to give a ruling on the issue of *torah im derekh eretz* as it related to the education of young Jews at the time. Rabbi Bloch prefaced his responsum with the following comment:

> In these matters it is difficult to give a clear halakhic response, because they concern issues which are largely based on ideological stances and opinions which are linked to aggadah, and which are therefore governed by the specific character of aggadic issues, as is the case in matters of opinion and ethics. Even though this is an area where there are several positive and negative biblical

---

31. Berakhot 35b.
32. Maimonides, *Commentary on the Mishnah*, Av. 4:7; Yad, *Talmud Torah* 3:10; *Tashbetz*, i. 142–48; see also *Kesef Mishneh* on Yad, *Talmud Torah* 3:10.
33. *Rema*, 5–7.

commands, nonetheless one cannot here establish fixed positions, as is the case in halakhah, and establish rulings that are appropriate to everyone. For the matter depends to a large extent on the temperament of the person concerned and his particular circumstances, as well as the variables of time, place, situation and environment.[34]

At most, Jewish law can yield boundary rules in such matters. There are positions that lie outside Judaism, and cannot be assented to by any halakhic authority. But within these boundaries there are legitimate differences. The debate about *torah im derekh eretz* was one such case. The controversies over Zionism and secession were others.

The arguments that have divided Orthodoxy in the last two centuries, then, are not new. What is new is their allocation into movements and ideologies which tacitly or vociferously exclude one another. The differences of opinion between what are called "Modern" and "traditionalist" Orthodoxy, between one school of thought and another, sometimes between one Hasidic group and another, have hardened into irreconcilable conflicts and mutual delegitimation. The fruits of modernity are sectarianization and adjectival Orthodoxy. And we are now in a position to define the transformation more precisely. It is the application of halakhah to the realm of aggadah. Halakhic positions exclude one another; aggadic positions do not. When arguments that have traditionally been open-ended become split between institutions and ideologies, each of which excludes alternatives, aggadic pluralism has been lost. In its place has come the concept of a single normative Torah view.

THE SEARCH FOR AUTHORITY

Why has this occurred? One of the most profound effects of secularization has been its assault on the concept of authority. Traditional societies are those in which many of the choices which individuals are called on to make, from religious affiliation to choice of occupation or

---

34. The responsum is cited in full in Yehudah Levi, *Sha'arei Talmud Torah* (Jerusalem: Feldheim, 1981), 296–301. It is summarized in the English translation of this work: id., *Torah Study* (Jerusalem: Feldheim, 1990), 275–77.

marriage partner, are shaped by norms, customs, and values embedded in the society of which they are a part. They preceded their birth; they will outlive their death. They are the given of their situation. Traditional thought is marked by the way in which conflict between the individual and society is seen as a marginal and deviant phenomenon. It knows that there are lawbreakers, rebels, apostates, and renegades. But for the most part there is a congruence between the ethos of the individual and that of society.

This congruence is torn asunder by the social and intellectual processes of modernity.[35] Much of what was hitherto given is now chosen. Individuals construct their own life-plan, not least their choice of values. Kantian ethics introduces this radical development in terms of a distinction between heteronomy (legislation from outside) and autonomy (self-legislation). To be ethical is to be autonomous, to accept only the authority of self. A consistent motif of post-Enlightenment ethics is the rejection of religious authority as an external command to which one submits. For this reason Hegel is sharply critical of the Jewish structure of law. "Of spirit," he writes of Judaism, "nothing remained save obstinate pride in slavish obedience."[36] Much of Nietzsche's work is a deepening set of variations on this theme. Judaism, he says, introduced "a God who *demands*."[37] The autonomous self, central to modern ethics, is radically incompatible with the structures of Jewish spirituality, built as they are on the concept of *mitzvah*, command.

The threat to tradition has therefore been not simply the dethronement of halakhah in favour of some other source of authority, but the loss of authority altogether. Against a cultural background in which religious authority was taken for granted, a distinction could be made between areas where Torah issued authoritative commands and those where a range of options was left open. In the modern situation it has seemed increasingly necessary to emphasize authority as such,

---

35. See the pertinent comments of MacIntyre, *After Virtue*, esp. 30. See also Berger, Berger, and Kellner, *The Homeless Mind*, for a sociological study of the same phenomenon.

36. *On Christianity: Early Theological Writings of Friedrich Hegel*, trans. T. M. Knox and R. Kroner (1948), 178. Quoted in Don Cupitt, *Crisis of Moral Authority* (London: SCM Press, 1985), 111.

37. Nietzsche, *Twilight of the Idols* and *The Anti-Christ*, 136.

even on questions to which authority had not hitherto been brought to bear. This was quickly apparent in the emergence of a new style of leadership amongst the Hasidim of the eighteenth century: the *tzadik* or *rebbe*. It appeared in the early nineteenth century in non-Hasidic East European Jewry in the form of the *rosh yeshivah*. Though, as is evident from a famous letter from Maimonides to Rabbi Shmuel ibn Tibbon,[38] the practice of consulting a Torah sage on matters outside halakhah is not new, its institutionalization was.[39] Opponents of the Hasidic movement often argued that the bond between a *rebbe* and his followers went beyond the bounds of the traditional relationship between teacher and disciple.

The issue of authority lay at the heart of Samson Raphael Hirsch's exchange of correspondence with Rabbi Seligmann Baer Bamberger on the question of secession. Hirsch argued that Bamberger had no right to interfere with his decision, and quoted the halakhic rule that "One cannot permit what one's colleague has forbidden." Bamberger replied that the rule was irrelevant to the case in hand. Hirsch's decision had not been accepted by the community. Moreover, there were scholars of equal or greater weight in Frankfurt who disagreed with it. Hirsch had cast aspersions on his opponents, men of unquestionable learning and piety. Bamberger in effect accused Hirsch of improper authoritarianism, and argued that he should have placed the issue before other rabbinical

---

38. English version in *Letters of Maimonides*, trans. Leon Stitskin (New York: Yeshiva University Press, 1982), 130–36.

39. This is evident in the comments of one of the early Hasidic leaders. In his "Igeret Hakodesh" Rabbi Shneur Zalman of Lyady, leader of what came to be known as the Chabad or Lubavitch movement, writes as follows: "Has this ever happened since the beginning of time, and where have you found a precedent for this custom in any of the books of the early or later sages of Israel, that there should be a custom and practice of *asking for advice in mundane matters, to know what to do in matters pertaining to the physical* [i.e., secular] *world*. Questions of this kind were not asked of even the greatest of the early sages of Israel, the tannaim and amoraim, 'from whom no secret was hidden' and 'all the paths of heaven were clear to them'": "Igeret Hakodesh," *Tanya*, ch. 22. Rabbi Shneur Zalman adds that a sage can give advice only in matters of Torah and the fear of heaven. Only a prophet can give advice in other things.

authorities rather than decide it himself.[40] The controversy turned not so much on the substantive issue of secession as on the authority of a congregational rabbi as *mara de'atra*, "master of the locality," empowered to make binding decisions on its behalf.

The collapse of the traditional *kehillah* meant that, in organizational terms, the power of religious authorities was greatly circumscribed. Functions which had previously been the responsibility of the Jewish community were taken over by the state. Others, though they were administered by the community, came increasingly under the control of secular or non-Orthodox majorities. As we saw, it was in response to these developments that secession seemed the only route to preserve the integrity of Orthodoxy. Traditional religious authority could be recreated within the enclosed environment of the Hasidic group or the yeshiva. Hirsch sought to do likewise within the highly integrated synagogue-school nexus he created in Frankfurt. In retrospect we can see his battle with Bamberger as an attempt to endow the congregational rabbinate with an authority roughly equivalent to that which had emerged in Hasidic and yeshiva circles.

Secession meant sacrificing community-wide influence in favour of a heightening of the rabbi's powers within the narrow ambit of his disciples. Jewish tradition had spoken of three modes of leadership, practical, intellectual, and ritual – the crowns of *malkhut* (kingship), *torah*, and *kehunah* (priesthood) respectively – which were standardly distributed among different groups within the community.[41] Within the total environment of the Hasidic group or yeshiva these functions were often concentrated in a single person, so that separatism, while fragmenting Orthodoxy, greatly intensified its focus of authority on charismatic figures.

This new authority found expression in a concept that surfaced with increasing prominence from the late nineteenth century onward:

---

40. Schwab, *The History of Orthodox Jewry in Germany*, 76–79; Liberles, *Religious Conflict in Social Context*, 221–24.

41. For a historical survey of Jewish political organization, in terms of the "three crowns," see D. J. Elazar and Stuart A. Cohen, *The Jewish Polity* (Bloomington, IN: Indiana University Press, 1985). See also Stuart Cohen's more recent and detailed study, *The Three Crowns* (Cambridge: Cambridge University Press, 1990).

da'at torah, "a, or the, Torah view."[42] *Da'at torah* bridged the gap between aggadah and halakhah. It lent unqualified authority to the views of a sage on precisely those issues of interpretation and evaluation that lay beyond the parameters of halakhah. The idea itself is deeply rooted in tradition. But it contains a fateful ambiguity. It may mean *a* Torah view or *the* Torah view. In principle, since the subjects with which it deals are not given to halakhic resolution, it means *a* Torah view. But in practice, since the institutions in which it is voiced are usually monolithic, it has come to mean *the* Torah view.

What *da'at torah* signifies is not always clear. One writer has defined it as "a special endowment or capacity to penetrate objective reality, recognise facts as they really are, and apply the pertinent halakhic principles. It is a form of *ruach hakodesh* [quasi-prophetic insight], as it were, which borders if only remotely on the periphery of prophecy."[43] Others see it as an extension of halakhic ruling; yet others as the consensus of the great sages of the generation, considered authoritative in virtue of their role as the collective conscience of the Jewish people. This much, however, is clear. First, *da'at torah* is invoked in areas where the halakhic guidelines are not unequivocal. Second, it is appealed to on precisely those matters which have been, in the past two centuries, the subject of ideological debate within the Orthodox community itself. It has been brought into the arguments, for example, over secular studies, attitudes to the State of Israel, national service for yeshiva students in Israel's armed services, Orthodox participation in rabbinical associations which include non-Orthodox members, and whether or not Israel may exchange land for peace. Third, a *da'at torah* view is usually presented as intuitive, oracular, and prophetic, rather than in the normal form of a halakhic ruling with sources, inference, argument, and rational consideration of contrary positions. *Da'at torah* is, in short, the extension of halakhic authority to matters which are

---

42. The phrase *da'at torah* is found in the Talmud (Chullin 90b). Its usage in the sense of authoritative ideology is, however, recent. See the controversial comments of Lawrence Kaplan, "Rabbi Isaac Hutner's '*Da'at Torah* Perspective' on the Holocaust: A Critical Analysis," *Tradition*, 18:3 (1980), 235–48, esp. nn. 5, 7.

43. Bernard Weinberger, "The Role of the Gedolim," *Jewish Observer* (Oct. 1963), 11.

not halakhic only but include elements of evaluation, ideology, and communal policy.

Da'at torah in a restricted sense is surely a Judaically well-founded idea. There are matters which lie outside halakhah which the sages none the less called Torah.[44] In such matters one might seek the advice of a sage, or emulate his example.[45] But in its unrestricted modern usage it is more problematic.[46] The status of intuition or prophetic insight in the halakhic process is highly controversial.[47] The Talmud contains the principle that the Torah is "not in Heaven,"[48] meaning that rulings are to be determined not by prophetic insight but by the majority vote of the sages. Maimonides adds that in a matter of Jewish law, a thousand prophets would be outweighed by a thousand and one sages.[49] Rabbi Zvi Hirsch Chajes differentiates between the legislative power of the sage and the prophet precisely in that while both have the power to make enactments "to protect" the institutions of Judaism, the sage must demonstrate the clear and beneficial consequences of his rule, while the prophet may rely on his intuition.[50]

Equally problematic is the concept of authority that *da'at torah* embodies. A rabbi certainly has authority over his disciple; a constituted Sanhedrin has authority over Israel; the great sage of a generation has authority in virtue of the informal consensus which recognizes his unrivalled erudition and judgement. The idea of *da'at torah* is, however, often used to make larger claims: to undercut the authority of other halakhists or to negate other Orthodox approaches.[51] Its development has gone hand in hand with an extension of the influence of the *rosh yeshivah* and the Hasidic leader as against the local rabbi and, in Israel,

---

44. Berakhot 62a.

45. See, e.g., Yad, *De'ot* 2:1, 6:2.

46. See J. Simcha Cohen, *Timely Jewish Questions, Timeless Rabbinic Answers* (Northvale, NJ: Jason Aronson, 1991), 78–93; Yehuda Amichai, "Da'at Torah Be'inyanim She'einam Halachti'im Muvhakim," *Techumin*, 11 (1991), 24–30.

47. The classic study is Ephraim Urbach, "Halakhah Unevuah," *Tarbitz*, 18 (1947), 1–27.

48. Bava Metzia 59b.

49. Maimonides, *Commentary on the Mishnah*, Intro.

50. Chajes, *Torat Hanevi'im*, ch. 5.

51. The idea of *da'at torah* must be distinguished from such concepts as the command to heed sages generally (Deut. 17:11), the authority of a rabbinic court of law, *emunat*

the chief rabbinate. It is not clear that Jewish tradition recognizes such authority in the absence of discipleship or formally constituted powers. Nor is it certain that Jewish law recognizes the exclusive authority of rabbinic bodies in policy issues that were traditionally the preserve of *keter malkhut,* monarchy, or *takanot hakahal,* communal governance.[52] At the very least, these are controversial issues which call for clarification.

The extension of authority implicit in modern uses of *da'at torah* means, in effect, excluding tradition's alternative voices. It leads to a view of Judaism from which what we have called aggadic pluralism is missing. It negates the idea, in other words, that there are areas of policy and evaluation where more than one view is possible and legitimate. It reduces all matters of Judaic significance to the status of halakhah, which is to say, matters on which there is one correct ruling applicable to all Jews in all times and all places. The areas where *da'at torah* have been invoked have been precisely those where different evaluations were possible within Orthodoxy and where different rulings were appropriate to different groups and circumstances. *Torah im derekh eretz,* for example, may have been the correct response for nineteenth-century German, but not Hungarian, Jewry. Different responses to Zionism were appropriate at different stages of its evolution. The "seamless robe" view of Judaism, whereby all questions faced by Jews have the same character and call for the same mode of resolution, is a modern phenomenon rather than a traditional one, and does injustice to rabbinic Judaism's internal subtlety. Above all, it suppresses its most effective means of handling diversity within the framework of unity.

It abolishes the distinction between what I have called the rules of the language and the many sentences possible within it. It means that all difference becomes fundamental and schismatic. The organizational and intellectual forms of sectarianization are mutually reinforcing. For the members of a given institution or group, *a* Torah view of social process

---

chakhamim ("faith in the sages"), and so forth. The question behind *da'at torah* is precisely how far these concepts extend, and how far they authorize one rabbinic opinion against others.

52. For a good survey in English of the concept of communal governance in Jewish law see *Encyclopaedia Judaica,* s.v. *Takkanot hakahal,* xv. 728–37.

and policy comes to seem the only authentic one. In extreme cases it leads one revered Torah sage to accuse another of heresy,[53] or traditionalists to speak of modernists as idolaters.[54] In most cases it means a marked lack of contact, dialogue, and kinship between the various Orthodox sectors who may be differentiated by nothing other than their affiliation to a particular yeshiva or Hasidic group. In the process, halakhic norms of personal relationships are either circumvented or abandoned.

Tradition clearly has the resource to handle diversity without disunity on the kind of issues which have divided Orthodoxy since the nineteenth century. Indeed, Orthodoxy's fragmentation has occurred precisely because traditional distinctions have been eroded in the search for new bases of authority. The invocation of *da'at torah* in the sense of a uniquely and universally correct solution to questions that admit of none is untraditional and destructive of other values that are unquestionably central to Torah, not least of *keneset Yisrael* itself. Its use could only be justified as a concession to crisis. That crisis existed in the early twentieth century, as Orthodoxy seemed to be facing defeat by the forces of secularity throughout central and eastern Europe. It existed in the decades of painful reconstruction after the ravages of the Holocaust. It is doubtful whether it exists today, at a time of unprecedented Orthodox revival. We can hope for aggadic pluralism gradually to be restored.

HALAKHIC UNIVERSALISM

A similar process has occurred in the domain of halakhah itself. This is not the place for a detailed investigation of halakhic decision making. It is sufficient to note that Jewish law, grounded as it is on revelation

---

53. This occurred before the Israeli general election of November 1988, when a rosh yeshivah levelled this accusation against the distinguished head of a Hasidic group. He refused to be associated with a political party, Agudat Yisrael, which had any connection with the group or accepted its advertisements in its party newspaper. Exclusion of other Orthodox rabbis on ideological grounds has marked Agudat Yisrael since its inception. See Schwab, *The History of Orthodox Jewry in Germany*, 115–26.

54. See the remark of Rabbi Elya Meir Bloch quoted in Chaim Dov Keller, "Modern Orthodoxy: An Analysis and a Response," in Reuven Bulka (ed.), *Dimensions of Orthodox Judaism* (New York: Ktav, 1983), 253.

and precedent, is not open-endedly flexible. On many questions there is a spectrum of halakhic opinion, but to be well founded, an opinion must be based on the canonical sources of Jewish law as interpreted by accepted principles of inference. The opinions themselves are subject to the narrowing process of consensus. And when doubt prevails, there are higher-order rules of when to be lenient, when strict.

This suggests that there is ultimately only one normative answer to any halakhic question. In many cases this may be so, but not in all. As in any legal system, hard cases arise. Sometimes they involve considerations of policy as well as precedent.[55] Not only past decisions but also future consequences must be taken into consideration. The question then arises: *What* are the values by which halakhic policy is to be judged? In its broadest sense, the answer is relatively clear. The sages are the guardians of the halakhic system. They act to ensure its realization and continuity through the vicissitudes of time. Maimonides states the aim of rabbinic legislation to be "to strengthen the religion and improve the world." The rabbis have power temporarily to suspend biblical laws "to bring the masses back to religion or save them from corruption."[56] But these propositions may be too broad to provide an answer to difficult questions. To pose a key dilemma of modernity: Which takes precedence, defence of the *content* or of the *constituency* of the halakhic system? If a strict ruling will enhance the commitment of the few but alienate the many, is it to be preferred to a lenient ruling that will include the many but compromise the religious intensity of the few?

Put in the context of the past, the question can probably have only one answer. Halakhah conceived as the constitution of a people necessarily aims at including all. A rabbinic decree to which the majority of the community was unable to adhere was *ultra vires*.[57] Many of the leniencies introduced into Jewish law – including those circumventing

---

55. I have dealt with this subject at greater length in the fifth Jakobovits Lecture, "Three Approaches to Halakhah" (unpublished). On the general jurisprudential point, Ronald Dworkin has suggestive things to say in his *Taking Rights Seriously* (London: Duckworth, 1978), 81–130; id., *A Matter of Principle* (Oxford: Clarendon Press, 1986), 72–103, 119–77; id., *Law's Empire* (London: Fontana, 1986).

56. Yad, *Mamrim* 1:2, 2:4.

57. Ibid., 2:5.

the prohibition on taking interest, and formalizing the sale of *chametz* (leaven) during Passover – were overtly or implicitly justified on the basis of economic necessity, itself considered a factor in halakhic policy on the ground that "the Torah treats protectively the money of Israel."[58] A Judaism economically unviable for many of its adherents would be exclusive. Wherever possible the halakhah was *in*clusive. Among the principles by which the Talmud justified its rulings were: "so as not to close the door to borrowers,"[59] "so as not to discourage penitents,"[60] and "so as not to put to shame those who lacked means."[61] Rabbi Shimon ben Adret justified one ruling on the grounds that it would "open the door to those who wished to perform *mitzvot*."[62] Those who wished to adopt a higher standard could do so voluntarily. The standard rubric was: "He who wishes to be strict with himself will receive blessing, but he who is lenient has not lost thereby."

Until the threshold of modernity, halakhah was the constitution of a people, in fact as well as theory. But throughout the nineteenth century this formulation became increasingly problematic. Emancipation meant that Jewish communities lost their coercive powers to secure adherence to halakhah. The spread of secularism and Reform meant that by the end of the century a majority of Europe's Jews saw themselves as outside its ambit. *De facto,* halakhah had become not the law of a people but the code of a voluntary elite. Nor was this all. The concentration of Torah in yeshivot, the separation of the yeshivot from the general community, and the independence of yeshiva heads and teachers from the congregational rabbinate meant, in effect, that Torah's primary constituency had become an elite of the elite.

What then had become of Maimonides' guiding objectives of the halakhic system? "To improve the world" had become in part the

---

58. See Mish. Nega'im 12:5, Yoma 39a and references cited there. For further examples of such legislation see Leo Jung, *Human Relations in Jewish Law* (New York: Jewish Education Committee, 1967), 106–13; Eliezer Berkovits, *Not in Heaven: The Nature and Function of Halakhah* (New York: Ktav, 1983), 14–19.

59. Sanhedrin 3a.

60. Gittin 55a; Bava Kama 94a–95a.

61. Ta'anit 31a.

62. *Rashba,* 581.

responsibility of the state, in part the province of Jewish communal organizations that were often unanswerable to Jewish law. "To bring the masses back to religion" had, in the frank assessment of many rabbinic leaders, become impossible. The masses were in full flight from religion. Rabbi Israel Meir Hacohen (the Chafetz Chayyim, 1838–1933), a leading halakhist and a figure of outstanding saintliness, put the dilemma simply. The honour of God, he writes, is being daily desecrated. The Torah and its commandments are being abandoned. He who cares for the sanctity of Torah cannot be silent. But what can he do? If he protests, he will not be heeded. The Chafetz Chayyim's response is to distinguish between those who are already effectively lost to the faith, and those who still have some kinship with it. One must attend to the latter. For the former, nothing can be done.[63]

For many halakhists, then, "to strengthen the religion" was the sole objective that remained, and it could best be achieved by strengthening *she'erit hapeleitah*, the faithful "remnant" that survived. The sense of being lonely survivors in a hostile world, born in the social and intellectual assaults of the nineteenth century, was immeasurably deepened by the experience of the Holocaust which all but completely destroyed the vast hinterlands of East European traditionalism and its outstanding centres of learning. The context and constituency of halakhah had been transformed. It was now being preserved by a minority to whom the outside world, Jewish and non-Jewish, had been uniformly hostile, and in whom lay the conscious, lonely task of ensuring Torah's survival. Necessarily, the guiding objective of halakhah was, under these circumstances, not the perfection of society or the Jewish people as a whole, but the perfection of the individual. The aim of inclusivity, which had moderated the system in favour of leniency, was in abeyance. The aim was now intensity for the faithful who remained.

THE SEARCH FOR STRINGENCY

Strict rulings have therefore come to dominate the halakhic system in recent decades. Norms that were halakhically acceptable to previous generations have come to seem inauthentic and compromising. In the

---

63. Israel Meir Hacohen, *Chizuk Hadat*, i.

1960s Rabbi Simcha Elberg, editor of the Orthodox journal *HaPardes*, gave a name to the phenomenon. He called it "Bnei Braqism," after the religious township in Israel. "The Bnei Braq concept embodies a major revolution in the very structure of religious life. Bnei Braq is looking for increased rather than decreased stringency.... A young yeshiva student... will, when approaching the *Shulchan Arukh* [Rabbi Joseph Caro's code of Jewish law], search out that opinion which forbids, which restricts, which is more stringent. He will not look for the phrase, 'and there are those who are more lenient' nor will he abide by that sort of decision, but will be on the watch for the words, 'there are those who are stricter.'" When he finds a new stringency, Rabbi Elberg adds in Yiddish, the student *iz zekh mechaye nefesh*; he "refreshes his soul."[64]

In some respects, this development runs not only against the overall tenor of the halakhic system but also against its traditional vehicles of continuity: family and local community practice. The halakhic literature generally embodies a respect for extant traditions, and tries where possible to vindicate them.[65] The revolution to which Rabbi Elberg refers implicitly involves a reversal of this process: a willingness to criticize the standards of previous generations. That this was possible is due to the confluence of several historical and social factors. First has been the growth, in Israel and America, of yeshivot on the East European model. Here, during the critical period of maturation, the student is separated from his family and local community. The yeshiva and its head act *in loco parentis* and the influence of local custom is lost. Second was the geographical dislocation of world Jewry – the mass migrations of 1880–1920 and 1930–40 – which ruptured the continuity of Jewish community life. Third was the impact of the Holocaust itself on the next generation. Lost worlds were being rebuilt by those who had themselves not experienced them. The living past, embodied in family and communal traditions, was thus replaced by a reconstructed past.[66]

---

64. Cited in Menachem Friedman, "Life Tradition and Book Tradition in the Development of Ultra-Orthodox Judaism," in Harvey Goldberg (ed.), *Judaism Viewed from Within and from Without* (Albany, NY: State University of New York Press, 1987), 235–36.

65. See, e.g., Rivash, 158.

66. See Friedman, "Life Tradition," and id., "Haredim Confront the Modern City," in

As a result, stricter norms have developed on such issues as modesty of dress, separation of the sexes, and *kashrut* (dietary laws). Traditional *shiurim*, measurements of size, weight, and volume in relation to Jewish law, have been displaced by the more stringent rulings of Rabbi Avraham Karelitz (the Chazon Ish, 1878–1953). The construction of *eiruvin* – devices to allow carrying in the streets on Shabbat – hitherto regarded as a religious imperative,[67] has increasingly come to be viewed as a dangerous leniency. Deepening scepticism has prevailed on the religious significance of secular education and the State of Israel. The bearers of contemporary culture – secular newspapers[68] and television – are forbidden. Factors which in the past tempered religious exclusivity – mixed neighbourhoods, and the need to earn a living – have been less in evidence. The urban ghetto facilitates homogeneous neighbourhoods. The development of the welfare state and rises in living standards have enabled the period spent in yeshiva study to be considerably extended.[69]

An élite religiosity has thus developed within Orthodoxy itself, in opposition not only to non-Jews and non-Orthodox Jews, but to Orthodox Jews who temper their spirituality with an involvement with the world. A sharp contrast is drawn between *benei torah* (scholars) and *baalebatim* (laymen) in such remarks as "the opinion of the *baalebatim* is the reverse of the opinion of the Torah," or "the truth is the opposite of what is believed by the masses."[70] Halakhic practice becomes emblematic of membership of the élite.[71] Stringency reinforces the conception of Judaism as an act of segregation from a corrupt and corrupting world.

Peter Medding (ed.), *Studies in Contemporary Jewry*, ii (Bloomington, IN: Indiana University Press, 1986), 74–96.

67. See, e.g., Chatam Sofer: *Orach Chayim*, 99.

68. The Netziv was an avid reader of newspapers. See Meir Bar-Ilan, *Mivolozhin ad Yerushalayim* (2 vols.; Tel Aviv, 1971), i. 138, 163.

69. See, in addition to Friedman's studies, Liebman and Don-Yehiya, *Religion and Politics in Israel*, 119–37.

70. Friedman, "Life Tradition," 243, 253.

71. This, of course, is a characteristic of sectarian religious organizations. See Wilson, *Religion in Sociological Perspective*, 89–120.

MODERATION AS A RELIGIOUS NORM

Charles Liebman, a sociologist of unusual insight, has concluded from these phenomena that "extremism" is a "religious norm."[72] He argues that "a propensity to religious extremism does not require explanation since it is entirely consistent with basic religious tenets and authentic religious orientations. It is religious moderation or religious liberalism, the willingness of religious adherents to accommodate themselves to their environment, to adapt their behavioural and belief patterns to prevailing cultural norms, to make peace with the world, that requires explanation." On this interpretation, the unexpected rise of centres of Orthodox intensity in the last two decades is not an anomaly. It is the reinstatement of classic Jewish values.

There is truth in this view, but not the whole truth. Jewish law aimed at the perfection of both society and the individual. To be sure, these did not wholly coincide. Maimonides developed two different typologies of the religious personality. He called them the *chakham* and the *chasid*, the sage and the saint.[73] The sage embodied in his character Judaism's social ideals. He mediated between conflicting claims. He pursued the "middle way," which Maimonides identified with the way of God. The concept of the *chakham* is closely linked with Maimonides' understanding of Jewish law and prophetic leadership as essentially political.[74] A religious leader must be able to "regulate the actions of man; he must complete every shortcoming, remove every excess, and prescribe for the conduct of all, so that the natural variety [of temperament within a society] should be counterbalanced by the uniformity of legislation, and the order of society be well established."[75] Reconciling opposites and resolving conflicts are the art of governance, and it is

---

72. Charles Liebman, "Extremism as a Religious Norm," *Journal for the Scientific Study of Religion*, 22 (Mar. 1983), 75–86.
73. Maimonides, *Shemoneh Perakim*, 4; Yad, *De'ot*, 1; see also *Guide of the Perplexed*, iii. 53–54.
74. See on this Leo Strauss, *Philosophy and Law* (Philadelphia: JPS, 1987), 79–110; Lawrence V. Berman, "Maimonides on Political Leadership," in Daniel Elazar (ed.), *Kinship and Consent* (Ramat Gan: Turtledove, 1981), 113–25.
75. *Guide of the Perplexed*, ii. 40.

through governance that man strives to imitate God.[76] The sage is one who has developed this skill, handling the conflicts within himself and his environment judiciously and with emotional detachment. He is the ideal type of the halakhic system considered as a social code.

The *chasid* or saint is altogether different. The term, for Maimonides, denotes excess.[77] The *chasid* does not base his ethic on imitating the ways of God. His virtue arises from the imperfections of the human personality. Because man is more easily inclined to cowardice than courage, or to miserliness than generosity, the *chasid* maintains a psychic equilibrium by tending somewhat to the opposite extreme. The sage acts according to the law, and the law maximizes social perfection; but the saint acts "beyond the letter of the law."[78] His saintliness is the product of victory in a constant struggle against baser emotions, something unnecessary for the sage, who acts out of judgement, not passion. The *chasid* is the ideal type of the halakhic system considered as a code of individual, not social, perfection.[79]

Considered in isolation, the saint is greater than the sage. But the halakhic system does not encourage us to consider individuals in isolation. The way of the sage is therefore normative – "We are commanded to walk in these middle ways, which are the good and right ways, as it is said, 'And you shall walk in his ways'"[80] – while the way of the saint is a concession to human emotion. But there are times, says Maimonides,

---

76. Ibid., 54.

77. *Commentary on the Mishnah*, Av. 5:6; *Guide of the Perplexed*, iii. 53.

78. Yad, *De'ot* 1:5.

79. It will be clear that I understand Maimonides in a somewhat broader context than does Aharon Lichtenstein, "Does Jewish Tradition Recognize an Ethic Independent of Halakhah?," in Menachem Kellner (ed.), *Contemporary Jewish Ethics* (New York: Sanhedrin Press, 1978), 102–23. Lichtenstein understands the chasid in terms of supererogation, but fails, I think, to do justice to Maimonides' general preference for the *chakham* over the *chasid*. On this point see *Igerot Harayah*, i, nos. 89, 99–100, on the distinction between *chakhemei* and *chasidei umot haolam*. For other interpretations see Norman Lamm, "Hechakham Vehachasid Bemishnat Harambam," in *Samuel Belkin Memorial Volume* (New York: Yeshiva University, 1981), 11–28; Marvin Fox, "The Doctrine of the Mean in Aristotle and Maimonides: A Comparative Study," in id., *Interpreting Maimonides* (Chicago: University of Chicago Press, 1990), 93–123.

80. Yad, *De'ot* 1:6.

when the way of the sage is unavailable as an ideal. The sage embodies social virtue. When society is irretrievably degenerate, social virtue is impossible. "If [virtuous men] saw that due to the corruption of the people of the city they would be corrupted through contact with them... and that social intercourse with them would bring about the debasement of their own moral habits, then they withdrew to desolate places where there are no evil men."[81] In his law-code Maimonides envisages the possibility that all societies at a particular time might be corrupt, "as is the case now."[82] When social perfection is impossible, individual perfection remains. When the times are out of joint, one must live as a saint.

We can now assess Charles Liebman's claim that extremism is a religious norm. It is so only from the point of view of the *chasid*. Strict rulings which go beyond the letter of the law, segregation from secular society, and total immersion in institutions of Torah are consummations devoutly to be wished from the perspective of individual perfection. Indeed, the vocabulary of the contemporary yeshiva ethic, stressing as it does personal "completeness," consistency, and a rejection of practical compromise, is intently focused on the individual. The flourishing today of institutions capable of producing such individuals in abundance is, after the assaults of the previous two centuries, little short of miraculous.

But the ethic of the *chasid* takes precedence over that of the *chakham* only in circumstances that are themselves deviant. Maimonides' philosophy of halakhah is a compelling statement of moderation as a religious norm. Jewish law is coextensive with the Jewish people. It is the constitution of Jewish society. It is therefore constrained from extremism. So seriously did Maimonides take this fact that he argued that biblical law itself was gradualist and made many concessions to the weaknesses of the Israelites in the wilderness. Every law, even divine law, must reckon with the human situation and must legislate for a real society, even as it aspires to an ideal one.[83]

---

81. *Shemoneh Perakim*, 4.
82. Yad, *De'ot* 6:1. Compare the closing passages of Maimonides' Epistle on Martyrdom and his letter to the sages of Lunel.
83. *Guide of the Perplexed*, iii. 32.

Liebman correctly notes that "in the past, rabbinical authorities, responsible for the entire community, were reluctant to interpret religious law in such a manner that the vast majority of Jews would find its observance excessively burdensome."[84] This was the primary moderating influence on halakhah. Where Liebman errs is in seeing this as accidental rather than essential to the halakhic enterprise. The halakhah of the sage aims at universality: it is bound by a desire to keep the entire community within the framework of law. The saint, who acts beyond halakhic duty, is constrained by no such limitation. He aims at personal intensity, not a universal order. Halakhah itself will only reflect the ethos of the saint under conditions of social breakdown, when rabbinic authorities are convinced that the majority would not observe Jewish law however leniently it was interpreted.

Throughout the nineteenth and early twentieth centuries there were halakhists of distinction who were less pessimistic. Rabbis David Zvi Hoffmann, Yechiel Weinberg, Yitzchak Elchanan Spektor, and Ben-Zion Uziel were among those who developed a more measured approach to Jewish realities, understanding the need for leniency wherever possible. Rabbi Yechiel Michal Epstein, author of the monumental halakhic code the *Arukh Hashulchan,* frequently defends extant practice even where its permissibility is tenuous. Others, most notably Rabbi Chaim Hirschensohn, advocated more radical halakhic accommodations, but the consensus was against them.

Just as we distinguished between halakhah and aggadah, then so we must distinguish between halakhah and the essentially extra-halakhic ethos of the saint. Tradition described the latter as going *lifnim mishurat hadin,* "beyond the letter of the law," and in other phrases of similar import. Halakhah aspires to universality, society-wide adherence, and "improving the world." Especially when the law lacks coercive sanctions, it must wherever possible prefer a lenient ruling that embraces many to a strict decision that is observed only by the few. Beyond halakhah there is unlimited scope for personal piety, but this is not to be confused with the halakhic norm itself. Only the most negative assumption that the majority are beyond the reach of the law, presently and potentially,

---

84. Liebman, "Extremism as a Religious Norm," 82.

would justify a systematic preference for the strictest available ruling. That assumption conflicts with a rabbinic faith that declared that "even the emptiest of Israel is as full of *mitzvot,* religious deeds, as a pomegranate is [of seeds]."[85]

The present tendency to conflate law and "beyond the letter of the law," like the tendency to conflate halakhah and aggadah, is a response to and evidence of religious crisis. But that crisis has reached its peak and already lies in the past. Halakhic Judaism no longer faces extinction. Its populations flourish. Its institutions thrive. We can expect the recovery of a more universalist approach to halakhah, and a renewal of the necessary distinction between halakhah and personal piety.

BEYOND SECTARIANISM

The two resources of tradition so far considered, aggadic pluralism and halakhic universalism, have a bearing only on Orthodoxy. The present Orthodox schisms are not unprecedented: we have only to recall the conflicts between supporters and opponents of Maimonides in the Middle Ages and between Hasidim and their opponents in the eighteenth century. But they are deeply destructive of traditional values and distinctions. Halakhah embodies the idea that the Jewish people is constituted as a community of belief and action. The primary content of revelation is law, not personal salvation or individual ethical choice. The primary function of law is to shape a society. The function of Jewish law is to bind and direct the Jewish people considered as an indivisible covenantal entity.

Halakhah unites. It is the Jewish equivalent of what Strawson called "social morality" as against "individual ideal." Above the community-forming structure of halakhah, one could build aggadic visions and voluntary codes of piety, both of which were pluralist by their nature, specific as they are to time, place, person, and perspective. But a confusion of the two, of halakhah with aggadah on the one hand, halakhah with *lifnim mishurat hadin,* or voluntary stringency, on the other, is to confuse the rules of the language with the sentences spoken within it. This destroys community and distorts the essential nature of the halakhic

---

85. Berakhot 57a, Eiruvin 19a, Sanhedrin 37a.

enterprise. Recovering the traditional distinctions would restore Orthodox unity without restricting Orthodox diversity.

But it would not address the deepest fissure of modernity, that between Orthodoxy and others. To this, therefore, we must now turn.

Chapter 6

Inclusivism

W e now come to the most sensitive stage of the argument. I have argued that Jewish tradition contains the resources to prevent Orthodoxy's disintegration into conflicting sects. But does it have the resources to span the quite different and vastly greater divide between Orthodoxy and non-Orthodoxy? Here schism – the division of Jewry into two peoples – is a real possibility. Can diversity coexist with unity even across the abyss of disagreement on fundamentals of faith and practice?

Let us first specify the terms in which we are to address the question. Firstly, it applies to all groups that lie outside Orthodoxy – to the various forms of liberal Judaism (Reform, Conservative, and Reconstructionist), and equally to the several modes of secular Jewish identity, from diaspora Jewish ethnicity to Israeli secular nationalism. The contours of the problem differ in each case, so in this and the next chapter we shall consider only the most difficult: the relationship between Orthodoxy and Reform, in particular radical Reform as it has developed in America. If this problem is insoluble, it does not imply that the others are. But if some resolution can be found here, it should be readily applicable elsewhere.

Secondly, what kind of solution do we seek? The Orthodox-Reform rift is readily bridged if certain conditions are fulfilled. Reform Jews might decide, in the present climate of the search for tradition, to become Orthodox Jews. Orthodoxy might discover a hitherto unsuspected possibility of halakhic pluralism. Reform Judaism, less dramatically, might reformulate its doctrinal position in ways that could allow its accommodation within an Orthodoxy broadly conceived. More modestly still, some shared procedure might be arrived at, agreeable to both sides, for at least the most basic halakhic determinants of personal status: conversion and divorce. A sufficient structure of Jewish unity might be built on the narrow base of consensus on who is a Jew and who may marry whom.

Practical solutions of this nature need constantly to be articulated, in the faith that at some stage some formula or development will emerge that will generate substantive convergence towards a common conception of Jewish peoplehood. That faith is not wishful thinking. It is in large measure what it is to have faith in *keneset Yisrael,* the covenantal community; and faith in the covenantal community is an essential element of Jewish messianic belief. I shall have more to say about such proposals in a later chapter. However, they are not the immediate concern. Instead, in this chapter I consider the worst-case scenario: that nothing changes in either Reform or Orthodox attitudes. Again, this minimalist strategy has advantages. If, with this initial assumption, we fail to make progress, then nothing is ruled out by way of faith that attitudes will change, or in terms of proposals to generate change. If, on the other hand, some reconciliation is possible even within present positions, we shall have achieved a small gain on which others might be built.

The problem, thus stated, seems insoluble. Orthodoxy, as I have argued throughout, does not recognize the possibility of denominational pluralism. It cannot concede legitimacy to Jewish interpretations that deny or secularize the fundamentals of faith. This is, indeed, what is meant by Orthodoxy, and why this particular term was chosen by its opponents. To use the metaphor of the previous chapter, Orthodox Jews are related to one another as speakers of a common language, though they speak different sentences and use different dialects. That language is determined by the ground-rules of halakhic authority and

the fundamentals of faith. Those who do not share those rules necessarily speak another language. The several languages may have words in
common, but they will not mean the same thing.

Orthodoxy parts company with Reform as it did with Samaritans, Christians, and Karaites. Judaism, as has often been noted, does
not attach the same significance to creed as it does to deed. Few of the
Talmud's thousands of pages are devoted to doctrine. Instead, overwhelmingly, they are concerned with the clarification of law. But, as is
less often noted, Judaism's great schisms have occurred over matters of
belief: the authority of the oral law, the inception of the messianic age,
and the divine, unmediated authorship of revelation.

That dogma should be rarely debated, analysed, and codified yet
none the less definitive is not a paradox. The principles of Orthodoxy
are its boundaries. Boundary disputes are generally rare but bitter. For
the most part, borders are taken for granted; life proceeds unreflectively
within them. Reform, though, in its gradual abandonment of halakhic
norms, halakhic authority, and belief in revelation, was necessarily judged
to have crossed the line separating the Judaism of revelation and tradition from another country, another language.

Our initial expectation of Orthodox-Reform reconciliation must
therefore be low. My argument, however, will be that this is a false interpretation of the facts. A traditional strategy is readily available to prevent
schism. The problem is not the lack of a resolution but the *perception* of
that resolution from two different perspectives. For, deeply rooted as it
is in tradition, it runs directly contrary to modern sensibilities. We shall
discover a deep conceptual gap between tradition and modernity. We
face what sociologists call a collision of consciousness. In this chapter,
we shall examine the solution. In the next, we shall consider how it is
perceived.

HALAKHIC INCLUSIVISM

In 1861, Rabbi Jacob Ettlinger, one of the foremost halakhic authorities
in Germany, was asked the following question. One who desecrates
the Sabbath in public is regarded as having placed himself outside the
community. According to some, he is regarded as a non-Jew and it is
forbidden to drink his wine. Does this apply to contemporary Jewish

transgressors? Ettlinger divides his answer into two sections, legal and factual. The law, he believes, is in accordance with those who rule strictly, that one may not drink the wine of one who publicly breaks the Sabbath. But the facts of contemporary Jewish life call for careful evaluation. "I find it difficult," he writes, "to know how to judge the Jewish sinners of our time. So far has the plague [of religious laxity] spread that the majority think it permissible to break the Sabbath. Perhaps, then, they are to be treated as one who believes, wrongly, that an act is permitted – who is regarded as almost, but not quite, a deliberate sinner. Some of them recite the Sabbath prayers and *kiddush* [sanctification said over wine], and then proceed to desecrate the Sabbath by doing work that is biblically and rabbinically forbidden."[1]

The reason why one who publicly desecrates the Sabbath is regarded as an apostate, continues Ettlinger, is that he denies creation and, by implication, the Creator. But in this case the individual has acknowledged God and creation in his prayers and *kiddush*. As for the children of such transgressors, they are to be regarded more leniently still, for they belong to the category of "merely following their fathers' customs" (*minhag avoteihem beyadeihem*) and "a child brought up by gentiles" (*tinok shenishbah*). Rabbi Ettlinger's conclusion is that it is halakhically defensible to drink the wine of a contemporary Sabbath-breaker, though "he who wishes to be strict will receive blessing."

The responsum touches on fundamentals. Judaism is the religion of a particular people. From this, two consequences follow. It is *inclusive* towards Jews, and *pluralist* towards other faiths. All Jews are embraced by the covenant of Sinai. But the covenant is not addressed to other nations, so that there is no equivalent in Judaism of the doctrine of *extra ecclesiam non salus*. One does not have to be a Jew to merit eternal life. These views would suggest a Judaism of extreme religious tolerance. But there are limits. Tradition maintains that there are Jews and non-Jews who have no share in the world to come. For Jews the most obvious exclusion is heresy, denial of one of the fundamentals of Jewish faith.[2] For non-Jews, it is denial of monotheism.

---

1. *Binyan Tzion*, NS 23.
2. Yad, *Teshuvah* 3:6–14.

Was it possible to be lenient, even so? It was. As far as non-Jews were concerned, the Talmud had recorded the dictum of Rabbi Jochanan that "the gentiles outside the land [of Israel] are not idolaters. They are merely following their fathers' customs [*minhag avoteihem beyadeihem*]."[3] This principle was used by Rabbenu Gershom,[4] along with other considerations, to defend the medieval Jewish practice of trading with gentiles on their festivals, something which the Mishnah had forbidden.[5] In relation to Jews, the Talmud had used the concept of "a child brought up by gentiles [*tinok shenishbah*]" to describe a situation in which a Jew might transgress Jewish law without being in a position to know that what he was doing was forbidden.[6] Maimonides had invoked the idea to rule that Karaites, other than those of the first generation, were not deliberate rebels against rabbinic Judaism. One should not shun them, but instead "draw them with words of peace" so that they repented and returned to the ways of Torah.[7]

The strategy in both cases is similar. It involves seeing the heresy concerned as inherited, not chosen. It represents habit, not conviction. It applies to belief systems the idea of duress (*ones*). One who acts under duress lacks the requisite intention. He is not the true author of his acts. So, too, there is a concept of cultural duress. One who is brought up in a tradition of erroneous beliefs is not the true author of those beliefs. In this case, heresy is due to outside influences and cultural conditioning, not to a personal act of rebellion against divine law. Rabbi Ettlinger applies both strategies to the Jewish transgressors of his day. They are acting out of habit and misguided parental influence. They are sinners, but not heretics. They remain within the halakhic community. One may therefore drink their wine. Following this precedent, Rabbi David Zvi Hoffmann ruled that one may count them in a quorum for prayer.[8] Rabbi Joseph Saul Nathansohn, author of the responsa *Shoel Umeshiv*,

---

3. Chullin 13b.
4. See Katz, *Exclusiveness and Tolerance*, 24–36.
5. Mish. Avodah Zarah 1:1.
6. See Shabbat 68b, Shevuot 5a.
7. Yad, *Mamrim* 3:3.
8. *Melamed Leho'il*, i. 29.

concurred.[9] Rabbi Chayyim Ozer Grodzinski included Ettlinger's reasoning in ruling that Sabbath-breakers might be counted in certain circumstances as valid witnesses.[10] Other authorities, among them Rabbi Abraham Karelitz[11] and Rabbi Kook,[12] ruled that the category of heretic was inapplicable today.

No more powerful inclusivist strategy could be conceived. These rulings provide a halakhic basis for seeing all Jews – Conservative, Reform, secular, and atheist – as still within *keneset Yisrael*, the covenantal community. It is a traditional solution to the problem of Jewish unity across even deep ideological divisions. But before we consider its implications, we must ask a more fundamental question.

There is a difference between halakhic possibility and halakhic actuality. There is a difference, in other words, between a legitimate halakhic opinion – based on the appropriate sources and inferences derivable from them – and ultimate halakhic ruling. Most arguments within the Talmud, for example, presuppose this distinction. Each side of the argument may be warranted, but only one becomes normative law. In the present instance, that inclusive rulings *could* emerge with regard to contemporary transgressors is a tribute to the scope of halakhic possibility. That they *did* emerge is evidence of something else, a series of evaluative judgements that have more to do with what we have called aggadah than halakhah. For it is clear that there was an alternative possibility. A person publicly desecrating the Sabbath had placed himself outside the community; so had a heretic. Against each of the inclusive rulings I have cited, an exclusive alternative was possible. Indeed the direct, uninterpreted application of text to circumstance would have favoured exclusivism. Reform, Conservative, and secular Judaisms were, in so far as they involved a denial of one or several principles of faith, halakhically to be regarded as heresies. Why then were individual adherents of these ideologies not regarded as heretics? Why was the line of inclusion not only available but actually chosen?

---

9. Cited ibid.
10. *Achi'ezer*, iii. 25.
11. *Chazon Ish* on *Yoreh De'ah* (Bnei Brak: Greineman, 1973), 2:16.
12. *Igerot Harayah*, i. 138.

INCLUSIVISM: THE RATIONALE OF COVENANT

Here we can only speculate. The halakhic literature, like other legal literature, generally hides its underlying evaluations. It is concerned to demonstrate that its conclusions follow from the antecedent sources, and that apparently conflicting texts neither contradict nor compromise the judgement reached. As Nachum Rabinovitch observes, "The purpose of a responsum is not primarily to explain why the law holds in a particular case. It is rather to prove that no matter how we look at a particular issue, the decision could not be otherwise.... Naturally when it comes to explaining the real motivations for the decision, the responsum may be downright misleading because the positive reasons for the law may not be adequately stressed."[13]

Let me say immediately what this does *not* imply. Reform thinkers have pointed to it as evidence of the "subjectivity" of halakhic decision making.[14] Conservative ideologists interpret it as evidence of halakhah's historicity.[15] A halakhic authority, they argue, is the product of his time, environment, and culture, and his rulings reflect the fact. Some Orthodox thinkers have been misrepresented as denying the phenomenon altogether, as if halakhic conclusions followed deductively from textual premises and there were no "hard cases" in Jewish law.[16]

All three interpretations, I believe, are wrong. There *are* hard cases in which the antecedent sources allow of more than one answer to a halakhic question. The question under review, the status of non-Orthodox Jews, is one. But in deciding which answer to adopt, the *posek,* the halakhic judge, relies neither on subjective considerations nor on values

---

13. Nachum Rabinovitch, "A Halakhic View of the Non-Jew," *L'Eylah,* 1:4 (1979), 18.

14. Eugene B. Borowitz, "Subjectivity and the Halakhic Process," *Judaism,* 13 (1964), 211–19.

15. See, e.g., Robert Gordis, "A Dynamic Halakhah: Principles and Procedures of Jewish Law," *Judaism,* 28 (1979), 263–82.

16. Some of J. David Bleich's presentations – e.g., his "Introduction: The Methodology of Halakhah," *Contemporary Halakhic Problems* (New York: Ktav, 1977), xiii–xviii, and "Halakhah as an Absolute," *Judaism,* 29 (1980), 30–37 – have been understood this way. See, e.g., David Singer, "Who Are Today's Modern Orthodox?," *Sh'ma,* 13:257 (Sept. 16, 1983), 112–15, and the ensuing debate.

drawn from contemporary non-Jewish culture. He relies, instead, on his understanding of the entire thrust of the antecedent tradition.

Ronald Dworkin, speaking of law generally, has made the point well:

> Any judge forced to decide a lawsuit will find, if he looks in the appropriate books, records of many arguably similar cases decided over decades or even centuries past by many other judges of different styles and judicial and political philosophies.... Each judge must regard himself, in deciding the new case before him, as a partner in a complex chain enterprise of which these innumerable decisions, structures, conventions, and practices are the history; it is his job to continue that history into the future through what he does today.... So he must determine, according to his own judgement, what the earlier decisions come to, what the point or theme of the practice so far, taken as a whole, really is.[17]

Applying this to the case in hand, what "point" or "theme" of Judaism, taken as a whole, sanctioned an inclusivist ruling in the case of modern non-Orthodox Jews?

The first, surely, is this. Halakhah is intrinsically inclusive because its object, *keneset Yisrael,* is a community of birth as well as faith. Michael Wyschogrod puts clearly a proposition that lies at the heart of classic Jewish self-definition. "The foundation of Judaism is the family identity of the Jewish people as the descendants of Abraham, Isaac and Jacob. Whatever else is added to this must be seen as growing out of and related to the basic identity of the Jewish people as the seed of Abraham elected by God through descent from Abraham. This is the crux of the mystery of God's election."[18] Wyschogrod draws this conclusion: "The house of Israel is therefore not a voluntary association defined by acceptance or rejection of a set of propositions."[19]

---

17. Dworkin, *A Matter of Principle,* 159.
18. Michael Wyschogrod, *The Body of Faith,* 57.
19. Ibid., 175.

This is a slight overstatement. It is possible, in traditional Jewish thought, to place oneself effectively outside the community by the rejection of a set of propositions, namely the principles of faith. But the fundamental point is valid. A Jew is born into obligations. There is no formal moment of acceptance of the commands. The born Jew is, as the Talmud put it, "already foresworn as from [the revelation at] Mount Sinai."[20] The presumption of Jewish law is therefore that the Jew remains within the halakhic community, without any need to demonstrate acceptance of its laws or creed. This remains so even if the individual systematically transgresses Jewish law.

Maimonides accordingly wrote that when a person belongs to *klal Yisrael*, the faith-community of Israel, "it is incumbent upon us to love him, to care for him, and to do all for him that God commanded us to do for one another in the way of affection and brotherly sympathy." He continued: "And this is so even if he were to be guilty of every transgression possible, by reason of power of desire or the mastery of base natural passions. He will receive punishment according to the measure of his perversity, but he will have a portion in the world to come, even though he be one of the transgressors in Israel."[21]

The principle was put to the test in an acute form in the Middle Ages. At various times and places, great pressures were put on Jews to convert to Christianity or Islam. Economic and political sanctions were used, including, on occasion, the threat of death if Jews did not comply. Some did. Many of those who did remained practising Jews in secret, *conversos* or *marranos* as they were called. The question arose whether they were still halakhically to be considered Jews. Did the Jewish acts they performed covertly still count as *mitzvot*, the religious deeds of members of the covenantal community? Were they to be admitted to or excluded from the synagogue?

The question came to Maimonides in the wake of the invasion of Spain by the Almohades, an aggressive Muslim sect that sought forced conversions to Islam. Maimonides' family had left Spain for this reason. Of those who remained, some chose to die. Others converted. A rabbi

---

20. Yoma 73b, Nedarim 8a, Shevuot 21b.
21. Maimonides, *Commentary on the Mishnah*, Sanh., ch. 10, Intro.

had ruled that the *conversos* were henceforth to be regarded as gentiles. Any Jewish religious act they now did would be not a *mitzvah* but an additional transgression. Maimonides, shocked by this ruling, wrote his *Epistle on Martyrdom* in reply. It remains one of the classic texts of halakhic inclusivism.[22]

Maimonides quotes a long series of texts and rabbinic interpretations to show that at various times in biblical history the people of Israel had been collectively guilty of cardinal sins, especially idolatry. Yet in each case, when the prophets complained of Israel's corruption they were rebuked by God. "If this is the sort of punishment meted out to the pillars of the universe – Moses, Elijah, Isaiah and the ministering angels – because they briefly criticized the Jewish congregation, can one have an idea of the fate of the least among the worthless who let his tongue loose against Jewish communities of sages and their disciples, priests and Levites, and called them sinners, evil-doers, gentiles, disqualified to testify, heretics who deny the Lord God of Israel?"

He goes further. Idolatry is less grave than heresy, and conversion undergone through duress is less grave still. None the less, even in the case of undoubted heretics – Maimonides cites Ahab, Eglon king of Moab, Nebuchadnezzar, and the biblical Esau as seen through rabbinic tradition – they were rewarded for the good deeds they did. "The Holy One, blessed be he, does not withhold the reward of any creature," says Maimonides, quoting an aggadic axiom.[23] "If these well-known heretics were generously rewarded for the little good that they did, is it conceivable that God will not reward the Jews, who despite the exigencies of forced conversion, perform commandments secretly?"

Maimonides concludes that Jews should leave and travel to a place where they will be free of persecution. Those who remain are sinful. Duress is a defence; but to choose to live under it rather than leave is culpable. None the less, whoever ignores his advice and decides to stay "must bear in mind that if he fulfils a precept, God will reward him doubly, because he acted for God only and not to show off or be accepted as an observant

---

22. The text is available in English translation in Halkin (trans.), *Crisis and Leadership*, 13–90.
23. Pesachim 118a, Nazir 23b, Bava Kama 38b, Horayot 10b.

individual." As for the community's relation to the *conversos,* he rules: "It is not right to alienate, scorn, and hate people who desecrate the Sabbath. It is our duty to befriend them and encourage them to fulfil the commandments. The rabbis regulate explicitly that when an evil-doer who sinned by choice comes to the synagogue, he is to be welcomed, not insulted."

The essay strikes a masterly balance between criticism and encouragement. Throughout we are reminded of Rabbi Meir's reply to Rabbi Judah on the meaning of the biblical phrase "You are sons of the Lord your God."[24] Rabbi Judah had argued that "when you behave as sons, you are called sons; when you do not, you are not called sons." Rabbi Meir insisted: "In either event, you are called sons."[25] The covenantal relationship was biological and unbreakable. Jews remained the children of God whether or not they acted accordingly.

Some such perception undoubtedly informs the rulings of Rabbi Ettlinger and others. The weight of Jewish values lay on the side of inclusion. If by a formal halakhic device the person publicly desecrating the Sabbath could be kept within the community, then it should be invoked. But this rationale, though powerful, is not enough. An analogy could not be drawn between idolatry and heresy. Idolatry was a sin. Heresy was a rebellion. One could worship idols and still be counted within the covenantal family. But heresy, wrote Maimonides, was an act of self-exclusion from the family.[26] In his code he had written that "the Torah is very solicitous for the lives of Israelites, whether they are righteous or wicked, *since* all Israelites acknowledge God and believe in the essentials of our religion."[27] The "since" was crucial. How then could one go further and include secular or liberal Jews, who did not accept "the essentials of our religion," within the scope of Jewish peoplehood, halakhically conceived?

THE COGNITIVE IMPACT OF SOCIAL CHANGE

It was here that the deeply negative view of contemporary culture taken by a number of Orthodox authorities had positive halakhic consequences.

---

24. Deut. 14:1.
25. Kiddushin 36a.
26. Maimonides, *Commentary on the Mishnah,* Sanh., ch. 10, Intro.
27. Yad, *Rotze'ach* 13:14.

Rabbi Moses Sofer and Rabbi Kook were, in their different ways, convinced that a diaspora synthesis of Judaism and secular culture – the model proposed by Samson Raphael Hirsch – was unworkable. The former advocated Orthodox seclusion; the latter, a total Jewish culture in Eretz Israel. But both agreed that emancipation threatened diaspora Jewish continuity at its foundations. Jews would be exposed to social and intellectual pressures that would prove irresistible. It was just this negation that was to prove the basis of a remarkable re-evaluation of the phenomenon of heresy.

The Talmud, as we have seen, had used the idea of cultural duress. It had spoken of a *tinok shenishbah*, a child brought up among gentiles and who could not therefore have been expected to know the law. But the concept meant what it said. It spoke of an exceptional occurrence: a child raised outside the Jewish community, lacking all knowledge of Judaism. Rabbi Moses Isserles had defined a *tinok shenishbah* as *eino yode'a mitorat Yisrael kelal,* one who "knows nothing at all of Jewish law."[28] The generalization of the concept to a broad spectrum of Jews who knew what Jewish law was and had chosen not to follow it was a radical halakhic stroke. The reasoning of Rabbi Kook and Rabbi Karelitz – an authority broadly within the school of Rabbi Moses Sofer – is illuminating in this context. Kook uses a closely related idea, that of passion considered as duress. The Tosafists[29] had employed this idea specifically in the case of sexual passion. To apply it to a cultural context is a daring generalization. But this is what Kook does. "The same [reasoning adopted by the Tosafists] applies to the "bad maid," the mood of the times, who has been permitted by the will of Heaven to exercise sway prior to being totally vanquished, and who has seduced many of our young children with all her many charms to whore after her. They were fully under duress, and God forbid that we judge them as acting voluntarily."[30] Kook does not predicate his defence of a rebellious generation on a lack of knowledge of Judaism. He bases it instead on the powerful counter-attractions of the secular culture to which they have been exposed.

---

28. *Rema* on *Yoreh De'ah* 159:6.
29. *Tosafot* on Sanhedrin 26b, s.v. *hechashud*; Gittin 41b, s.v. *kofin*.
30. *Igerot Harayah*, i. 138.

Rabbi Karelitz uses two arguments, one social, the other spiritual, to render the concept of heresy inapplicable in the modern age. The first is this. Jewish law permits one to hate the wrongdoer.[31] But this is so only after he has rejected rebuke.[32] Rebuke is impossible nowadays.[33] Therefore, one must love the wrongdoer.[34] This is essentially a sociological argument, based on the demise of traditional structures of religious authority. Though it rests wholly on talmudic and medieval sources, the inference it draws is characteristically modern. Indeed, on the basis of the same sources, a medieval authority had come to precisely the opposite conclusion: in the face of widespread transgression one should redouble one's efforts to rebuke, even beyond the limits laid down in the Talmud.[35] Rabbi Karelitz is writing in an age in which coercion and persuasion lack power. The concept of rebellion is intimately related to that of authority. When authority wanes, there ceases to be rebellion as traditionally understood.

The second argument is the most radical recorded in the literature. The severe punishment meted out to the heretic belonged, he argues, to a world in which divine providence was evident to all. Not only was heresy under such circumstances an unpardonable rebellion, but its

---

31. Pesachim 113b.
32. See Yad, *Rotze'ach* 13:14; *Hagahot Maimoniyot* on Yad, *De'ot* 6:3; *Sefer Hachinukh* (Venice, 1523), 245.
33. See Arakhin 16b.
34. *Chazon Ish* on *Yoreh De'ah* 2:28. The reasoning is cited here and elsewhere in the name of the Maharam of Lublin, citing his responsum 13. That ruling, however, though it deals with the subject of rebuke, does not make the point advanced by the Chazon Ish. It can, however, be inferred from the sources cited above.
35. Ritva, cited in *Shitah Mekubetzet* on Beitzah 30a. The Talmud there had formulated the principle "Let Israel go their way. Better that they sin unwittingly than that they sin deliberately." This placed a limit on rebuke. Under certain circumstances, where one's words would not be heeded, it was better to be silent than to speak. The medieval authorities debated the precise location of this limit. Ritva, however, in the name of "a distinguished Ashkenazi rabbi," cites the view that "this principle was intended only for those times. In the present generation, however, when people are lax about many matters, one should rather make a 'fence around the Torah.' Even when the transgression is only of rabbinic law, we should protest and impose penalties so that people sin neither unwittingly nor deliberately." Ritva adds that this seems to him to be correct.

punishment was perceived by the community as contributing to its own welfare. People knew that a community which left heretics unpunished would itself be punished by sword and pestilence. Nowadays, however, the ways of providence are hidden. Far from contributing to social order, the punishment of heretics would seem, to the majority of Jews, to be an unwarranted act of destructive authoritarianism. Instead of mending the breach of observance, it would widen it. Therefore we must try instead to draw back unbelievers not through punitive sanction but through "the bonds of love."[36]

These lines of argument are unprecedented prior to modernity. To be sure, some traces of them can be found in the talmudic literature. Rav Ashi, about to expound on King Manasseh's exclusion from the world to come, is visited by a dream in which the king assures him, "Had you been there, you would have caught up your cloak and run after me."[37] Biblical and rabbinic legislation is shot through with the perception that Jewish conduct is influenced by social contact. One of its central motifs is the need to maintain a distance between the Jew and non-Jewish cultures. But it was just this "fence" around Jewish identity that emancipation threatened to remove, and the halakhic authorities had renounced or been deprived of the power to enforce it. Precisely the awareness that halakhic observance had, in modernity, become voluntary led to a corresponding realization that *lack* of observance had in a certain sense become *in*voluntary.

The rulings of Rabbis Ettlinger, Kook, and Karelitz reveal a finely honed insight into what in a secular context would be called the sociology of knowledge. The religious beliefs of Orthodoxy were no longer objectified in the structures of Jewish social reality. In the traditional situation, "the world as defined by the religious institution in question was *the* world, maintained not just by the mundane powers of the society and the instruments of social control, but much more fundamentally maintained by the 'common sense' of the members of that society."[38]

---

36. *Chazon Ish* on *Yoreh De'ah* 2:16.
37. Sanhedrin 102b.
38. Berger, *The Sacred Canopy*, 134. See also Peter L. Berger and Thomas Luckmann, *The Social Construction of Reality* (London: Pelican, 1987).

Heresy in such an environment is necessarily deviant, a rebellion against a self-evident world order. But emancipation had broken the congruence between Jewish belief and external reality. Tradition lost "the quality of self-evident intersubjective plausibility."[39] As Ettlinger and Hoffmann put it: how could Sabbath-breaking be evidence of a denial of faith when most Jews regarded it as permitted? As Kook and Karelitz argued, in the contemporary cultural context heresy itself could no longer be regarded as culpable, even if it remained heresy. The leniency of these rulings is directly related to the seriousness with which Orthodoxy took the assault of modernity. Those like Samson Raphael Hirsch who were more inclined to take modernity in their stride were, as we shall see in the next chapter, dramatically less sympathetic to doctrinal deviance.

INCLUSIVITY AND THE DESIRE TO BE INCLUDED

So behind halakhic inclusivism lay covenantal consciousness on the one hand, sociological insight on the other. But these two factors might not have been enough without the presence of a third, perhaps the hardest to define halakhically. It was noted in an earlier chapter that Maimonides, in discussing the law that a court may coerce a husband to grant a divorce, had used a significant phrase: "since he wishes to be a Jew [*rotzeh liheyot miYisrael*] and wishes to fulfil all the commandments."[40] The disjunction of these two clauses was inconceivable prior to modernity. To wish to be a Jew *was* to wish to fulfil the commands. To cast off the yoke of the commands was to wish to leave the Jewish community. The liberal and secular Jew thus raised a question never before confronted in quite this form. Did the wish to remain a Jew, severed from the desire to keep the traditional commands, carry halakhic significance?

The authorities so far cited do not refer directly to the issue, though Rabbi Ettlinger was struck by the existential contradiction of the Sabbath-breaker who before setting out to work on the day of rest sanctified it in his prayers. He wished to remain within the community of the Sabbath without obeying its laws. It is not surprising that Rabbi Ettlinger confesses that it is "difficult to know how to judge" such

---

39. Berger, *The Sacred Canopy*, 151.
40. Yad, *Gerushin* 2:20.

conduct. But there are suggestions here and there in the literature that lead us to conjecture that the wish to remain a Jew was a fact possessing independent religious dignity. Once again, it is Maimonides who points the way.

The Talmudic literature had distinguished between "an apostate with respect to one law" and an "apostate with respect to the whole Torah."[41] Maimonides' treatment of the two concepts is theologically masterful. In Jewish law, both had forfeited their share in the world to come. What then was the need for the idea of an "apostate with respect to the whole Torah" if apostasy in respect of a single one of its laws had the same effect? Maimonides' answer is that they represent two different kinds of rebellion. The apostate with respect to one law – sinning not out of weakness but out of defiance – acts as if part of the Torah has ceased to apply to him. He offends against the ninth principle of faith, that the Torah is eternal. The apostate with respect to the whole Torah, by contrast, may perhaps not commit a single transgression. Instead he is one who "at a time of persecution converts to another religion, allying his fate with theirs, saying, 'What advantage is it to me to remain part of the people of Israel, seeing that they are humiliated and persecuted? It is better for me to join my destiny to those who have power.'" He offends against the eleventh principle of faith, belief in reward and punishment and the ultimate justice of humanity under providence.[42]

Maimonides, in other words, regards desertion of the Jewish people as a religious offence independently of any transgression committed in the process. This is more strikingly evident in his interpretation of another passage. The Talmud speaks of "sectarians, informers, scoffers, those who reject the Torah and deny the resurrection of the dead, and those who separate themselves from the community [*shepirshu midarkhei hatzibur*].[43] Rashi is puzzled by the last phrase, for he understands it as a generic description of the preceding cases. To separate oneself from the community is, for Rashi, to be guilty either of a cardinal transgression or

---

41. Chullin 5a.

42. Yad, *Teshuvah* 3:9. See the excellent commentary of Nachum Rabinovitch, *Yad Peshutah*, ad loc. (Jerusalem: Feldheim, 1977), 55–60.

43. Rosh Hashanah 17a.

of heresy. Maimonides, however, regards it as a quite distinct offence. It refers to one who "even if he does not commit any transgression, none the less separates himself from the congregation of Israel, does not fulfil commands together with them, is indifferent to their distress, does not share in their fasts, and goes his own way as if he were a member of another nation, not theirs."[44]

These negative rulings imply a positive corollary. If leaving the Jewish people, regardless of transgression, is itself a fundamental sin, a determination *not* to leave the Jewish people must in itself be a fundamental virtue. This proposition was never explicitly formulated in the classic literature, but how, prior to modernity, could the question have arisen? To be a Jew was the paradigm of an involuntary state of being. One was born a Jew. One was defined as a Jew by the internal and external reality-- definitions of Jewish minority existence in a Christian or Islamic culture. There was what sociologists call "a total identification of the individual with his socially assigned typifications."[45] Being a Jew was an identity, not a role. It was given, not chosen. Virtue presupposes choice. Since Jewish affiliation was not chosen, it was not a virtue but a state.

But Jewish law recognized one instance of choosing to be a Jew, namely, the case of the convert. It is here that identification with the Jewish people emerges as a significant motif in its own right. In a remarkable passage, the Talmud describes the procedure by which the court interviewed a prospective convert. "If at the present time a person wishes to become a proselyte, he is to be asked, "What reason do you have for wishing to become a proselyte? Do you not know that Israel at the present is persecuted and oppressed, despised, harassed, and overcome by afflictions?" If he replies, "I know, and I am unworthy," he is accepted immediately."[46] Conversion, to be sure, also involved acceptance of the commands. But the passage bespeaks a deep awareness that becoming a Jew is, not least, an act of identification with a people and its destiny,[47] and that – given the tragic nature of its history "at the present time" – such

---

44. Yad, *Teshuvah* 3:11.

45. Berger and Luckmann, *The Social Construction of Reality*, 108.

46. Yevamot 47a.

47. On this see Soloveitchik, *Divrei Hagut Veha'arakhah*, 43–48.

an act is a moving gesture of faith. In this the rabbis were doing no more than mirroring the biblical archetype of the convert, Ruth, whose words of affiliation were both national and religious: "Your people shall be my people, and your God my God."[48]

Which brings us to the crucial transformation of Jewish identity under emancipation. To be a Jew, for one born a Jew, is not a matter of *halakhic* choice. But there are situations of cultural crisis when it becomes an *existential* choice. Jews throughout Europe were invited to submerge their identities in a neutral, enveloping secular citizenship. Overwhelmingly they resisted the terms of that transaction. There were periods, it is true, when significant numbers of Jews converted to Christianity, especially in the last decades of the eighteenth century and the first of the nineteenth, especially, too, among the upper strata of wealth and culture. In 1799 a leading Berlin Jewish intellectual, David Friedlander, put forward a general proposal. Jews should join the Protestant church. They would be baptized. But they would not confess Christian dogma in its entirety. They would subscribe only to the religion of nature.[49] That this proposal gained little assent, that the early wave of conversions subsided, and that Jews, liberal or secular, remained Jews and sought ways of expressing their Jewishness, are facts of monumental significance.

For the most part, Jews did *not* say, "What advantage is it to me to remain part of the people of Israel, seeing that they are humiliated and persecuted? It is better for me to join my destiny to those who have power." They declared their willingness *liheyot miYisrael*, to be counted among Israel. The Reform movement, despite its legitimation of assimilatory modes of conduct, was at the same time, in the minds of many of its theorists, a consciously counter-assimilatory force.[50] Secular Zionism, with some exceptions, was even more avowedly particularist: from Moses Hess onwards it displayed a ferocious national pride. Such were the complex interplays of emancipation and antisemitism in the nineteenth century that even assimilatory gestures had dissimilatory

---

48. Ruth 1:16.
49. See Katz, *Out of the Ghetto*, esp. 115–23.
50. See id., *Jewish Emancipation and Self-Emancipation*, 3–74.

consequences. The "Science of Judaism" movement, whose purpose, according to Moritz Steinschneider, was "to give the remains of Judaism a decent burial,"[51] produced among other things a rise in Jewish historical consciousness which lent impetus to Zionism. The children and grandchildren of assimilated European Jews – among them Martin Buber, Franz Rosenzweig, Gershom Scholem, and Jiri Langer – discovered, in their encounter with the Jews of Eastern Europe, an integrity and vitality that produced further variants of the dialectic between acculturation and Jewish affirmation.[52]

These were not facts that could be regarded as evaluatively neutral, as if once religious faith and halakhic authority were abandoned it was a matter of indifference whether Jews converted, assimilated, or found alternative modes of Jewish identity. But here was a dilemma for which rabbinic thought provided no clear precedent. On the one hand, liberal Judaisms and secular Zionism were Jewish affirmations in an age of real and seductive alternatives. On the other, they were revolutionary deviations from the only terms in which tradition had defined the Jewish vocation and destiny. The former fact called for positive recognition. The latter called for negation. How to give religious expression to the value of Jewish identification *per se* without at the same time legitimating a secularization of Jewish identity is the problem that exercised many of the leading Orthodox thinkers of the twentieth century.

I surveyed several of these approaches in the chapter on Orthodoxy and Jewish peoplehood. Rabbi Reines solved the problem by distinguishing acts between man and God from those between man and man. The former required religious motivation; the latter did not. Secular Jews, working as they did for the amelioration of the Jewish condition, were thus fulfilling a religious command regardless of their intent. Rabbi Hirschensohn accorded an independent significance to Jewish peoplehood even as secularly conceived. Rabbi Soloveitchik, through his concept of the two covenants, those of the Exodus and Sinai, history

51. Gershom Scholem, *The Messianic Idea in Judaism* (New York: Schocken, 1972), 307.
52. See, e.g., Shulamit Volkov, "The Dynamics of Dissimilation: *Ostjuden* and German Jews," in Reinharz and Schatzberg (eds.), *The Jewish Response to German Culture*, 195–211.

and destiny, was able to locate feelings of Jewish solidarity and collective responsibility on the map of biblical and rabbinic values.

Perhaps Rabbi Kook went furthest in his distinction between the two components of Jewish consciousness, *nefesh* and *ruach,* "soul" and "spirit" respectively. "The *nefesh* of those Jewish transgressors who, in this pre-messianic era, join themselves lovingly to matters of collective Jewish concern – Eretz Israel and national rebirth – is more developed than the *nefesh* of the wholly pious ones of Israel who do not have the same inner feeling for the collective good and the rebuilding of the people and the land. Those who fear God and keep his commands have, though, a more developed *ruach*."[53] Here was inclusivism transfigured into mysticism. But the thrust is unmistakable. There is a sense in which those who identify with Israel's collective identity, even if they do so on secular premises, have a religious virtue that many of the religious do not possess. Kook, of course, believed that the paradox would be resolved in a messianic synthesis. The dynamic of Israel's national renaissance would lead to a new symbiosis. The secularists would give of their *nefesh* to the religious, who in turn would endow the secular with *ruach,* spirituality.

Each of these philosophies is an attempt to accord religious significance to the phrase *rotzeh liheyot miYisrael,* to the mere wish to be a Jew, even when severed from its nexus in the life of the commands. For in modernity the wish was not "mere." It represented a choice in the felt presence of alternatives. The dialectical tensions in these Orthodox readings of peoplehood are acute and inescapable. To affirm the covenant of Exodus without that of Sinai, or *nefesh* without *ruach,* or commands between man and man without those between man and God, was impossible. But to affirm that, in each case, the former was nothing without the latter was also impossible.

The inclusivist strategy resolves the tension by valuing the desire to participate in the Jewish destiny while devaluing liberal and secular interpretations of that destiny. This is the essence of Rabbi Ettlinger's responsum on the Sabbath-breaker, as it was of all subsequent inclusivist rulings. The contemporary Sabbath-breaker presented the halakhic system with an apparent contradiction: he wished to be part of

---

53. Abraham Isaac Kook, *Arpelei Tohar* (Jerusalem: Mosad Harav Kook, 1983), 11.

the Sabbath community without obeying its laws. An exclusivist ruling would take the second fact as definitive. Since he rejects the law, he in turn is rejected by the law. An inclusivist ruling takes the first fact as decisive. Since he wishes to be included, he is still part of the community. The fact that he rejects halakhah is to be explained away as a culturally conditioned error. And what applied to the Sabbath specifically applied to the covenantal community generally. Those who manifested a wish to be included within Israel, by their affirmation of Jewish identity, were to be included. But the construction they placed on that inclusion – liberal, secular, ethnic, nationalist, or cultural – was not to be legitimated. It too was an excusable error, but an error none the less.

INCLUSIVISM AND POST-HOLOCAUST THEOLOGIES

Inclusivism, then, uses classic halakhic strategies – variants on the themes of *minhag avoteihem beyadeihem* (habit, not belief) and *tinok shenishbah* (excusable ignorance) – to include within the covenantal community those whose beliefs and practices would, if taken at their face value, place them outside. It is an extraordinarily powerful device, capable of neutralizing the schismatic impact of almost any Jewish ideology at odds with tradition. Its method, considered as a formal halakhic device, is to isolate the liberal or secular Jew from his beliefs. The beliefs remain heretical but those who believe them are not heretics, for they do not ultimately or culpably believe them. Liberal and secular Jews remain Jews, even though neither liberal nor secular Judaism is Judaism.

Deviant belief is to be attributed to the impact of a secularizing culture, the collapse of religious authority, and the absence of compelling religious role models, rather than to willed and conscious rebellion. Needless to say, the halakhic authorities so far considered did not *endorse* any departure from tradition. What they did was to search for ways to *excuse* it.

I have argued, though, that the *availability* of formal halakhic devices in no way explains their actual *application*. Exclusive rulings were at least as readily available as inclusive ones. Behind the decision to include rather than exclude, I have suggested, lay three perceptions: one of principle, two of empirical assessment. The principle was that Judaism classically favours inclusion rather than exclusion since *keneset Yisrael* is a community of birth as well as faith. The born Jew remains a Jew and the onus of halakhic argument is to try to continue to see him as such.

The two empirical assessments amounted to a shrewd evaluation of the impact of modernity on Jewish identity. On the one hand, so overwhelming were the combined intellectual, social, cultural, and political assaults on tradition that individual abandonments of Orthodoxy could no longer be judged by normal halakhic criteria. Halakhah generally focuses on the individual and his intentions, but here was a phenomenon that could only be understood against a vast historical backdrop. On the other hand – once the initial shock of Reform had subsided – it began to be seen that deviant modes of Jewish identity were none the less defiant modes of Jewish affirmation. They were a refusal to accept conversion or total assimilation. Not only *could* heresy be excused; there were grounds for thinking that it *ought* to be excused.

Here, then, was tradition contemplating the phenomenon of its collapse among large sections of the Jewish population that had undergone the experience of modernity. The response was complex: necessarily so, given the deep conflict between the desire to maintain Jewish unity and the equally passionate desire to maintain Jewish belief and practice uncompromised. So inclusivity went hand in hand with a fierce Orthodox battle against all dissenting ideologies and an increasing tendency to follow the German-Hungarian model of secession from organizations that included the non-Orthodox. Preserving Jewish unity and Orthodox integrity seemed existentially incompatible. The triumph of inclusivism was to show that theoretically at least they were compatible.

Inclusivism, though, is a classic strategy of tradition. It embodies an Orthodox view of Jewish unity. In contrast to it we must set a contemporary version of unity which likewise attaches religious value to the desire of Jews to remain Jewish, but which does so from the non-traditional perspective of *pluralism*. This has been a leading theme of post-Holocaust Jewish theology. In what way does it differ from inclusivism? Early on in the argument we considered the position of Irving Greenberg, itself a variant on the work of the most influential theologian of the Holocaust, Emil Fackenheim. To these two thinkers we must now briefly turn.

Fackenheim is most famous for his statement that after Auschwitz, "the authentic Jew of today is forbidden to hand Hitler yet another, posthumous victory" by failing to survive as a Jew. Reminding us that according to tradition Torah issued the Jew with 613 commandments, Fackenheim calls this a new, 614th command. It is this that unites the secularist and the religious Jew. Not only does each hear the imperative of Jewish survival, but each hears it in a strikingly similar way. Hitherto the believer was conscious of both *mitzvah* and *metzaveh,* the command and the commander, while the secularist rejected both. Now, however, even the secularist hears a "command" while even the believer finds it impossible to hear the "commander." The Holocaust resists religious interpretation, and yet from it emerges a kind of fragmentary revelation that the Jewish people must survive, for not to do so would be, as it were, passively to accede to the Final Solution. "It may well be the case," argues Fackenheim, "that the authentic Jewish agnostic and the authentic Jewish believer are closer today than at any previous time."[54]

Fackenheim's understanding of contemporary Jewish unity is based on three premises. The first is that "a Jew today is one who, except for an historical accident – Hitler's loss of the war – would have either been murdered or never been born."[55] All Jews today share the same defining knowledge of post-Holocaust existence, that of being "an accidental remnant." Second, religious faith is no longer possible as it was before the Holocaust. Faith in the covenant presupposes "an unbroken historical continuity from past to present." That continuity has been decisively "ruptured" by the Holocaust in which the covenantal people came face to face with the possibility that it might cease to be.[56] Third, the secular Jewish response to the Holocaust, especially as evident in the State of Israel, is a defiant commitment to Jewish survival that can only adequately be described as religious: "For this commitment is *ipso facto* testimony that there can be, must be, shall be, no second Auschwitz anywhere; on this testimony and this faith the secular Jew no less than

---

54. Emil Fackenheim, *The Jewish Return into History: Reflections in the Age of Auschwitz and a New Jerusalem* (New York: Schocken, 1978), 19–24.

55. Id., *To Mend the World,* 295.

56. Ibid., 260.

the religious stakes his own life, the lives of his children, and the lives of his children's children. A secular holiness, side by side with the religious, is becoming manifest in contemporary Jewish existence."[57]

The old dichotomies between secular and religious are therefore inapplicable. Religious Jews, their faith "ruptured," have to that extent become secular. Secular Jews, forced into acknowledging their "singled-out" condition, have to that extent become religious. It is this shared domain of what Fackenheim calls "secular holiness," and what Greenberg calls "holy secularity," that constitutes the substantive common ground of contemporary Jewish life.

Irving Greenberg, we recall, builds on these premises to argue that, after Auschwitz, the covenant itself has become "voluntary." The covenant called Jews to be witnesses to the divine presence in history. The Holocaust made Jews witnesses to a divine absence in history. "What then happened to the covenant? I submit that its authority was broken but the Jewish people, released from its obligations, chose voluntarily to take it on again."[58]

Greenberg, like Fackenheim, takes as his affirmative starting-point the fact that Jews have decided to continue to be Jews. But they do so on radically new terms. "As long as the covenant was involuntary, it could be imposed from above in a unitary way.... In the new era, the voluntary covenant is the theological base of a genuine pluralism.... [This] is a recognition that all Jews have chosen to make the fundamental Jewish statement at great personal risk and cost."[59] Orthodoxy can no longer refuse to recognize other interpretations of Judaism, for religious authority has been shattered by the Holocaust. Instead, all forms of Judaism must be seen as legitimate variants on the attempt to live by the covenant.

How much of this analysis is or could be shared by Orthodoxy? In one respect, a great deal. As we have seen, *before* the Holocaust halakhic authorities had already come to similar conclusions. Emancipation and secularization had made Jewish commitment existentially, if not halakhically, voluntary. The authority of faith and halakhah remained,

---

57. Id., *The Jewish Return into History*, 54.
58. Irving Greenberg, *Voluntary Covenant*, 17.
59. Ibid., 22.

but its *Sitz im Leben*, its traditional social setting, had been transformed and, for many, destroyed. Against this backcloth, the affirmation of *any* Jewish identity was to be taken as ground for inclusion within the covenantal community. The secular Jew's rejection of Judaism was not to be taken at its face value. He had chosen to make "the fundamental Jewish statement" of remaining a Jew, and in so doing had made a religiously significant commitment. Orthodoxy confronted the covenantal crisis prior to the Holocaust, and in this respect Fackenheim and Greenberg's argument for the sanctity of even secular Jewish survival had already been anticipated by Rabbis Ettlinger and Kook.

What Orthodoxy cannot share is the argument that the Holocaust has decisively changed the terms of Jewish existence. Neither theologically nor empirically is this so. Empirically it is refuted by the fact that the same patterns of assimilation and counter-assimilation evident before the Holocaust are evident today. As Arthur Hertzberg has pointed out, "a generational clock has ticked over and over again in the open society. Whether in New York and Philadelphia in 1840, in Paris and Bordeaux in the 1850s, in Budapest around the turn of the century, in Berlin and Vienna in the 1920s, and now in the United States in the 1970s, it tells the same frightening time."[60]

The Holocaust has not changed the trends of diaspora Jewish life, its rates of affiliation or attrition. Nor has it changed its institutions and ideologies. As Jacob Neusner has noted: "The twentieth century has produced no important and influential Judaic systems. The Judaisms that flourish today...all took shape in the nineteenth century."[61] It has been implicit in my argument throughout that the fragmentation of Jewry is best understood in terms of social processes, not historical events, even those as decisive as the Holocaust and the rebirth of Israel. It is a phenomenon of the nineteenth century no less than the twentieth. This is not to deny the significance of Holocaust theology, but to insist that its intellectual force is symbolic rather than explanatory.

---

60. Arthur Hertzberg, "The Emancipation: A Reassessment after Two Centuries," *Modern Judaism*, 1:1 (1981), 48.
61. Jacob Neusner, *Understanding Seeking Faith*, 101.

In particular, one phenomenon in contemporary Jewish life is unintelligible on Greenberg and Fackenheim's theology. For it is just those Jews who maintained that the covenant is neither "ruptured" nor "broken" who have most flourished in the post-Holocaust world. Institutionally and demographically, the strongest and most rapidly growing group in the contemporary Jewish world is Orthodox Jewry itself. It is they who overwhelmingly fulfilled Fackenheim and Greenberg's criterion of commitment to Jewish survival, by having Jewish children and demonstrating the faith to bring new generations of Jews into a hostile world. This suggests an opposite conclusion to that drawn by the theologians. For the Holocaust – more seriously than its threat to faith in the covenant – shattered faith in the benign, humanist, and universalist assumptions of the Enlightenment.

It is not that "the commanding voice of Auschwitz" issued a 614th imperative that the Jewish people should survive. That command had always been implicit in the other 613, and had been seen as such even by anti-religious thinkers from Spinoza to Jacob Klatzkin. What had happened, rather, is that during the nineteenth century the universalist thrust of the Enlightenment made an unprecedented assault on the particularism of Jewish survival. It was naive faith in the Enlightenment that was called into question at Auschwitz. In the ensuing search for meaning, the commanding voice of Sinai could once again be heard.

Theologically, too, the argument does injustice to tradition. This is not to deny that the Holocaust represents an extraordinary crisis of faith. Historically it may be, as Fackenheim has argued, "unique." Theologically, though, it is not unique. At rare but identifiable moments, a terrible question comes to the forefront of Jewish consciousness. Why continue to be Jewish? Why be bound by a covenant sealed long ago in an ancient wilderness between a redeemed people and its redeeming God? Can the obligations of covenant persist when its terms appear to be refuted by history? Does it survive the exile and persecution of the covenantal people?

The question was asked by the prophet Ezekiel confronting Babylonian exile.[62] It was asked again by the sages in the wake of Roman

---

62. Ezek. 20:32–35.

destruction and oppression.[63] It was asked again by Judah Halevi and Nachmanides at the beginning of the medieval religious persecutions.[64] It was asked, most searchingly, by Isaac Arama and Don Isaac Abarbanel in the midst of the fifteenth-century Spanish oppression and widespread Jewish conversions to Christianity.[65] There was a time when the Talmud itself came to the conclusion that "by rights we should issue a decree that we should not marry and have children, and let the children of Abraham come to an end."[66]

On each occasion, however, the terms of the covenant were reaffirmed by those who survived and remained Jews. For it bound not only those who "stand here with us today" but also those who are "not here with us today."[67] The covenant was *involuntary* – such is the thrust of the response from Ezekiel to Abarbanel – and spans all generations. There is, in Isaiah's phrase, no "bill of divorce."[68] There will be moments when a rational theologian will conclude, as Greenberg puts it, that "we are entering a period of silence in theology";[69] the Torah itself puts it more strongly: "Many disasters and distresses will come upon them and they will then ask, 'Have not these disasters come upon us because our God is not among us?' And I will surely hide my face on that day."[70] But this (such is the prophecy) will lead not to a desertion but to a renewal of the covenant.

Post-Holocaust Jewish existence – the "new Jewish stand" of Israel's rebirth and the diaspora's persisting ethnicity – can be interpreted as a miraculous confirmation of covenantal history no less than as a radical discontinuity with the past. Tradition, therefore, is strengthened in its inclusivism. Those who choose to make a Jewish affirmation in the late twentieth century, in whatever form, make a covenantal gesture of heroic proportions. Above all, the Holocaust makes *exclusivism* morally

---

63. Sanhedrin 105a – a midrashic amplification of the passage from Ezekiel above.
64. See, e.g., Judah Halevi, *Kuzari*, 4:20–3; Nachmanides on Gen. 32:26, Lev. 18:25.
65. Akedat Yitzchak, and Isaac Abarbanel on Deut. 29:12–14 in *Mirkevet Hamishneh*.
66. Bava Batra 60b.
67. Deut. 29:13–14.
68. Isa. 50:1.
69. Greenberg, *The Third Great Cycle*, 16.
70. Deut. 31:17–18.

invidious. Attempted genocide binds Jews, a generation later, in an indissoluble covenant of fate. Precisely because the Final Solution was addressed to the biological, not the theological, community of Jews, it reinforced the traditional understanding of *keneset Yisrael* as a community of birth, not faith alone. If the covenant of hate did not distinguish between religious and secular Jews, believers and heretics, neither can its only possible redemption, the covenant of love. Halakhic inclusivism predated the Holocaust and is independent of it. But the Holocaust lent it overwhelming emotive force.

Pluralism rests on the dethronement of tradition. Fackenheim and Greenberg predicate Jewish unity on the fact that religious certainty and authority are no longer available. All Jews stand on the common ground of a merely fragmentary faith. But inclusivism rests on tradition. It rejects the rewriting of the covenant in the language of uncertainty, and has cogent reasons for doing so. The covenant cannot be philosophically renewed at the cost of its essential destruction. Tradition views a lack of faith in the post-Holocaust situation as excusable, intelligible, even the most logical inference from the facts of history, but as none the less wrong. Faith is not invulnerable to historic crisis; but it survives it through the strength of its own counter-factual, even obstinate, loyalty. The two ways of understanding Jewish unity are opposed and incompatible.

Tradition sees unity in terms of inclusivism. And therein lies the problem. For inclusivism is in direct conflict with the dominant mode of contemporary thought on the question of the relationship between different interpretations of faith. That mode is pluralism. The question before us therefore is: Can the inclusivist vision be translated into a pluralist consciousness? Does the traditional solution to schism founder on the conceptual ground of modernity?

Chapter 7

A Collision of Consciousness

The previous chapter described the halakhic strategy for preserving Jewish unity in the face of division over fundamentals and termed it *inclusivist*. But it raises a number of questions. Why can there be no halakhic strategy along the lines favoured by those outside Orthodoxy, namely *pluralism*? If Judaism recognizes pluralism along a number of axes, why not halakhic pluralism? And if it should emerge that inclusivism is the only available strategy, is it indeed a formula for Jewish unity? Does it not fail by its own unacceptability to those outside of Orthodoxy? To answer these questions, we must first be clear what the terms mean.

John Hick, discussing the relationships between one faith and another, defines three possibilities: exclusivism, inclusivism, and pluralism. Exclusivism is the view that "one particular mode of religious thought and experience (namely one's own) is alone valid, all others being false." Inclusivism is the view that "one's own tradition alone has the whole truth but that this truth is nevertheless partially reflected in other traditions." Pluralism is the view that "the great world faiths embody different perceptions and conceptions of, and correspondingly different responses to, the Real or the Ultimate."[1]

Let me put the distinction more precisely as it concerns Judaism. Inclusivists and exclusivists share the view that there is only one authoritative set of religious truths and imperatives. They hold, in other words, the classic rabbinic position that every Jew is bound by the principles of faith and the rules of halakhah. These are the boundaries of Judaism. But they move on from this starting-point in opposite directions. An *exclusivist* takes rejection of these norms at its face value. Karaites who rejected rabbinic law, *conversos* who out of fear embraced Christianity or Islam, and liberal or secular Jews who broke with halakhah had placed themselves outside the community of faith. They were heretics. They had no share in the world to come. The good deeds and Jewish rituals they performed were not *mitzvot*.[2] They or their children, at least in some respects, had forfeited their status as Jews.

Inclusivists do not take rejection at its face value. As the term implies, they seek to *include* within the faith those who apparently stand outside. Thus Maimonides saw *conversos* and the children of Karaites as Jews still within the ambit of salvation. Sometimes an inclusivist will give an interpretation of deviant conduct different from that which its agent would give himself. So Rabbi Kook saw secular Jews as implicitly religious. So, too, Chabad Hasidism sees all Jews as wishing, in their innermost selves, to be connected with God and Torah. It would be going too far to make a principled division between exclusivists and inclusivists as if these were two distinct strands in Jewish law and thought. Halakhic authorities judged each case by its circumstances. None the less, as we have seen, the central thrust of Jewish law in modern times has been towards inclusivism, for reasons that have equally to do with the character of modernity and with principles that are embedded deep in the logic of Judaism.

Pluralism takes issue with both exclusivism and inclusivism. It asserts that there is no single authoritative definition of Judaism. Instead

---

1. John Hick, *Problems of Religious Pluralism* (London: Macmillan, 1985), 91.
2. See, e.g., Elchanan Wasserman, *Kovetz Ma'amarim* (Jerusalem: Wasserman, 1963), 67.

there are many valid interpretations, none of which excludes or necessarily includes others. Pluralism is not the same as subjectivism, the idea that there is no objective truth in ethics or theology. It suggests, instead, that the same objective reality may be interpreted in different but equally valid ways, because it can be seen from different perspectives, with different purposes and through different cultural traditions. Pluralists are fond of illustrating their point by imagining blind men trying to describe an elephant. One feels its leg and identifies it as a tree. Another feels its trunk and concludes that it is a snake. A third feels the tail and says it is a rope. Theologies may seem to conflict, yet they may be perceptions of the same thing under different aspects.

The difference between Jewish inclusivism and pluralism, then, is this. Inclusivism asserts that there is an authoritative set of beliefs that constitute Jewish faith. It involves, among other things, belief in the divine revelation of the Torah and the authority of rabbinic tradition, interpretation, and law. Denial of these propositions cannot be understood, as pluralists would argue, as an equally legitimate way of understanding the covenant. It is, instead, an error. But – and this is the crux of inclusivism – it is an excusable error, not to be attributed to defiance or rebellion. Inclusivism preserves Orthodoxy while not excluding the non-Orthodox from the covenantal community.

A Jewish pluralist, on the other hand, would argue that liberal, Reform, Conservative, and secular Judaisms are equally legitimate ways of understanding the Jewish destiny. None is an error. He or she might flesh out this proposition by pointing to the different values each particularly exemplifies. It used to be argued, for example, that while Orthodoxy concentrated on Torah, Conservative Judaism focused on the Jewish people, while Reform Judaism was more concerned with theology and God. In terms of their decision-making processes, the alternatives might be stated somewhat differently. Reform attaches more weight to the individual, Conservative Judaism to the Jewish community in the present, and Orthodoxy to the Jewish people in its unbroken continuity. Regardless of how the different movements are characterized, pluralism argues that none is false. Each emphasizes some covenantal values. Each to some extent underemphasizes others. They are related to the transcendent realities of Jewish faith as are, say, paintings by Monet,

Cezanne, and Van Gogh to the landscape they depict. To call one correct and the others erroneous is to fail to understand the essential multiplicity of interpretation.

Inclusivism, then, is compatible with Jewish tradition. Is pluralism?

PLURALISM AND TRADITION

Rabbinic Judaism, I have argued, is pluralist in a number of respects. First, it recognizes the validity of at least some other religious traditions. *Chasidei umot haolam*, the pious of the nations of the world, have a share in the world to come.[3] Islam, most authorities agreed, is pure monotheism. Rabbi Menachem Hameiri extended this validation to all nations "who are disciplined in the ways of religions and civilization."[4] Maimonides saw both Christianity and Islam as facets of the divine plan of history, in which both religions served to prepare the world for the messianic age.[5] Rabbi Kook spoke of the "brotherly love of Esau [Christianity] and Jacob, of Isaac and Ishmael [Islam]," and of Judaism's respect for religious diversity.[6] To be sure, a Jew is not allowed to abandon Judaism, but non-Jews are not called on to embrace it. There are other equally legitimate ways of serving God.

Secondly, as we have seen, rabbinic Judaism is pluralist with regard to matters that lie outside halakhah. There are many striking statements to this effect within the tradition. There is prophetic pluralism. "The same communication is revealed to many prophets, but no two prophesy in the same style."[7] There is interpretative pluralism. There are "seventy faces" to the Torah.[8] "Just as perfume gives forth many scents, so when a verse is expounded you find in it many senses."[9] The

---

3. *Tosafot*, Sanhedrin 13:1; Yad, *Melakhim* 8:11.
4. *Beit Habechirah* on Bava Kama 37b–38a; see Katz, *Exclusiveness and Tolerance*, 114–28; Nachum Rabinovitch, "A Halakhic View of the Non-Jew," 18–23.
5. Yad, *Melakhim*, end of ch. 11 (uncensored eds.). See Lawrence Kaplan, "Maimonides on Christianity and Islam," *L'Eylah*, 22 (1986), 31–34.
6. *Igerot Harayah*, i. 112.
7. Sanhedrin 89a.
8. Nachmanides on Gen. 8:4.
9. Song of Songs Rabbah 4:10.

divine reality and the divine word both overflow any particular attempt to capture them in concepts. Infinity cannot be caught in the language of finitude. The reluctance of tradition to authorize precise articulations of faith or a single reading – even a single *style* of reading – of the biblical text is testimony to its sense of the inadequacy of language in the face of the Infinite.

Thirdly, rabbinic Judaism admitted cognitive pluralism. There is more than one way of knowing the world. Rabbi Soloveitchik's early work, *The Halakhic Mind*, is an essay on this theme.[10] "Sober epistemological facts," he writes, "demonstrate the heterogeneity and pluralistic character of the most basic cognitive methods." The concept of knowledge cannot be dissociated from the *telos* or purpose with which it is sought. Because human purposes are many and various, so are the forms of knowledge. "Systematic knowledge means the understanding and grasping of the universe in consonance with a definite *telos*.... Pluralism asserts...that the object reveals itself in manifold ways to the subject, and that a certain *telos* corresponds to each of these ontical manifestations."[11] An artist, a scientist, and a man of faith may see a sunset in different ways because they approach it with different frames of reference.

Soloveitchik writes as if cognitive pluralism were a peculiarly modern cultural phenomenon. But classic Jewish thought contains many examples. The biblical narrative of Joseph, for example, is an extraordinarily subtle example of shifting perspectives, in which a single sequence of events is seen now under the aspect of human intention, now under the guidance of an overarching providence. The text relating to the third plague in Egypt – when the Egyptian magicians, unable to produce lice by their magic arts, declare, "It is the finger of God"[12] – is almost a philosophical essay on different ways of understanding the miraculous: as that which is sent by God or that which cannot otherwise be explained. The rabbis, distinguishing between Torah and *chokhmah*

---

10. Joseph Soloveitchik, *The Halakhic Mind* (New York: Seth Press 1986). See Jonathan Sacks, "Rabbi J. B. Soloveitchik's Early Epistemology," *Tradition*, 23:3 (1988), 75–87.
11. Soloveitchik, *The Halakhic Mind*, 14–16.
12. Ex. 8:19.

(wisdom), recognized an independent domain of secular knowledge.[13] The halakhic system, with its elaborate structure of legal constructs, drew clear lines between empirical and legal facts.[14] Even legal facts could not be disentangled from their purposes. For example, a barrier might be considered a wall by the law of *sukkah* (the temporary dwelling used on the festival of Tabernacles), but not by the law requiring separation of the sexes in the synagogue. Not only divine reality, then, but the world of the senses also was given to plural modes of knowledge.

Fourthly, there was the pluralism of halakhic argument. In any given case there may be only one normative halakhic ruling, but there may be several equally well-founded halakhic opinions. A view which is rejected is not necessarily a view which is false. The schools of Hillel and Shammai both represent "the words of the living God." "The words of those who prohibit and of those who permit," said Rabbi Joshua, are "all of them given from one Shepherd."[15] Rabbinic Judaism recognizes the integrity of "argument for the sake of Heaven."[16] Rabbi Menachem Hameiri praises intellectual conflict as the means of arriving at truth.[17] Rabbi Kook goes further and sees conflict as the most complete representation of a truth that is necessarily many-sided.[18]

THE SOCIAL CONTEXT OF PLURALISM

Some forms of pluralism, then, are compatible with tradition. But clearly not all. The concept of Orthodoxy (or as the Mishnah puts it, beliefs the denial of which involve forfeiting a share in the world to come)[19] presupposes the possibility of heresy. The idea of halakhah – Judaism as law, binding on all its members – involves the possibility of rebellion as well as transgression. One can place oneself outside the law, as well as break it. Tradition sees Jews as constituting a covenantal community, and a community is defined by boundaries. Boundaries may be sharply

---

13. See *Entziklopediah Talmudit*, xv. 55–80.
14. On this see Soloveitchik, *Halakhic Man*.
15. Chagigah 3b.
16. Mish. Avot 5:17.
17. *Beit Habechirah* on Mish. Avot 5:17.
18. Kook, *Olat Rayah*, i. 330.
19. Mish. Sanhedrin 10:1.

or loosely defined, but there must exist a territory outside them for them to be boundaries at all. Not everything can count as a legitimate interpretation of faith or practice. Were it otherwise, Judaism would have no substantive content as the religion of a people.

Religious pluralism, far from being a self-evident phenomenon, in fact calls out for explanation. To be sure, all non-sectarian religious systems will tolerate differences of opinion on matters considered inessential to the definition of the faith community. Rabbinic Judaism, defining its faith community in terms of revealed law, was pluralist in the ways described above, precisely because they did not impinge on the halakhic system. But at the heart of any traditional religion lie ultimate claims about reality and authority. Religious belief is understood in terms of an objective truth that excludes alternatives. The great religious schisms, Jewish or otherwise, were fought on the ground of conflicting truths. The idea of pluralism – that ultimate truths are *not* incompatible, merely alternative expressions of the same reality – is revolutionary and sharply at odds with religious history. Certainly the great ideological battles of the nineteenth century between Orthodoxy and Reform, diasporism and Zionism, and the religious and secular interpretations of Zionism itself were fought on absolutist grounds. The radical reformers and secularists, far from maintaining that theirs was merely one possible interpretation of tradition, held that it was the only rational response possible to the times.

Jewish denominational pluralism is a specific phase in the dialectic of tradition and modernity. The initial period is marked by movements of radical accommodation to modernity. For Reform, this was the first half of the nineteenth century, for secular Zionism the period between 1880 and 1930. The ideology, if not the practical politics, of both movements defined itself in opposition to the antecedent tradition. Reform was the negation of the religion of the ghetto. Zionism was the negation of the diaspora. Each saw itself as throwing off the yoke of an outworn past, and as the sole survivor of modernity. Pluralism has no place in the mood of these times.

By the late twentieth century, however, the vision has been succeeded by achievement: social integration and acceptance in the diaspora, and the creation of the State of Israel. The initial impetus to radicalism has become a distant memory. The radicals, moreover, turn out not to be the sole inheritors of the future. Orthodoxy survives. So does the diaspora. More unexpectedly still, Orthodox Jews are at home in secular culture. Diaspora Jews are Zionists. The either-or of ideological radicalism no longer describes the way Jews act or think. To this must be added the powerful thrust lent by the Holocaust and Israel to the sensed reality of Jewish peoplehood. It becomes more plausible to think in terms of what unites rather than divides Jews, and more urgent.

But even these processes would not explain the emergence of pluralism as an ideology of the late twentieth century without one further factor: the deepening impact of secularization. Modernity privatizes the religious domain. Liberal theologies, accommodating themselves to social and intellectual change, translate statements about external reality into propositions about believers themselves, and propositions about authority into the vocabulary of personal choice. Religious language, instead of describing a given external and objective order, now designates a chosen internal and subjective reality. Once this move is made, pluralism becomes an intellectual possibility. Statements of objective truth clash in a way that statements about subjective perception do not. When religion no longer contests the public domain, coexistence takes the place of conflict. Because ultimate realities have been internalized, religious movements can see their differences as matters of interpretation rather than truth. "The phenomenon called "pluralism" is a social-structural correlate of the secularisation of consciousness."[20]

Denominational pluralism, then, is neither a feature of Jewish tradition nor even a first response to modernity. It occurs, argues Peter Berger, when religious authority is demonopolized and different groups have to compete for commitment in an open market.[21] It is, suggests Bryan Wilson, the result of a crisis of secularization. Inter-denominational co-operation, he writes, "is not in itself a revival of religion, nor a reconversion of society. It is the turning in on itself of institutionalized religion as its hold on the wider social order has diminished."[22]

---

20. Berger, *The Sacred Canopy*, 126.
21. Ibid., 126–53.
22. Wilson, *Religion in Secular Society*, 202.

It emerges when revolutionary movements persist beyond the circumstances that brought them forth; when the ideological wars of the first confrontation with change have subsided; when movements discover that their opponents, scheduled for oblivion, have survived; when the shared experience of modernization brings the realization that religious groups across the ideological spectrum have much in common; when religion has been marginalized to the point that its internal discords are less prominent than the difference between those of *any* religious commitment and those of none; when religions have sacrificed the language of truth for that of choice; and when the idea of objective authority has been replaced by that of self-fulfilment.

Necessarily, then, Orthodoxy cannot subscribe to pluralism in the contemporary sense, for Orthodoxy is the decision to continue to understand tradition *in the traditional way*, as objective truth and external authority. Pluralism arises when a movement initially conceived in opposition to a tradition seeks to reaffirm its links with that tradition within the framework of a non-traditional consciousness. It involves a revisionary translation of the tradition into new terms of reference. Jewish pluralism, as an argumentative strategy, consists in recategorizing issues that had hitherto been grounds for schism into one or other of the areas where the tradition had allowed for more than one interpretation. It involves seeing debates that had previously been central to the definition of Judaism as in fact marginal. To see how this happens, and why Orthodoxy cannot accede to it, let us consider one example of the pluralist case: the argument from argument.

HALAKHIC ARGUMENT, HALAKHIC DECISION

The argument is this.[23] Liberal Judaism differs from Orthodoxy in its practices. To a greater or lesser extent it will permit what halakhah forbids. In the early pre-pluralist stage of its ideological development, this

---

23. On Jewish pluralism see Greenberg, *Toward a Principled Pluralism*; Reuven Kimmelman, "Judaism and Pluralism," *Modern Judaism*, 7:2 (1987), 131–50; Jacob Petuchowski, "Plural Models within the Halakhah," in Bulka (ed.), *Dimensions of Orthodox Judaism*, 149–61, and Walter Wurzburger, "Plural Models and the Authority of Halakhah," ibid. 162–74; David Dishon, *Tarbut Hamachloket Beyisrael* (Tel Aviv:

fact was explained by arguing that sections of the halakhah had become inapplicable to the present moment. The new dispensation was not seen as *halakhic* behaviour. Its legitimation lay elsewhere. Pluralism, however, seeks to re-traditionalize it *as* halakhic behaviour of a kind. It belongs to a halakhah which is answerable – and which, it is argued, was always answerable – to personal autonomy (Reform) or the ethics of the age (Conservative). Clearly, though, this is not halakhic behaviour as Orthodoxy understands the term. The conflict must be explained. But this is simple (so the pluralist contends) given what we know of the traditional pluralism of halakhic argument. The differences between liberal and Orthodox halakhah are exactly akin to those between the schools of Hillel and Shammai, or the other arguments of which the Talmud is full. These and those are the words of the living God. Halakhah itself is pluralist.

The argument itself is specious. It involves confusing halakhic argument with halakhic decision. The schools of Hillel and Shammai each interpret the words of the living God, but the law follows Hillel. One can, to be sure, discern a genuine difference of opinion throughout the rabbinic literature between realists and positivists, between those who see halakhic argument as converging on the truth and those who see it eventuating in a decision.[24] For the former, rejected opinions are

---

Schocken, 1984); David Hartman, "Halakhah as a Ground for Creating a Shared Spiritual Language," in his *Joy and Responsibility* (Jerusalem: Ben-Zvi Posner, 1978), 130–61.

24. The view that the schools of Hillel and Shammai both represented "the words of the living God" suggests positivism, namely, that both are true but that one must make a decision between them. *Tosafot*, Chagigah 2:9, however, suggests that halakhic controversy arose between the two schools only because the disciples did not sufficiently attend on their masters. On this view, controversy is not intrinsic to the halakhic process but instead represents a failure in the transmission of tradition.

The realist view – realist meant here in a Platonic sense, that halakhah corresponds to truth – is suggested by Nachmanides in his remarks to the effect that the spirit of God is always present among the judges of Israel (Commentary on Deut. 17:11, 19:19). However, Nachmanides' way of putting it, that "the Holy One, blessed be he, assents to the verdict" of the human court, is consistent with positivism and the view that the binding power of halakhah is a matter not of truth but authority.

One talmudic passage, Rosh Hashanah 24b–25b, adopts an explicitly positivist stance. The date of the new moon is determined by the decision of the court even if

false. For the latter, they may be true but non-normative. But for both, halakhic argument converges on a single authoritative ruling. Halakhic argument may be pluralist. Halakhic practice is not.

There were, of course, divergences in practice. As early as the talmudic period, Jews in Palestine and Babylon had distinctive customs.[25] From these emerged the different Ashkenazi and Sephardi traditions.[26] There were numerous minor local differences.[27] These flowed from the absence of a central supreme halakhic authority. "So long as the Great Sanhedrin was in existence," writes Maimonides, "there were no controversies in Israel.... After the Great Sanhedrin ceased, disputes multiplied in Israel, one declaring "unclean" and giving a reason for his ruling, another declaring "clean" and giving a reason for his ruling."[28] In the post-Gaonic period, no single authority was regarded as having global jurisdiction.[29] Rabbinic decrees and enactments could have only local force. But the system retained its coherence through defined limits of legal procedure, argument, and decision. There was consensus on fundamental issues of substance, on what were the authoritative halakhic texts, methods of argumentation, and limits of judicial autonomy. A ruling could be adjudged simply wrong if it ignored agreed precedent.[30]

---

it is in error. See also the interesting distinction made by Rabbi Akiva Eger in *Gilyon Hashas* on Makkot 5a between situations where obligations are created by acts, and those where they are created by decisions of the court. See also below in the present chapter, on the case of the rebellious elder.

For further discussion, from different perspectives, see Norman Lamm and Aaron Kirschenbaum, "Freedom and Constraint in the Jewish Judicial Process," *Cardozo Law Review*, 1 (1979), 99–133; Yochanan Silman, "Hikba'uyot Halakhtiot Bein Nominalizm Verealizm: Lyunim Bephilosophiah Shel Hahalakhah," *Dinei Yisrael*, 12 (1985), 249–66; H. Ben Menahem, "Is There Always One Uniquely Correct Answer to a Legal Question in the Talmud?" *Jewish Law Annual*, 6 (1986), 164–75; Bernard Jackson, "Jewish Law or Jewish Laws," ibid., 8 (1989), 15–34.

25. Joel Mueller, *Chiluf Minhagim Bein Benei Bavel Livenei Eretz Yisrael* (Vienna, 1878).

26. H. J. Zimmels, *Ashkenazim and Sephardim* (Oxford: Oxford University Press, 1958).

27. For examples from the early rabbinic period see Shabbat 130a; Pesachim 50b–51a, 55b–56a.

28. Yad, *Mamrim* 1:4.

29. See Yad, Intro.

30. *Shulchan Arukh, Yoreh De'ah* 242:31. See *Entziklopediah Talmudit*, ix. 333–9; Nachum Rabinovitch, *Hadar Itamar* (Jerusalem: Mosad Harav Kook, 1972), 1–10.

Halakhic practice was not pluralist. Rather, it resembled a legal system in which certain domains were delegated to local legislatures. To call liberal norms that accord weight to personal autonomy or the ethics of the age "halakhah" is to equivocate between local variations in a single legal system and two different legal systems altogether.

Where then does the argument gain its plausibility? By the secularization of the idea of halakhah. Halakhah is law, binding on the Jewish people in its totality. But when religious law loses its coercive power, as happened to Jewish law during emancipation, it loses the institutional context that made its character as law self-evident. Traditional behaviour comes to seem expressive of less formal commitments: private ethical persuasion,[31] or historically endorsed habit,[32] or even a code of social belonging.[33] Each of these can be overridden as law cannot. Each admits of pluralism as law does not. Halakhah becomes "tradition," which is to say the sacred past rather than the commanding present.[34] Halakhic pluralism is, in short, a symptom of the secularization of religious behaviour. This is why it is self-evidently plausible to modern consciousness and at the same time necessarily incompatible with Orthodoxy. For Orthodoxy is the refusal to transform Jewish law from the revealed constitution of the covenant into a self-defined code of personal autonomy or an evolving historical process.

31. Thus, the Reform theologian Eugene Borowitz writes, "I do not see how, even in principle, Jewish law can be imposed on such a Jewish self. Rather, with autonomy essential to selfhood, I avidly espouse a pluralism of thought and action stemming from Jewish commitment": "The Autonomous Jewish Self," *Modern Judaism*, 4:1 (1984), 47. For Borowitz, halakhah represents a "resource" for the modern Jew, not law.

32. "Yes, it is true, in a sense, that the whole of Torah is *minhag*, custom, growing through the experience of human beings and interpreted by them in response to particular conditions in human history": Louis Jacobs, *A Jewish Theology* (London: Darton, Longman and Todd, 1973), 224.

33. Thus Jack J. Cohen, a Reconstructionist, calls halakhah the repository of "the mind and character of the Jewish people": "Halakhah and the Life of Holiness," *Rabbinical Assembly Annual*, 30 (1958), 90. This is his version of Mordecai Kaplan's position that instead of Jewish law, we should speak of Jewish "folkways."

34. See Jaroslav Pelikan, *The Vindication of Tradition* (New Haven, CT: Yale University Press, 1984).

PLURALISM OR INCLUSIVISM?

Pluralism, then, proposes a mode of Jewish unity acceptable to modern consciousness. But it is *ipso facto* unacceptable to Orthodoxy. It succeeds only if the terms of Orthodoxy are false. This is why the most persuasive theologies of pluralism – those of Emil Fackenheim and Irving Greenberg considered in the previous chapter – are so insistent that traditional faith is impossible in the post-Holocaust age. But pluralism fails within the terms it sets itself. For it sought to accommodate liberal and Orthodox Judaisms within the same universe of discourse. They were variant interpretations of the same covenantal truth. But Orthodoxy cannot be so accommodated. Only an Orthodoxy misconceived as an ultra-traditional liberalism can. Orthodoxy is defined in terms of truth and authority, not interpretation and option. This fact cannot be translated into pluralism.

We are left with the traditional alternative, inclusivism. But we are now faced with a critical problem. Inclusivism proposes a mode of Jewish unity acceptable to traditional consciousness. But this threatens to make it *ipso facto* unacceptable to liberalism. The reason is this. From the point of view of a liberal Jew, inclusivism has a benefit and a price. The benefit is that it allows Orthodoxy to relate to him or her in a spirit of kinship and shared fate. The price is that this happens through a deliberate and systematic conflict of interpretations.[35] Reform Jews, for example, will see their willingness to drive on the Sabbath, eat non-kosher food, or appoint a woman cantor as part of a principled understanding of Judaism. Orthodox Jews, if they are inclusivist, will see such willingness as a culturally conditioned error. Inclusivism involves a refusal to accept the self-evaluation of those outside tradition. This is its strategic crux.

Attaching no significance to liberal Jews' description of their own actions and intentions allows Orthodoxy to include individuals within the halakhic community while excluding their ideologies. In so doing, it bypasses the conflict between communal unity and doctrinal integrity.

---

35. The point has been made frequently by Eliezer Schweid in his writings on Kook. See, e.g., his *Hayehudi Haboded Vehayahadut* (Tel Aviv: Am Oved, 1975), 178–93; *Hayahadut Vehatarbut Hachilonit* (Tel Aviv: Hakibbutz Hame'uchad, 1981), 110–42; "Two Neo-Orthodox Responses to Secularization."

It is, as we have seen, a device that allows enormous inclusivity. But it does so by devaluing the legitimacy of any interpretation of Judaism that lies outside the parameters of traditional faith. It is a strategy of which non-Orthodox Jews might understandably not wish to avail themselves. Explicitly or implicitly, they will feel that it assaults their authenticity. Reform Jews, defending their integrity, wish to be understood not as transgressing the law through excusable error, but as adhering to another conception of Jewish law, or if not law, then another conception of Judaism as ethics, or ethnicity or autonomy.

The Reform Jew seeks no less than a pluralist approach to Judaism, one that will concede the legitimacy of alternative interpretations of halakhah and the fundamentals of faith. But Judaism, as classically conceived, admits of pluralism in this sense only in respect of other faiths. This, then, generates the tragic paradox that Orthodoxy can only accede to the Reform Jew's request at the cost of seeing Reform as another religion altogether. Some Orthodox authorities have indeed suggested just this. In response to the Reform rabbinate's demand for official recognition in Israel, they have argued that it should be granted on the basis that Reform, like the Samaritans and Karaites, is sufficiently distinct from Judaism to constitute a separate religious community.[36] Reform would then be recognized, like Christianity and Islam, as a religion explicitly independent of Judaism. This would formalize a total and probably irreparable schism. Pluralism, *when translated into the categories of tradition,* achieves a result directly opposite to that sought by the liberal Jew.

This is what I meant when, in an early chapter, I noted that in the contemporary Jewish world the pursuit of unity is inherently divisive. Pluralism denies the self-definition of Orthodoxy. Inclusivism denies the self-definition of non-Orthodoxy. Were liberal Jews to accept Orthodoxy at its face value, they would be forced to abandon the terms of pluralism and argue that Orthodoxy is false. Were Orthodoxy to accept liberal Jews on their own terms, they would be forced to conclude that they lay outside the covenantal community. Inclusivist and pluralist conceptions

---

36. J. David Bleich, "Parameters and Limits of Communal Unity from the Perspective of Jewish Law," *L'Eylah,* 21 (1986), 31–6. The same suggestion has been reported in the name of the former Ashkenazi chief rabbi of Israel, Shlomo Goren.

of unity are incompatible. The one cannot absorb the other. We here come face to face with one of the most profound collisions between tradition and modernity.

The problem, to restate it, is that inclusivism assaults the self-respect of the liberal Jew. It rests on a distinction between liberal Jews and liberal Judaism. To legitimate the former it must delegitimate the latter. To include dissenting individuals it must exclude dissenting ideologies. Tradition can only interpret the covenantal community as a community of faith and practice. To include those who stand outside the boundaries of traditional faith and practice, it must see their stance as non-essential, the result of environmental influence and excusable error. What is essential is their desire to be counted in the community, to be identified as Jews, even on terms to which they do not explicitly subscribe. Inclusivism, in driving a wedge between the dissenting individual and his or her beliefs, deliberately marginalizes the central virtues of modernity: authenticity, integrity, the deep congruence be- tween the self and its expressions. Liberal Judaism asks Orthodoxy to respect its integrity. That is precisely what Orthodoxy, for the sake of Jewish unity, proposes not to do.

Is the problem insuperable? What is happening in this confrontation? Is it that Orthodoxy in fact believes that non-Orthodox Jews do not sincerely believe what they profess? Or is it that Orthodoxy does not recognize sincerity, authenticity, or integrity as values? It is, I contend, neither of these things. Instead we are caught in a conceptual impasse, the result of an intellectual revolution that threatens to render the values of tradition untranslatable into the language of modernity. To understand the problem in its proper perspective we must consider the changing ideas of self and society. We can then approach the question of integrity, or the dignity of dissent.

THE MODERN SELF

In traditional societies, the individual is identified by his or her membership of a variety of social groups and by occupancy of a set of roles. In a stable and long-standing culture, these roles - of spouse, parent, child, occupation, social class, and so forth - carry with them established duties and responsibilities. The scope for individual choice, sometimes even with respect to marriage partner,[37] is relatively circumscribed. As Michael Oakeshott has pointed out, in such traditional communities "the moral life does not spring from the consciousness of possible alternative ways of behaving." Instead, "we acquire habits of conduct in the same way as we acquire our native language."[38] The self is largely defined by society.

By contrast, the individual in the contemporary urban setting typically occupies a series of roles that are experienced as not given but chosen. Nor are they definitive of personal identity. Sociologists have observed that modern identities are peculiarly "open-ended, transitory, liable to ongoing change."[39] As a result, "biography is...apprehended both as a migration through different social worlds and as the successive realization of a number of possible identities."[40] Religious or ideological commitments too become forms of role of which we may choose several, successively or simultaneously. No longer universes we inhabit, they become positions we adopt. Life-worlds become lifestyles. The self is distanced from its social roles.

As the social world becomes pluralized and fragmented, self, not society, becomes the main bearer of reality. But the modern self, unlike its traditional counterpart, has no specific content. Little is given to it by way of birth, culture, or preordained role. In Erving Goffman's sociology, for example, the self becomes a mere peg on which various roles are hung. In Jean-Paul Sartre's existentialism, the self has no "essence" and is, instead, the perpetual awareness of possibilities. "This democratised self which has no necessary social content and no necessary social identity can then be anything, can assume any role or take any point of view, because it *is* in and for itself nothing."[41] The self is "deinstitutionalized."

This has profound implications for ethics. Virtues are sometimes untranslatable from one social context to another. An example: the verse in Psalms "Gird your sword upon your side, O mighty one; clothe yourself with splendour and majesty" invokes a code of military distinction.

---

37. See Egon Meyer, *Love and Tradition* (New York: Plenum Press, 1985).
38. Michael Oakeshott, "The Tower of Babel," *Cambridge Journal*, 2:2 (1948), 69.
39. Berger, Berger, and Kellner, *The Homeless Mind*, 74.
40. Ibid., 73.
41. MacIntyre, *After Virtue*, 30.

It belongs to a period of warrior kings. By the time we reach the talmu-dic period, however, we find it understood by Rabbi Kahana to refer to words of Torah.[42] The sword as a symbol of military honour had become incomprehensible in a rabbinic culture of quietism and scholarship. What was the weapon of a scholar? His words of Torah. The verse used a vocabulary of virtue that had, by the time of the Babylonian sages, to be translated into an altogether different social frame of reference.

Or consider an example directly relevant to the transformation we are considering. In a scintillating essay, the sociologist Peter Berger discusses "the obsolescence of the concept of honour."[43] The notion of *honour*, and the closely associated one of chivalry, belong in the main to stable and hierarchical societies in which the individual is defined by preordained roles. Honour has to do with the conduct owed to a person in respect of a position. The concept which has supplanted it, *dignity*, belongs to an era in which the individual self is seen as something apart from its various enactments. Dignity has to do with conduct owed to a person as such. "The concept of honour," Berger writes, "implies that identity is essentially, or at least importantly, linked to institutional roles. The modern concept of dignity, by contrast, implies that identity is essentially independent of institutional roles." The idea of honour is simply inapplicable to a world in which the language of ethics has become detached from the fulfilment of socially established roles.

Alasdair MacIntyre has noted that it is this deinstitutionalized self that lies at the heart of contemporary moral philosophy. "It is in this capacity of the self to evade any necessary identification with any particular contingent state of affairs that some modern philosophers, both analytical and existentialist, have seen the essence of moral agency." The self of modern moral theory stands apart from any particular tradi-tion. "To be a moral agent is, on this view, precisely to be able to stand back from any and every situation in which one is involved...and to pass

---

42. Ps. 45:4; Shabbat 63a.
43. Peter Berger, "On the Obsolescence of the Concept of Honour," *European Journal of Sociology*, II (1970), 339–47; repr. in Michael Sandel (ed.), *Liberalism and its Critics* (Oxford: Blackwell, 1984), 149–58, and in Berger, Berger, and Kellner, *The Homeless Mind*, 78–89.

judgement on it from a purely universal and abstract point of view that is detached from all social particularity."[44] The weight given in contemporary moral philosophy to individual freedom, authenticity, and rights is thus the product of a particular social transformation and of that detraditionalized entity, the modern self.

THE TRADITIONAL JEWISH SELF

This mode of discourse and consciousness collides with classic Jewish assumptions at several points. First there is the constitutive idea of Judaism itself, that Jews are *born into obligations*. Jewish identity commits what in modern moral thinking is seen as a fallacy: it fuses fact with value, "is" with "ought." A Jew is a Jew by virtue of birth. But this fact carries with it certain duties and obligations. Membership of the Jewish community is thus simultaneously a biological and ethical proposition. Jews do not choose the commands by which they are bound. This assertion is untranslatable into Kantian or Sartrean ethics. The previous chapter mentioned Irving Greenberg's suggestion that today Jews are bound only by a "voluntary covenant." We now sense the deep conceptual tensions that lead to such an idea, radically at odds as it is with tradition. For the notion of an *in*voluntary covenant conflicts with the characteristically modern view that only obligations that are voluntarily undertaken are ethically binding.

Secondly, within Judaism itself there are *distinctions* of obligation which follow from birth rather than choice. There is the special sanctity of the *kohen,* which precludes him, among other things, from marrying a divorcée. There are the distinctive roles of men and women in the religious life. There are the disabilities of the *mamzer,* the child born of an adulterous or incestuous relationship. These become moral cruxes in liberal Judaism precisely because they are not consequences of choice on the part of the person concerned.

Thirdly, the specificities of Jewish law conflict with what, on liberal assumptions, would be deemed to be matters of personal choice. The prohibitions against homosexuality or intermarriage, for example, seem to intrude into domains which are peculiarly personal. They become

---

44. MacIntyre, *After Virtue,* 30.

difficult to justify within the categories of modern secular ethics. Indeed, they concern areas of conduct to which, to the liberal mind, the concept of law as such is inapplicable. These too are issues on which some exponents of liberal Judaism have felt morally bound to part company with tradition in the name of autonomy.

Above all, the *otherness* of Jewish law as something given by God and interpreted by an authoritative rabbinic tradition runs counter to the fundamental thrust of modernity. This, as we have seen, has been central to the philosophical critique of religious ethics as heteronomous – legislated from outside the self – since Kant. Indeed, this proved to be the critical issue which divided Orthodoxy from all other modern constructions of Judaism: its insistence on the *givenness* of Torah and halakhah.

So modernity and Jewish tradition seem to conflict in their deepest assumptions about the self. Tradition postulates an objective order, differentiating in role if not in status between Jew and non-Jew, man and woman, that clashes with the contemporary premiss that the only significant roles are those we choose. It places religious-ethical authority outside the self, while modern ethical theory makes the self its own legislator. If the Jew of tradition lived in the free choice of whether or not to obey the law, the post-traditional Jew lives in the free choice of what law to obey. Not surprisingly, the most problematic of all traditional ideas for the modern Jew is that of Torah as revealed legislation, given at Mount Sinai and binding subsequent generations without their consent.

THE AUTONOMOUS SELF AND JUDAISM

Perhaps the simplest way of indicating the revolution of consciousness involved is to note that *authenticity,* in the twentieth-century sense of genuinely doing that which is right in one's own eyes, is the central existentialist virtue[45] and the archetypal biblical vice.[46] The word "authentic" originally meant "genuine," "authoritative," or "justified." Recently it has come to mean something like "that with which we genuinely identify." The transition between the two is simple to trace. An authentic da Vinci is one which he himself painted, as opposed to a counterfeit, fake, or

---

45. See John Macquarrie, *Existentialism* (London: Pelican Books, 1973), 135–72.
46. Deut. 12:8; Judg. 17:6, 21:25.

forged da Vinci. Authentic, in this sense, means really proceeding from its author. The transformation comes when we perceive ethics, or Judaism, as bearing the same relationship to the self as a painting to its painter, namely: a free creation, essentially unpredictable, whose authentication lies in its trueness to self.[47]

In the Bible, the supreme virtue is to do that which is right "in the eyes of God." To do that which is right in one's own eyes is the paradigm of lawlessness. Post-Kantian ethics reverses these values. Mere obedience is inauthentic. Moral agency means to be the author of one's own behavioural code. From the perspective of the autonomous self, then, halakhic existence is inauthentic because it flees from making personal choice the centre of its universe. From the perspective of tradition, much of contemporary ethics is inauthentic precisely *because* it makes personal choice the measure of all things.

Certainly, neither art nor ethics nor liberal Judaism moves in unmediated freedom. But we face a Copernican revolution none the less. This is evident when we consider the work of the most distinguished contemporary liberal Jewish theologian, Eugene Borowitz.[48] Borowitz

---

47. The point can be put more philosophically. Peter Geach distinguishes between *attributive* and *predicative* adjectives; see his "Good and Evil," *Analysis*, 17 (1956), 33–42. "Yellow" is a predicative adjective, for the sentence "That is a yellow bird" can be analysed into "That is a bird and it is yellow." But the adjective "good" in the sentence "He is a good cricketer" cannot be analysed into "He is a cricketer and he is good." "Good" in this sense is attributive. Bernard Williams calls an attributive adjective one that is "logically glued to the substantive it qualifies": *Morality: An Introduction to Ethics* (Harmondsworth: Penguin Books, 1973), 54.

One of the problems with the word "authentic" is whether it is predicative or attributive. Is the phrase "an authentic Jew" analysable into two distinctive and separate components – being a Jew and being, independently, authentic – or is "authentic" attributive? Is the meaning of authenticity determined by the meaning of Judaism?

The issue addressed in the text is the slow transition from attributive to predicative authenticity, from an authenticity determined by objective criteria to one determined by trueness to self. This, as I argue, is part of a wider cultural process in which personal identity, and with it the key terms of ethics, shifts from determination by roles to free-standing selfhood. See Alasdair MacIntyre, *A Short History of Ethics* (London: Routledge and Kegan Paul, 1967), 84–109.

48. Most of the quotations below are drawn from his most complete presentation thus far: Borowitz, "The Autonomous Jewish Self." Some are drawn from his other pre-

wishes to give an account of "the autonomous Jewish self" that is at the same time close to tradition. Autonomy, he argues, "makes sense only in terms of the self's actualization of God's will since God is the source and standard of its own being." Moreover, the contemporary Jewish self has a "direct, primary, ethnic form." It is "structured by an utterly elemental participation in the Jewish historical experience of God." The Jew is bound to a particular community, and this rules out extremes of individualism. Aiming, too, at a unified life, the Jew cannot value spontaneity over all else. "Form, habit, institution and structure have a necessary role to play."

This is, by previous standards of liberal Judaism, an extremely traditionalist portrait. Nineteenth-century Reform was universalist and humanist, and valued ethics over ritual. By complete contrast, Borowitz declares that the need now is to "recapture a compelling particularism." Reform's "confidence in humankind and in western civilization" has "been shattered." Religious discipline is needed to overcome liberal Judaism's "drive to anarchy." A highly traditional Jewish life could be incorporated within this philosophy. With one exception.

The liberal Jew is permitted to break with tradition when conscience so dictates. He is guided by precedent but "not to the point of dependency or passivity of will." Borowitz's traditionalism "does not rise to the point of validating law in the traditional sense, for personal autonomy remains the cornerstone of this piety." It is, in short, tradition without halakhah. Halakhah, I argued, was Judaism's equivalent of Strawson's "social morality." It shapes a people into a community of action. It is the domain in which universal norms take precedence over individual ideal. For Borowitz there is no such domain. Faced with a conflict between society and self, norm and conscience, the self must reign supreme.

Borowitz's philosophy is a lucid example of how tradition is transformed when translated into the terms of the modern self. Tradition itself is turned from halakhah – community-creating law – into a

---

sentations of the same subject: *A New Jewish Theology in the Making* (Philadelphia: Westminster Press, 1968), 177–213, and *Choices in Modern Jewish Thought* (New York: Behrman House, 1983), 243–72.

catalogue of "resources one can draw on to meet one's personal needs." The autonomous self is not simply one motif of modern thought among many which can be added to Judaism as cosmetic ornamentation. Once introduced into the system, inevitably it moves to a place of controlling power, shaping all else to its contours. When the autonomous self rules, the values associated with it – integrity and authenticity – become fundamental. So the liberal Jew's request of Orthodoxy, that it respect his or her integrity, is more than a matter of etiquette or even ethics. It is a fundamental issue of self-definition. The question we must now ask is: Is tradition itself capable of admitting such an idea, namely a respect for the integrity of those who refuse to obey halakhah out of principle?

INTEGRITY AND FUNCTION

At first sight the answer must be an overwhelming No. Firstly, the idea is utterly destructive of halakhah. A system of law cannot admit into itself the systematic right to disengage from it. Secondly, the intellectual world of halakhah is at odds with the mode of consciousness in which integrity in this modern sense figures as a virtue. As law, halakhah presupposes a congruence between self and society. As divine law it presupposes an even deeper congruence between self and the source of the commands. "Authenticity" as the priority of the individual over social or divine imperative is, in this context, not integrity but rebellion. Halakhic man, writes Rabbi Soloveitchik, finds authenticity precisely in obeying the command. It "seems to him as though he discovered the norm in his innermost self, as though it were not just a commandment that had been imposed upon him but an existential law of his very being."[49] There will, surely, be moments when he faces a command to which he cannot assent. But then, like Abraham at the binding of Isaac, faith reigns. Man acknowledges his finitude in the presence of the Infinite. He experiences the "victory of defeat." Man, says Rabbi Soloveitchik, "defeats himself by accepting norms that the intellect cannot assimilate into its normative system."[50] This is an idea

---

49. Soloveitchik, *Halakhic Man*, 65.
50. Id., "Majesty and Humility," *Tradition*, 17:2 (1978), 37.

almost impossible to make compelling to a modern sensibility, but it cannot be edited out of the tradition.[51]

This is not to say that a benign attitude to liberal Judaism is impossible from the perspective of Orthodoxy. It is possible. But not in terms of integrity. Orthodoxy might, for example, draw a distinction between liberal Jewish theology and practice. Thus one observer has noted that "the bulk of American Jews regard Reform rabbis...as having a function which Orthodox and Conservative rabbis cannot and need not have as long as there are Reform rabbis, namely the sanctifying of life-cycle events which are halakhically invalid but which the community feels, albeit reluctantly, it must approve." Intermarriage is a good example. No Judaism, halakhic or otherwise, can sanction marriages between Jews and non-Jews without threatening traditional Jewish continuity at its foundations. Such, however, is the rate of intermarriage in highly acculturated Jewish communities that exclusion of the outmarried can equally be perceived as a demographic disaster. In this conflict between *de jure* norm and *de facto* reality, "the Reform rabbi...serves the larger Jewish community by sanctifying non-halakhic but communally sanctioned behaviour."[52]

In principle, Orthodoxy might concede that the existence of Reform has beneficial consequences even while dissenting completely from its ideology. This is no paradox. No clearer precedent exists than Maimonides' attitude to Christianity. On the one hand, few Jewish thinkers have taken a more negative view of Christian theology than did Maimonides. On the other hand, few were more positive in their estimate of the consequences of Christianity. Because of it, "the messianic hope, the Torah, and the commandments have become familiar topics of conversation among the inhabitants of distant isles."[53] The analogy

---

51. David Hartman's *A Living Covenant: The Innovative Spirit in Traditional Judaism* (New York: Free Press, 1985) is an attempt to do so. My argument is that the attempt must fail.

52. Norman Mirsky, "Mixed Marriage and the Reform Rabbinate," *Midstream*, 16 (Jan. 1970), 44.

53. Yad, *Melakhim* 11 (uncensored eds.). See Lawrence Kaplan, "Maimonides and Christianity and Islam."

is invidious, but the point is clear. Historical or sociological function is one thing, respect for integrity another.

INTEGRITY AND TRADITION

But it is precisely this approach that is likely to scandalize the liberal Jew. He or she wishes to be respected for principles held, not consequences created. Liberal Jews wish to be understood at their own valuation, namely, as individuals who have rejected halakhic precedent as a matter of conscience and integrity, not *de facto* pragmatism. This is a reasonable request. What is more, tradition has room for it. First impressions notwithstanding, the rabbinic concept of integrity is more complex than it seems. It accords an ethical dignity to principled dissent. But it is just here that we can see most clearly why such an idea, if invoked, would have consequences opposite to those sought by the liberal Jew.

The idea of the integrity of principled dissent is not altogether absent from the halakhic literature. Jewish law, for example, distinguishes between a *meshumad lete'avon* and a *meshumad lehakhis*, one who habitually sins because of "appetite" or weakness of will, and one who does so out of rebellion. The latter is more serious than the former, for while the weak-willed breaks the law, the rebel places himself outside it altogether. A view is none the less expressed in the Talmud (though it was not taken up as law) that in one respect principled rebellion is preferable to self-indulgent transgression. Rava argues that the rebel is qualified to give testimony in a Jewish court of law.[54] The "sinner out of appetite" is suspected of being willing to perjure himself for gain. The "sinner out of principle" is not. Perhaps this is as near as Jewish law comes to recognizing an independent virtue of integrity even when expressed as rebellion.

Thus far halakhah. But aggadah, the realm of value and theory, presents a more subtle picture. The paradigm of principled defiance was the case of the "rebellious elder." This was a qualified judge who dissented from a ruling of the supreme court and gave a contrary ruling

---

54. Sanhedrin 27a. The law, though, follows Abbaye, that a rebel is disqualified from testimony. To be sure, Abbaye may not disagree with the logic of Rava's position, but he understands the verse "Do not accept the wicked as witness" (Ex. 23:1) more widely to include even those who are not wicked for gain.

in accordance with his own reading of the law. Biblical law prescribed capital punishment in such a case, albeit hedged with qualifications.[55] Aggadically, however, how was such a rebel to be regarded? Was the supreme court the legislator of truth, so that a rebellious elder was guilty of obstinate error? Or was the issue the quite different one of authority? On this interpretation, the rebel may have been as justified in his ruling as the court, perhaps more so. He is punished not because he is wrong, but because he refuses to accept the authority of the majority verdict.

There were certainly those, such as Nachmanides, whose writings suggest the idea that providence attends the deliberations of a Jewish court, so that its verdicts are always true.[56] But there were those, Maimonides among them, who saw the law of the rebel as a matter of judicial authority alone. "Even though he [the rebellious elder] judges and they judge, he has received traditions and they have received traditions, none the less the Torah has ascribed honour [i.e. authority] to them. If the court wishes to forgo its honour and leave him be, it may not do so, so as not to multiply disputes in Israel."[57] Nachmanides, too, seems to accept this idea. One is obliged to accept the ruling of a court even if one is convinced that it is wrong, because otherwise "disputes would multiply and the one Torah would become many Torahs."[58]

This opens the way to a potentially tragic dilemma for the individual judge. What if he is certain – on the basis of his received tradition itself – that the majority are wrong? On the one hand, the Torah has given authority to the majority consensus and commanded that it be obeyed.[59] On the other hand, Judaism does not allow the individual to transgress what he knows to be the law merely because others have commanded him to do so. There is no "agent for wrongdoing," no defence that one was merely obeying orders. "When the words of the master conflict with the words of the pupil, whose words are to be obeyed?" the Talmud asks, rhetorically.[60] When the word of God conflicts with

---

55. Deut. 17:12; Yad, *Mamrim* 3:4–7.
56. *Commentary* on Deut. 17:11; 19:19. See also Judah Halevi, *Kuzari*, 3:41.
57. Yad, *Mamrim* 3:4; see also *Guide of the Perplexed*, iii. 41.
58. *Commentary* on Deut. 17:11.
59. Deut. 17:11.
60. Kiddushin 42b.

the word of man, the word of God must take precedence. All authority recognized by halakhah, including that of a king over his subjects[61] and a parent over his child,[62] is qualified by this: that it does not take precedence over the authority of the divine word. Here then is a judge who believes the divine word indicates one course of action, while the court believes it indicates another. How shall he act?

The dilemma provides the rabbinic literature with some of its most haunting scenes of moral conflict. Let me give two examples. When "testimonies" were being taken on rabbinic traditions, Akavia ben Mehalalel found himself in disagreement with the majority of his colleagues on four issues. The Mishnah reports,[63] "They said to him: Akavia, withdraw what you have been saying on these four things and we will make you *av beit din*, father of the court. He said to them: It is better for me to be called a fool all my days than that I should become, even for an hour, a wicked man in the sight of God. And let not men say that he withdrew his opinions for the sake of achieving power." The Mishnah concludes, "They excommunicated him and he died while under excommunication, and the court stoned his coffin." A deathbed scene is recorded between Akavia and his son. "In the hour of his death, he said to his son: Retract from the four opinions I used to declare. His son said to him: Why then did you not retract? He replied: I heard them from the mouth of the many and they heard them from the mouth of the many. I stood firm by my tradition, and they held firm by theirs. But you have heard [my views] from the mouth of a single individual and [their views] from the mouth of the many. It is better to leave the opinion of a single individual and hold by the opinion of the many."

The Mishnah finishes with Akavia insisting to the end on individual integrity. "His son said to him: Father, commend me to your colleagues. He replied: I will not commend you. His son said: Have you found some fault in me? He replied: No. But your own deeds will bring

---

61. Yad, *Melakhim* 3:9. On this subject much has been written. See, e.g., Moshe Greenberg, "Rabbinic Reflections on Defying Illegal Orders: Amasa, Abner and Joab," in Kellner (ed.), *Contemporary Jewish Ethics*, 211–20.
62. Yad, *Mamrim*, 6:12.
63. Mish. Eduyot 5:6–7.

you close [to them] or cause you to be far [from them]." We are left in no doubt as to the moral heroism of Akavia's stand. The Mishnah itself records the tribute that "the Temple Court never closed before anyone in Israel equal to Akavia ben Mehalalel in wisdom and the fear of sin." The logic of his position, too, is clear. Giving testimony, he must report the facts as he remembers them. His colleagues remember them otherwise, but he cannot withhold the truth as he sees it. Here, then, is one instance of the integrity of principled dissent.

The other concerns one of the most famous passages in the entire rabbinic literature, the argument between Rabbi Eliezer ben Hyrcanus and the sages on the ritual cleanliness of a broken and reconstituted oven. Rabbi Eliezer declared it clean; the sages ruled against him. He "brought all the proofs in the world" for his view but none was accepted. After invoking several miracles, he finally appealed to Heaven itself, "whereupon a Heavenly Voice was heard saying: Why do you dispute with Rabbi Eliezer, seeing that in all matters the halakhah agrees with him?" This proof too was rejected, on the grounds that "It [the Torah] is not in heaven." Once the Torah has been given, its interpretation depends not on revelation but on the majority vote. Rabbi Eliezer was then excommunicated.

Attention is often given to the continuation of the passage, in which the Talmud celebrates the principle of rabbinic authority. Rabbi Nathan meets the prophet Elijah, who reports to him the reaction of Heaven to its defeat by the sages. "The Holy One, blessed be he...laughed [with joy], saying: my sons have defeated me, my sons have defeated me." But there is a further sequel, describing what happened when Rabbi Eliezer was excommunicated:

> He [Rabbi Eliezer] tore his clothes, removed his shoes, and sat on the earth. Tears streamed from his eyes. The world was then smitten: a third of the olive crop, a third of the wheat, and a third of the barley crop.... A *tanna* [sage] taught: Great was the calamity that befell that day, for everything on which Rabbi Eliezer cast his eyes was burned up. Rabban Gamliel too was travelling in a ship when a great wave arose to drown him. "It appears to me," he said, "that this can only be on account of Rabbi Eliezer ben

Hyrcanus." He arose and said, "Master of the Universe, you know full well that I have not acted for my honour, nor for the honour of my father's house, but for your honour, so that disputes should not multiply in Israel." The storm subsided.

The passage ends on a tragic note. Rabbi Eliezer prays to God about the incident. Rabban Gamliel dies. Rabbi Eliezer's wife, who was the sister of Rabban Gamliel, comments: "All gates [of prayer] may be locked, except the gates of wounded feelings."

The aggadic conflict is clear. Heaven appears, first on the side of Rabbi Eliezer, then on the side of the majority, and finally again on the side of the excommunicated Rabbi Eliezer. Rabbi Eliezer is one of the great tragic heroes of the rabbinic literature. Rabban Jochanan ben Zakkai, his teacher, declared that if all the sages of Israel were in one scale of the balance and Rabbi Eliezer in the other, he would outweigh them all.[64] When he died, Rabbi Akiva declared, "You have left the whole generation orphaned."[65] A tradition maintained that "when Rabbi Eliezer died, the scroll of Torah was hidden away."[66] Neither here nor elsewhere are we left in any doubt that his integrity was awe-inspiring. Heaven takes his side.[67] The excommunication is a tragedy. But it is an inevitable tragedy. The assertion of authority is necessary "so that disputes should not multiply in Israel."

THE PARADOX OF INTEGRITY

None of these sources endorses the idea of an autonomous "conscience."[68] Akavia, Rabbi Eliezer, and the rebellious elder do not act on the basis of moral intuition. They act on the basis of the tradition as they received or interpreted it. But it is the structure of the conflict that concerns us. At an aggadic level, their principled dissent is accorded an unmistakable

---

64. Mish. Avot 2:8.
65. Y. Shabbat 2:6.
66. Sotah 49b.
67. See also Shabbat 130a for another interesting example.
68. Michael Wyschogrod has explored the issue of conscience as such in his "Judaism and Conscience," in Asher Finkel and Lawrence Frizzel (eds.), *Standing before God* (New York: Ktav, 1981), 313–28.

ethical dignity. We admire their courage in defence of conviction. The literature invites us to. At the same time we recognize that there is no alternative to their exclusion from the community if halakhic authority is to remain. The conflict is not between right and wrong but between two kinds of right: individual and collective. Akavia and Rabbi Eliezer act rightly from the point of view of individual ideal. Their opponents act rightly from the point of view of social morality. There is no ethical resolution to this conflict. But there is a practical one. They are excommunicated. Halakhah is the constitution of a community, not a code of individual perfection. In a conflict between the integrity of the individual and the integrity of the legal system, the latter must win, even if Heaven aligns itself with the former.

The conclusion to which we are driven is this. The liberal Jew wishes Orthodoxy to respect the integrity of his abandonment of tradition. We have seen that integrity in the sense in which he uses the word – as the affirmation of the autonomous self – cannot be admitted as a virtue within the halakhic system. Here we are faced with an irresolvable conflict between traditional and modern consciousness. But tradition itself recognized another form of individual integrity, which arose when an individual read the tradition differently from the majority of his peers. This might have served as a model for a contemporary version of the dignity of dissent. But it is just this precedent that warns us of the consequences. Along with the dignity of dissent comes exclusion from the community. Dissent threatens halakhic authority humanly, as the autonomous self does conceptually. The liberal Jew associates integrity with *in*clusion in the covenantal community. Tradition associates it with *ex*clusion from that same community. Were Orthodoxy to accede to the liberal Jew's request, the consequences would be the reverse of what was sought.

Historically, this was in fact the case. Inclusivism was adopted by those halakhic authorities who were least inclined to take Reform or secular Judaisms at their face value. There were other Orthodox thinkers who were far more sympathetic to the Enlightenment culture out of which Reform arose. They understood Reform in its intellectual context. They took it seriously, judging it by its own standards of integrity. It was they who abjured inclusivism and sought instead to brand Reform as heresy and exclude it altogether.

Samson Raphael Hirsch took a positive view of emancipation and secular culture. He was educated at a secular high school and went to university. In his student days at the University of Bonn he had been a close friend of Abraham Geiger, the future Reform leader. Initially they had formed a preaching society together.[69] Hirsch none the less became the most zealous and unyielding critic of Reform in nineteenth-century Jewry. He was the leading spirit of Orthodox secession, the refusal to participate with Reform representatives in joint communal organizations, arguing that "the enforced unity of the community...is nothing but an empty, meaningless form."[70]

Rabbi Zvi Hirsch Chajes (1805–55), an outstanding Orthodox rabbinic scholar, was deeply sympathetic to the Enlightenment. He was one of the few traditionalist rabbis of his day to obtain a university doctorate,[71] and he was in close contact with other Enlightenment enthusiasts like Nachman Krochmal and Rabbi Solomon Judah Rapoport. But in his *Minchat Kenaot* (1849), a response to the radical Reform conferences of the 1840s, he made the most extreme exclusivist proposal of the nineteenth century. He argued that Reform Jews, or at least their leaders, be formally declared total gentiles like the Samaritans. It should be forbidden to marry them, mix socially with them, or mourn them.[72]

Hirsch and Chajes were men who understood Reform through its own categories. They had had the same exposure to the intellectual currents of their day as had the radical Reformers, Geiger and Holdheim. As a result they were far less inclined to be inclusive than the more traditional rabbinate. This, then, is the paradox of the Orthodox-Reform relationship. Reform, committed to pluralism, seeks Orthodox legitimation of its own principled integrity. But if this point of view were accepted by Orthodoxy it would lead to exclusivism and schism. Those like Hirsch and Chajes who were most able to see it as it saw itself were the most inclined to sever all relations with it. The alternative is

---

69. Liberles, *Religious Conflict in Social Context*, 116–24; Rosenbloom, *Tradition in an Age of Reform*, 61–5.
70. Liberles, *Religious Conflict in Social Context*, 202.
71. See *Encyclopaedia Judaica*, v. 327.
72. Z. H. Chajes, *Kol Sifrei Maharatz Chayes* (2 vols.; Jerusalem: Divrei Hachomim, 1958), 975–1031.

Orthodox delegitimation of Reform, which assaults Reform sensitivities but at the same time allows Reform Jews as individuals to be included within the halakhic community.

Pluralism conceives Jewish unity in terms of modern consciousness. Inclusivism conceives it in terms of traditional consciousness. The two, as we have seen, collide at the most fundamental conceptual level. Statements about the self, society, authority, autonomy, halakhah, integrity, and dissent that are made in the one mode cannot be translated into the other without dramatic reversals of meaning. The point made in the first chapter is here disclosed in its full and tragic depth: contemporary Jews are divided by a common language. Inclusivism cannot embrace the terms of liberal Judaism. Pluralism cannot incorporate Orthodoxy.

It is here that philosophical and sociological analysis reaches its limit. To have defined the problem is not to have solved it. Nor is it to have rendered it insoluble. It is, instead, to show that neither the traditional nor the modern approaches can achieve a complete solution. Each leaves a remainder unaccounted for. Pluralism cannot fully confront the language of tradition: objective truth and halakhic authority. Inclusivism cannot confront on its own terms the autonomous self. Each renders part of the problem theoretically and systematically invisible. The aim of analysis is to restore the remainders to visibility.

Do we then face tragedy? If not a schism, then the fated mutual incomprehensibility of tradition and modernity, Orthodoxy and liberal Judaism? Can there be conversation across this conceptual abyss? Or coexistence? Or convergence? Are the two versions of unity, the inclusivist and the pluralist, destined to divide the Jewish people?

Chapter 8

Schism?

I have described what seems to be the inexorable unfolding of tragedy. It is not merely that Orthodoxy and Reform are drifting further apart as the one rejects, the other adapts to, an increasingly secular and individualist culture. It is that the desire for unity is itself inherently and paradoxically divisive. The reason is that each side holds a different concept of unity: one inclusivist, the other pluralist. These two ideas are incompatible. They systematically exclude one another. The result is that the more vigorously unity is pursued, the further it recedes. An apparently shared wish that Jewry be "one people" is, it seems, destined to be frustrated by conceptual impasse and mutual incomprehension.

Was and is this inevitable? It is the result, let us recall, of the impact of enlightenment, emancipation, and secularization on a people that had hitherto been defined by halakhah, the constitution of Jewish law. This gave rise, initially in Germany and Austria and subsequently in America, to a series of religious denominations – Reform, Liberal, Conservative, and Reconstructionist – each of which involved a reinterpretation of the key terms of Jewish existence, especially of halakhah. Judaism had previously known differences and disputes: between Ashkenazim and Sephardim, rationalists and mystics, followers and critics of Maimonides, Hasidim and their opponents. But however acrimonious the arguments, the commitment of both sides to halakhah had prevented their deterioration to the point of schism.

Differences of a larger order, between Jews and early Christians, Rabbanites and Karaites, the rabbinic mainstream and the seventeenth- and eighteenth-century messianic movements of Shabbatai Zvi and Jacob Frank, had eventuated in fundamental splits that could not be contained within a single religious order. There is no precedent since Second Temple times for the coexistence of denominations, rival systems, fundamentally differing interpretations of Judaism. Nor does the Second Temple period, with its internecine rivalries and wars, provide a reliable model on which to predicate the present. Is there, then, a different route by which the collision between tradition and modernity might be negotiated, one that does not involve the fragmentation of Jewry into denominations? If so, might it yet be taken? If not, what are the implications?

ROSENZWEIG AND FACKENHEIM

One possibility of what one might call a non-denominational non-Orthodoxy is suggested by the thought of one of the most profound twentieth-century Jewish thinkers, Franz Rosenzweig (1886–1929). Born to highly assimilated parents in Kassel, Germany, Rosenzweig came to the brink of conversion to Christianity. What diverted him from this course was an experience of Orthodoxy in Berlin, and he was led further back towards tradition by his encounter, during the First World War, with Eastern European Jewry.[1]

Rosenzweig died young and never completed his full "return" to tradition. Nor was this his exact intention. The twentieth-century European Jew was, he argued, a child of his time and could not escape his cultural situation as heir to post-Enlightenment thought. As he put it

---

1. Franz Rosenzweig's major work is *The Star of Redemption* [1921], trans. William Hallo (London: Routledge and Kegan Paul for the Littman Library, 1971). The best introduction to his life and work is N. N. Glatzer, *Franz Rosenzweig: His Life and Thought* (New York: Schocken, 1961). A book of essays has recently been published: Paul Mendes-Flohr (ed.), *The Philosophy of Franz Rosenzweig* (Hanover, NH: University Press of New England, 1988). See esp. the essay by Ernst Simon, "Rosenzweig: Recollections of a Disciple," ibid. 202–13.

in his speech at the opening of his new house of learning, the Frankfurt *Freies Jüdisches Lehrhaus*, the Jew returning to tradition "must not give up anything, renounce anything," but should instead "lead everything back to Judaism."[2] He must find his way back without ceasing to be a "modern" Jew. Part of this was relatively straight-forward, though revolutionary enough for someone of Rosenzweig's background and time. The texts of the Jewish heritage were no longer to be considered part of a discarded past. They were to be studied as the resources through which the Jew defines his present. But learning was one thing, doing was another. It was here that Rosenzweig confronted the central problem of Jewish modernity. Was it possible to find room for the idea of halakhah? The past might be studied, even experienced, but did it still have the power to command?

Rosenzweig's colleague, Martin Buber, thought not. Revelation, for Buber, did not have propositional content. It did not yield *law*. Law was universal. Revelation was immediate and specific. It was, in the phrase he coined, an "I-Thou" encounter. Rosenzweig challenged Buber in an open letter, published as *The Builders: Concerning Jewish Law*.[3] Law, he argued, lay at the heart of Judaism. One could not translate it out and still be faithful to Judaism's historic character. It was no longer possible to treat the law as if it were given and self- evident, but it was still possible to experience it in its inwardness, to have an I-Thou experience of halakhah. But this could only come about by trying to keep it. The law "cannot be known like knowledge, but can only be done."[4]

Rosenzweig, as a characteristically modern thinker, places the self – not community or law – at the heart of his system. But the individual can still turn "law" (*Geselz*) into "commandment" (*Gebot*) by experiencing it not as a cold, external rule but as a living imperative addressed to the self. This is not the "autonomous" self of modern Reform Judaism, self-legislating and choosing which laws to keep and which not. Rosenzweig's self does not make its own laws. Instead it attempts to listen to the

---

2. Glatzer, *Franz Rosenzweig*, 231.
3. Franz Rosenzweig, *On Jewish Learning*, ed. N. N. Glatzer (New York: Schocken, 1955), 72–92.
4. Ibid., 82.

law of Torah as a commandment "which he must fulfil, simply because he cannot allow it to remain unfulfilled."[5]

Not everyone will be able to keep all the laws this way. Each person will come to his own discovery, necessarily unique and private, of what he can keep and what not. But (and this is the crux) it will not be a matter of what he *chooses* to do, but a matter of what he *can* do. The "selection does not depend on the will but on our ability." Rosenzweig's philosophy of law is an attempt to break away from autonomy towards theonomy, the recognition that the command comes from outside the self even as it is appropriated and internalized by the self. "The deed is created at the boundary of the merely do-able, where the voice of the commandment causes the spark to leap from 'I must' to 'I can.'"[6] This sentence is a kind of modern midrash on the biblical phrase in which the Israelites at Sinai accepted the commands: "We will do and we will listen." For Rosenzweig, "doing" becomes a form of "listening."

A very similar position, philosophically more explicit, was advanced by Emil Fackenheim in an essay written in 1938, though published only recently. Fackenheim is the most impressive of the post-Holocaust liberal theologians. His thought, as we saw in an earlier chapter, is consciously incompatible with tradition in its insistence that the Holocaust represents a "hermeneutic rupture," an unbridgeable abyss, between the Jewish past and the Jewish present. But shortly before leaving Nazi Germany, Fackenheim addressed himself to the question posed by Rosenzweig. Can the contemporary Jew, without sacrificing his contemporariness, confront Jewish law? His paper "Our Position toward Halakhah" gives an answer in the affirmative.[7]

Fackenheim begins by recognizing the form of the problem. The twentieth-century man of faith approaches religion from the outside. He judges it "in terms of standards he already brings to it." The result is that "religion is measured by the nature of the one who does the judging."

---

5. Ibid., 86.
6. Ibid.
7. In *The Jewish Thought of Emil Fackenheim: A Reader*, ed. Michael Morgan (Detroit: Wayne State University Press, 1987), 21–25. See Fackenheim's own comments on the article, ibid. 8. Fackenheim's most recent statement still adheres to this position. See his *What Is Judaism?* (New York: Collier, 1987), 145–46.

Halakhah fares badly in this process, but Fackenheim identifies two ways of salvaging it for the modern mind. He calls them, respectively, the "religious" and the "national." The "religious" way is to see Jewish law as arousing religious feelings or satisfying religious needs. This is the classic liberal strategy, one that results when religion is privatized and translated from external truth to internal experience. The "national" way is to see Jewish law as the creation and binding force of the Jewish people as a whole. It is an expression of peoplehood. Fackenheim does not identify these two approaches further, but we recognize them as the broad strategies, respectively, of Reform Judaism on the one hand, and Mordecai Kaplan's Reconstructionism on the other.

Both salvage elements of traditional halakhic behaviour, but not the idea of halakhah itself. For Jewish law, on either version, "is viewed as a spiritual creation of earlier Jewish generations, and nothing more." Revelation and command are left out of the equation. Traditional conduct becomes no more than "custom and ceremony." It ceases to be halakhic, for halakhah "confronts us as *Commandment*, Commandment therefore *given by the other*." It demands to be actualized in daily life, not just as an aesthetic means to religious experience or as a sociological instrument of group survival. For halakhah to be possible, one must be willing and able to let oneself be addressed by the Other. The self must break out of its autism. Here, then, Fackenheim faces the problem Rosenzweig confronted. Can the modern Jew transcend the autonomous self and hear the commanding voice of Sinai?

Jews in the past did just this. The Jewish people "has always attempted *not to say it* [the command] *to itself but to let itself be addressed*." The contemporary Jew does not have the same faith as his predecessors. All he has is a "readiness to faith." Yet he desires to hear the same "Word" as his ancestors, spoken at Sinai, explicated by unbroken centuries of rabbinic interpretation. In seeking to recover the bond with the past he must therefore be ready to admit the idea of "the Other as Demanding." The present generation "must seek to recover a bond with its ancestors, in order thus to be able, as it were, to stand at Sinai itself, i.e., in order thus genuinely to become *Klal Yisrael* not only horizontally but vertically as well." In order to do this, Jews must begin with deeds, with "some of the doing of our ancestors." As Rosenzweig, too, had warned, not all of tradition will be "do-able." But it is in the leap of action that the contemporary Jew transcends his doubts. "Whether or not our doing will answer to the Demanding we cannot know. All we can do is be ready, and in this readiness *attempt to do even as we remain questioners.*"

How then does the thought of Rosenzweig and Fackenheim bear on the subject at hand, the division of Jewry into denominations? Each recognized the gap between modernity and tradition, especially as it affected the understanding of revelation and halakhah. But neither sought to bridge it by a synthesis of two essentially opposed cultures. Neither, in other words, sought a solution in terms of a religious movement, a denomination. Instead they acknowledged that halakhah exists: not a new Reform or Conservative halakhah, but the halakhah of tradition, the written and oral laws of Sinai. To be sure, the contemporary non-Orthodox Jew is alienated from it. Only by great striving can he or she confront it at all. But halakhah is Jewishly unavoidable. Around it and its concepts – revelation, covenant, the oral law – the Jewish people had constituted itself in the past. Only by accepting the givenness and otherness of halakhah can the abyss between present and past be overcome so that the Jew can once again be in dialogue with Hillel and Rabbi Akiva, Rashi and Maimonides. Without halakhah there can be no Judaic continuity.

Their solution to the contradiction between divine command and human autonomy is philosophically close to the position taken by many Orthodox thinkers, among them Rabbi Soloveitchik in *Halakhic Man*. In hearing the command, the Jew "does not experience any consciousness of compulsion accompanying the norm. Rather, it seems to him as though he discovered the norm in his innermost self, as though it was not just a commandment that had been imposed upon him, but an existential law of his very being."[8] Two things, however, differentiate Rosenzweig and Fackenheim from Soloveitchik. The first is that what for Soloveitchik is already a state of mind is for them an aspiration, an end-point to be reached. Soloveitchik speaks from within a traditional consciousness. Rosenzweig and Fackenheim see that frame of mind as not yet theirs, though they wish as far as possible to make it so.

---

8. Soloveitchik, *Halakhic Man*, 64–65.

The second, and more obviously significant, is that Rosenzweig and Fackenheim both predict that, for the modern Jew, not everything will be "do-able." Neither thinker is willing to lay down criteria in advance of what commands can be done and what left undone. That would have been wholly at odds with their philosophical purpose. They believed this question could only be answered by the individual. Even the same individual would give different answers at different stages of his or her religious development. It is this, though, that separates them from Orthodoxy. The Orthodox thinker takes as a paradigm Abraham at the binding of Isaac. When faced with a conflict between command and conscience, command takes precedence. Rosenzweig's point is that we are not Abraham. There are times when we cannot "hear" the command, even though we know it.

So Rosenzweig and Fackenheim did not restate Orthodoxy. They did something conceptually more interesting. They reformulated liberal Judaism into a not-yet-Orthodoxy. Taking as their contemporary starting-point the detraditionalized self, they outlined a way in which such a self might attempt the road back to revelation and halakhah. They gave an account of what it would be for modern consciousness to, as it were, stand in the presence of tradition. This is a project whose religious integrity Orthodoxy should not find impossible, or even difficult, to recognize.[9] For it addresses the very issue which Orthodoxy itself must address, albeit from the opposite perspective.

The alienation of the majority of contemporary Jews from tradition is a fact with which Orthodoxy has had to reckon. Though the covenant is not "voluntary," any contemporary Jewish thinker must find room for the fact that halakhic observance, even Jewish identification, in open societies is experienced as voluntary to a degree unknown in the pre-modern *kehillah.* "It is much more probable today than ever before that a Jew who remains faithful to the covenant...is acting out

---

9. See, e.g., the tributes paid to Rosenzweig by Orthodox writers: Schwab, *The History of Orthodox Jewry in Germany,* 127; Eliezer Berkovits, *Major Themes in Modern Philosophies of Judaism* (New York: Ktav, 1974), 37–38; David Miller, "Traditionalism and Estrangement," in Phillip Longworth (ed.), *Confrontations with Judaism* (London: Blond, 1967), 209–11.

of conscience instead of social conformity."[10] The gap between the real and the ideal, the contemporary Jew and traditional Judaism, has been bridged in twentieth-century Orthodox thought in essentially the same way as Rosenzweig and Fackenheim proposed, namely by invoking the idea of *teshuvah* or "return." *Teshuvah* occupies a central place in the thought of both Rabbi Soloveitchik[11] and Rabbi Kook,[12] and in both it carries a wider, more biblical resonance than it had in rabbinic thought. *Teshuvah* is not simply or even primarily repentance for transgression. It is a return of the alienated self to tradition.

Rosenzweig and Fackenheim provide the basis for a not-yet-Orthodoxy which does not seek to *legitimate* deviations from halakhah and thus in effect create alternative communal norms. One could imagine both Reform and Conservative practice reconceived along these lines. Rather than taking the autonomous self or the ethics of the age as their central values, they would instead ask the question: How much of tradition can be actualized by this individual, or this congregation, at this moment? The fact that some of it could not, would not be justified *de jure,* but conceded *de facto.* Halakhah would exist as an absolute and an ideal, but the existential situation of contemporary Jewry would, at the same time, be granted its own integrity. Not all of the tradition can be appropriated by today's Jews, but neither it nor its authority is to be rejected. Instead, Judaically, the times are out of joint. The commanding voice of Sinai is only imperfectly heard in the distorting atmosphere of an individualistic culture. The modern Jew lives in the relativities of his time, but through them he can occasionally respond to the absolute. He observes as much of Judaism as he can, and aspires to do more. The rest is "not yet" rather than "not ever."

Such a philosophy, if adopted, would not alter the *fact* of the widespread abandonment of halakhah, but would prevent its *institutionalization* into separate movements and denominations. Why, then, has this route not been taken?[13] Clearly, it has not answered to the ideological

---

10. Wyschogrod, "Judaism and Conscience," 326.
11. Soloveitchik, *Al Hateshuvah.*
12. Kook, *Orot Hateshuvah.*
13. It is, however, advocated in Dennis Prager and Joseph Telushkin's popular work,

commitments of many Reform and Conservative leaders. For them, the encounter with post-Enlightenment philosophical, political, and historical thought has been decisive.[14] In their view, Judaism is not an absolute, presently experienced in the midst of a relativizing culture. Rather, contemporary culture yields its own absolutes (the autonomous self, or the ethics of the age), against which tradition must be seen as relative.

Inexorably, too, the pressures of social integration in the West seemed to call for institutional rather than merely individual accommodation. In the nineteenth century this involved, for radical Reform, massive changes, including the abolition of circumcision, the permission of work on the Sabbath, the abandonment of Jewish laws of divorce, and substantial liturgical innovations. Today, for American Reform and British Liberal Judaism, they include acceptance of intermarriage, legitimation of homosexuality, and a rejection of all laws differentiating men and women. If the realities of acculturated Jewish life were to be given religious expression, it would have to be *de jure* rather than merely *de facto*. The tensions between halakhic ideal and the real lives of Jews were too great to be held in balance. They called for justification that would allow Jews a sense of consistency. The varieties of liberal Judaism provided it. In their different ways they validated the actual transformations of Jewish life by proposing new criteria of religious behaviour. The path made available by Rosenzweig and Fackenheim was not taken. One does not need to doubt the integrity of those concerned to see that this was a fateful development. Alternative norms of Jewish conduct were proposed. Rivals were established to the halakhic system. One possibility of a non-denominational modern Jewry was declined.

HIRSCHENSOHN AND KOOK

So was another, this time from the opposite direction – from that of the halakhic community itself. Jewish law could and can be seen from two perspectives, each of which has ample representation in the early and medieval rabbinic literature. It could be understood as the divine

---

The Nine Questions People Ask about Judaism (New York: Simon and Schuster, 1981), 159–61.

14. See, e.g., Borowitz, *Choices in Modern Jewish Thought*, 243–72.

will, through obedience to which an *individual* achieves perfection. Or it could be understood as the divine constitution of a covenantal people, through which a *nation* achieves sanctification. For a prolonged period, between the first and nineteenth centuries CE, the differences between these two conceptions was neither pronounced nor critical. Both motifs, for example, are present in the philosophical writings of Moses Maimonides. On the one hand, for Maimonides, the commandments are social and political in intent. They shape, directly or obliquely and through the course of time, a society built on virtue and truth.[15] On the other hand, their performance, if accompanied by intense meditative concentration, brings about a wholly personal union between the human mind and God.[16] Halakhah, then, was both private and public. At Sinai, said the sages, a covenant was enacted with the people as a whole and with each individual separately.[17]

So long as Jewish law retained its primacy over Jewish life, these two ideas were not in conflict. But with modernity, they split asunder. Halakhah now became the code not of a people but of a section of it, namely those who adhered to Orthodoxy. What then became of the idea of halakhah as the constitution of a nation? As we saw in the chapters on Orthodoxy, a marked divergence of views was possible. There were those, spanning the spectrum from Samson Raphael Hirsch to the disciples of Rabbi Moses Sofer, who emphasized the priority of Torah over peoplehood and who were willing, as a result, to secede from the wider Jewish community. But there were others who attached greater weight to the Jewish people as an indivisible nation,[18] and as a result saw Torah and halakhah as inseparable from the collective life of Jews.

The natural focus of their thoughts was the land of Israel. In the diaspora, as a result of emancipation, Judaism had been made private. It could no longer represent a total culture. The return of Jews to Israel, though, offered the hope of covenantal renewal. Torah might once again

---

15. *Guide of the Perplexed*, ii. 40, iii. 27–49.
16. Ibid., iii. 51.
17. See *Tosafot*, Sotah 8:10–11.
18. See *Tana Devei Eliyahu*, 14: "My son, most people think that the Torah comes first, but I tell you that Israel comes first": *Tana Devei Eliyahu*, ed. M. Friedmann (Jerusalem: Bonberger and Wahrman, 1960, 71).

become the constitution of a nation, through the instrumentality of a Jewish state. Admittedly, the Zionist movement itself and those moved by it to join the early waves of immigration were predominantly secular. But here lay the challenge: to reinterpret Jewish law in such a way as to make it viable as the code of a modern society.

In the early decades of the twentieth century this line of thought was explored by Rabbi Chaim Hirschensohn.[19] Torah, for him, was essentially covenantal: the agreement of the Israelites, binding on their descendants, to be governed by divine law. It was this that constituted Jewry as a nation. Other nations had been forged through race or territory. Jewry had not, for it accepted converts from other races and had lived out most of its history in dispersion. The connection between Torah and peoplehood was axiomatic. An emergent Jewish state must necessarily, then, have a distinctive constitution. Other states were governed by a social contract, an agreement between their members. Israel was governed by a divine covenant, an agreement between the people and God. But this in turn demanded that the covenant be viable. It must be a code by which most of its members could live. The restrictive legislation by which the sages had protected biblical law was now counter-productive. It was effective for a people suffering the onslaught of Greek and Roman power. But it was ill-suited to a population celebrating, after eighteen hundred years, a return to free national life. Hirschensohn was a committed halakhist, deeply opposed to Reform Judaism. But he believed that the halakhic system itself contained both the mandate and the flexibility to adapt to modernity. In particular, he defended democracy and the participation of women in elective government on halakhic grounds.

A similar approach has more recently been argued by Yeshayahu Leibowitz and Eliezer Berkovits. Leibowitz, while convinced of the immutability of halakhah in relationships between man and God and man and man, believes that development is possible and necessary in the case of relationships between man and state. There is, he maintains, a distinction between laws which bring institutions into existence and those which merely regulate pre-existing practices. The Jewish laws of prayer created the possibility of prayer, but the Jewish laws of slavery

---

19. Hirschensohn's thought is well summarized in Schweid, *Demokratiah Vehalakhah*.

did not create slavery. Halakhah in its social and political dimension took institutions already extant and proceeded to regulate and transform them. It must do so now in the context of a Jewish state. Halakhic innovation was necessary because rabbinic Judaism, which gave Torah law its systematic exposition, reached its full flowering after the demise of Jewish sovereignty with the destruction of the Second Temple. Rabbinic law takes for granted the absence of Jewish responsibility for an economy and a defence force. Even the code of government contained in Maimonides' "Laws of Kings" is a theoretical construction, never tested against the exigencies of political power. The observance of Jewish law in the State of Israel is, Leibowitz argued, currently predicated on the fact that many of its essential services will be performed by non-observant or secular Jews, who are thus cast into the role of gentiles. But this means that halakhah currently fails its own test of universalizability, namely that it should be capable of being fulfilled by all Jews simultaneously.[20]

Eliezer Berkovits draws a somewhat different distinction. For him the central feature of Jewish law is its conception of a dual Torah. The written law, recorded in the Pentateuch, is timeless and universal. The oral law is time-specific and particular. Its task is to translate Torah into the immediacies of a given situation. The essence of the oral law is that it is not written down. It could not be, because the rulings appropriate to one generation may not be relevant to the next. In exile, both Jewish law and Jewish life had been frozen into stasis. One of the symptoms of this was that the oral law had been written down, codified, and thus deprived of its essential responsiveness to change. Jews had now returned to Israel, but halakhah remained in exile. Berkovits argued the case for a recovery of the flexibility that oral law had once had in the hands of its early practitioners. In particular, he emphasized the role of reason and ethics in the judicial process. Considerations of justice and Jewish unity, he argued, should now lead halakhists to reconsider the role of women in religious life, to adjust the laws of marriage so that a woman could

---

20. Yeshayahu Leibowitz, *Yahadut, Am Yehudi, Umedinat Yisrael* (Jerusalem: Schocken, 1979); id., *Emunah, Historiah, Ve'arakhim* (Jerusalem: Academon, 1982).

not be held captive by a husband who refused to grant her a divorce, and to liberalize the laws of conversion.[21]

Each of these approaches was, in effect, an attempt to move beyond "Orthodoxy," as the religion of a minority, to Torah, as the effective law of an entire nation. In a very different way from Rosenzweig and Fackenheim's, these thinkers were likewise engaged in a battle against the *de facto* denominalization of Jewish life. They too failed. In part, doubtless, this was because their proposals were too radical. They involved stretching halakhah to its limits and beyond. The weight of precedent was against them. With the end of the Sanhedrin, the compilation of the Mishnah, the closure of the Talmud, and the absence of a body with formal and global legal authority, Jewish law had evolved in an increasingly conservative direction. New legislation or reinterpretation of the scope envisaged by Hirschensohn, Leibowitz, and Berkovits was almost certainly fated to be deemed *ultra vires*. Some thinkers, most notably Rabbi Judah Leib Maimon, vested their hopes in a reconstitution of the Sanhedrin in the new state, a project which Maimonides had intimated was possible.[22] But this would have required wide-spread consensus, and it was not forthcoming.

But in part, the failure of Hirschensohn and others to secure support for their proposals was due to the same fragmenting forces that left Rosenzweig, too, a lonely figure. Secularization has divided Jews in Israel no less than in the diaspora, perhaps more so. So long as halakhah was the lived, enforced code of the Jewish people, there were considerations, recognized by the halakhah itself, rendering it responsive to crises in Jewish life. There were rulings based on the principle of the economic viability of Judaism, "the Torah treats protectively the money of Israel."[23] There were others based on the need to maintain peaceful relations with the majority population: the halakhic principles of "the ways of

21. Eliezer Berkovits, *Crisis and Faith* (New York: Sanhedrin, 1976); id., *Hahalakhah, Kochah Vetafkidah* (Jerusalem: Mosad Harav Kook, 1981); id., *Not in Heaven*; id., *Jewish Women in Time and Torah* (Hoboken, NJ: Ktav, 1990).

22. J. L. Maimon, *Chidush Sanhedrin Bimedinatenu Hamechudeshet* (Jerusalem: Mosad Harav Kook, 1951).

23. See *Entziklopediah Talmudit*, xi, s.v. *Hatorah chasah al mammonam shel Yisrael*, 240–45.

peace" and "the avoidance of animosity."[24] There were limits imposed on martyrdom at times when it seemed as if the leadership of the Jewish community might choose on religious grounds to die rather than to live.[25] There were limits to the divisive impact of religious teachings and sanctions in the face of non-observance of Jewish law. The Talmud had established rules of tactical silence. "Just as it is a command to say that which will be heeded, so it is a command not to say that which will not be heeded" was one.[26] "Let Israel go their way: better that they sin unwittingly than knowingly" was another.[27] Halakhic authorities had to consider carefully the effects of the imposition of punishments such as excommunication. Should they still be implemented if they might have the effect of driving the offender to apostasy, or, as the rabbis called it, *tarbut ra'ah,* "bad ways"? Rabbi Moses Isserles ruled that they should;[28] others disagreed;[29] Rabbi David ibn Abi Zimra (Radbaz) concluded that the court had to weigh the consequences in each instance.[30]

Each of these principles had the effect of moderating halakhic rulings to preempt a possible divorce between Jewish law and the realities of Jewish life. They operated within defined limits: they could be invoked only when the halakhah itself granted its exponents discretionary power. But they operated, too, within a specific environment, namely the adherence of Jews to Jewish law. Once that ceased, a fundamental change took place in the *Sitz im Leben,* the life-setting, of halakhah. Jewish law became, in effect if not in principle, the voluntary code of a self-selecting elite. Those who remain within Orthodoxy can *ipso facto* live by its standards. Those who abandon it, do not turn to it for solutions which can be found, with less difficulty, in Conservative, Reform,

---

24. For a survey of these principles and their application see *Entziklopediah Talmudit,* vol. i, s.v. *Eivah,* 228–30, and vol. vii, s.v. *Darkhei shalom,* 716–24.

25. Sanhedrin 74a. See also David Daube, *Collaboration with Tyranny in Rabbinic Law* (Oxford: Oxford University Press, 1965).

26. Yevamot 65b.

27. Beitzah 30a, Shabbat 148b.

28. *Shulchan Arukh, Yoreh De'ah* 334:1.

29. See *Turei Zahav* on *Yoreh De'ah* 334:1; *Chatam Sofer* on *Yoreh De'ah,* 322; *Pachad Yitzchak,* s.v. "Gilui Arayot"; Zvi Hirsch Chajes, *Darkhei Hora'ah,* ch. 6, in his *Kol Sifrei,* 269–80, and *Minchat Kenaot,* ibid. 1021–27.

30. *Radbaz,* i. 187.

or secular Israeli versions of Jewish life. The delicate interplay between Jewish law and the Jewish people – the collective, covenantal dimension of the halakhah – has been disrupted by the seismic effects of modernity. The result has been that there have been few left to support the proposals advocated by Hirschensohn and others. Their programme lacks a constituency. The bifurcation they sought to avoid, between those within and those outside the halakhic system, has occurred, and its divisive potential grows with time.

What has emerged in Israel in recent years is not a convergence but a confrontation between secular and religious publics.[31] The Orthodox voice that has gained most power has not been that of religious Zionism with its vision of societal harmony under the sovereignty of Jewish law. Instead it has been that of groups who explicitly see Orthodoxy as one sectional interest among others. Orthodoxy as a whole has moved towards more sectarian forms of organization and thought, and to adversarial stances towards secular culture and non-Orthodox Jewry. The dynamic of division and denomination, once introduced into Jewish life, is tenacious and self-reinforcing. Orthodoxy is driven to define itself increasingly as a movement of resistance, while those outside are progressively convinced that halakhah does not speak to their situation.

The most complex, haunting response to the crisis of halakhah and modernity was given by Rabbi Abraham Kook, himself an exotic combination of radical mystic and traditional halakhist. He wrote:

> Sometimes, when there is a need for a [temporary] transgression of the words of Torah and the generation lacks a figure who can show the [halakhic] way, the result comes about instead by rebellion [*hitpartzut*]. It is none the less preferable that it should happen by unwitting transgression. This is the basis for the principle "Better that they sin unwittingly than that they sin knowingly." Only when prophecy exists in Israel is it possible to remedy the

---

31. See Liebman and Don-Yehiya, *Religion and Politics in Israel*; Charles Liebman (ed.), *Religious and Secular: Conflict and Accommodation between Jews in Israel* (Jerusalem: Keter, 1990). For a secular reaction see Uri Huppert, *Back to the Ghetto* (New York: Prometheus, 1988).

situation by a temporary ruling [*hora'at sha'ah*], so that the result occurs through permission and the open fulfilment of a religious command [*bederekh heter umitzvah begalui*]. When the light of prophecy is screened, the remedy [*tikun*] comes about through rebellion, which grieves the heart in itself, but gladdens it by its ultimate result.[32]

These are remarkable sentiments; indeed, for an Orthodox thinker, they are unique.[33] They embody Kook's conviction that Divine providence was at work in the changes being brought about by secularists; above all, the Jewish rebirth in the land of Israel. Yet they precisely pose the alternatives. How are halakhists to respond to a situation where Jewish law and life have drifted apart?

There are, as Kook notes, three possibilities. The first is temporary halakhic accommodation, *hora'at sha'ah*. The second is tactical silence, letting transgressors sin unwittingly. The third is active denunciation, which creates rebellion. One who fully believes in providence will have the faith that the results of all three strategies will be the same. That which Heaven wishes to happen will happen. But Kook leaves us in no doubt as to his preferred alternative, *hora'at sha'ah*, a temporary, emergency adjustment of the law to the times. He is equally clear as to why it is the route not taken. The generation is unworthy. The prophetic spirit is in eclipse. Halakhic leadership of that transcending order, he profoundly believed, lay in the future, not the present. Jewish law, in other words, cannot function with the full flexibility of tradition until it recovers its traditional constituency; until Jews once again become a people of halakhah.

---

32. Kook, *Arpelei Tohar*, 15.

33. In fact, in their original version they were more radical still. The last sentence in the quotation, for example, originally read: "When the light of prophecy is screened, the remedy comes about through rebellion, which grieves the heart *because of its external form*, but gladdens it *because of its inner essence*." On this version, rebellion against halakhah might possess an inner sanctity. The antinomian potential of this remark is obvious, and the text was amended by the editors when the work was republished. See Binyamin Ish-Shalom, *Harav Kook: Bein Ratzionalizm Lemistikah* (Tel Aviv: Am Oved, 1990), 190–91 and 321, n. 115. On antinomian Jewish mysticism see Scholem, *The Messianic Idea in Judaism*, 78–141.

TWO JEWRIES?

Rabbi Kook leaves us with short-term pessimism and long-term optimism. The two ways in which a rift between Orthodoxy and others might conceivably have been avoided were routes not taken. Liberal Judaism did not adopt the approach of Rosenzweig. Orthodoxy did not take the path of Rabbi Hirschensohn. Kook's pessimism has been vindicated. Has his optimism? Given the schismatic tendencies in contemporary Jewish religious life, what is the likely outcome?

Two problems dominate all others: divorce and conversion. In Jewish law the requirements of *get*, a bill of divorce, are highly exacting, demanding great halakhic expertise. Already in the 1840s, however, German Reform was beginning to abandon the religious procedure of *get* altogether in favour of accepting a civil divorce as sufficient. Samuel Holdheim had argued that, with emancipation, "whatever has reference to interhuman relationships of a political, legal and civil character" was no longer the province of biblical or rabbinic law. Instead the rabbinic principle that "the law of the land is law" was to be applied.[34] The entire structure of Jewish family law was to be dismantled. This became accepted practice in the American Reform movement.

The problem that arises is this. If a woman remarries without obtaining a valid divorce from her first husband, her children by her second marriage are illegitimate, *mamzerim*, in Jewish law. Jewish law has a narrower definition of illegitimacy than most forms of secular law. A child is not illegitimate by being born out of wedlock. It is a *mamzer* only if born as the result of an incestuous or adulterous union. In the present instance, the woman is regarded as still married to her first husband until validly divorced. A new relationship is therefore adulterous, and children born from it are *mamzerim*. As such they carry a stigma with tragic consequences: they may not marry a legitimate Jew.

The Reform abandonment of halakhic divorce thus creates a halakhic fact of illegitimacy which excludes children of remarriages from themselves marrying any but a minority of Jews. The potential for human grief is enormous. Why, though, if the problem has existed since the 1840s, has it only recently become critical? For two reasons. First

---

34. Graff, *Separation of Church and State*, 121–23.

is the unexpected persistence of both Orthodoxy and Reform. Within each group the problem does not arise. Within Orthodoxy, the requirement of *get* remains in place. Within Reform, the law of the *mamzer* was abandoned along with religious divorce. The problem arises at the boundaries: when a Reform Jew wishes to marry an Orthodox Jew. Neither group seriously contemplated this possibility. Orthodoxy saw Reform as destined for extinction by its rapid assimilation. Reform saw Orthodoxy as scheduled for eclipse by the inevitable tide of modernity. Each now realizes that the other has survived. The question of marriage across the boundaries is real.

The second reason is the rising incidence of divorce itself. The Jewish community had traditionally been known for the stability of its marriages. In recent decades, however, the national divorce rate in America and other Western countries has risen sharply, and the Jewish pattern has more closely approximated the national norm (though still below it). By 1971, for example, the National Jewish Population Survey discovered that among the 25- to 29-year-old group, 15 per cent of all households were separated or divorced.[35] This, combined with the fact that non-Orthodox groups constitute a majority of American Jews, has led Irving Greenberg to estimate that there will be 100,000–200,000 *mamzerim* in America by the year 2000.[36] The figure has been challenged by the sociologist Steven M. Cohen as an overestimate,[37] but even he projects two thousand cases a year. The problem is qualitative as well as quantitative. Each case represents a potential tragedy. Each, too, adds to the likelihood of a complete schism between Orthodoxy and Reform, for it brings nearer the point at which, formally or informally, marriage across the divide will become precarious.

The second problem – that of conversion, or more generally "Who is a Jew?" – arises thus. According to Jewish law, to be a Jew is to be born of a Jewish mother. A halakhic procedure is necessary only for one who *becomes* a Jew, namely, a convert. The halakhic criteria of

35. Samuel C. Heilman, "The Jewish Family Today: An Overview," in Jonathan Sacks (ed.), *Tradition and Transition* (London: Jews' College Publications, 1986), 197.

36. Greenberg, *One Jewish People?*

37. Steven M. Cohen, "The One in 2000 Controversy," *Moment*, 12:1 (1987), 11–17.

conversion are straightforward: immersion in a *mikveh*, circumcision for males, and *kabalat hamitzvot*, acceptance of the commands.[38] The problem, however, arises with non-Orthodox conversions. In American Reform, for example, these often involve neither immersion nor circumcision. Even when both are undertaken, there is the question of acceptance of the commands. Since Reform denies the binding character of Jewish law, and even Conservative Judaism rejects some of its tenets, this will be questionable in most cases.[39] In addition, the conversion procedures must be undergone in the presence of a court of law. One composed of non-Orthodox rabbis who dissent from fundamental principles of Jewish faith would not be halakhically recognized.[40] Finally, conversion must represent the acceptance of Judaism for its own sake, not for ulterior motive.[41] Since many conversions outside Orthodoxy are prompted by prospective marriage to a Jewish partner, this too constitutes an obstacle to their recognition.

As with divorce, the problem is of long standing, but its impact is relatively recent. The key factor here is intermarriage between Jews and non-Jews. Intermarriage rates in American Jewry had been estimated as no more than 1 per cent in the 1920s. By the 1980s they had risen sharply. Rates varied from city to city, and according to age-group and educational background, but they converged on the figure of one in three. By 1991 a survey revealed that half of those married below the age of 30 had outmarried. Attitudes to intermarriage were also changing. The 1975 Boston survey revealed that acceptance of the phenomenon was growing rapidly; it had lost its taboo for the young. Those who married out were no longer inclined to see this as their exit from Judaism. They wished still to be identified as Jews.[42] This posed a formidable problem for Reform, who were suffering most from the attrition.

---

38. Yad, *Isurei Bi'ah* 13–14; *Shulchan Arukh, Yoreh De'ah* 268.

39. See *Achi'ezer*, 3:26; *Igerot Mosheh, Yoreh De'ah*, i. 157, 160.

40. See J. David Bleich, "Permitting Use of a *Mikveh* for Non-Orthodox Conversion," *Tradition*, 23:2 (1988), 88–95.

41. *Shulchan Arukh, Yoreh De'ah* 268:12.

42. The statistical evidence is surveyed in Jonathan Sacks, "Towards 2000: The American Experience," *L'Eylah*, 23 (1987), 23–27.

A series of radical policies emerged. The requirements for conversion of the non-Jewish spouse were scaled down. An active outreach policy was developed towards the outmarried. What, though, of the cases where the non-Jewish partner is unwilling to convert? Although officially discouraged, some 40 per cent of Reform rabbis will officiate at mixed marriages where there has been no conversion of the non-Jewish partner. A further 30 per cent will not do so themselves, but will refer the couple to a rabbi who will.[43]

The problem then arose as to the status of the children of such marriages. In 1983, the Reform rabbinate ratified its commitment to the principle of patrilineal Jewish identity, whereby a child is presumed Jewish if either of its parents is Jewish, the presumption being established by "timely and appropriate acts of identification with the Jewish faith and people." This came close to an official acceptance of intermarriage, for even where the non-Jewish mother did not convert, the children could still be considered Jewish if they so chose. More even than in the case of divorce, the numerical impact of these policies is vast. Their tragic potential, too, is immense, for it means that by now some hundreds of thousands of individuals who have received Reform conversions or patrilineal Jewish identity, or are the children of women who have, consider themselves Jewish and halakhically are not.[44]

It is over Reform policies on personal status more than any other issue that religious schism threatens Jewry. Jewish history records two precedents illustrative of the course of conflict. One is the tension between the schools of Hillel and Shammai, during which, according to the Talmud, "disputes multiplied and the Torah became like two Torahs."[45] The Mishnah none the less records that "though one school prohibited and the other permitted, the schools of Hillel and Shammai did not refrain from marrying one another."[46] A final breach was avoided.

43. Bulka, *The Coming Cataclysm*, 44.
44. To be sure, Jewish status is not quite as sharply either-or as the argument in the text suggests. See Lichtenstein, "Brother Daniel and the Jewish Fraternity"; Moshe Yeres, "Burial of Non-Halakhic Converts," *Tradition*, 23:3 (1988), 60–74; and see below in the text.
45. Sanhedrin 88b.
46. Mish. Eduyot 4:8; Yevamot 1:4; *Tosafot* on Yevamot 1:10. See, however, Yevamot

The other is the separation of Judaism and Christianity. In a recent scholarly study, Professor Lawrence Schiffman has shown that the earliest Christians were regarded by the rabbis as apostates but still Jews. "The ultimate parting of the ways for Judaism and Christianity took place when the adherents to Christianity no longer conformed to the halakhic definitions of a Jew."[47] When gentiles could become Christians without the halakhic requirements for conversion, the rabbis stopped seeing the members of the new sect as deviant Jews and started seeing them as members of a different and alien religious community. The rift was complete and final.

The outcome of these two conflicts turned on issues of Jewish status and eligibility for marriage. The prospect is that the relationship between Orthodoxy and Reform in America is unlikely to follow the model of Hillel and Shammai. It is already advanced along the path taken by Jews and early Christianity.

The problem exists primarily in America. Ironically, though, schism is likely to be precipitated by Israel, where there is no significant Reform presence. The reason is this. In American Jewry, as in other diasporas, there is no central Jewish authority recognized by all sides as having the competence to rule on matters of collective concern. Reform and Orthodoxy continue to drift apart, but there is no arena of confrontation. Instead, each operates within its own parameters. Orthodoxy, by definition, follows the rules of halakhah in both conversion and divorce. American Reform recognizes its own converts, and has abandoned the law of *mamzerut*. The problem, as we noted, arises only at the borders, when a Reform Jew and an Orthodox Jew wish to marry in a ceremony conducted according to halakhah. As the two communities continue on their separate, divergent orbits, these occasions grow rarer. Jewry

---

14a–b, Y. Yevamot 1:6, where several different explanations are given as to why the two schools intermarried despite the fact that they upheld different laws in relation to mamzerut. They are (1) that both schools in practice followed the ruling of the school of Hillel; (2) that divine intervention brought it about that neither school married individuals forbidden to them by their own rules; (3) that the two schools kept one another informed about disputed cases.

47. Lawrence H. Schiffman, *Who Was a Jew? Rabbinic and Halakhic Perspectives on the Jewish-Christian Schism* (Hoboken, NJ: Ktav, 1985), 77.

can separate into two peoples slowly, gradually, and without a dramatic moment of denouement.

The State of Israel, however, brings the problem into sharply delineated crisis. Central to its self-definition as the state of the entire Jewish people is the Law of Return. By this, any Jew who decides to live in Israel can become a citizen immediately without undergoing a naturalization procedure. As amended in 1970, the law defines as a Jew one born to a Jewish mother or one who has been converted to Judaism, but does not itself clarify what constitutes conversion. Since then there have been periodic attempts by religious parties to have the clause amended to read "converted according to halakhah." Though this would affect only a handful of cases each year – Reform converts seeking Israeli citizenship – it would, by implication, constitute a declaration by the State of Israel of non-recognition of the American Reform and Conservative rabbinate, the largest denominations in the largest diaspora Jewish community. The most recent attempt to amend the law, following Israel's 1988 general election, sent shock waves throughout the Jewish world. The attempt was abandoned, but not without exposing deep tensions between Orthodoxy and others and between Israel and the diaspora, normally quiescent but capable of sudden volcanic eruption. The moment revealed how tenuous and fragile Jewish unity is.

RESOLUTIONS

How, then, are these crises likely to be resolved? The problem of divorce and illegitimacy is potentially the more intractable, for the disability of *mamzerut*, once acquired, cannot be removed and is transmitted to future generations. None the less, a solution exists within halakhah. It is the *character of* the solution, though, which deserves careful analysis. It is a classic example of what I have called halakhic inclusivism. For this reason it collides headlong with pluralist sensibilities.

The late Rabbi Moses Feinstein, the leading halakhic authority of his generation, delivered a ruling in 1956 which at a stroke dissolved the problem of the status of children of Reform second marriages.[48] Reform

---

48. *Igerot Mosheh*, vol. i, no. 76. See also nos. 75, 77.

marriages, he ruled, were not halakhically valid. Therefore they needed no valid divorce. It followed that children from remarriages were not *mamzerim*.

It was a bold piece of reasoning. The marriage ceremony itself could be invalidated if it was not observed by two witnesses qualified to testify in a Jewish court. Since those present were likely to be Reform Jews themselves, it was probable that they transgressed Jewish law in ways that disqualified them as witnesses. Rabbi Feinstein's innovative reasoning, though, was that even the subsequent cohabitation did not establish marriage. Previous authorities had held that regardless of the validity of the ceremony, the fact that the couple openly proceeded to live together established marriage by cohabitation. Rabbi Feinstein's reasoning was that this was so only where there was intent. Here, however, cohabitation cannot have been intended to establish the marriage, since everyone assumed that the marriage had already been established by the synagogue ceremony. This ruling, if generally adopted, had the consequence of solving the entire problem of divorce and halakhic illegitimacy arising from Reform marriages.

Its formal structure is typical of the inclusivist strategy. It includes individuals by delegitimating ideologies. By, in effect, annulling all Reform marriages, it vitiated the need for divorce. It freed the Reform divorcée to marry an Orthodox man in an Orthodox synagogue, and it removed illegitimacy from the children of remarriages where the first marriage had been conducted under the auspices of Reform. Its reasoning, too, was consistent. By abolishing the need for halakhic divorce, the Reform rabbinate had established that their ceremonies were not intended to create halakhic marriage. They formalized a union of a kind, but not a union "according to the laws of Moses and Israel." Rabbi Feinstein's ruling utilized the Reform abandonment of halakhah to establish a stunningly inclusivist conclusion. If a Reform marriage did not create a positive halakhic fact, neither could it create a negative one.

The ruling scandalized many, though not all, of the non-Orthodox rabbinate. Some, like Eugene Borowitz, recognized its beneficial consequence in removing one of the major barriers across the religious divide. Others, however, were affronted, for it proposed to view Reform marriages as halakhically non-existent. One leading Conservative theologian described the responsum as "politics masquerading as religion." Another declared that the cure was more harmful than the malady.[49] The ruling met the fate of all inclusivist strategies when they encounter pluralist consciousness. It was held to be a denial of Reform's authenticity and self-evaluation. Indeed it was, for this is how the inclusivist avoids schism.

The responsum and the reactions it arouses are a test case of the fraught encounter between inclusivism and pluralism. What is at stake? Traditional and modern consciousness at their point of deepest difference, namely objectivity, self, and the description of action. Traditional consciousness, of which halakhah is a supreme example, takes the historic community and its norms as definitive. In the case of Judaism, an act has religious significance if and only if it meets the objective requirements of religious law. No subjective consideration can endow an act with religious properties if it lacks the necessary halakhic requirements. Thus Rabbi Feinstein was able to rule that Reform marriages fail to meet the criteria of a union terminable only by a halakhic divorce. Modern consciousness, however, grants the self authority over the description of its acts. The couple have married since that was their intention and since they and the officiant believed that the ceremony would have this effect.

How then should one proceed when two incommensurate worlds conflict? The answer, I suggest, is that *decisions should be judged by their consequences, not by the construction placed upon them.* It is not the formal strategy of Rabbi Feinstein's ruling that should be considered, but its effects. On the internal workings of Reform, it had no effect whatsoever. Those who married and divorced within the movement looked for their legitimation not to halakhic authorities but to the Reform rabbinate. The validity of their marriages, within their own terms of reference, was unaffected. On the internal workings of Orthodoxy, likewise, Rabbi Feinstein's ruling had no effect. It related to Reform marriages, not Orthodox ones. Its impact was solely at the boundary: where a Reform Jew and an Orthodox Jew sought to marry. There its consequence was

---

49. David Novak, "A Response to the Recent Proposal of Rabbi Dr. Sidney Brichto," *Jewish Law Annual*, 8 (1989), 289–99.

unequivocally benign. It enabled the marriage to take place without halakhic obstacle. It achieved what all parties sought.

To be sure, it implied Orthodox non-recognition of the Reform rabbinate. But the Reform rabbinate does not seek to derive its legitimacy from Orthodox recognition. Its self-definition is unaffected, and on its own principles, self-definition is pluralism's supreme value and human right. Reform protests against the ruling are therefore misconceived. Judging decisions by their consequences, not by their intent or inner logic, would remove much of the pain of confrontation. This is not to say that the end justifies or legitimates the means. It does not. The Jewish tradition is concerned with consequences,[50] but not to the point of making them the sole criterion of action. None the less, the recognition that even approaches with which one fundamentally disagrees may have results that one can welcome is a route to partial reconciliation. When total reconciliation is impossible, this is not an insignificant achievement.

The problem of conversion and patrilineal status is less easily resolved. There have been calls by Reform, Conservative, and Orthodox religious leaders for a reversal of the American Reform rabbinate's decision on patrilineal descent and for a unified conversion procedure and court.[51] It is hard to see how either will become possible. Compelling institutional logic led American Reform to its policy of accommodation towards mixed marriages. Now that these comprise one in two marriages

---

50. The most famous example is the logic behind the rule that saving a life overrides the laws of the Sabbath: "Let one Sabbath be broken in order that many be kept in the future" (Yoma 85b). Consequentialism also underlies Maimonides' explanation of the rule that the court may order the temporary suspension of a biblical law in order to restore the rule of biblical law generally. It is, he writes, like amputating a limb in order to save a life (Yad, *Mamrim* 2:4). The positive consequences outweigh the negative.

51. See Petuchowski, "Plural Models within the Halakhah"; Robert Gordis, "To Move Forward, Take One Step Back," *Moment*, 11:5 (1986), 58–61; Bulka, *The Coming Cataclysm*; Norman Lamm, "Seventy Faces," *Moment*, 11:6 (1986), 23–28; Haskel Lookstein, "Mending the Rift: A Proposal," *Moment*, 11:3 (1986), 58–61. A similar proposal was made in England by the Liberal Rabbi Sidney Brichto, "Halakhah with Humility," *Jewish Chronicle*, Oct. 2, 1987, 29. For responses to Brichto's proposal see the articles by Louis Jacobs, Moshe Zemer, Berel Berkovits, and David Novak in *Jewish Law Annual*, 8 (1989), 253–99.

involving young American Jews, a more stringent policy would cause massive depletions in Reform's numbers.

A unified conversion procedure, quite apart from the problems it would raise as to the composition of the rabbinical court, would be shipwrecked on the rock of the requirement, on the part of the convert, for "acceptance of the commands." It is difficult, perhaps impossible, to envisage a criterion that would simultaneously satisfy Reform and Orthodox interpretations of that phrase. Admittedly there have been thinkers, notably Eliezer Berkovits, who have advocated extreme leniency.[52] The condition itself is left vague in the halakhic literature. Historically and currently, different rabbinic courts have adopted different policies.[53] Some, most notably the Israeli rabbinate, have been less demanding than others,[54] while some, the Sephardi Syrian community, for example, have at times refused to accept converts at all.[55] The Talmud, in a famous passage, records a series of instances in which Hillel accepted as converts individuals whom Shammai had driven away.[56] Hillel, according to Rashi and the Tosafists,[57] relied on his own judgement that they would eventually accept the whole of Jewish law even if they did not do so now. On this basis Rabbi Joseph Caro ruled that conversion, in such doubtful cases, was left to the discretion of the court.[58] In theory, then, grounds for leniency exist.

But this discretion accorded to rabbinic courts requires that each case be treated in its context. Is there a sincere desire to accept Judaism for its own sake? Are there grounds for the belief that the convert will

52. Berkovits, *Not in Heaven*, 106–12.
53. See *Aseh Lekha Rav*, vol. i, no. 23; and see also the fuller exposition, ibid., vol. iii, no. 29. On the general history of conversion policies in Judaism see William G. Braude, *Jewish Proselytizing* (Providence, RI: Brown University, 1941); Bernard Bamberger, *Proselytism in the Talmud* (New York, 1968); Joseph R. Rosenbloom, *Conversion to Judaism* (Cincinnati: Hebrew Union College Press, 1978).
54. This, though, has not been without controversy. See *Sha'arurit Hagiyurim Hamezuyafim* (Israel, 1989) (no publisher or author's name given).
55. See S. Zevulun Lieberman, "A Sephardic Ban on Converts," *Tradition*, 23:2 (1988), 22–25.
56. Shabbat 31a.
57. Rashi on Shabbat 31a, s.v. *gayereih*; *Tosafot* on Yevamot 109b, s.v. ra'ah.
58. *Beit Yosef* on *Tur, Yoreh De'ah* 268, and see *Aseh Lekha Rav*, vol. i, no. 23.

ultimately accept its religious obligations? If not, conversion is not a benefit conferred by the court but a liability. As the Talmud puts it, joining the Jewish people involves heavy duties and participation in what has often been a tragic fate, neither of which can be lightly undertaken. For the sake of the individual concerned, the court must act responsibly and with integrity, unmoved by demographic or institutional policy. Courts in Israel have taken into account the fact that a convert who lives there will be surrounded by a Jewish culture and society in which halakhic norms govern major sectors of public life. Precisely this is absent in the diaspora situation where the problem of Reform conversions arises. There neither the public secular culture nor the values of liberal Judaism are supportive of halakhic practice. The same argument – defining "acceptance of the commands" in terms of an anticipated future – militates in favour of a more open policy in Israel and a more restrictive one in the diaspora. Grounds for leniency cannot be transferred from one context to another.[59]

The most important single step to avoid schismatic confrontation would be, instead, to remove the question of "Who is a Jew?" from Israel's political agenda. This has been advocated by, among others, Lord Jakobovits and Rabbis J. David Bleich and Nachum Rabinovitch.[60] Jewish status, as a halakhic issue, is beyond the competence of Israel's secular parliament and agencies to determine. It is to be decided by rabbinic courts alone. The Law of Return could then be amended to apply to born Jews only, with the further stipulation that "state officials, without in any way passing judgement on matters of halakhah," might consider "even technically invalid conversions as evidence of a convert's sincere desire to identify with the aspirations and common destiny of the citizens of the State of Israel."[61]

---

59. See, e.g., Berel Berkovits, "Comments on Rabbi Dr. Brichto and Rabbi Dr. Jacobs," *Jewish Law Annual*, 8 (1989), 269–88.

60. See Immanuel Jakobovits, *The Timely and the Timeless* (London: Vallentine, Mitchell, 1977), 215–17; Nachum Rabinovitch, "On Religion and Politics in Israel," in Jonathan Sacks (ed.), *Orthodoxy Confronts Modernity* (New York: Ktav, 1991), 123–35; Bleich, "Parameters and Limits of Communal Unity."

61. Bleich, "Parameters and Limits of Communal Unity," 36.

This would not amount to a solution of the problem, but to a decision to let it remain unresolved. Perhaps at present it is insoluble. It may be that contemporary Jewry is in the not unprecedented situation whereby the Jewish status of particular groups is for a time in doubt, as occurred in the case of the Samaritans, Idumeans, early Jewish Christians, and Karaites. At times there were half-converts, variously described as "God-fearers," "devout ones," or "worshippers of God," who appear to have accepted some of Judaism's laws and tenets but not others.[62] Josephus speaks of Greeks who accepted Judaism but who, "lacking the necessary endurance, have again seceded."[63] At such times there is no single answer, agreeable to all sides, to the question "Who is a Jew?"

In the context of a legal exposition,[64] Maimonides writes that during the reign of David and Solomon no converts were officially accepted, the presumption being that applicants were driven by ulterior motives. None the less, many were unofficially converted by *hedyotot*, "laymen." The supreme court held open the possibility that these conversions might be valid, "neither driving them [the converts] away since they had immersed themselves, nor drawing them close," until the course of time proved their sincerity or lack of it. Here then was an instance where the Jewish status of certain individuals was indeterminate and only became clarified by their subsequent behaviour.

For the foreseeable future, therefore, it may be that the problem of patrilineal Jews and non-Orthodox converts will simply be dealt with on a case-by-case basis when such individuals seek Orthodox recognition.[65] Nor is it necessarily the case that a non-Orthodox conversion has no Jewish significance even though it lacks halakhic validity. I noted Rabbi Bleich's suggestion that such conversions might be taken, by the

---

62. See Rosenbloom, *Conversion to Judaism*, 42–43, 51 and the literature cited there.
63. Josephus, *Against Apion*, 2:123, quoted ibid. 48.
64. Yad, *Isurei Bi'ah* 13:14–16.
65. One option recently explored by halakhists is the conversion of children, while still minors, born to mothers whose Jewish status is not halakhically recognized. See Jack Simcha Cohen, *Intermarriage and Conversion: A Halakhic Solution* (Hoboken, NJ: Ktav, 1987); Nachum Rabinovitch, "Kol Yisrael Arevin Zeh Bazeh," *Techumin*, II (1991), 41–72.

Law of Return, as prima-facie evidence of identification with the State of Israel and its citizens. In respect of the laws of burial, some halakhists have suggested that a non-Orthodox convert is not to be classed as a non-Jew.[66] One writer has suggested a distinction between *shem Yisrael* and *kedushat Yisrael*, roughly speaking, between "intermediate Jewish identity" and full halakhic status.[67]

Indeed, Rabbi Joseph Soloveitchik has related conversion to the broader issue of Jewish identity in modern times.[68] The process of conversion has two elements, best summarized in the words of Ruth to Naomi, "Your people shall be my people and your God my God." Jewry is a people defined by a religion. Therefore to become a Jew involves both an acceptance of the commandments and an identification with a people. According to the Talmud, a prospective convert is instructed on both counts. He or she is told of Israel's history ("persecuted and oppressed, despised, harassed, and overcome by afflictions") and informed of its commands. These represent the two covenants, of Exodus and Sinai, or fate and destiny, which together constitute Jewish existence. The two elements of the conversion process themselves reflect this duality. The act of circumcision symbolizes entry into a people (the covenant of fate) while immersion signifies acceptance of the commands (the covenant of destiny). Rabbi Soloveitchik argues that today Jewry is united by a sense of shared fate, but not yet by a collective religious destiny. Following his analysis through to its conclusion, one might say that the gesture implicit in a non-Orthodox conversion – a desire formally to be included within the Jewish people – is not without its positive significance even though it may possess no halakhic validity.

Nor is this an academic speculation only. No clearer demonstration could have been provided than this: that there were few Jews worldwide who were not moved and enthralled by the recent immigration to Israel of the Jews of Russia and Ethiopia, despite the fact that in both cases, for different reasons, there were considerable doubts

---

66. The literature is surveyed in Yeres, "Burial of Non-Halakhic Converts."
67. See ibid., 73 n. 44.
68. Soloveitchik, *Divrei Hagut Veha'arakhah*, 9–56.

about their halakhic status as Jews. The sense of Jewish peoplehood is sometimes wider, deeper, and stronger than the parameters of halakhah would suggest.[69]

A DIVIDED UNITY

What emerges from the developments surveyed in this chapter is a not unremarkable paradox. The most significant propositions about modern Jewry concern not what has happened but what has not happened. On the one hand Jews did *not* take the two available paths that might have pre-empted religious schism. Liberal Judaism did not adopt Rosenzweig's "not yet" approach to halakhah. Orthodoxy did not take Rabbi Hirschensohn's path to halakhic innovation. These facts testify to the unabated divisions of contemporary Jewry and to a fragmentation too deep to be contained within the boundaries of tradition, however conceived.

On the other hand, on the edge of the abyss, Jews did *not* proceed to schism. Rabbi Feinstein might, on grounds of halakhic principle or policy, have ruled that the children of Reform second marriages were *mamzerim*. Orthodox parties in Israel might have pressed to its conclusion their claim for an amendment to the Law of Return. Above all, Orthodoxy might have taken the route contemplated by Rabbis Moses Sofer[70] and Zvi Hirsch Chajes,[71] that of declaring Reform Jews to be non-Jews with whom it was forbidden to marry or mix. That none of these occurred testifies to the continuing power over the Jewish imagination of the idea of "one people."

Rabbi Kook, playing on the talmudic saying that the messiah would come to a generation that was either wholly righteous or wholly wicked, once asked what could be said of his own unique generation, which was *both* wholly righteous *and* wholly wicked.[72] Today's Jewry is

---

69. See esp. the responsum of Moshe Feinstein published in *Techumin*, 12 (1992), 98. Rabbi Feinstein writes: "Even if according to law [the Jews of Ethiopia] are not Jews, none the less *since they regard themselves as Jews and are willing to make self-sacrifices for their Judaism*," they are to be saved as Jews even though they require conversion.
70. See *Chatam Sofer*, vi. 39.
71. Chajes, *Kol Sifrei*, 975–1031.
72. Abraham Isaac Kook, *Eder Hayakar Ve'ikvei Hatzon* (Jerusalem: Mosad Harav Kook, 1967), 108.

both uncompromisingly divided and unprecedentedly united: divided by religious difference, but united by a powerful sense – reinforced by the Holocaust and the State of Israel – of a shared history, fate, and responsibility. In this tense equilibrium between opposing forces, Jewry faces its as yet uncertain future.

Chapter 9

The Future of a People

Twice before, the people of Israel came apart. After the reign of Solomon the nation was divided into two, a northern and a southern kingdom. Eventually the northern kingdom was conquered and sent into exile, where, lacking the inner means to survive as a distinct group, its population assimilated and disappeared from the script of Jewish history: the lost ten tribes. After the Babylonian exile, a second struggle took place over several centuries between secular and religious, syncretist and particularist tendencies within Jewry. A period of political autonomy, beginning with the Maccabean revolt and ending with the destruction of the Temple, opened and closed with what in effect were wars of Jew against Jew.

The Jewish people, forged in exile, gaining its purpose in the wilderness, has been able to survive dispersion and powerlessness, passivity and persecution. What it has not been able to negotiate without massive self-inflicted injury is freedom and empowerment. In the modern era, emancipation offered the first, the State of Israel the second. The result has been that the Jewish people is coming apart again.

The present study has focused on only one axis of that disintegration, the intractable differences between Orthodoxy and Reform. This is a problem primarily of the diaspora. But there are at least two other axes that should be considered. One is between religious and secular groups in Israel. This is far more fraught with direct and ugly confrontation: the burning of bus shelters and stoning of cars travelling on the Sabbath by *charedim* (pietists), retaliatory acts of vandalism against yeshivot by secularists, and an escalating war of words.

Admittedly, these clashes paint an exaggerated picture. For the most part, religious and secular publics live in relative peace. Newsworthy incidents mask the underlying reality of coexistence. None the less, the project of the return to Zion contained, almost from the beginning, deeply opposed expectations. For one group it signalled the return of Jewry to Judaism. For another it meant the liberation of Jewry from Judaism. For the former Israel was a place where the Jewish people might reconsecrate itself away from the assimilatory forces of Europe. For the latter it was the arena within which Jews could develop a national life freed from the "abnormality" of minority status and the need for religion to provide a basis for identity and continuity.

There were and are more moderate views on both sides. But the nature of the state forces the argument into political and cultural conflict. In the diaspora, different groups of Jews can coexist without their lives impinging on one another. In a Jewish state, when all groups are party to the political process, a direct contest can hardly be avoided. For what is at stake is the character of the public domain, and given the nature of the ideologies in contention, the state cannot be neutral between them. Each specific case raises issues of global principle, between religious coercion and individual freedom as the secularists see it, or between the Jewish character of the state and secularization as the religious see it. For both sides a war of cultures is already in progress. A survey in Jerusalem in 1988 revealed that while 23 per cent of those questioned saw the city's most serious problem as Jewish-Arab relations, 58 per cent identified it as the religious-secular divide between Jews.[1] In Yeshayahu Leibowitz's judgement, "Perhaps we will reluctantly arrive at a separation into two nations...each going its historic way imbued by intense hatred [of the other]."[2]

---

1. Liebman, *Religious and Secular*, xi.
2. Quoted in Huppert, *Back to the Ghetto*, 40.

The second line of fracture lies between Israel and the diaspora. Here too the argument has escalated in recent years, though its roots lie in the nineteenth century. One strand within Zionist thought, itself composed of many shades and nuances, has always been that the diaspora is scheduled for extinction. Jews survived in exile, albeit tenuously, so long as social and religious forces preserved them as a people apart. That no longer applies in the free and open societies of the west. Diaspora Jewish survival is threatened whether the surrounding environment is benign or malign. If the former, it is endangered by assimilation; if the latter, then by antisemitism. In different hands the argument becomes by turns sociological (attrition by intermarriage), cultural (the impossibility of an authentic Jewish creativity in a non-Jewish milieu), or political (the vulnerability of Jews as a minority). What these have in common, though, is clear: *shelilat hagolah*, a "negation of the diaspora" as a viable locus of Jewish continuity.[3]

The argument on the other side is more complex. There is the religious anti-Zionist case that the State of Israel represents a presumptuous, premature return to sovereignty before the messianic age. There is the secular anti-Zionist proposition that statehood is a betrayal of the Jews' historic role as exemplary exiles, iconoclasts of nationalism and power.[4] There is the case, mounted with vigour by Jacob Neusner, that America rivals Israel as a place of Jewish freedom, security, and intellectual fertility.[5] And there is the view, argued by Arthur Koestler and Georges Friedmann, that the two Jewries are simply drifting apart, the diaspora into individual assimilation, Israel into collective assimilation.[6] Inevitably, as Israel develops its autonomous culture, and as Jewries elsewhere become more integrated into their surrounding societies, each will have less in common with the other until they are no longer recognizable as a single people.

---

3. See Eisen, *Galut*.
4. This is the case argued consistently by George Steiner.
5. Jacob Neusner, *Who, Where and What Is Israel?* (Lanham, MD: University Press of America, 1989).
6. Arthur Koestler, *Promise and Fulfilment* (London: Macmillan, 1949); Georges Friedmann, *The End of the Jewish People?* (London: Hutchinson, 1967).

David Vital's recent analysis is simpler still. The interests of Israel and American Jewry cannot forever coincide. This of itself will force them apart. The process, he claims, has already begun. His conclusion is that "the Jewish world...is now coming apart. Where there was once a single, if certainly a scattered and far from monolithic people – indeed a nation – there is now a sort of archipelago of discrete islands composed of rather shaky communities of all qualities, shapes, and sizes, in which the Island of Israel, as it were, is fated increasingly to be in a class by itself."[7]

It is not my concern here to analyse these other conflicts. I have done so elsewhere.[8] The question before us in this final chapter is simply this: Given that Jewish unity is a value for many Jews, what sort of value is it? Not, surely, a unity of culture, for there is no common cultural denominator between the Jews of Cochin, Cincinnati, Manchester, and Madrid. Nor is it a unity of interests, for, David Vital's analysis notwithstanding, Jews have shown themselves capable of *sacrifice* of interest for the sake of threatened Jewries elsewhere. It is not a unity of race, as the merest glance at arriving Russian and Ethiopian Jews in Ben-Gurion airport will demonstrate. Nor is it a political unity, for Jews outside Israel live under a variety of governments, none of them Jewish. Unity is, as it always was, a *religious* value: a fact of covenant, a mutual commitment and faith. That it has become problematic should therefore occasion no surprise. It is a symptom of the tenuous hold of religion over the modern Jewish mind. But that it remains as a value is perhaps the most telling evidence that Jewry has not yet abandoned its religious roots. Habits of thought, senses of obligation, and gestures of action can persist long after the beliefs which gave them cogency have lost their hold. The concept of Jewry as "one people" is a religious idea; surviving in a secular age, it is in need of resuscitation.

As an Orthodox Jew, pained by the conflicts and contradictions in contemporary Jewish life, I want in this concluding analysis to set forth the idea of "one people" as I understand it, and spell out its implications for those still moved by its vision, still summoned by its call.

---

7. Vital, *The Future of the Jews*, 147.
8. Sociologically in my *Arguments for the Sake of Heaven* (Northvale, NJ: Jason Aronson, 1991); theologically in *Crisis and Covenant*.

THE REJECTION OF REJECTION

Jewish self-understanding begins with the book of Genesis. For eleven chapters it sets out the prehistory of mankind. For the rest it chronicles the lives of the patriarchal families, the prehistory of Israel. One of its recurring themes, perhaps even its *leitmotiv,* is sibling rivalry, fraternal conflict. Cain and Abel, Lot and Abraham, Isaac and Ishmael, Jacob and Esau, Joseph and his brothers: the scene recurs in seemingly endless variations as if to say that this above all would haunt the future, repeatedly threatening the threefold harmony of the divine design, between man and God, man and man, and man and nature.

Genesis establishes the nature of human existence in the presence and under the sovereignty of God. Neither God nor man is as portrayed by paganism in antiquity or science in modernity. They are not forces of nature, subject to deterministic laws. Instead, God is free and personal and desires the worship of free, morally choosing human beings. The two are linked not through nature but through the free choice of mutual, moral commitment: in a word, through *covenant.* The "law" which is to occupy so central a place in the religion of Israel is not the law of mythology or science, a law of description, explanation, and thus manipulation. Instead it is the law which links a free God to free human beings through their common commitment to justice and compassion: a law of ethics and sanctification, issued in commands and consummated in human response to those commands.

But because humanity is granted free will, the divine design is repeatedly subverted. Disobedience is possible and soon becomes actual. However, the world is not to be abandoned to chaos. Repeatedly, God is called on to intervene to redirect and reinstruct humanity. The conflicts of Genesis are, from a human point of view, all too understandable. *Homo sapiens,* that unstable mixture of "dust of the earth" and the "breath of God," is prey to desires, envies, rivalries, and violence which threaten social, even cosmic, order. Less understandable, though, is the sequence of divine interventions as they concern a particular kind of act, namely *choice.*

A free God is one who chooses. Throughout Genesis, God chooses those who best respond to and thus exemplify his call. But this has consequences, quite different from those which might have occurred had humanity responded to its vocation as the image of God. Rather than directing man to God's presence and purpose, divine choice renews human conflict. What then is the divine response?

The two sections of Genesis, the prehistory of mankind and that of Israel, are symmetrically structured. Each is told in a sequence of three choices in which the third reverses the pattern of the previous two. Implicit in this narrative is a theological proposition of immense significance which, thus far unstated, has animated and shaped the argument of this book.

The first choice takes place after the exile of Adam and Eve from Eden. Cain and Abel, the first human children, each bring offerings to God. Abel's is accepted, Cain's is not. Cain is angry. Though warned by God, his resentment grows until, alone in the field with his brother, he attacks and kills him.

The spirit of Cain haunts humanity until "the earth was corrupt in God's sight and was full of violence." This time a second choice takes place. Not an individual, but almost everything that lives, is now rejected. Noah alone finds favour in God's eyes, and only he and those with him in the ark survive. There is a flood, and the universe is momentarily returned to its initial chaos: waste and void and darkness over the face of the deep.

In these two narratives, choice implies rejection. The third, however, is quite different. After the flood, God vows never again to reject and thus destroy mankind. Humanity sins again, this time by building the tower of Babel. God frustrates the plan but does not punish the perpetrators. Human language is confused, mankind is scattered, and civilization splits into a multiplicity of cultures. God now chooses again: this time Abraham and his children. But in this third act of choice *there is to be no rejection.* Instead, in and through Abraham, "all the families of the earth will be blessed."

With Abraham, the whole focus of the Bible shifts from humanity as a whole to a single exemplary family. Again there are to be three choices. In the first, Abraham has a child, Ishmael, by Sarah's handmaid Hagar. Twice Ishmael is displaced: once before he is born, when Sarah treats Hagar harshly and she runs away; a second time after Isaac is born, when mother and son are sent into the wilderness and nearly die.

Abraham is attached to Ishmael. When first told by God that another son would be heir to the covenant, he says, "Would that Ishmael might live by your favour!" Later, when Sarah demands that Ishmael be sent away, "The matter distressed Abraham greatly." None the less, God affirms that Isaac has been chosen, not Ishmael.

In the second generation, Isaac and Rebecca have twins, Esau and Jacob. Isaac loves Esau, but already before the children had been born an oracle had announced to Rebecca that the choice would lie elsewhere: "The older will serve the younger." Twice Jacob uses cunning to obtain the signals of special favour, the birthright and the blessing. Isaac is distressed. Jacob, he says, has used "deceit." Isaac had intended to bless Esau. None the less, the choice is confirmed. It is Jacob who will carry the covenant.

It is crucial to understand that in these two episodes choice does not imply rejection: such is the post-Babel equation. Isaac and Jacob have been chosen, but Ishmael and Esau have not been rejected. Three times the Torah stresses that Ishmael will be blessed. He will be "too numerous to count." He will be "the father of twelve chieftains." He will be "a great nation." Esau too is thrice blessed. Isaac promises him "the fat of the earth and the dew of heaven above." When the brothers meet after long estrangement, Esau has grown powerful, declaring "I have much." Later, when Moses leads the Israelites towards the land of Canaan, God tells him not to wage war against the descendants of Esau: "I will not give you of their land so much as a foot to tread on; I have given the hill country of Seir as a possession to Esau." The Torah details their genealogies, as if to say that Ishmael and Esau have each acquired the dignity of destiny. Here is the origin of Judaism's pluralism towards other nations and faiths.

But *choice is experienced as rejection.* In two extraordinary portrayals of the other side of choice, the Torah sets forth its human cost. The scenes of Ishmael, left to die under a bush in the desert, and of Esau, entering Isaac's tent to take his blessing and discovering that Jacob has received it, are among the most emotionally moving in the entire Bible. There is no choice without tragedy and without giving rise to conflict. Ishmael is destined to be "a wild ass of a man, his hand against everyone and everyone's hand against him." Esau and Jacob, who "struggle in the womb," are fated to rivalry. Isaac, blessing Esau, tells him that "when you grow restive you shall break his [Jacob's] yoke from your neck." Divine choice and fraternal conflict, the two great themes of Genesis, are interlinked.

The scene is now set for the culminating drama, one whose significance can be measured by the fact that it occupies almost half of the book of Genesis: the story of Jacob and his children. As with the first triad, so with the second: the third episode reverses the direction of the previous two. Until now, the father has favoured the older child, while God has chosen the younger. Now Jacob favours the younger. He loves Rachel, the younger sister. He loves Joseph and Benjamin, the youngest sons. Consistently, however, his choices are frustrated. He works seven years for Rachel, but is given Leah in marriage. He loves Rachel, but it is Leah who has children, and Rachel who dies prematurely. He loves Joseph, but Joseph is taken from him, leaving only a bloodstained coat.

An equation, thus far implicit, is now spelled out. *The love which is choice is experienced as rejection by the unloved.* In two key passages, the biblical text highlights the inexorable transition from love to hate. The first concerns Jacob's wives. Jacob "*loved* Rachel also, more than Leah.... And God saw that Leah was *hated*." The second concerns Jacob's children. "Now Israel *loved* Joseph more than all his other sons.... When his brothers saw that their father *loved* him more than any of them, they *hated* him and could not speak to him in peace." The *less* loved feels *un*loved, and thus hated; and thus hates.

Despite its thematic complexity, the story of Jacob and his children is a dense cluster of reversals. Jacob chooses his youngest sons, but in fact all his children will be chosen. The fraternal rivalry which leads the brothers to plan to kill Joseph leads instead to the exile of the whole family to Egypt, where they become a single nation. By the beginning of the book of Exodus, all of Jacob's children are called God's firstborn, "Israel." The book of Genesis ends on a note of reconciliation which momentarily reverses all of its earlier discords. Adam and Eve had eaten of the tree of knowledge that they might be like God; but Joseph tells his brothers, "Am I in place of God?" Cain had killed Abel, the brothers had sought to kill Joseph, but Joseph assures them that there will be no more strife: "You planned evil against me, but God meant it for good."

In the days of Noah, human civilization had been threatened by rain. In the days of Joseph it is threatened by lack of rain. Both the flood and the drought strike "the face of all the earth." But Joseph does what Noah did not do: he "saves many people alive." The symmetries are exact.

Cain and Abel, and Noah and the flood, set forth the thesis of choice and rejection. The story of Babel and the call to Abraham are the antithesis: choice without rejection. This is embodied twice, in Isaac and Ishmael, Jacob and Esau. But choice without rejection is none the less *perceived* as rejection: not only by Ishmael and Esau but by Leah and Joseph's brothers as well. Genesis ends with a new and final thesis. *From here onward there are to be no more choices.* There will be no more dramas of chosen sons. When, at the time of the golden calf, and again after the episode of the spies, God threatens to destroy the people, leaving only Moses, Moses reminds him of his covenant with the patriarchs. For now there is a chosen family, none of whose members may be unchosen. God and Israel have entered a binding covenant. The choice, once made, cannot be unmade. God has joined His destiny with all of Israel. All of Israel has pledged itself to God. The concluding thesis to which the whole of the book of Genesis is the argument is *the rejection of rejection.* Here is the origin of Jewish inclusivism. Israel is henceforth to be one indivisible people, the collective firstborn child of the One God.

AN IDEA IN CRISIS

It is a crucial thesis which, as an axiom of faith, governs Israel's understanding of its own history. The covenant cannot be broken. Rejection is at an end. None the less, the covenantal relationship suffers horrifying vicissitudes. Israel rebels and is sent into exile. There it experiences the full desolation of a life outside God's protection. Israel is an unfaithful wife, says Hosea, therefore she has been sent away.[9] But, insists Isaiah, the covenantal partners, though separated, are still married. "Where is your mother's certificate of divorce with which I sent her away?"[10] God and Israel are still bound to one another. God hides his face, but he still watches. The people are disobedient, but will one day repent and return.

---

9. Hos. 1–3.
10. Isa. 50:1.

Israel, though it suffers and seems vulnerable, is as eternal as the covenant. In spite of its rebellions and exiles, pledges God, "when they are in the land of their enemies, I will not reject them or abhor them so as to destroy them completely, breaking my covenant with them."[11] But here an epistemological crisis occurs. From Israel's rebellions and dispersions, *not all return*. Individuals, communities, and tribes vanish. Of Solomon's united kingdom, only the confederation of Judah and Benjamin ultimately survives. Ten tribes, the northern kingdom, are conquered and disappear. Thus begins a series of secessions and assimilations, some forced, others voluntary, that persist to the present day. Of each generation, only a fragment endures to beget the next. So, in the prophetic literature, we meet the concept of *she'erit Yisrael*, the remnant of Israel. "A remnant will return," says Isaiah, "the remnant of Jacob, to the mighty God. Though your people, O Israel, be like the sand of the sea, only a remnant will return."[12] How is this fact to be understood? How can it be that all Israel is chosen, yet not all survive as Israel? This is the crisis.

There are two possible answers. Those who survive are either an *accidental remnant* or a *chosen remnant*. If those who endure as Israel are an accidental remnant, then Jewish history bespeaks the ravages of life under the hiding of the face of God. Unprotected, the righteous and the innocent suffer alike. The enemy strikes arbitrarily. Individuals are lost, but the people survives. Those who live are not specially chosen, not necessarily more righteous than those who die. The divine promise is that some will remain, and from them a people will be rebuilt. "As a shepherd saves from the lion's mouth only two leg bones or a piece of an ear," says Amos, "so will the Israelites be saved."[13] The remnant of Israel will be like "a brand snatched from the fire."[14]

The idea of an accidental remnant dominates prophetic thought. Israel suffers grievously for its sins. The people are scattered, threshed, beaten, refined. But those who, bruised and injured, return represent the people as a whole. Rabbinic midrash, and later Nachmanides,

---

11. Lev. 26:44.
12. Isa. 10:21–22.
13. Amos 3:12.
14. Amos 4:11; Zech. 3:2.

describe this history in an image drawn from Genesis.[15] Israel in its trials of survival is Jacob wrestling with the angel. Jacob must struggle with an adversary through the long night until the dawn of redemption breaks. He is tenacious; he survives. But afterwards, he limps. The persecutions, crusades, inquisitions, and pogroms all leave their mark. Yet "Jacob returns whole."

But here and there an alternative model surfaces. According to this, those who survive are those who are truly chosen. The real Israel is only a part of the apparent Israel, the grain that remains after the chaff is blown away. The decimations of history are not random but retributive. The wicked die; the righteous live. "Shall I not avenge myself on such a nation as this?" asks God through Jeremiah. "Go through her vineyards and ravage them, but do not destroy them completely. Strip off her branches, for these people *do not belong to the Lord.*"[16]

This view might seem to run against the argument of Genesis, that all of Israel is chosen and cannot be unchosen. But at this point we notice a curious omission. The prophets frequently had recourse to metaphors drawn from the Pentateuch. In a process known to rabbinic tradition as *midrash,* described by modern scholars as "inner biblical exegesis," the later literature of Judaism is an extended process of reinterpretation of themes already present in the Mosaic books.[17] In the present instance, a perfect metaphor for the idea of a chosen remnant lay directly at hand, in the narratives of Genesis. For not all the children of the patriarchs were children of the covenant. Surely, then, those who vanished through Israel's catastrophes and attritions were Ishmaels and Esaus, whilst those who survived were the true Isaac and Jacob. In fact, however, the prophets systematically *avoided* this image: a telling indication of how deeply Genesis argues against it. After Jacob, no child of Israel lies outside the covenant. When the prophets search for a metaphor of Israel's infidelity they find it, instead, in Sodom and Gomorrah,[18] or the

---

15. Genesis Rabbah 77:4; *Commentary* on Gen. 32:26.

16. Jer. 5:9–10.

17. Michael Fishbane, *Biblical Interpretation in Ancient Israel* (Oxford: Clarendon Press, 1985).

18. See, e.g., Isa. 1:9–10, 3:9; Jer. 23:14, 49:18; Ezek. 16:46–56; Amos 4:11; Lam. 4:6.

rebellious generation of the wilderness.[19] But both comparisons invite consolation, for Abraham prayed on behalf of Sodom, and the children of those who perished in the wilderness were destined to enter the land. Thus the covenant survived its first crisis. The inclusive interpretation of "one people" was preserved.

AGAINST COVENANTAL DUALISM

But the *exclusivist* concept of a saving or righteous remnant, a "true Israel" amongst the mixed multitude, appeared with disruptive force during the second covenantal crisis: the long period of internal strife from the Maccabean revolt in the second century BCE to the destruction of the Temple and the collapse of the Bar Kochba rebellion in 135 CE. A fundamental dualism between the saved and the condemned appears in the apocalyptic writings, the documents of the Qumran sect, and the literature of the Gnostics. In the Dead Sea Scrolls it takes the form of a cosmic struggle between the "children of light" and the "children of darkness." Dan Jacobson sums up the tendency thus: "One can guess that at all times during the historic periods covered by these texts, particular groups must have cherished the belief that they were in fact more chosen than others among the chosen people.... In all these [early post-biblical] texts one finds sects which believed passionately that they represent the worthy remnant of which the prophetic literature of their ancestors had spoken: a small, truly chosen group surviving precariously but decisively within a counterfeit Israel, a nation composed of sinful leaders, evil priests and misled masses."[20]

One development in particular was to have fateful consequences. For the metaphor so conspicuously avoided by the prophets finally made its devastating appearance. Not all Jews are children of the covenant. "Not all who are descended from Israel are Israel. Nor because they are his descendants are they all Abraham's children." The proof? Ishmael was not chosen, though he was Abraham's child. Nor was Esau, though he was born to Isaac and Rebecca. God is free to choose and unchoose. Prophetic texts – including Isaiah's "only a remnant will return" – are

---

19. Ezek. 20:30–38.
20. Dan Jacobson, *The Story of the Stories* (London: Seeker and Warburg, 1982), 123.

reinterpreted to show that not all Israel will be saved. "It is not the natural children who are God's children, but it is the children of the promise who are regarded as Abraham's offspring."[21] Not every Jew is chosen. The author of these words was Paul, architect of a Christian theology which deemed that the covenant between God and his people was now broken. Torah as law had been repealed. A new Israel had been elected to replace the old. Those within Jewry who did not accept the new dispensation were unsaved. No doctrine has cost more Jewish lives. Pauline theology demonstrates to the full how remote from and catastrophic to Judaism is the doctrine of a second choice, a new election.

What, then, was the response of the Pharisees and the emergent rabbinic mainstream? They too faced epistemological crisis. Until the collapse of Jewish autonomy in Israel, the doctrine of "one people" had a natural plausibility. To be sure, there were Jewish diasporas, and there were deep divisions within Israel itself. But a nation, territorially concentrated and to some extent self-governing, conspicuously shares a fate. When it is attacked, oppressed, or suffers setbacks, all its inhabitants suffer. It has focuses of national unity. Kings, priests, Jerusalem and its aura, the Temple and its rites all served to remind a population that the nation had institutional embodiment. The collectivity had its visible symbols. But by the second half of the second century CE all these were in ruins. With the brutal suppression of the Bar Kochba revolt, the rabbis were aware that, for the foreseeable future, there were to be no more Jewish kings and no speedy rebuilding of the Temple. The messianic hope remained. But in the meanwhile a long dispersion was beginning, one that had no parallel in Jewish history. How then, deprived of the formal structures and institutions of national unity, were Jews to remain "one people"?

Jews still had a faith, of course. But a faith community is not a people. It is not the *family* of Abraham, the *children* of Israel. One *becomes* a member of a community of faith but one is *born* a Jew. It was at this point that the sages articulated an idea implicit in the covenant from the beginning but which had not, until now, needed to be spelled out. Israel

---

21. Rom. 9. On modern interpretations of this passage, see Hyam Maccoby, *Paul and Hellenism* (London: SCM Press, 1991), 155–79.

is, according to the *Mekhilta Derabbi Shimon bar Yochai*, "a single body and a single soul ... when one is smitten, all feel pain."[22] They are united not by the institutions of monarchy or the Temple but by the covenant itself. In the famous principle set out in the *Sifra*, "All Israel are sureties for one another."[23] The covenant is more than a series of vertical commitments linking individual Jews with God. It is also a set of horizontal bonds linking Jews with one another in collective responsibility. Thus the concept of nationhood survived the collapse of Israel's central institutions and the dispersion of its population. It rested on Torah as the constitution of a people.

Jewish peoplehood was never an absolutely inclusive idea. One could place oneself outside the community by idolatry or heresy. There was even a benediction against heretics in the liturgy. But the sages construed peoplehood in such a way as to rule out its restriction to an exclusive elite. All Israel, they said, has a share in the world to come.[24] A fast which does not include transgressors is not a fast.[25] The "four species" of Tabernacles – the palm-branch, citron, myrtle, and willow – refer to the four kinds of Jew, those with and without learning, with and without good deeds. "The Holy One, blessed be he, declares that they should all be bound together as a single bunch so that they may atone for one another."[26] In these and other statements the sages cast the idea of peoplehood as widely as possible within the parameters of faith.

Admittedly, not everyone agreed. Commenting on a classic "chosen remnant" text – Jeremiah's prophecy that God will take "one of you from every town and two from every clan and bring you to Zion" – Resh Lakish declared that the verse was to be understood literally. Only the righteous few would survive. But Rabbi Jochanan dissented. Instead, Jeremiah meant that one individual would, by his merits, save a whole town, and two an entire clan.[27] On the phrase "You are sons of the Lord your God," Rabbi Judah said, "When you behave as sons you are called

22. *Mekhilta Derabbi Shimon bar Yochai* on Ex. 19:6.
23. *Sifra* on Lev. 26:37.
24. Mish. Sanhedrin 10:1.
25. Keritot 6b.
26. Leviticus Rabbah 30:12.
27. Sanhedrin 111a.

sons; when you do not behave as sons you are not called sons." Chosenness is thus conditional. It must be earned and can be undone. But Rabbi Meir demurred. "In either case [however Israel behaves] you are called sons."[28] Chosenness is ontological, written into Israel's being. Rabbi Meir's and Rabbi Jochanan's view prevailed. "Even though they [the Jews] are impure, the divine presence is among them," affirmed the *Sifra*.[29] "Even though they have sinned, they are called Israel," said Rav.[30] This last aggadic statement was to have halakhic ramifications. Even an apostate – so ruled Rabbenu Gershom and Rashi – remains a Jew.[31]

There are few suggestions in early rabbinic thought that those who survive are the chosen few and those who rebel are not the true Israel. The idea does occur. Whoever is not merciful, said the sages, is not a child of Abraham.[32] Whoever is shameless, his ancestors were not present at Sinai.[33] Those who act without compassion are children of the "mixed multitude" who left Egypt with Israel.[34] But such statements are rare and marginal. The majority view was that "even the emptiest of Israel is as full of *mitzvot*, religious deeds, as a pomegranate is of seeds."[35] Indeed, in a breathtaking interpretation, Rabbi Zera drew the same lesson from the moment when Isaac blessed Jacob, who was wearing Esau's clothes. The text reads, "Isaac smelled the smell of his garments and blessed him." Rabbi Zera comments: "Read not 'his garments' [*begadav*] but 'his betrayals' [*bogedav*]."[36] The message is clear. Though Israel wears Esau's clothes and bears the aroma of betrayal, he is still blessed.

There is, however, one fully developed instance of the "chosen remnant" theory in the rabbinic literature. It occurs in Maimonides' *Epistle to Yemen* of 1172. The Jewish community of Yemen was under

---

28. Kiddushin 36a.
29. *Sifra* on Lev. 16:16.
30. Sanhedrin 44a.
31. For a history of these rulings see Katz, *Exclusiveness and Tolerance*, 67–81; Blidstein, "Who Was Not a Jew?"
32. Beitzah 32b.
33. Nedarim 20a.
34. Beitzah 32b.
35. Berakhot 57a; Eiruvin 19a; Sanhedrin 37a; Song of Songs Rabbah 4:5; Genesis Rabbah 32:10.
36. Sanhedrin 37a.

threat of forced conversion to Islam. Some of its members had suc-cumbed. Those who had not were anxious and confused. They turned to Maimonides for advice. His reply is a monument of reassurance. "As it is impossible for God to cease to exist, so is our destruction and disap-pearance from the world unthinkable." What then of the Jews who have yielded to threats and converted? Maimonides here advances an idea that will strengthen the resistance of those who have not. The repeated persecutions of Jews, he says, are trials "designed to purify and test us, so that only the saints and the pious men of the pure and undefiled lin-eage of Jacob will adhere to our religion and remain within the fold." God has promised that the children of those who stood at Sinai would have faith until the end of time. "Consequently, let everyone know who spurns the religion that was revealed at that theophany, that he is not an offspring of the folk that witnessed it."[37]

Here, unmistakably, is theological Darwinism: the survival of the religiously fittest. Those who convert to Islam are not now, nor ever were, true Jews. But we cannot separate the statement from its context. For Maimonides himself, in another context – the *Epistle on Martyr-dom* – had delivered the most powerful of all statements of inclusivism. There he had declared the *conversos* to be true Jews. The religious deeds they did in secret would be doubly rewarded. The difference between the two epistles is simple. There he addresses those who have converted; here he speaks to those who have not. Isidore Twersky is surely correct in his judgement that *"she'erit hapeleitah* [the surviving remnant] is a consolatory concept but it is not an ideology which one consciously and resignedly embraces *ab initio*."[38]

Against a sectarian dualism which divided Israel into the saved and the condemned, the sages insisted that the covenant addressed a people, not an elite. The sinning Jew may be punished and may lose rights within the halakhic system, but he remains a Jew, a child of the covenant, beloved of God. Those who disappear in the course of history are not the "counterfeit Israel" who are being punished and whose loss

---

37. Translation taken from Halkin, *Crisis and Leadership*, 102–3.
38. Isidore Twersky, "Survival, Normalcy, Modernity," in Moshe Davis (ed.), *Zionism in Transition* (New York: Arno Press, 1980), 350.

may go unmourned. On the contrary, the liturgies of lamentation in the Middle Ages express the fact that it is the righteous who suffer. Those who survive are an accidental remnant. The covenant is inclusive. For it was made with a people, the entire "congregation of Jacob."

THE THIRD CRISIS

This faith disintegrated in modernity. Michael Wyschogrod reports that Martin Buber once declared that *keneset Yisrael*, the Jewish people as a single entity, no longer existed. They were too fragmented, too divided over fundamentals. *Keneset Yisrael* had "come to an end sometime around the Enlightenment, which undermined classical Jewish self-understanding. From then on, the concept of the Jewish people as one entity standing before God was problematic."[39]

In a sense, Buber was right. The many Jewish visions of the nineteenth century were neither inclusivist nor pluralist, but exclusivist. Each saw itself as the only route to a Jewish future, and confidently foresaw the demise of the alternatives. Reform Jews saw Orthodoxy as an anachronism of the ghetto, a vestige of an earlier age that would not survive exposure to the open air of an open society. Orthodoxy saw Reform as another name for assimilation. It was a halfway house to intermarriage, and its adherents would disappear as Jews within three generations. Zionists, both secular and religious, saw the diaspora as fated for extinction by assimilation or antisemitism. Critics of early Zionism saw it as a quixotic gesture destined to failure, meanwhile threatening the situation of diaspora Jewry by the spectre of dual loyalties. Religious critics added that it was even worse than Reform, for it threatened collective assimilation and the complete secularization of Jewish life. Each group saw itself as Jewry's saving remnant.

The language of Jews in the nineteenth and early twentieth centuries has no precedent since Second Temple times. Quite apart from the Jew-hating literature of such lapsed or ex-Jews as Ludwig Borne, Karl Marx, Walter Rathenau, and Fritz Mauthner,[40] even the writings

---

39. Wyschogrod, *The Body of Faith*, 239.
40. See Sander Gilman, *Jewish Self-Hatred* (Baltimore, MD: Johns Hopkins University Press, 1986).

of affirming Jews is dualistic, built on oppositional stereotypes between "good" and "bad" Jews. The enlightened Jews of Germany in the 1830s, embarrassed by their Yiddish-speaking brothers, said that they "create a sense of disgust in their correligionists."[41] By the 1880s, as Jews from the East began to enter Germany, a Jewish newspaper could write, "The Russian Jews have multiplied in Germany like frogs." They "evoke the justified German hatred for the Jews."[42]

The most virulent rhetoric came from the secular Zionists. In 1905 Jabotinsky outlined his plan for a new "Hebrew" identity that would negate what he called the *yid* of exile. The *yid* is "ugly, sickly, and lacks decorum." He is "trodden on and easily frightened," "despised by all," and has "accepted submission."[43] Earlier, Theodor Herzl had drawn a yet more savage caricature. *Mauschel*, the exilic Jew, is "a distortion of human character, unspeakably mean and repellent." He "feels miserable fear," is "impudent and arrogant," and pursues "only his own dirty business." It is, added Herzl, "as if in a dark moment of our history some mean strain intruded into and was mixed with our unfortunate nation."[44] The racist slurs of pre-state Zionism led Yechezkel Kaufmann, himself an ardent Zionist, to accuse the movement of a "vocabulary of abuse" that was "paralleled only in overtly antisemitic literature of the worst kind."[45]

Seen in the full perspective of Nazism and anti-Zionist Islamic fundamentalism, the fact that Jews could use such language about each other is little less than shocking. Clearly there were extenuating factors. In an age of antisemitism, Jews had internalized gentile perceptions of the Jew to devastating effect. What is therefore doubly chilling is that the vocabulary persists today. A recent survey of the *charedi* (Orthodox pietist) press in Israel, for example, revealed a sharp dualism between "Jews" and "Israelis" (secular Jews). "Israelis" were seen as Jewish gentiles, even antisemites. One newspaper spoke of a conflict between the

---

41. Ibid., 160–61.
42. Ibid., 284.
43. Quoted in Amnon Rubinstein, *The Zionist Dream Revisited* (New York: Schocken, 1984), 4.
44. Quoted in Gilman, *Jewish Self-Hatred*, 239.
45. Yechezkel Kaufman, "The Ruin of the Soul," in Michael Selzer (ed.), *Zionism Reconsidered* (London: Macmillan, 1970), 117–30.

"sons of the light of Torah" against the "sons of secular darkness." Another asked, "Which is worse, Zionism or Nazism?," and answered, "The Nazis burned the bodies of the community of Israel and the Zionists burned the souls of the community of Israel, and one who leads another to sin is worse than one who murders."[46] A parallel survey of the secular press disclosed equally brutal stereotypes. *Charedim* are "evil, primitive, mindlessly brainwashed." They are bent on extortion, opposed to democracy; they are embodiments of "khomeinization" or fanatical religious rule.[47] One recent book, Uri Huppert's *Back to the Ghetto*, portrays Israeli religious groups as totalitarian enemies of a free society.[48]

Few observers of contemporary Jewry have failed to note the deep bitterness that periodically surfaces between secular and religious Jews in Israel, Orthodox and Reform Jews in America, diaspora and Israeli Jewry, and within Orthodoxy itself between "modernists," Hasidic groups, and yeshiva leaders. But with this, we come to the crux. There may have been a time, during the nineteenth and early twentieth centuries, when such estrangement was inevitable. Today it is not. The early struggles to establish a Jewish state are over. So is the battle to secure Jewish admission to the societies of the West. The forces which gave rise to fragmentation lie, for the most part, in the past. Israel is not threatened by the diaspora, nor the diaspora by Israel. Reform is not endangered by Orthodoxy. Orthodoxy, through its powerful structures of education, is secure against assimilation. A rhetoric of negation brings neither strategic advantage nor psychological security. No group gains by the injuries it inflicts on others. Each wins adherents by its own vision and power, not by the denigration of alternatives.

The time has come to call a halt to the sectarian dualism of the saved and the condemned, and to the Darwinism which calmly contemplates the extinction of some group of Jews. For four reasons. If, after the Holocaust and the attacks on the State of Israel, gentile antisemitism is

46. Amnon Levi, "The *Haredi* Press and Secular Society," in Liebman (ed.), *Religious and Secular*, 21–44.
47. Samuel Heilman, "Religious Jewry in the Secular Press: Aftermath of the 1988 Elections," in Liebman (ed.), *Religious and Secular*, 45–66.
48. Huppert, *Back to the Ghetto*, 40.

morally unacceptable, so too is Jewish antisemitism. Secondly, Jewish Darwinism is sociologically unrealistic. Within its own criteria, no major grouping within Jewry is about to disappear. Thirdly, it is historically blind. The modern era has recapitulated the disastrous divisions of two earlier crises in Israel's past, and it would be folly indeed, in the rabbis' phrase, "to have seen [what happened before] and not to learn the lesson." Fourthly and above all, the idea of "one people" forms the very core of Jewish faith in the covenant between God and a chosen nation. That idea has been assailed by crisis before. But it survived. If, in an age of freedom and sovereignty such as Jews have only rarely experienced in three and a half thousand years of history, it were to collapse, the tragedy would resound through all future Jewish generations.

The idea of "one people" is a religious commitment that cannot be given coherence in any other frame of discourse. Jews are not linked horizontally across continents and vertically through time as a community of culture, interests, race, or ethnicity. They do not share a political system, a territory, or a language. Nor, though this is often taken for granted, is it self-evident that Jews share a "history" and a "fate." The narratives of the Jewish past told by, for example, Rabbi Joel Teitelbaum, Rabbi Abraham Kook, Simon Dubnow, Gershom Scholem, and David Ben-Gurion are not the same history. Nor is the fact that, say, British Jews feel implicated in the fate of Soviet and Ethiopian Jewry merely instinctual. It is an instinct born of an essentially religious commitment: that Jews are responsible for one another and are thus bound to come to one another's aid. That idea belongs not to nature, race, or politics, but to covenant. Jews might have decided, as did the late Arthur Koestler on the founding of the State of Israel, that henceforth their history and fate would diverge. That for the most part they did not is testimony to the power of faith over even the most secular Jewish imagination.

But the paradox of modern Jewry is that religion, which historically united Jews, today divides them. The axiom on which Judaism was predicated was the inseparability of Torah and the people Israel. But they have become separated. That was a possibility uncontemplated in the rabbinic literature.[49] There might be individual secessions from halakhah,

49. See *Akedat Yitzchak*, Gate 29.

even large-scale defections as in Spain and Portugal in Inquisition times. But these were conscious departures. All concerned knew that a line had been crossed, an exit taken. That a majority of Jews might define themselves as Jews without reference to religious belief or halakhic practice would have seemed, until a century ago, a contradiction in terms.

PLURALISM, EXCLUSIVISM, INCLUSIVISM

How, then, is this fact to be responded to? We have argued that an internal Jewish pluralism that would *de jure* acknowledge different religious denominations is ruled out by the classic terms of Judaism. Precisely because Judaism is the religion of a nation, one of its central terms is halakhah, law. Law translates faith into the structures of common life. It turns the Sabbath from a time of private recreation into a day of public rest. It turns the ethical imperative from a chaos of individual choices into a shared code of righteousness. The immutable nature of the commandments joins each Jew not merely to God but to God as responded to by generations of Jews in every place of their dispersion. Seemingly fragile, unenforced by political power, halakhah united Jews across centuries and continents and gave them identity as a nation. A pluralism that would formally recognize the obsolescence of halakhah (Jewish secularism) or its subjection to the autonomous self (Reform) or the local ethic of time and place (Conservative) would not be a proposal to unite Jewry but, instead, to announce its dissolution.

I have argued, too, that exclusivism, though it has had advocates in the Jewish past, runs against the main thrust of Jewish tradition. Its power cannot be denied. Israelis who negate the diaspora, diaspora Jews who see statehood as a betrayal of Judaism, secularists who regard religion as a force for evil, religious Jews who see secularists as pagans and idolaters, Reform Jews who believe Orthodoxy to have been refuted by the Enlightenment, and Orthodox Jews who see Reform Jews as gentiles – all have the great virtue of intellectual purity. History, on this view, is a war of truth against falsehood, and we can be certain that we are the sole possessors of truth. The Dead Sea Scrolls testify to the attraction of this idea, and it has hypnotic potency in confused times. But the chronicles of human tyranny tell how much blood has been shed in its name, and Jewry has not been without its own internal wars.

When God was about to create man, said the rabbis, the angels of truth and peace objected. God then took truth and threw it to the ground, bidding it spring up from the earth.[50] At most, so the midrash implies, we can aspire to truth as it is on earth, not as it is in Heaven. Only by acknowledging this are peace and coexistence possible.

The alternative is inclusivism. My reading of the Jewish sources, which may of course be faulty, suggests that God, in choosing Israel, made a covenant with an entire people. This was not his only choice. Before the flood, he chose a single righteous individual, Noah. After the flood, he made a covenant with all humanity. But in choosing Abraham, Isaac, Jacob, and Jacob's children, he chose to link his name with a particular family. In Rabbi Akiva's words: all mankind is in God's image, but Israel are called God's children.[51] Israel in turn, by accepting the covenant at Sinai, agreed to be bound for all time to be a "kingdom of priests and a holy nation." Like most relationships between fathers and sons in the Bible, that between God and Israel has frequently been tense. There is no suggestion in the Torah that it would be otherwise. A covenant, like parenthood or marriage, involves risk. God accepts the risk that Israel will be unfaithful. Israel faces the risk that God will hide his face. But they are bound to one another by the unbreakable force of mutual undertaking. Jewish history is the record of that relationship. Its epic drama, stretching from Abraham and Sarah to the Holocaust and the return of Jews to the promised land, is still unfolding.

Inclusivism is the belief that the covenant was made with a people, not with righteous individuals alone. One may leave or enter the people by apostasy on the one hand, conversion on the other. But the normal mode of faith is through birth, community, and the transmission of tradition across the generations. That is why the central institutions of Judaism are the family, the *kehillah* (community), and education as induction (*chinukh*) into a people, its past and laws. Western modernity, by contrast, has given peculiar weight to the individual and the state, a dichotomy into which Judaism cannot be translated. This either-or was internalized in Jewry's two most striking innovations: Reform (the

---

50. Genesis Rabbah 8:5.
51. Mish. Avot 3:18.

individual) and secular Zionism (the state). Neither, I believe, if pursued with consistency, represents continuity with the Jewish past or a formula for "one people" in the Jewish present.

Inclusivism understands the present alienation of many Jews from Torah as neither a mandate to fragment the covenant (pluralism) nor justification for a clash of competing exclusive truths. Instead it is evidence of the overwhelming force of a secular culture in which many of Judaism's truths are unstatable. It does not accord this culture the status of revelation. But neither does it regard it as non-existent. Judaism demands of Jews, now as always in the past, that they go against the current of the times. But it understands that those who go with it are not necessarily acting out an individual renunciation of Judaism. The Talmud describes a dream in which Rav Ashi meets King Manasseh, one of the Bible's great idolaters. The king teaches the rabbi a halakhah he did not know. Why then, asks the rabbi, did you worship idols? Had you lived in my time, answers the king, you would have caught up your cloak and run after me.[52] Rabbi Jochanan taught: whoever denies that Manasseh has a share in the world to come is guilty of demoralizing those who would return.[53]

This perception lies behind the inclusivist ruling that Jews today who abandon halakhah are for the most part to be judged *tinokot shenishbu*, subjects of cultural duress. In one form or another this was the view advocated by Rabbis Jacob Ettlinger, David Zvi Hoffmann, Abraham Kook, Chaim Ozer Grodzinski, Joseph Saul Nathansohn, and Abraham Karelitz, and was based on a ruling of Maimonides about second-generation Karaites. I have suggested in this chapter that its roots are to be found much earlier in Jewish history, in the argument of the book of Genesis. Inclusivism involves a denial of truth to secular and liberal Judaisms (much as these Judaisms involve a denial of truth to Orthodoxy). But it insists that secular and liberal Jews are part of the covenant, participants in Judaism's bonds of collective responsibility, to be related to with love, dignity, and respect. This offends the modern self, which demands to be respected not for what it is but for what it believes and

---

52. Sanhedrin 102b.
53. Ibid. 103a.

does. It is, in terms of modern consciousness, an imperfect solution. But perfect solutions are not to be found this side of messianic time.

Inclusivism is not another name for Modern Orthodoxy. Modern Orthodoxy is a statement of Jewish *ideology*. Inclusivism is a statement of Jewish *ecology*, of the complex totality of Jewish peoplehood. I have argued that Orthodoxy is not a denomination. It is instead a boundary, defined by halakhah and the principles of Jewish faith, within which many types of philosophy and piety are possible. Modern Orthodoxy is one of them, but not the only one that lays legitimate claim to the attentions of the modern Jew. There are differences of evaluation, style, and orientation that have not in the past received, nor do they in the present call for, halakhic resolution, despite their deep religious significance. There are forms of behaviour (self-imposed stringency, "beyond the letter of the law") which have religious dignity but are not to be confused with the halakhic norm itself. The Judaism of halakhah and faith is a language within which many sentences are possible. There is an open-ended number of ways and contexts in which God can be served and his name sanctified, and inclusivism does not seek to decide between them. There are inclusivists within the yeshiva tradition and the Hasidic world as well as within modern Orthodoxy. Common to them is a deep love of and reluctance to divide the Jewish people.

INCLUSIVIST IMPERATIVES

What, then, would an inclusivist advocate in the present? Firstly, a deep sensitivity to the language in which we speak of other Jews. The Jewish tradition attached the highest significance to speech. God spoke and the universe was: the world was created by words. Human beings, too, create or destroy social worlds with words. Language, for Judaism, is the medium of revelation. Indeed, the Targum translates the phrase in the second chapter of Genesis, "and man became a living soul," as "and man became a speaking soul."[54] For Jewish consciousness, words are life. In this context we can understand the rabbinic insistence that *lashon hara,*

---

54. *Targum Onkelos* on Gen. 2:7.

evil speech, is tantamount to the three cardinal sins of murder, immorality, and idolatry combined.[55]

We may not speak of other Jews except in the language of love and respect. Rabbinic tradition taught collective solidarity and the prophetic obligation to speak well (*lelamed zekhut*) of the congregation of Israel. When Moses declared of the Israelites, "They will not believe in me," God, according to the Talmud, replied, "They are believers, the children of believers, but you ultimately will not believe."[56] The Talmud states that when God said to Hosea, "Your children have sinned," he should not have agreed, but instead should have said, "They are Your children, the children of your favoured ones.... Be compassionate to them."[57] Rabbi Shimon bar Yochai taught: Even when a generation curses its father and does not bless its mother [when it rejects God and Jewish tradition], "slander not a servant to his master."[58] There is a covenantal obligation to search out and articulate the good in fellow Jews. To be sure, Jewish law recognizes exceptions to the rule against "evil speech." Heresy is one. But the inclusivist, by insisting that non-believing Jews today are *tinokot shenishbu,* has ruled out this clause in almost all cases.

There is, admittedly, a biblical obligation to reprove wrongdoing.[59] But according to many authorities it does not apply when it is certain that reproof will not be heeded.[60] According to talmudic principle it does not apply when a person, originally acting in ignorance, is likely to continue to transgress, now knowingly.[61] There were mishnaic teachers who maintained that the whole institution of reproof was at times impossible to sustain. A generation might be unworthy: either it lacked the will to respond to criticism or it lacked individuals who could

55. Y. Pe'ah 1:1; Yad, *De'ot* 7:3.
56. Shabbat 97a; Exodus Rabbah 3:12.
57. Pesachim 87a.
58. Ibid. 87b. See also Song of Songs Rabbah 1:6. On the general theme see Urbach, *The Sages,* 554–64.
59. Lev. 19:17. On the subject generally see Jonathan Sacks, "Rabbinic Conceptions of Responsibility for Others: A Study of the Command of Rebuke and the Idea of Mutual Suretyship," Ph.D. thesis (University of London, 1982).
60. *Tosafot,* Shabbat 55a, s.v. *Ve'af al gav; Hagahot Maimoniyot* on Yad, *De'ot* 6, n. 3.
61. Beitzah 30a, Shabbat 148b.

administer criticism persuasively.[62] In any event, rules Maimonides, reproof must be delivered "gently and tenderly" and must not put the other person to shame.[63]

Secondly, the inclusivist would not seek to use coercive means to bring Jews back to tradition. Admittedly, the halakhic system recognizes coercion. Maimonides speaks of the messianic king using it to enforce religious law.[64] But its valid use implies underlying public assent. In the one passage in which the rabbis suggested that the commandments were given to Israel against their will (according to which God suspended Mount Sinai over the Israelites and told them that if they did not assent, they would die) Rav Acha bar Yaakov responded: "This constitutes a strong objection to the Torah."[65] Rabbi Abraham Karelitz argued that at the present time coercive punishments would be seen by a secular population as unwarranted. They would therefore not improve but worsen the religious environment.[66]

In the Middle Ages, Gersonides contrasted Torah with the laws of the nations in that while the Torah invites assent, the laws of other faiths "do not conform to equity and wisdom...so that people only obey them because of compulsion, fear, and the threat of punishment and not because of their essence."[67] In the nineteenth century Samson Raphael Hirsch welcomed an age of religious freedom.[68] More recently, Rabbi Nachum Rabinovitch has argued that the sages "perceived in every reduction of the power of coercion a step forward in preparing the world for

---

62. Arakhin 16b.
63. Yad, *De'ot* 6:8. To be sure, there are circumstances in which, according to Maimonides, one is allowed to put others to shame. But this presumably only applies if there is reason to suppose that such a strategy will be effective in securing repentance. See the literature cited in Sacks, "Rabbinic Conceptions of Responsibility for Others," 304–78.
64. Yad, *Melakhim* 11:4.
65. Shabbat 88b.
66. *Chazon Ish* on *Yoreh De'ah* 2:16.
67. Gersonides on Isa. 42:1–4.
68. Hirsch, *Nineteen Letters*, Letter 18: "I rejoice that the scales hang free, held by God alone, and that only intellectual efforts mutually balance each other, but that no temporal power can interpose the sword to check the freedom of the swinging." Hirsch believed that a free society would lead to the purification of religion.

the Heavenly kingdom." The whole thrust of Judaism is, he suggests, of a gradual society-wide education towards the uncoerced acceptance of halakhah.[69] The inclusivist, sensitive to these arguments, seeks to draw Jews back not by legislative or political means but by "words of peace"[70] and "cords of love."[71]

Thirdly, the inclusivist understands the supreme importance Judaism attaches to education. For it is through constant study that Torah is transformed from external law to internalized command. Knowing that Torah is a law not of nature but of revelation, he is aware that acceptance of it does not come naturally.[72] God seeks not only the deed, but also the heart. But that means an informed heart and instructed emotion. The inclusivist recognizes that education must speak to the cultural situation of the student; as the Bible puts it, it must answer the questions asked by the child. He knows that "learning leads to doing," that education is Judaism's classic alternative to coercion, and that secular culture can only be confronted – as it was by the sages in Greek and Roman times – by an intensification of Jewish learning.

Above all, he believes that only through universal Jewish education can Jews satisfy the first requirement of a people: that its members share a language of discourse.[73] He agrees with Alasdair MacIntyre's statement: "An educated community can exist only where there is some large degree of shared background beliefs and attitudes, informed by widespread reading of a common body of texts which are accorded a canonical status within that particular community" and when there is also "an established tradition of interpretative understanding of how those texts are to be read and construed."[74] Throughout their dispersion

69. Nachum Rabinovitch, "Darkhah shel Torah," in B. Brenner, O. Kapach, and Z. Shimshoni (eds.), *Ma'alei Asor* (Ma'aleh Adumim: Ma'aliot, 1988), 8–42; for an abridged English trans. see "The Torah Way," in Shubert Spero and Yitzchak Pessin (eds.), *Religious Zionism after Forty Years of Statehood* (Jerusalem: WZO, 1989), 277–308.

70. Yad, *Mamrim* 3:3.

71. *Chazon Ish* on *Yoreh De'ah* 2:16.

72. See Cynthia Ozick, "On Living in the Gentile World," in Nahum Glatzer (ed.), *Modern Jewish Thought* (New York: Schocken, 1977), 167–74.

73. See Hartman, "Halakhah as a Ground for Creating a Shared Spiritual Language," in his *Joy and Responsibility*, 130–61.

74. Alasdair MacIntyre, "The Idea of an Educated Public," in Graham Haydon (ed.),

Jews were linked by texts. Heine called the Torah the "portable father-land" of the Jews. It was their shared territory, their central point of reference. Their arguments and speculations were all couched in the form of concentric commentaries to its words. Without the acquisition of a shared textual heritage it is difficult to see how Jews can begin to communicate as "one people with one language."[75]

Fourthly, while not advocating halakhic change along the lines argued by Rabbi Chaim Hirschensohn or Eliezer Berkovits, the inclusivist seeks to apply halakhah to its widest possible constituency. To the extent that precedent and consensus allow, the inclusivist is mindful of the metahalakhic principles recorded in the Talmud: that Jewish law should, as far as possible, not be beyond the reach of the poor; that it should be sensitive to the needs and rights of women; and that it should not bar the way to religious return.[76] He recalls one of Maimonides' principles of rabbinic authority, that it be used "to bring the many back to religion or to save the many from stumbling in other transgressions."[77] Where judicial discretion is available, he uses it to "open the doors to those who wish to perform *mitzvot*,"[78] and to preempt Jews being driven away from Judaism (*tarbut ra'ah*).[79] He seeks to create an environment in which Jews will bring their problems to halakhah rather than to some other system for solution, and he is mindful of Maimonides' statement that "the ordinances of the Torah were meant to bring upon the world not vengeance, but mercy, loving-kindness, and peace."[80]

Fifthly, the inclusivist seeks a nuanced understanding of secular and liberal Jews. He refuses a dualism that divides Jewry into unmixed

---

Education and Values (London: Institute of Education, 1987), 15–36.

75. On the general state of Jewish literacy see Ruth Wisse, "The Hebrew Imperative," *Commentary* (June 1990), 34–39; Paul Mendes-Flohr, *Divided Passions* (Detroit: Wayne State University Press, 1991), 413–23.

76. I.e., the principles of *hatorah chasah al mamonam shel Yisrael, hefsed merubah; mishum agunah; shakdu chakhamim al takanat benot Yisrael; takanat hashavim,* etc.

77. Yad, *Mamrim* 2:4.

78. Rashba, 581.

79. See the summary of positions in Chajes, *Kol Sifrei*, 1021–27.

80. Yad, *Shabbat* 2:3.

categories of good and evil. He is aware that there are some authorities who maintain that even the good deeds of those who reject halakhah have no religious value.[81] None the less, he interprets this as applying to heretics in the past, not to the Jews of today. In so doing, he relies on the general inclusivist argument that secular and liberal Jews are not to be judged as deliberate rebels but as unwitting (*shogeg*) or coerced (*anus*)[82] products of their environment. Or he maintains the distinction argued by Rabbi Isaac Reines, that halakhic intent is required only for commands between man and God, not for those between man and man.[83]

More strongly still, the inclusivist follows the argument of Maimonides in the *Epistle on Martyrdom*. There Maimonides invokes the talmudic principle that "the Holy One, blessed be he, does not withhold the reward of any creature"[84] to show that Jews who, under duress, convert to Islam still gain merit by performing Torah commandments. Maimonides cites aggadic texts which show that God recompenses the greatest wrongdoers – Esau, Ahab, Eglon, Nebuchadnezzar – for the smallest good deed they do. "If these well-known heretics were generously rewarded for the little good that they did, is it conceivable that God will not reward the Jews who despite the exigencies of forced conversion perform commandments secretly?" [85] Maimonides goes further. Even one who could escape religious persecution but chooses not to is still rewarded for his good deeds. "If he fulfils a precept, God will reward

---

81. Rabbi Zvi Hirsch Chajes argues that even though we have a rule that *mitzvot ein tzerikhot kavanah*, "the fulfilment of the commands does not require intention," this applies only to the specific intention to fulfil a particular command (*kavanah peratit*). For an act to count as the fulfilment of a command, it must none the less be accompanied by the general intention (*kavanah kelalit*) which comes from religious belief. If this belief is lacking, the act lacks halakhic significance as religious behaviour. See Chajes, *Kol Sifrei*, 1012. A similar conclusion was arrived at independently by Rabbi Elchanan Wasserman (*Kovetz Ma'amarim*, 67). Wasserman invokes the halakhic category of *mitasek*, where the agent is unaware of the nature of his act, to characterize the religious behaviour of Jews who deny the fundamentals of faith.

82. See in this context Radbaz, 1258.

83. Isaac Reines, *Shenei Hame'orot* (Pietroków, 1913), 19.

84. Pesachim 118a, Nazir 23b, Bava Kama 38b, Horayot 10b.

85. Trans. in Halkin, *Crisis and Leadership*, 23.

him doubly, because he acted for God only, and not to show off or be accepted as an observant individual."[86]

With these principles in mind, the inclusivist shares the judgement of Rabbi Abraham Kook that secular Zionists and Israelis are engaged in fulfilling the command of "settling the land" which the sages and Nachmanides regarded as "equal to all the other commands combined."[87] He respects the fact that most Jews worldwide retain a high commitment to charity, another act to which the sages attached the highest value. To this he adds Maimonides' comment that one who performs even a single precept, for its own sake and out of love, is promised a share in the world to come.[88]

The inclusivist attaches positive significance to the fact that liberal Judaisms have played their part in keeping alive for many Jews the values of Jewish identity, faith, and practice. These are not identity, faith, and practice as he understands them, but he recalls Maimonides' ruling that even Christianity and Islam had served "to prepare the whole world to worship God with one accord" by spreading knowledge of the messianic age, the Torah, and the commandments, even though these were not as Judaism understood them.[89] How much more does this apply to movements which have served to retain Jews within Jewry who might otherwise have drifted into another faith or no faith at all.

Sixthly, believing as he does in divine providence, the inclusivist strives to recognize the positive consequences of Jewish liberalism and secularism even as he refuses to recognize their truth or ultimate viability. He recalls the statement of Rabbi Kook, quoted in the last chapter, that "when the light of prophecy is screened" good [*tikun*] sometimes comes about through means which one would not have chosen *ab initio*. As a result of the many reforming or secularizing movements of the

---

86. Ibid., 33.

87. *Sifre* on. "Re'eh," 80; Nachmanides, *Hasagot* on Maimonides, *Sefer Hamitzvot*, positive command 4; see also his commentary on Lev. 18:25. On Kook see Yaron, *Mishnato shel Harav Kook*, 231–84.

88. Maimonides, *Commentary on the Mishnah*, Makkot 3:17.

89. Yad, *Melakhim* 11. The passage is censored in standard printed editions. An English translation is given in Isidore Twersky (ed.), *A Maimonides Reader* (New York: Behrman House, 1972), 226–27.

nineteenth century, Jews negotiated the traumas of social change and antisemitism without mass conversions to Christianity or widespread abandonment of identity. Within each of these movements there was a complex dialectic of assimilation and counter-assimilation, a desire for "normality" alongside fierce pride in religious or national difference. Even the "Science of Judaism" movement, conceived by some of its founders as a means of "giving the remains of Judaism a decent burial," led to a renewed interest in Jewish history and texts, and thus indirectly to the revival of the love of Zion and Jewish scholarship.

Each of these groups, while dissenting from tradition, none the less gave new life to some aspect of tradition. Secular Zionism reminded Jews that political activity, not only passivity, was part of Judaism. Indeed, Maimonides had written to the sages of Marseilles that Jerusalem had fallen because the Jews of the time neglected "the art of martial defence and government."[90] Other secularists and liberals revived the Hebrew language, the Jewish national idea, and the prophetic passion for social justice. Some strove to reach a new "hearing" of the biblical text. Others renewed interest in rabbinic aggadah and in medieval Jewish thought and poetry. Where such movements did not exist, Jews estranged from tradition either passively abandoned Judaism altogether or actively joined secular revolutionary causes.

Even on the most negative view, that the new forms of Jewishness hastened the flight from tradition, none the less they kept alive the future possibility of return. Nathan Glazer, an acute critic of the secularization of Jewish life, noted that the mere fact that Jews had remained Jews meant that "the Jewish religious tradition is not just a subject for scholars but is capable now and then of finding expression in life. And even if it finds no expression in one generation or another, the commitment to remain related to it still exists. Dead in one, two, or three generations, it may come to life in the fourth."[91] Glazer wrote those words in 1957. Since then the religious return of thousands of children of the fourth generation has proved the accuracy of his insight. In short, even

---

90. English version in Twersky, *A Maimonides Reader*, 465.
91. Nathan Glazer, *American Judaism*, 2nd ed. (Chicago: University of Chicago Press, 1972), 144.

as the inclusivist is pained by the fragmentation of Jews and Judaism, he recognizes its part in the divine design. He says, with Rabbi Akiva, "This too was for good."[92] In retrospect, halakhic Judaism might say to its opponents what the biblical Joseph said to his brothers: "You intended to harm me, but God intended it for good to accomplish what is now being done, the saving of many lives."[93]

Seventhly, the inclusivist, because he sees the shadings, not just the black and the white, in contemporary Jewish life, calls on liberal and secular Jewish leaders to act responsibly in the context of the totality of Judaism and the Jewish people. He does not judge their decisions indifferently. He values modern Reform Judaism's partial return to religious practice, Jewish education, a sense of peoplehood, the Hebrew language, and a love of the land of Israel. He respects secular Israelis' new interest in the Jewish history and literature of the past eighteen hundred years, the softening of early Zionism's negation of rabbinic Judaism, and the discovery that Israel is not called to be – perhaps can never be – "like all the nations."

At the same time, he discerns and is bound to warn against conflicting tendencies. Within Reform, the laxity of conversions, the decision on patrilineal descent, the endorsement of homosexuality, premarital sex, and abortion on demand are fateful breaks not only with the letter but with the whole spirit of Jewish law. They increase the likelihood that at some time Orthodoxy will see Reform as it saw Christianity: as a separate religion. Within Israeli secularism the growing hostility to Judaism, the resurrection of Spinoza as a hero of Jewish thought, and frequent acts of provocation towards the religious public all intensify the force of confrontation over that of reconciliation. The inclusivist welcomes those such as Jakob Petuchowski within Reform and Eliezer Schweid within secularism who argue that no Jewish movement can or may sever its links with Jewish tradition or the rest of the Jewish people.

The inclusivist understands in advance that Jews outside Orthodoxy will find his position "patronizing" or "imperialistic." That is the fate of inclusivism in the modern world. The Reform or secular Jew wishes

---

92. Berakhot 60b–61a.
93. Gen. 50:20.

to be respected for what he is, not for what potentially he might become. Indeed, extremists on all sides prefer extremist opponents, because each reinforces the other's prejudices. The inclusivist knows that his refusal to accept pluralism or dualism will find favour with no side. None the less, his decision to view non-Orthodox Jews as *tinokot shenishbu* flows from his deep love of the Jewish people, his respect for the sanctity of every Jew, and his sensitivity to the covenantal imperative not to divide where division is avoidable. He asks non-Orthodox Jews at least to make the effort to understand the logic of his position, and why no other is available within the terms of a tradition which he believes to be true, revealed, and binding. That is what I have tried to do in this book.

Eighthly, the inclusivist makes a parallel plea for understanding to exclusivist Orthodoxy. He does not stand midway between Orthodoxy and Reform, halakhah and the rejection of halakhah. On the contrary, he is committed to the same principles of faith and law as the exclusivists. His God is their God, his halakhah their halakhah, his reverence for the sages, past and present, the same as theirs. Moreover, he acknowledges in the yeshiva and Hasidic movements one of the great miracles of Jewish history. Over the past two hundred years, their resistance to secularization, their renewal of Jewish learning and piety, their succession of sages and saints, above all their astonishing reconstruction of Jewish life after the Holocaust are, for him, models of religious heroism before which he stands awestruck in admiration.

But he recalls with pain that during the same period the great inclusivists were judged by their rabbinic contemporaries with suspicion, disdain, and sometimes worse. The Hasidic movement, which spread piety to the masses of East European Jewry, aroused the deep hostility of rabbinic leaders. So did the efforts of Rabbi Azriel Hildesheimer in Eisenstadt and Rabbi Isaac Reines in Lida, to create seminaries to train rabbis for a new age. So did the willingness of Reines and other Orthodox rabbis to work with the non-religious in the Zionist movement. So did Rabbi Abraham Kook's attempt to bridge the abyss between secular Zionists and Judaism. Religious hostility towards inclusivism has not ceased. The recent attacks on such diverse figures as the leader of Chabad, Rabbi Menachem Mendel Schneerson, the talmudist and mystic Rabbi Adin Steinsaltz, and the leader of modern Orthodoxy,

Rabbi Norman Lamm, all fall within a by now lamentably predictable pattern. Inclusivism – the desire to bring Jews back to one another and to Torah – is seen as compromising religious purity, mixing with heretics and transgressors, and the thin end of a wedge of reform.

While respecting the deep integrity and halakhic provenance of such a view, the inclusivist defends his own position. He is obeying one of Judaism's most famous imperatives, Hillel's advice to "love peace, pursue peace, love people and bring them close to Torah." He recalls Maimonides' responsum on the Karaites, where he rules that one should behave towards them with respect, humility, honesty, and peace so long as they do not speak disrespectfully of Israel's past and present sages.[94] He heeds Maimonides' statement that "it is not right to alienate, scorn, and hate people who desecrate the Sabbath. It is our duty to befriend them and encourage them to fulfil the commandments.[95]

The inclusivist adds that, historically, the fears of contagion by association proved unjustified. The Hasidic movement did not break with halakhah. The Judaisms of Rabbis Hildesheimer, Reines, Kook, and others did not degenerate into secularism or reform. Indeed, in an instructive responsum, the fifteenth-century halakhist Rabbi Elijah Mizrachi ruled that one should allow Karaites to enter Jewish schools. Despite the fact that he had forbidden Jews to marry Karaites, Mizrachi insisted that their admission to the academies raised standards even among the Jewish students, and that the misplaced zeal which had led rabbis to exclude them had had a catastrophic effect on both sides.[96] That view surely applies today. Rabbi Yechiel Weinberg requested those opposed to efforts to draw marginal Jews back to Judaism to recall that those who engaged in such efforts were also driven by the same love and reverence for Torah.[97] It is that effort of understanding that the inclusivist calls for from his Orthodox critics. He does not ask exclusivists

---

94. Maimonides, *Responsa*, ed. J. Blau (Jerusalem: Mekitze Nirdamim, 1958), 449.
95. Maimonides, *Epistle on Martyrdom*, end.
96. Rabbi Elijah Mizrachi, *Responsa*, 57. I am indebted for this reference to Nachum Rabinovitch, "Kol Yisrael Arevin Zeh Bazeh" – a superlative example, incidentally, of halakhic inclusivism.
97. *Seridei Esh*, iii, 93, end.

to become inclusivists. He merely asks them not to destroy what he is labouring to build.

Ninthly, the inclusivist calls on all Jews to respect the sanctity of the Jewish people, collectively and individually. There is a prayer Jews say at the beginning of the morning service. "Not because of our righteousness do we lay our prayers before you.... What are we? What is our life? What is our kindness? What is our righteousness?" It is a litany of human worthlessness, followed by a transfiguring "but": "*But* we are your people, the children of your covenant." We may be without value, achievements, or good deeds, but we are beloved of God. Such is the message of the prayer. And if it applies to one Jew it applies to all. That is the irreducible minimum of a sense of covenantal peoplehood.

Each Jew must know this: that those others of his people with whom he disagrees carry with them the indivisible history of generations of Jews who survived the slings and arrows of outrageous fortune and yet chose to remain Jews. Every Jew is heir to a succession of tragedies and deliverances, trials and affirmations, unparalleled by any other nation. The Talmud rules that we must rise in respect for age, whether the elderly is wise or unwise, because the mere personal accumulation of history accords dignity to its possessor.[98] That, metaphorically if not halakhically, applies to the Jewish people as a whole. Every Jew today who, after the tragedy of the Holocaust, the attacks on the State of Israel, and the ravages of assimilation, chooses to stay a Jew and have Jewish children is making a momentous affirmation that may not be dishonoured. Even if we must sometimes reject the beliefs and deeds of an individual Jew, none the less he or she is a fragment of the *shekhinah*, the divine presence which dwells in the midst of Jews wherever and whatever they are. For the inclusivist believes with perfect faith that the covenant binds all Jews to one another, and that a Jew who remains attached to the chosen people cannot be unchosen.

Lastly, the inclusivist calls on Jews to hear the divine call in history. The Final Solution made no distinctions between religious and secular, affirming and assimilated Jews. If Hitler scheduled all Jews for death, may we do less than affirm all Jews for life? Communist and

---

98. Kiddushin 33a; Yad, *Talmud Torah* 6:9.

anti-Zionist assaults made no discrimination between traditional and atheist, diaspora and Israeli Jews. May we? May we protest against gentile antisemitism without practising Jewish philosemitism, *ahavat Yisrael*? May we ask the nations of the world to live at peace with Jews without first learning to live at peace with one another? After the self-inflicted divisions of the nineteenth century, tragedy in the twentieth century has brought Jews to the knowledge that they are involved inescapably, each in the fate of all. If history is a commentary on the covenant, can we avoid the conclusion that the past unspeakable century has been summoning Jews to return to one another and to God?

Twice before, at times of crisis, the people of Israel has split apart. Today it is threatening to do so again. But it has not yet done so. None of the current tendencies in Jewish life is on the verge of disappearance. Orthodoxy is resurgent. Reform is growing in numbers in both America and Britain. Religious groups in Israel have achieved prominence and power. The secularization of Israeli society proceeds apace. The State of Israel has survived the many attacks upon it, and has become the focus of diaspora life. The diaspora has shown a remarkable persistence, and has even witnessed a cultural and religious revival. Each, within its own terms of reference, can claim to be an heir to the Jewish future. The possibilities of fracture are immense.

And yet, among many Jews of all kinds there is a genuine desire for unity even if it is expressed in incompatible ways. Inclusivism and pluralism, let us recall, are both ways of stating that aspiration, despite the fact that they are destined to collide. Far more than in the early years of the state, Jews in Israel and in the diaspora are likely to see their fortunes as interlinked. Orthodoxy and Reform, Israel and the diaspora, religious and secular, despite their fierce antagonisms, have thus far held back from the final step of separation. There are centripetal as well as centrifugal pressures in contemporary Jewish life, driving together as well as forcing apart. The future, then, is peculiarly open, tense with conflicting forces of breaking and mending.

The primal scene of Jewish history is of the Israelites in the wilderness, fractious, rebellious, engaged in endless diversions, yet none the less slowly journeying towards the fulfilment of the covenantal promise. No image seems to me more descriptive of contemporary Jewry. There is no agreement on the route. But unmistakably, Jews are returning: some to a faith, others to a way of life, some to a place, others to a sense of peoplehood. For eighteen hundred years of dispersion, Jews prayed for freedom, the ingathering of exiles, the restoration of sovereignty, and the rebuilding of Jerusalem. Today they have them. If faith implies anything – faith in God, or the Jewish people, or the covenant that binds one to the other as a "kingdom of priests and a holy nation" – it implies this: that Jews having come thus far will not now disintegrate, so advanced along the journey which Abraham began nearly four thousand years ago. The inclusivist faith is that Jews, divided by where they stand, are united by what they are travelling towards,[99] the destination which alone gives meaning to Jewish history: the promised union of Torah, the Jewish people, the land of Israel, and God.

---

99. See Yeshayahu Leibowitz, *Emunah, Historiah, Ve'arakhim*, 112–18. Leibowitz argues persuasively that Jewish unity is not a fact but a task of Torah.

Bibliography

A. WORKS IN ENGLISH

Avineri, Shlomo, *Moses Hess: Prophet of Communism and Zionism* (New York: New York University Press, 1985).

Bamberger, Bernard, *Proselytism in the Talmud* (New York, 1968).

Ben Menahem, H., "Is There Always One Uniquely Correct Answer to a Legal Question in the Talmud?," *Jewish Law Annual*, 6 (1986), 164–75.

Berger, Peter L., *Facing up to Modernity* (New York: Basic Books, 1977).

———— "On the Obsolescence of the Concept of Honour" [1970], repr. in Michael Sander (ed.), *Liberalism and Its Critics* (Oxford: Blackwell, 1984), 149–58; also in Berger et al., *The Homeless Mind*, 78–89.

———— *A Rumour of Angels* (London: Allen Lane, 1970).

———— The Sacred Canopy: Elements of a Sociological Theory of Religion (New York: Doubleday, 1967).

Berger, Peter L., and Luckmann, Thomas, *The Social Construction of Reality* (London: Pelican, 1987).

Berger, Peter L., Berger, Brigitte, and Kellner, Hansfried, *The Homeless Mind: Modernization and Consciousness* (London: Pelican, 1974).

Berkovits, Berel, "Comments on Rabbi Dr. Brichto and Rabbi Dr. Jacobs," *Jewish Law Annual*, 8 (1989), 269–88.

Berkovits, Eliezer, *Crisis and Faith* (New York: Sanhedrin Press, 1976).

———— *Jewish Women in Time and Torah* (Hoboken, NJ: Ktav, 1990).

———— *Major Themes in Modern Philosophies of Judaism* (New York: Ktav, 1974).

———— *Not in Heaven: The Nature and Function of Halakhah* (New York: Ktav, 1983).

Berman, Lawrence V., "Maimonides on Political Leadership," in Daniel Elazar (ed.), *Kinship and Consent* (Ramat Gan: Turtledove, 1981), 113–25.

Bernstein, Louis, "Orthodoxy: Flourishing but Divided," *Judaism*, 36:2 (1987), 174–78.

Besdin, Abraham R., *Reflections of the Rav: Lessons in Jewish Thought Adapted from the Lectures of R. Joseph B. Soloveitchik* (Jerusalem: World Zionist Organization, 1979).

Black, Eugene C., *The Social Politics of Anglo-Jewry, 1880–1920* (Oxford: Blackwell, 1988).

Bleich, J. David, *Contemporary Halakhic Problems* (New York: Ktav, 1977).

———— "Halakhah as an Absolute," *Judaism*, 29 (1980), 30–37.

———— "Parameters and Limits of Communal Unity from the Perspective of Jewish Law," *L'Eylah*, 21 (Spring 1986), 31–36.

———— "Permitting the Use of a *Mikveh* for Non-Orthodox Conversion," *Tradition*, 23:2 (1988), 88–95.

Blidstein, Gerald, "Who Was Not a Jew? The Medieval Discussion," *Israel Law Review*, 11 (1976), 369–90.

Borowitz, Eugene B., "The Autonomous Jewish Self," *Modern Judaism*, 4:1 (1984), 39–56.

———— *Choices in Modern Jewish Thought* (New York: Behrman House, 1983).

———— *A New Jewish Theology in the Making* (Philadelphia: Westminster Press, 1968).

———— "Subjectivity and the Halakhic Process," *Judaism*, 13 (1964), 211–19.

Braude, William G., *Jewish Proselytizing* (Providence, RI: Brown University, 1941).

Brichto, Sidney, "Halakhah with Humility," *Jewish Chronicle*, Oct. 2, 1987, 29.

Bulka, Reuven P., *The Coming Cataclysm* (Oakville, Ontario: Mosaic Press, 1984).

Cesarani, David (ed.), *The Making of Modern Anglo-Jewry* (Oxford: Blackwell, 1990).

Cohen, Jack J., "Halakhah and the Life of Holiness," *Rabbinical Assembly Annual*, 30 (1958).

Cohen, Jack Simcha, *Intermarriage and Conversion: A Halakhic Solution* (Hoboken, NJ: Ktav, 1987).

—— *Timely Jewish Questions, Timeless Rabbinic Answers* (Northvale, NJ: Jason Aronson, 1991).

Cohen, Steven M., *American Assimilation or Jewish Revival?* (Bloomington, IN: Indiana University Press, 1988).

—— "The One in 2000 Controversy," *Moment*, 12:1 (1987), 11–17.

Cohen, Stuart, *The Three Crowns* (Cambridge: Cambridge University Press, 1990).

Cowen, Anne and Roger, *Victorian Jews through British Eyes* (Oxford: Oxford University Press for the Littman Library, 1987).

Cuddihy, John Murray, *The Ordeal of Civility: Freud, Marx, Levi-Strauss and the Jewish Struggle with Modernity*, 2nd ed. (Boston: Beacon Press, 1987).

Cupitt, Don, *Crisis of Moral Authority* (London: SCM Press, 1985).

Daube, David, *Collaboration with Tyranny in Rabbinic Law* (Oxford: Oxford University Press, 1965).

Domb, I., *The Transformation: The Case of the Neturei Karta* (London: Hamadfis, 1958).

Dorff, Elliot N., and Rosett, Arthur, *A Living Tree* (Albany, NY: State University of New York Press, 1988).

Dworkin, Ronald, *Law's Empire* (London: Fontana, 1986).

—— *A Matter of Principle* (Oxford: Clarendon Press, 1986).

—— *Taking Rights Seriously* (London: Duckworth, 1978).

Eckardt, A. Roy, *Jews and Christians: The Contemporary Meeting* (Bloomington, IN: Indiana University Press, 1986).

Ehrmann, S., "Moses Sofer," in Leo Jung (ed.), *Jewish Leaders* (New York: Bloch, 1953), 117–38.

Eisen, Arnold, *The Chosen People in America: A Study in Jewish Religious Ideology* (Bloomington, IN: Indiana University Press, 1983).

—— *Galut: Modern Jewish Reflection on Homelessness and Homecoming* (Bloomington, IN: Indiana University Press, 1986).

————— "Off Center: The Concept of the Land of Israel in Modern Jewish Thought," in Lawrence A. Hoffman (ed.), *The Land of Israel* (Notre Dame, IN: University of Notre Dame Press, 1986), 263–96.

Elazar, Daniel J., "The New Sadducees," *Midstream* (Aug.–Sept. 1978), 20–25.

————— *People and Polity* (Detroit: Wayne State University Press, 1989).

Elazar, Daniel J., and Cohen, Stuart A., *The Jewish Polity* (Bloomington, IN: Indiana University Press, 1985).

Endelman, Todd M., "The Englishness of Jewish Modernity in England," in Jacob Katz (ed.), *Toward Modernity: The European Jewish Model* (Oxford: Transaction Books, 1987), 225–46.

————— *The Jews of Georgian England* (Philadelphia: The Jewish Publication Society, 1979).

————— *Radical Assimilation in English Jewish History, 1656–1945* (Bloomington, IN: Indiana University Press, 1990).

Epstein, Barukh Halevi, *My Uncle, the Netziv* [1928], trans. Moshe Dombey (Jerusalem: Artscroll, 1988).

Esh, Shaul, "The Dignity of the Destroyed," in Y. Gutman and L. Rothkirchen (eds.), *The Catastrophe of European Jewry* (Jerusalem: Yad Vashem, 1976), 346–66.

Fackenheim, Emil, *The Jewish Return into History: Reflections in the Age of Auschwitz and a New Jerusalem* (New York: Schocken, 1978).

————— *To Mend the World: Foundations of Future Jewish Thought* (New York: Schocken, 1982).

————— *What is Judaism?* (New York: Collier, 1987).

Finestein, Israel, "Anglo-Jewish Opinion during the Struggle for Emancipation," *Transactions of the Jewish Historical Society of England,* 20 (1964), 113–43.

————— *Post-Emancipation Jewry: The Anglo-Jewish Experience,* The Seventh Sacks Lecture (Oxford: Oxford Centre for Postgraduate Hebrew Studies, 1990).

Fisch, Harold, *The Zionist Revolution: A New Perspective* (New York: St. Martin's Press, 1978).

Fishbane, Michael, *Biblical Interpretation in Ancient Israel* (Oxford: Clarendon Press, 1985).

Fox, Marvin, *Interpreting Maimonides* (Chicago: Chicago University Press, 1990).

———— "Nahmanides on the Status of Aggadot: Perspectives on the Disputation at Barcelona, 1263," *Journal of Jewish Studies*, 11:1 (1989), 95–109.

Friedman, Menachem, "Haredim Confront the Modern City," in Peter Medding (ed.), *Studies in Contemporary Jewry*, ii (Bloomington, IN: Indiana University Press, 1986), 74–96.

———— "Life Tradition and Book Tradition in the Development of Ultra-Orthodox Judaism," in Harvey Goldberg (ed.), *Judaism Viewed from Within and from Without* (Albany, NY: State University of New York Press, 1987), 235–56.

Friedman, Norman L., "Boundary Issues for Liberal Judaism," *Midstream*, 19:9 (1973), 47–52.

Friedmann, Georges, *The End of the Jewish People?* (London: Hutchinson, 1967).

Geach, Peter, "Good and Evil," *Analysis*, 17 (1956), 33–42.

Gilman, Sander, *Jewish Self-Hatred* (Baltimore: Johns Hopkins University Press, 1986).

Glatzer, N. N., *Franz Rosenzweig: His Life and Thought* (New York: Schocken, 1961).

Glazer, N., *American Judaism*, 2nd ed. (Chicago: University of Chicago Press, 1972).

Glock, Charles, and Stark, Rodney, *Religion and Society in Tension* (Chicago: Rand McNally, 1965).

Goldscheider, Calvin, *The American Jewish Community* (Providence, RI: Brown University Press, 1986).

———— *Jewish Continuity and Change: Emerging Patterns in America* (Bloomington, IN: Indiana University Press, 1986).

Goldscheider, Calvin, and Zuckerman, Alan, *The Transformation of the Jews* (Chicago: University of Chicago Press, 1984).

Gordis, Robert, "A Dynamic Halakhah: Principles and Procedures of Jewish Law," *Judaism*, 28 (1979), 263–82.

———— "To Move Forward, Take One Step Back," *Moment*, 11:5 (1986), 58–61.

Graetz, Michael, "The History of Estrangement between Two Jewish Communities: German and French Jewry during the Nineteenth Century," in Jacob Katz (ed.), *Toward Modernity: The European Jewish Model* (Oxford: Transaction Books, 1987), 159–70.

Graff, Gil, *Separation of Church and State: "Dina demalkhuta dina" in Jewish Law, 1750–1848* (Tuscaloosa, AL: University of Alabama Press, 1985).

Greenberg, Irving, "Cloud of Smoke, Pillar of Fire: Judaism, Christianity and Modernity after the Holocaust," in Eva Fleischner (ed.), *Auschwitz: Beginning of a New Era?* (New York: Ktav, 1977), 7–56.

———— *The Ethics of Jewish Power* (New York: National Jewish Resource Center, n.d.).

———— *On the Third Era in Jewish History: Power and Politics* (New York: National Jewish Resource Center, 1980).

———— *The Third Great Cycle in Jewish History* (New York: National Jewish Resource Center, 1981).

———— *Toward a Principled Pluralism* (New York: National Jewish Center for Learning and Leadership, 1986).

———— *Voluntary Covenant* (New York: National Jewish Resource Center, 1982).

———— *Will There be One Jewish People by the Year 2000?* (New York: National Jewish Center for Learning and Leadership, 1986).

Greenberg, Moshe, "Rabbinic Reflections on Defying Illegal Orders: Amasa, Abner and Joab," in Menachem M. Kellner (ed.), *Contemporary Jewish Ethics* (New York: Sanhedrin Press, 1978), 211–29.

Greilshammer, Ilan, "Challenges to the Institutions of the Jewish Community of France during the Nineteenth and Twentieth Centuries," in Stuart Cohen and Eliezer Don-Yehiya (eds.), *Conflict and Consensus in Jewish Political Life* (Ramat Gan: Bar-Ilan University Press, 1986), 31–60.

Grunfeld, L, *Three Generations* (London: Jewish Post Publications, 1958).

Halivni, David Weiss, *Midrash, Mishna, and Gemara* (Cambridge, MA: Harvard University Press, 1986).

Hammond, Phillip E. (ed.), *The Sacred in a Secular Age* (Berkeley: University of California Press, 1985).

Hartman, David, A Living Covenant: The Innovative Spirit in Traditional Judaism (New York: Free Press, 1985).

———— *Joy and Responsibility* (Jerusalem: Ben-Zvi Posner, 1978).

Heilman, Samuel C., "The Jewish Family Today: An Overview," in Jonathan Sacks (ed.), *Tradition and Transition* (London: Jews' College Publications, 1986), 179–207.

———— "The Many Faces of Orthodoxy," *Modern Judaism*, 2:1 (1982), 23–52; and 2:2 (1982), 171–98.

———— "Religious Jewry in the Secular Press: Aftermath of the 1988 Elections," in Charles Liebman (ed.), *Religious and Secular: Conflict and Accommodation between Jews in Israel* (Jerusalem: Keter, 1990), 45–66.

Heinemann, Isaac, "Marcus Horovitz," in Leo Jung (ed.), *Jewish Leaders (1750–1940)* (New York: Bloch, 1953), 261–72.

Herberg, Will, *Protestant-Catholic-Jew* (Garden City, NY: Doubleday, 1956).

Hertzberg, Arthur, "The Emancipation: A Reassessment after Two Centuries," *Modern Judaism*, 1:1 (1981), 46–53.

———— (ed.), *The Zionist Idea* (New York: Atheneum, 1981).

Hess, Moses, *Rome and Jerusalem* [1862], trans. Maurice J. Bloom (New York: Philosophical Library, 1958).

Hick, John, *Problems of Religious Pluralism* (London: Macmillan, 1985).

Hill, Michael, *A Sociology of Religion* (London: Heinemann, 1973).

Hirsch, Samson Raphael, *The Nineteen Letters on Judaism* [1836], trans. Bernard Drachman (New York: Feldheim, 1960).

———— *Judaism Eternal*, trans I. Grunfeld (2 vols.; London: Soncino, 1959).

Huppert, Uri, *Back to the Ghetto* (New York: Prometheus, 1988).

Jackson, Bernard, "Jewish Law or Jewish Laws," *Jewish Law Annual*, 8 (1989), 15–34.

Jacobs, Louis, "Comment on the Brichto Proposals," *Jewish Law Annual*, 8 (1989), 253–8.

———— *A Jewish Theology* (London: Darton, Longman and Todd, 1973).

———— *A Tree of Life* (Oxford: Oxford University Press for the Littman Library, 1984).

Jacobson, Dan, *The Story of Stories* (London: Secker and Warburg, 1982).

Jakobovits, Immanuel, *The Timely and the Timeless* (London: Vallentine, Mitchell, 1977).

—— "*Torah im Derekh Eretz* Today," *L'Eylah*, 20 (1985), 36–41.

Johnson, Paul, *A History of the Jews* (London: Weidenfeld and Nicolson, 1987).

Jung, Leo, *Human Relations in Jewish Law* (New York: Jewish Education Committee, 1967).

Kaplan, Lawrence, "Maimonides on Christianity and Islam," *L'Eylah*, 22 (1986), 31–34.

—— "Rabbi Isaac Hutner's '*Da'at Torah* Perspective' on the Holocaust: A Critical Analysis," *Tradition*, 18:3 (1980), 235–48.

Kaplan, Mordecai M., *Judaism as a Civilization* [1934] (Philadelphia: The Jewish Publication Society, 1981).

Katz, Jacob, "Contribution towards a Biography of R. Moses Sofer," in *Studies in Mysticism and Religion Presented to Gershom Scholem* (Jerusalem: Magnes Press, 1967), 115–48.

—— *Exclusiveness and Tolerance* (Oxford: Oxford University Press, 1961).

—— *Jewish Emancipation and Self-Emancipation* (Philadelphia: The Jewish Publication Society, 1986).

—— *Out of the Ghetto: The Social Background of Jewish Emancipation 1770–1870* (Cambridge, MA: Harvard University Press, 1973).

Katz, Steven T., "An Agenda for Jewish Philosophy in the 1980s," in Norbert M. Samuelson (ed.), *Studies in Jewish Philosophy* (Lanham, MD: University Press of America, 1987), 61–100.

Kaufman, Yechezkel, "The Ruin of the Soul," in Michael Selzer (ed.), *Zionism Reconsidered* (London: Macmillan, 1970), 117–30.

Keller, Chaim Dov, "Modern Orthodoxy: An Analysis and a Response," in Reuven Bulka (ed.), *Dimensions of Orthodox Judaism* (New York: Ktav, 1983), 253–71.

Kellner, Menachem, *Dogma in Medieval Jewish Thought* (Oxford: Oxford University Press for the Littman Library, 1986).

—— "Is Contemporary Jewish Philosophy Possible? – No," in Norbert M. Samuelson (ed.), *Studies in Jewish Philosophy* (Lanham, MD: University Press of America, 1987), 17–28.

Kimmelman, Reuven, "Judaism and Pluralism," *Modern Judaism*, 7:2 (1987), 131–50.

Koestler, Arthur, *Promise and Fulfilment* (London: Macmillan, 1949).

Lamm, Norman, *Faith and Doubt* (New York: Ktav, 1971).

—— "Seventy Faces," *Moment*, 11:6 (1986), 23–28.

—— *Torah Umadda* (Northvale, NJ: Jason Aronson, 1990).

Lamm, Norman, and Kirschenbaum, Aaron, "Freedom and Constraint in the Jewish Judicial Process," *Cardozo Law Review*, 1 (1979), 99–133.

Levi, Amnon, "The *Haredi* Press and Secular Society," in Charles Liebman (ed.), *Religious and Secular: Conflict and Accommodation between Jews in Israel* (Jerusalem: Keter, 1990), 21–44.

Levi, Yehudah, *Torah Study*, translation of *Sha'arei Talmud Torah* (Jerusalem: Feldheim, 1990).

Levy, Marion J., *Modernization and the Structures of Societies* (Princeton, NJ: Princeton University Press, 1965).

Liberles, Robert, *Religious Conflict in Social Context: The Resurgence of Orthodox Judaism in Frankfurt am Main 1838–1877* (Westport, CT: Greenwood Press, 1985).

Lichtenstein, Aharon, "Brother Daniel and the Jewish Fraternity," *Judaism*, 12:3 (1963), 260–80.

—— "Does Jewish Tradition Recognize an Ethic Independent of Halakhah?," in Menachem Kellner (ed.), *Contemporary Jewish Ethics* (New York: Sanhedrin Press, 1978), 102–23.

—— "The State of Orthodoxy: A Symposium," *Tradition*, 20:1 (1982), 47–50.

Lieberman, S. Zevulun, "A Sephardic Ban on Converts," *Tradition*, 23:2 (1988), 22–25.

Liebman, Charles, *The Ambivalent American Jew* (Philadelphia: The Jewish Publication Society, 1973).

—— "Extremism as a Religious Norm," *Journal for the Scientific Study of Religion*, 22 (Mar. 1983), 75–86.

—— "Orthodox Judaism Today," in Reuven Bulka (ed.), *Dimensions of Orthodox Judaism* (New York: Ktav, 1983), 106–20.

—— "Orthodoxy in American Jewish Life," in Reuven P. Bulka (ed.), *Dimensions of Orthodox Judaism* (New York: Ktav, 1983), 33–105.

———— "Religion and the Chaos of Modernity: The Case of Contemporary Judaism," in Jacob Neusner (ed.), *Take Judaism, for Example* (Chicago: University of Chicago Press, 1983), 147–64.

———— (ed.), Religious and Secular: Conflict and Accommodation between Jews in Israel (Jerusalem: Keter, 1990).

Liebman, Charles, and Don-Yehiya, Eliezer, *Civil Religion in Israel: Traditional Judaism and Political Culture in the Jewish State* (Berkeley: University of California Press, 1983).

———— *Religion and Politics in Israel* (Bloomington, IN: Indiana University Press, 1984).

Lipman, Vivian, *A History of the Jews in Britain since 1858* (Leicester: Leicester University Press, 1990).

Lookstein, Haskel, "Mending the Rift: A Proposal," *Moment*, 11:3 (1986), 58–61.

Maccoby, Hyam, *Judaism on Trial: Jewish-Christian Disputations in the Middle Ages* (London: Associated University Presses for the Littman Library, 1982).

———— *Paul and Hellenism* (London: SCM Press, 1991).

MacIntyre, Alasdair, *After Virtue: A Study in Moral Theory* (London: Duckworth, 1981).

———— "The Idea of the Educated Public," in Graham Haydon (ed.), *Education and Values* (London: Institute of Education, 1977), 15–36.

———— *A Short History of Ethics* (London: Routledge and Kegan Paul, 1967).

Macquarrie, John, *Existentialism* (London: Pelican Books, 1973).

Maimonides, Moses, *The Epistle on Martyrdom*, trans. Abraham Halkin, in *Crisis and Leadership: Epistles of Maimonides* (Philadelphia: The Jewish Publication Society, 1985), 13–90.

———— *Guide for the Perplexed*, trans. M. Friedlander (New York: Dover, 1956). Also *Guide of the Perplexed*, trans. Shlomo Pines (2 vols.; Chicago: University of Chicago Press, 1963).

———— *Responsa*, ed. J. Blau (Jerusalem: Mekitze Nirdamim, 1958).

———— *Letters of Maimonides*, trans. Leon Stitskin (New York: Yeshiva University Press, 1982).

Mendelssohn, Moses, *Jerusalem* [1783], trans. Allan Arkush (Hanover, NH: University Press of New England, 1983).

Mendes-Flohr, Paul, *Divided Passions* (Detroit: Wayne State University Press, 1991).

—— (ed.), *The Philosophy of Franz Rosenzweig* (Hanover, NH: University Press of New England, 1988).

Mendes-Flohr, Paul, and Reinharz, Jehuda (eds.), *The Jew in the Modern World: A Documentary History* (New York: Oxford University Press, 1980).

Meyer, Egon, *Love and Tradition* (Schocken: New York, 1987).

Meyer, Michael A., *Response to Modernity: A History of the Reform Movement in Judaism* (New York: Oxford University Press, 1988).

Mill, John Stuart, "On Liberty," repr. in H. B. Acton (ed.), *Utilitarianism, Liberty, Representative Government* (London: Dent, 1987).

Miller, David, "Traditionalism and Estrangement," in Phillip Longworth (ed.), *Confrontations with Judaism* (London: Blond, 1967), 197–231.

Mirsky, Norman, "Mixed Marriage and the Reform Rabbinate," *Midstream*, 16 (Jan. 1970), 40–46.

Morgan, Michael (ed.), *The Jewish Thought of Emil Fackenheim: A Reader* (Detroit: Wayne State University Press, 1987).

Mosse, George L., "Jewish Emancipation: Between *Bildung* and Respectability," in Jehuda Reinharz and Walter Schatzberg (eds.), *The Jewish Response to German Culture* (Hanover, NH: University Press of New England, 1985), 1–16.

Neusner, Jacob, From "Judaism" to "Torah": An Essay in Inductive Category Formation (New York: Hunter College, 1986).

—— *Understanding Seeking Faith* (Atlanta: Scholars' Press, 1986).

—— *Who, Where and What is Israel?* (Lanham, MD: University Press of America, 1989).

Nietzsche, Friedrich, *The Anti-Christ* [1895], trans. R. J. Hollingdale (London: Penguin Books, 1968).

—— *Twilight of the Idols* [1889], trans. R. J. Hollingdale (London: Penguin Books, 1968).

Novak, David, "A Response to the Recent Proposal of Rabbi Dr. Sidney Brichto," *Law Annual*, 8 (1989), 289–99.

Oakeshott, Michael, "The Tower of Babel," *Cambridge Journal*, 2:2 (1948), 67–83.

Ozick, Cynthia, "On Living in the Gentile World," in Nahum Glatzer (ed.), *Modern Jewish Thought* (New York: Schocken, 1977), 167–74.

Pelikan, Jaroslav, *The Vindication of Tradition* (New Haven, CT: Yale University Press, 1984).

Petuchowski, Jacob, "Plural Models within the Halakhah," in Reuven P. Bulka (ed.), *Dimensions of Orthodox Judaism* (New York: Ktav, 1983), 149–61.

Plaut, W. Gunther, *The Rise of Reform Judaism: A Sourcebook of its European Origins* (New York: World Union for Progressive Judaism, 1963).

Podhoretz, Norman, *Making It* (New York: Random House, 1967).

Prager, Dennis, and Telushkin, Joseph, *The Nine Questions People Ask about Judaism* (New York: Simon and Schuster, 1981).

Rabinovitch, Nachum, "A Halakhic View of the Non-Jew," *L'Eylah*, 1:4 (!979), 18–23.

—— "On Religion and Politics in Israel," in Jonathan Sacks (ed.), *Orthodoxy Confronts Modernity* (New York: Ktav, 1991), 123–35.

—— "The Torah Way," in Shubert Spero and Yitzchak Pessin (eds.), *Religious Zionism after Forty Years of Statehood* (Jerusalem: World Zionist Organization, 1989), 277–308.

Reines, Hayyim Z., "Isaac Jacob Reines," in Leo Jung (ed.), *Jewish Leaders (1750–1940)* (New York: Bloch, 1953), 275–93.

Robertson, Roland, *The Sociological Interpretation of Religion* (Oxford: Blackwell, 1970).

Rosenbloom, Joseph R., *Conversion to Judaism* (Cincinnati: Hebrew Union College Press, 1978).

Rosenbloom, Noah, *Tradition in an Age of Reform* (Philadelphia: The Jewish Publication Society, 1976).

Rosenzweig, Franz, *On Jewish Learning*, ed. N. N. Glatzer (New York: Schocken, 1955).

—— *The Star of Redemption* [1921], trans. William Hallo (London: Routledge and Kegan Paul, 1971).

Roth, Joel, *The Halakhic Process* (Jewish Theological Seminary of America, 1986).

Rubenstein, Amnon, *The Zionist Dream Revisited* (New York: Schocken, 1984).

Sacks, Jonathan, *Arguments for the Sake of Heaven* (Northvale, NJ: Jason Aronson, 1991).

———— *Crisis and Covenant: Jewish Thought after the Holocaust* (Manchester: Manchester University Press, 1992).

———— *The Persistence of Faith* (London: Weidenfeld and Nicolson, 1991).

———— "Rabbi J. B. Soloveitchik's Early Epistemology," *Tradition*, 23:3 (1988), 75–87.

———— "Rabbinic Conceptions of Responsibility for Others: A Study of the Command of Rebuke and the Idea of Mutual Suretyship," Ph.D. thesis (University of London, 1982).

———— "Three Approaches to Halakhah," Fifth Jakobovits Lecture (unpublished).

———— "Towards 2000: The American Experience," *L'Eylah*, 23 (Spring 1987), 23–27.

———— *Tradition in an Untraditional Age* (London: Vallentine, Mitchell, 1990).

Schachter, Jacob J., "Haskalah, Secular Studies and the Close of the Yeshiva in Volozhin in 1892," *The Torah U-Maddah Journal*, 2 (1990), 76–133.

Schiffman, Lawrence H., *Who Was a Jew? Rabbinic and Halakhic Perspectives on the Jewish-Christian Schism* (Hoboken, NJ: Ktav, 1985).

Schnapper, Dominique, "The Jews and Political Modernity in France," in S. N. Eisenstadt (ed.), *Patterns of Modernity*, vol. i: *The West* (London: Frances Pinter, 1987), 157–71.

Scholem, Gershom, *The Messianic Idea in Judaism* (New York: Schocken, 1972).

Schwab, Hermann, *The History of Orthodox Jewry in Germany* (London: Mitre Press, 1950).

Schweid, Eliezer, *Israel at the Crossroads* (Philadelphia: The Jewish Publication Society, 1973).

———— *The Land of Israel: National Home or Land of Destiny* (London: Associated University Presses, 1985).

———— "Two Neo-Orthodox Responses to Secularisation," *Immanuel*, 20 (1986), 107–17.

Shokeid, Moshe, *Children of Circumstances: Israeli Emigrants in New York* (Ithaca, NY: Cornell University Press, 1988).

Silber, Michael, "The Historical Experience of German Jewry and its Impact on the Haskalah and Reform in Hungary," in Jacob Katz (ed.), *Toward Modernity: The European Jewish Model* (Oxford: Transaction Books, 1987), 107–58.

Silberman, Charles, *A Certain People: American Jews and their Lives Today* (New York: Summit Books, 1985).

Simon, Ernst, "Rosenzweig: Recollections of a Disciple," in Paul Mendes-Flohr (ed.), *The Philosophy of Franz Rosenzweig* (Hanover, NH: University Press of New England, 1988), 202–13.

Singer, David, "Who Are Today's Modern Orthodox?," *Sh'ma*, 13:257 (Sept. 16, 1983), 112–15.

Soloveitchik, Joseph, *Halakhic Man*, trans. Lawrence Kaplan (Philadelphia: The Jewish Publication Society, 1983).

———— *The Halakhic Mind* (New York: Seth Press, 1986).

———— "The Lonely Man of Faith," *Tradition*, 7:2 (1965), 5–67.

———— "Majesty and Humility," *Tradition*, 17:2 (1978), 25–37.

Spero, Shubert, and Pessin, Yitzchak (eds.), *Religious Zionism after Forty Years of Statehood* (Jerusalem: World Zionist Organization, 1989).

Spinoza, Baruch, *Tractatus Theologico-Politicus* [1670], trans. R. H. M. Elwes (New York: Dover, 1951).

Stark, Rodney, "Church and Sect," in Philip E. Hammond (ed.), *The Sacred in a Secular Age* (Berkeley: University of California Press, 1985), 139–49.

Steinberg, Stephen, "Reform Judaism: The Origin and Evolution of a Church Movement," *Journal for the Scientific Study of Religion*, 5 (1965), 117–29.

Strauss, Leo, *Philosophy and Law* (Philadelphia: The Jewish Publication Society, 1987).

Strawson, P. F., *Freedom and Resentment* (London: Methuen, 1974).

Twersky, Isidore (ed.), *A Maimonides Reader* (New York: Behrman House, 1972).

——— "Survival, Normalcy, Modernity," in Moshe Davis (ed.), *Zionism in Transition* (New York: Amo Press, 1980), 347–66.

Unna, L, "Esriel Hildesheimer," in Leo Jung (ed.), *Guardians of Our Faith* (New York: Bloch, 1958), 215–31.

Urbach, E. E., *The Sages: Their Concepts and Beliefs* (Jerusalem: Magnes Press, 1975).

Vital, David, *The Future of the Jews* (Cambridge, MA: Harvard University Press, 1990).

Volkov, Shulamit, "The Dynamics of Dissimilation: *Ostjuden* and German Jews," in J. Reinharz and W. Schatzberg (eds.), *The Jewish Response to German Culture* (Hanover: University Press of New England, 1985), 195–211.

Weinberger, Bernard, "The Role of the *Gedolim,*" *Jewish Observer* (Oct. 1963), 11.

Williams, Bernard, *Morality: An Introduction to Ethics* (Harmondsworth: Penguin Books, 1973).

Williams, Bill, *The Making of Manchester Jewry, 1740–1875* (Manchester: Manchester University Press, 1976).

Wilson, Bryan, "An Analysis of Sect Development," *American Sociological Review,* 24:1 (1959), 3–15.

——— *Religion in Secular Society* (London: Pelican Books, 1969).

——— *Religion in Sociological Perspective* (Oxford: Oxford University Press, 1982).

——— *Sects and Society* (London: Heinemann, 1961).

Wisse, Ruth, "The Hebrew Imperative," *Commentary* (June 1990), 34–39.

Woocher, Jonathan, *Sacred Survival: The Civil Religion of American Jews* (Bloomington, IN: Indiana University Press, 1986).

Wurzburger, Walter, "Plural Models and the Authority of Halakhah," in Reuven P. Bulka (ed.), *Dimensions of Orthodox Judaism* (New York: Ktav, 1983), 149–74.

Wyschogrod, Michael, *The Body of Faith: Judaism as Corporeal Election* (Minneapolis, MN: Seabury Press, 1983).

——— "Judaism and Conscience," in Asher Finkel and Lawrence Frizzel (eds.), *Standing before God* (New York: Ktav, 1981), 313–28.

Yeres, Moshe, "Burial of Non-Halakhic Converts," *Tradition*, 23:3 (1988), 60–74.

Yinger, John Milton, *The Scientific Study of Religion* (London: Collier-Macmillan, 1970).

Zemer, Moshe, "Halakhah: Developmental and Pluralistic," *Jewish Law Annual*, 8 (1989), 259–68.

Zimmels, H. J., *Ashkenazim and Sephardim* (Oxford: Oxford University Press, 1958).

B. HEBREW SOURCES CITED

Note: This list does not necessarily include the classical sources, which are cited in the standard editions. Citations of responsa and commentaries have been annotated to indicate when the author lived.

Abrabanel, Isaac b. Judah, *Mirkevet Hamishneh* (Apulia, 1496).

Achi'ezer. Responsa by Chaim Ozer Grodzinski (1863–1940) (Vilna, 1922–39).

Akedat Yitzchak. Commentary by Isaac Arama (*c.* 1420–94) on the Pentateuch.

Amichai, Yehuda, "Da'at Torah Be'inyanim She'einam Halakhti'im Muvhakim," *Techumin*, 11 (1991), 24–30.

Aseh Lekha Rav. Responsa by Chaim David Halevi (b. 1929), 9 vols. (Tel Aviv, 1976–89).

Bar-Ilan, Meir, *Mivolozhin ad Yerushalayim*, 2 vols. (Tel Aviv, 1971).

Bat-Yehuda, Geulah, *Ish Hame'orot* (Jerusalem: Mosad Harav Kook, 1985).

Beit Habechirah. Commentary by Menachem b. Solomon Meiri (1249–1300) on the Talmud.

Beit Yosef. Commentary by Joseph b. Ephraim Caro (1488–1575) on *Tur*.

Berkovits, Eliezer, *Hahalakhah, Kochah Vetafkidah* (Jerusalem: Mosad Harav Kook, 1981).

Binyan Tzion. Responsa by Jacob Ettlinger (1798–1871).

Chajes, Zvi Hirsch, *Kol Sifrei Maharatz Chayes*, 2 vols. (Jerusalem: Divrei Hachomim, 1958).

Chatam Sofer. Responsa by Moses Sofer (1762–1839): *Orach Chayim* (Budapest, 1863); *Yoreh De'ah* (Pressburg, 1841); *Choshen Mishpat* (Pressburg, 1872).

Chazon Ish. Commentary by Abraham Karelitz (1878–1953) on the *Shulchan Arukh* (Bnei Brak: Greineman, 1973).

Dishon, David, *Tarbut Hamachloket Beyisrael* (Tel Aviv: Schocken, 1984).

Eleh Divrei Haberit [Altona, 1819], trans. in Mendes-Flohr and Reinharz (eds.), *The Jew in the Modern World* (New York: Oxford University Press, 1980), 150–56.

Etz Yosef. Commentary by Hanokh Zundel ben Yosef (d. 1867) on *Ein Ya'akov.*

Feinstein, Moshe, *Igerot Mosheh*, 6 vols. (New York: Moriah, 1959–82).

―――― Responsum published in *Techumin*, 12 (1992), 98.

Gaon, Hai, *Otzar Hageonim*, vol. iv, ed. B. M. Lewin (Jerusalem: Hebrew University Press, 1931).

Gaon, Sa'adia (882–942), *Emunot Vede'ot* (Constantinople, 1562). Trans. from Arab. by S. Rosenblatt as *The Book of Beliefs and Opinions* (New Haven, CT: Yale University Press, 1948).

Gilyon Hashas. Notes by Akiva Eger (1761–1837) on the Prague ed. of the Babylonian Talmud (1830–4), and later on the Vilna ed.

Hacohen, Israel Meir, "Chizuk Hadat," in *Kol Kitvei Chafetz Hayyim Hashalem* [Piotrokow, 1905], (New York, n.d.).

Hacohen, Malakhi, *Yad Malakhi* [1767] (New York: Bet Hasefer, 1974).

Hagahot Maimoniyot. Commentary by Meir Hakohen on Maimonides' *Yad Chazakah*, printed in most editions.

Halevi, Isaac b. Judah, *Pane'ach Raza* [1607] (Warsaw, 1860), ch. 7:1.

Hanaggid, Shmuel, *Mavo Hatalmud*, printed at the end of the Vilna ed. of tractate *Berakhot.*

Hirschensohn, Chayyim, *Malki Bakodesh*, 6 vols. (St. Louis, MO: Moirester Printing Co., 1919–28).

Igerot Harayah. See Kook, Abraham Isaac.

Igerot Mosheh. See Feinstein, Moshe.

Ish-Shalom, Binyamin, *Harav Kook: Bein Ratzionalizm Lemistikah* (Tel Aviv: Am Oved, 1990).

Katz, Jacob, "Af Al Pi Shechata, Yisrael Hu," *Tarbitz*, 28 (1958), 203–17.

Kesef Mishneh. Commentary by Joseph b. Ephraim Caro (1488–1575) on Maimonides' *Yad Chazakah.*

Kitvei Ramban. See Nachmanides.

Kook, Abraham Isaac, *Arpelei Tohar* (Jerusalem: Mosad Harav Kook, 1983).

———— *Eder Hayakar Ve'ikvei Hatzon* (Jerusalem: Mosad Harav Kook, 1967).

———— *Igerot Harayah,* 3 vols. (Jerusalem: Mosad Harav Kook, 1962–5).

———— *Olat Rayah,* 2 vols. (Jerusalem: Mosad Harav Kook, 1962).

———— *Orat Hateshuvah* (Jerusalem: Yeshivat Or Etzion, 1966).

Lamm, Norman, "Hechakham Vehachasid Bemishnat Harambam," in *Samuel Belkin Memorial Volume* (New York: Yeshiva University, 1981), 11–28.

Leibowitz, Yeshayahu, *Emunah, Historiah, Ve'arakhim* (Jerusalem: Academon, 1982).

———— *Yahadut, Am Yehudi, Umedinat Yisrael* (Jerusalem: Schocken, 1979).

Levi, Yehudah, *Sha'arei Talmud Torah* (Jerusalem: Feldheim, 1981).

Magid Mishneh. Commentary by Vidal Yom Tov of Tolosa (second half of 14th cent.) on Maimonides' *Yad Chazakah.*

Maimon, J. L., *Chidush Sanhedrin Bimedinatenu Hamechudeshet* (Jerusalem: Mossad Harav Kook, 1951).

Maimonides, *Shemonah Perakim.* For an English trans., see *The Eight Chapters of Maimonides on Ethics,* trans. J. Gorfinkle (1966).

———— *Yad Chazakah (Mishneh Torah).* For an English trans. see *The Code of Maimonides* (Yale Judaica Series, 1949–).

Mekhilta Derabbi Shimon bar Yochai, ed. J. Epstein and E. Z. Melamed (Jerusalem, 1955).

Melamed Leho'il. Responsa by David Tzvi Hoffman (1843–1921) (Frankfurt: Hermon, 1926).

Melammed, Ezra Zion, *Mefarshei Hamikra* (Jerusalem: Magnes Press, 1975).

Meshiv Davar. Responsa by Naphtali Tzvi Judah Berlin (1817–93; the Netziv) (Warsaw, 1894).

Mueller, Joseph, *Chiluf Minhagim Bein Benei Bavel Livenei Eretz Yisrael* (Vienna, 1878).

Nachmanides, *Kitvei Ramban*, ed. C. D. Chavel (Jerusalem: Mosad Harav Kook, 1964).

Pachad Yitzchak. Rabbinical encyclopedia by Isaac Lampronti (1679–1756), 10 vols. (Bnei Brak, 1981).

Rabinovitch, Nachum, "Darkhah Shel Torah," in B. Brenner, O. Kapach, and Z. Shimshoni (eds.), *Ma'alei Asor* (Ma'aleh Adumim: Ma'aliot, 1988), 8–42.

———— *Hadar Itamar* (Jerusalem: Mosad Harav Kook, 1972).

———— "Kol Yisrael Arevin Zeh Bazeh," *Techumin*, 11 (1991), 41–72.

———— *Yad Peshutah* (Jerusalem: Feldheim, 1977).

Radbaz. Commentary by David b. Solomon ibn Abi Zimra (1459–1573) on Maimonides' *Yad Chazakah*.

Rashba. Responsa by Solomon b. Abraham Adret (1235–c. 1310) (Bnei Brak, 1958–9).

Reines, Isaac, *Shenei Hame'orot* (Piotrokow, 1913).

Rema. Glosses by Moses b. Israel Isserles (1525 or 1530–1572) on the *Shulchan Arukh*.

Rivash. Responsa by Isaac b. Sheshet Perfet (1326–1408).

Schweid, Eliezer, *Demokratiah Vehalakhah* (Jerusalem: Magnes Press, 1978).

———— *Hayahadut Vehatarbut Hachilonit* (Tel Aviv: Hakibbutz Hame'uchad, 1981).

———— *Hayehudi Haboded Vehayahadut* (Tel Aviv: Am Oved, 1975).

Sefer Hachinukh. Attributed to Aaron Halevi of Barcelona (late 13th–early 14th cent.); ed. C. D. Chavel (Jerusalem: Mosad Harav Kook, 1962).

Seridei Esh. Responsa by Y. Weinberg (1885–1966) (Jerusalem: Mosad Harav Kook, 1977).

Sha'arurit Hagiyurim Hamezuyafim (Israel, 1989; no publisher or author given).

Shitah Mekubetzet. Compilation of talmudic commentaries by Bezalel Ashkenazi (c. 1520–91/4).

Silman, Yochanan, "Hikba'uyot Halakhtiot Bein Nominalizm Verealizm: Lyunim Bephilosophiah Shel Hahalakhah," *Dinei Yisrael*, 12 (1985), 249–66.

Sofer, Moses, *Derashot*, ed. by J. N. Stern, 2 vols. (Klausenberg: Friedman and Weinstein, 1929).

Soloveitchik, Joseph, *Al Hateshuvah*, ed. P. Peli (Jerusalem: World Zionist Organization, 1974).

———— *Chamesh Derashot* (Jerusalem: Tal Orot, 1974).

———— *Divrei Hagut Veha'arakhah* (Jerusalem: World Zionist Organization, 1981).

Tana Devei Eliyahu, ed. M. Friedmann (Jerusalem: Bonberger and Wahrman, 1960).

Tanya. See Zalman, Rabbi Shneur of Lyady.

Tashbetz. Responsa by Simeon b. Zemach Duran (1361–1444) (Amsterdam, 1738–41).

Turei Zahav. Commentary by David b. Samuel Halevi (1586–1667) on the *Shulchan Arukh* (Berlin, 1766).

Urbach, Ephraim, "Halakhah Unevuah," *Tarbitz*, 18 (1947), 1–27.

Wasserman, Elchanan, *Kovetz Ma'amarim* (Jerusalem: Wasserman, 1963).

Wessely, Naftali Herz, *Divrei Shalom Ve'emet* (Berlin: 1782).

Yaron, Zvi, *Mishnato shel Harav Kook* (Jerusalem: World Zionist Organization, 1974).

Zahavi, Y. Zvi, *Mehachatam Sofer ve'ad Herzl* (Jerusalem: Hasifriyah Hatzionit, 1966).

Zalman, Rabbi Shneur of Lyady, *Likutei Amarim: Tanya* [1797] (London: Soncino Press, 1973).

Index

Abarbanel, Don Isaac, 159
Abbaye, 184n54
abortion, 256
Abraham (patriarch), 140, 159, 182, 199,
    229, 230–231, 233, 236–237, 239, 246,
    261
acculturation, 3, 33, 40, 151
Acha bar Yaakov, Rav, 250
Achad Ha'am, 34, 81
Adler, Chief Rabbi Nathan Marcus, 77,
    79
After Virtue: A Study in Moral Theory
    (MacIntyre), 1, 115n35
aggadah, 113, 114
    compared with halakhah, 107–112,
        118, 130–131, 138, 184–185
    and principled defiance, 185–188
    rabbinic, 255
Agudat Yisrael, 5, 59. 90–91, 93, 95, 121n53
Akavia ben Mehalalel, 186–187, 188, 189
Akiva, Rabbi, 171n24, 188, 198, 246, 256
Alkalai, Yehuda, 5, 57
am Yisrael, 3. *See also* peoplehood
ambiguity. *See* language

*American Assimilation or Jewish
    Revival?* (Cohen), 13
antisemitism, xv, 227, 241, 242, 255
    French, 31
    gentile, 243–244, 260
    German, 77, 80
    in the nineteenth century, 150–151
    Jewish, 244
    modern, 41
    racial, xiv, 3, 25
    traumas of, 255
apostasy, 38, 67, 103, 148, 206, 246
Arama, Isaac, 103–104, 104n3, 159
"argument for the sake of heaven", 166
Ashi, Rav, 146, 247
Ashkenazim, 25, 107, 193. *See also*
    Sephardim
assimilation, 3, 16, 25, 55, 59, 68, 78, 82,
    154, 157, 210, 227, 239, 241, 243
    as defined by Cuddihy, 11
    See also intermarriage; secular
        culture and secularization
Aszod, Judah, 69
authenticity, xv, 15, 174, 175, 178, 179,
    180n47, 182, 216

authority, religious:
decline of, 145, 153, 156, 168
and principled dissent, 184–189
rejection of, 115
search for, 114–121
traditional, 117
autonomous self:
incompatible with *mitzvah*, 115
and Judaism, 179–182
and paradox of integrity, 188–191
and Reform, 95–96
See also modern self
Avodah Zarah (tractate), 67
Azulai, Rabbi Chayyim Yosef, 76–77

Babylonian exile, xvi, 158, 225
Back to the Ghetto (Huppert), 243
Bamberger, Rabbi Seligmann Baer, 92,
93, 116, 117
Bar-Ilan, Meir, 90
Bar Kochba rebellion, 22, 236, 237
Berger, Peter L., 28, 29, 95, 168, 177
berit goral (covenant of fate), 7, 89, 90,
98
berit ye'ud (covenant of destiny), 89
Berkovits, Eliezer, 203, 204, 205, 218, 252
Berlin, Naftali Zvi Yehuda (Netziv), 82,
90
Bernstein, Rabbi Louis, 46
Bildung (education in character), 61
Bleich, Rabbi J. David, 219, 220–221
Bleich, Prof. Judith, 64n35
Bloch, Rabbi Abraham Isaac, 113–114
Bloch, Rabbi Elya Meir, 121n54
"Bnei Braqism", 125
Borne, Ludwig, 241
Borochov, Ber, 5
Borowitz, Eugene, 172n31, 180–182, 215
Brenner, Joseph Chayyim, 5
Breuer, Isaac, 58, 71, 93, 95
Breuer, Rabbi Solomon, 58, 93

Brichto, Rabbi Sidney, 217n51
Britain, Jews of:
decorum in synagogue, 62, 78
English emancipation, 76–79, 90
and Ethiopian Jewry, 244
Liberal Judaism, xviii, 169–170, 175,
201, 209, 222
Orthodox Judaism, xvii
Reform Judaism, xvii, 260
and Soviet Jewry, 244
Buber, Martin, 16, 151, 195, 241
The Builders: Concerning Jewish Law
(Buber), 195
burial, laws of, 221

canonicals, 62, 77
Caro, Rabbi Joseph, 125, 218
Chabad, 86–87, 89, 116n38, 162, 257
"*chadash asur min hatorah*" (the new is
biblically forbidden), 68
Chajes, Rabbi Zvi Hirsch, 119, 190, 222,
253n81
chakham and *chasid* (sage and the
saint) typologies, 127, 128n79, 129
change, interpreting, 54–59
Chanina, Rabbi, 23
charedim (pietists), 226, 243
charity, 254
Chasidim. *See* Hasidim
Chatam Sofer. *See* Sofer, Rabbi Moses
Chazon Ish. *See* Karelitz, Rabbi
Abraham
Chibbat Zion movement, 82
chosen people, concept of, 75. *See also*
remnant of Israel
Christianity:
Maimonides on, 164, 254
separation from Judaism, 213
"church," as sociological term, 37, 103
circumcision (*milah*), xvii, 13, 201, 211,
221

"civil Judaism", 10, 12, 17–18, 42
Clermont-Tonerre, Count of, 30–31, 58,
    101
coercion, abnegation of, 38–39, 88, 145,
    226, 250–251
cohen. See *kohen*
Cohen, Jack J., 172n33
Cohen, Steven M., 13, 117n41, 210
collision of consciousness, 161–191
    commandment (*mitzvah*), xvii, 3,
        9, 37, 38–39. 42, 52, 83, 104, 196,
        111n27, 124, 142–143, 147, 155, 182,
        183, 245, 250, 253, 254, 259, 258
    acceptance of, 13, 141, 149, 211, 218,
        219, 221
    and autonomous self, 115
    Maimonides on, 202
    Rosenzweig and Fackenheim on,
        194–201
common language, Jews divided by, 6,
    191
compartmentalization, 63, 65
    Neo-Orthodox, 72
confrontation and conflict:
    halakhic resolutions, 214–222
    imperatives to resolve, 248–261
    in Israel, 145n35, 206, 225–228, 243,
        256
    nineteenth-century Jewish self-
        definition, 15–16
    in Orthodoxy, 45–46, 73, 131–132, 243
    See also fragmentation; schism
congruence:
    between self and its expressions,
        174–175
    between self and society, 126, 182
consequences, legal decision and, 108–
    109, 110
Conservative Judaism in United States,
    xvii

characterized, 163
    and conversion, 11, 201, 214, 217
    differences with Orthodoxy, 13,
        53–54, 169–170
    emergence, 28–29, 35, 51
    and "not-yet-Orthodoxy", 199, 200
    and pluralism, 245
    See also Jewish Theological
        Seminary
conversion to Judaism:
    "acceptance of the commands", 149,
        211, 218, 221
    talmudic passage on, 149–150,
        218–219
    See also "Who is a Jew?"
        controversy
conversion, forced, from Judaism, 141,
    142, 240, 253
converses, 38, 141, 142, 143, 162, 240. See
    also *marranos*
covenant:
    in Book of Genesis, 229, 233
    conservation of the, 52–54
    crises of: first, 233–236; second, 236–
        241; third, 241–245
    direction and scope of, 54, 60–63
    dualism, and "chosen remnant",
        236–241
    faith and practice, 175
    inclusivism as rationale of, 139–143,
        246–247
    keneset Yisrael as bearer of, 75
    in post-Holocaust theology, 43,
        156–160
    See also *berit goral; berit ye'ud;
        keneset Yisrael*
Cuddihy, John Murray, 11, 61
cultural duress and excusable error, 137,
    144, 247. See also *tinok shenishbah*
culture, Torah as. See *derekh eretz*

da'at torah (a, or the, Torah view), 118–121, 118n42, 119–120n51

Darwinism, theological, 240, 243–244

David ibn Abi Zimra, Rabbi (Radbaz), 206

Dead Sea Scrolls, 236–244

denominations, Jewish:
  adjectival Judaism, 29–41
  as defined, 28–29
  Judaism and, 35–36
  and misunderstanding about nature of Orthodoxy, 36–40, 51
  See also Conservative Judaism; Liberal Judaism; Orthodox Judaism; Reconstruction Judaism; Reform Judaism

derekh eretz and Torah,
  Jewish or secular, 66–70
  destiny, Jewish, xv, 5, 10, 17, 44, 54, 98, 152, 163. *See also* Jewish history

Deutz, Emanuel (*grand rabbin de France*), 78

diaspora:
  and Holocaust, 8, 157–158
  and Israel, 8–10, 227–228, 243, 260
  and Law of Return, 214, 219
  and peoplehood, 11–12
  survival of, 167–168, 259–261
  and Zionism, 227, 241–245
  See also *galut*

Disputation of Barcelona (1263), 107, 109n17

dissent. *See* integrity

dissent, principled, 184, 187, 188–189
  divisiveness, fault-lines of, xv

divorce:
  Berkovitz on, 204–205
  and British Reform, xvii
  civil, xvii, 209
  halakhic, 209
  and the *kohen*, 178
  and radical nineteenth-century Reform, 33, 201
  schismatic tendencies with regard to, 209–210
  search for agreement on, 214–217
  in the United States, 13

Dreyfus affair, 31, 81

dual Torah, Berkovits on, 204

Dubnow, Simon, 244

Durkheim, Emil, 27, 34, 61

Dworkin, Roland, 123n55, 140

East European Jewry, 90, 116, 257. *See also* Hasidim

Eckardt, A. Roy, 9

ecology, Jewish, 248

education, Jewish:
  day schools, 63, 69, 97
  and Hirsch, 63–66, 68
  as induction (*chinukh*), 246
  and Reines, 83
  supreme importance of, 251–252

eiruvin, construction of, 46, 126

Elazar, Daniel, 11, 41, 48

Elberg, Rabbi Simcha, 125

Eliezer ben Hyrcanus, Rabbi, 187–188

Elijah (prophet), 44, 94, 110, 142, 187

elitism. *See* sects and religious elitism

emancipation:
  in Eastern Europe, 80–85, 90
  in England and France, 76–79
  of European Jewry, xiv, 3, 29–31, 101
  and Holocaust, 8
  in Hungary and Germany, 90–94
  and Jewish identity, 15–16, 150
  Orthodox responses to, 55–57, 61–63, 143–147, 189–191

England, Jews of. *See* Britain

Enlightenment, 2–3, 11–12, 26, 30–31, 41,
    55, 60, 101, 115, 158, ʾ89, 193, 194, 201,
    240, 245
    Buber on, 241
    in Eastern Europe, 80
    and Holocaust, 158
    and Jewish identity, 15–16
    maskilim, 70, 82, 83
    Orthodox responses to, 190
Epistle on Martyrdom (Maimonides),
    88, 129n82, 142, 240, 253
Epistle to Yemen (Maimonides),
    239–240
Epstein, Rabbi Yechiel Michal, 130
Eretz Yisrael, 3. *See also* Israel
Esau, 142, 164, 229–230, 233, 235, 236,
    239, 253
Ethiopian Jewry, 244
ethnicity, xvi, 4, 11, 35, 133, 159, 174, 244
Ettlinger, Rabbi Jacob, 57, 135–136, 137–
    138, 143, 146, 147–148, 152–153, 157, 47
exclusivism, 245–248
excommunication, 30, 31, 186, 188, 206
excusable error. *See* cultural duress
exile. See *galut*
exorcisms, Jewish, 3
Ezekiel (prophet), 56–57, 158, 159, 159n63

Fackenheim, Emil, 7, 9, 154–156, 157, 158,
    160, 173;
    Rosenzweig and, 194–201
faith:
    after Holocaust, 155–156, 160
    and obedience to command, 182
    in practical consensus, 134–135
    traditional and practice, 175
faithful remnant. *See* remnant of Israel
Feinstein, Rabbi Moses, 214, 215, 216, 222,
    222n69
fences:
    around Jewish identity, 146

for the Torah, 68, 69, 145n35
Final Solution. *See* Holocaust
"four cubits":
    of halakah, 72, 72n52
    of Jewish culture, 66
France, Jews of, 31, 32, 62
    emancipation, 76–79, 90
Frank, Jacob, 194
Frankel, Zecharias, 34
Frankfurt, Jews of, 63, 65, 66, 69, 71,
    91–93, 95, 116, 117, 195
Freud, Sigmund, 61
Friedlander, David, 150
Friedmann, Georges, 227
fundamentalism, 27, 242. *See also* sects
    and religious elitism
fund-raising, 12, 41
Furtado, Abraham, 31
The Future of the Jews (Vital), xviii

galut (exile)3, 4, 9, 59. *See also* diaspora
Gamliel, Rabban, 187–188
Geach, Peter, 180n47
Geiger, Abraham, 190
Gemeinde Orthodoxy, 93, 102
Genesis (book), analysis, 229–233, 235,
    247, 248
Germany, Jews of:
    and antisemitism, 77, 80
    debate among, in nineteenth
        century, xvii, 60–63, 71, 76–77
    Orthodox secession, 90–98
    Protestrabbiner, 58
    Reform movement, 33–34, 58, 209
    self-derogation by Jews, 241–242
Gershom, Rabbenu, 137, 237
Gersonides, 250
ge'ulah (redemption), 3
gezerot. *See* halakhah
Glazer, Nathan, 255
Goffman, Erving, 176

Goldscheider, Calvin, 14
Graetz, Heinrich, 55
Graetz, Michael, 62, 78–79
Greenberg, Irving, 9, 42, 43, 44, 154, 156, 157, 158, 159, 160, 173, 178, 210
Grodzinski, Rabbi Chayyim Ozer, 158, 247
Guttmacher, Rabbi Elijah, 57n15, 87

Hacohen, Rabbi Israel Meir (Chafetz Chayyim), 124
halakhah:
    argument and decision in, 169–172
    as architecture of Jewish life, 25
    as constitution of a nation, 201–208
    compared with aggadah, 107–112, 118, 130–131, 138, 184–185
    and *da'at torah*, 117–120
    and definition of Jewishness, 13
    and *derekh eretz*, 87–88
    as divisive shibboleth, 41
    as "fence for the Torah", 68
    and German Reform, 33–34
    givenness of, 179
    Hirschensohn on, 89
    inclusivism, 135–138
    and integrity, 182–191
    leniency of, 124, 126, 130, 147, 218, 219
    metahalakhic principles, 252
    and moderation, 127–131
    pluralism within, 166
    and restrictive legislation (*geserot*), 88
    strategy on Jewish unity within, 161
    and stringency, 124–126
    universalism, 121–124
    See also Orthodoxy; Torah
Halakhic Man (Soloveitchik), 198
Halakhic Mind, The (Soloveitchik), 165
Halivni, David Weiss, 108n13
Hame'asef (periodical), 61

Haman complaint to Ahasuerus, 32
Hamburg, Jews of, 32–33, 33n23, 54, 63
Hameiri, Rabbi Menachem, 164, 166
hashkafah (outlook), 112
Hasidim:
    divisions in past, 25
    divisions in present, 46, 96, 242–243
    Hess on, 82
    and inclusivism, 248
    leadership, 116–117, 119–120
    variations, 106–107
    See also Chabad; Satmar
Hebrew language, revived, 22, 255, 256
Hegel, Friedrich, 115
Heilman, Samuel, 67
Heine, Heinrich, 61
Hellenizers, 23, 45. *See also* zealots
Herberg, Will, 35
heresy:
    benediction against heretics, 238
    and boundaries of faith, 175
    and Chajes, 189–190
    and *da'at torah*, 120
    excused, 154
    exclusivist view, 162
    inclusivist view, 135–147, 252–253
    and Reform, 39–40
    rule against evil speech, 248–249
    See also excommunication
Hertzberg, Arthur, 15, 157
Herzl, Theodor, 31, 58, 81, 83, 242
Heschel, Abraham Joshua. 16
Hess, Moses, 58, 80–82, 84, 150
Hick, John, 161–162
"hiding of face of God", 3, 4, 8, 42, 234, 246
Hildesheimer, Rabbi Azriel, 57n15, 93, 257, 258
Hillel, 170, 198, 218, 258

Hillel and Shammai, schools of, 47, 109, 110, 166, 170, 170n24, 212, 213, 213n46
Hirsch, Samson Raphael:
  early years, 79
  on emancipation and secular culture, 190–191
  followers of, 57, 71–72, 73
  and Neo-Orthodoxy, 16, 66
  on Orthodox as term, 36
  and Orthodox secession, 92–94, 116–117, 147
  and religious freedom, 250–251
  on revelation, 53–54
  and *Torah im derekh eretz*, 62–68
Hirschensohn, Rabbi Chaim, 87, 88, 89, 90, 130, 151, 201, 203, 203n19, 205, 207, 209, 222, 252
Hoffmann, Rabbi David Zvi, 130, 137, 147, 247
Holdheim, Samuel, 33, 40–41, 190, 209
Holocaust, xiv, xv
  and *berit goral*, 70, 90, 98
  Final Solution, 7, 8, 155, 160, 259–260
  Greenberg on, 42–43
  interpretations of, 7–8
  and Jewish consciousness, 7, 8, 11, 158
  loss of tradition, 126
  Orthodox recovery from, 97, 257
  and sense of isolation, 124
homosexuality, 178, 201, 256
Horovitz, Rabbi Marcus, 92
Hosea (prophet), 233, 249
Hungarian Jewry, 62, 68, 69, 76, 90–94, 96, 120, 154
Huppert, Uri, 243

Ibn Ezra, 108
identity crisis of modern man, 27
illegitimate descent in Jewish law. See *mamzerut*

inclusivism:
  and Book of Genesis, 247–248
  and desire for inclusion, 147–153
  and divorce, 215–216
  and exclusivism, 245–248
  halakhic, 135–138
  impact of social change, 143–147
  imperatives to resolve conflict, 248–261
  and paradox of integrity, 188–191
  and pluralism, 173–175, 193, 245–248
  and post-Holocaust theologies, 153–160
  principle of inclusivity, 103
  and rationale of covenant, 139–143
  as religious term, 162–164
integrity:
  and function, 182–184
  paradox of, 188–192
  and tradition, 184–188
intermarriage, 13, 14, 178, 183, 201, 211, 212, 227, 241
Isaac (patriarch), 164, 182, 199, 229, 230–232, 233, 235, 236, 239, 246
Isaiah (prophet), 64, 142, 159, 223, 234, 236
Ishmael, 164, 229, 230–233, 235, 236
Ishmael, Rabbi, 22, 111n28, 113
Islam, 38, 40, 141, 162, 164, 174, 240, 242, 254
Israel:
  and *berit goral*, 98
  birth of, xiv, xv, 4–5, 7, 25, 42–43
  current tendencies, 260
  da'at torah issues, 117–121
  Declaration of Independence, 4, 6
  growth of Orthodoxy, ix,
  and Jewish unity, 41–44
  Orthodox attitudes to, 45–46, 97

Russian and Ethiopian immigrants, 221–222
and secular and religious confrontation, 205–206, 225–226, 243–244, 256–257
significance of, 8–10
and the Six-Day War, 8, 89
yoredim, 12
See also diaspora; Law of Return, Zionism; "Who is a Jew?" controversy
Israel Meir Hacohen, Rabbi (the Chafetz Chayyim), 124
Isserles, Rabbi Moses, 113, 144, 206

Jabotinsky, Vladimir, 242
Jacob (patriarch), 140, 164, 229, 231–233, 234, 235, 239, 240, 241, 246
Jacobs, Rabbi Louis, 172
Jacobson, Dan, 236
Jakobovits, Lord Immanuel, 219
Jeremiah (prophet), 56, 57, 109n15, 235, 238
Jewish denominations. *See* denominations
Jewish faith. *See* faith
Jewish fragmentation. *See* fragmentation of Jewry
Jewish history:
divine call in, 259–260
divisions and dispersions, 80–81, 234, 260
at times of crisis, xvi, 260
See also destiny, Jewish
"Jewish problem, the", 3
Jewish self, traditional, 156–157
Jewish Theological Seminary of America, 34
Jewish thought, strategies of, 15–18
"Jewishness", definition of, 12, 14. *See also* "Who is a Jew?"

Jewry, fragmentation of:
as divine design, 255–256
and Jewish values, 98
and obsolescence of conflict, 243
and social processes, 157
See also confrontation and conflict; schism
Jochanan, Rabbi, 111, 137, 238, 239, 247
Jochanan ben Zakkai, Rabban, 188
Joseph, 165, 229, 232–233, 256
Josephus Flavius, 220
Judah Halevi, 55, 86, 159
Judah, Rabbi, 110, 143, 205, 238–239
Judaism as a Civilization (Kaplan), 34
Judaism:
boundaries of, 15, 79, 114, 135, 162, 166–167, 175, 210, 222
and denomination, 35–36
meaning of the word, 61
mission of, 58
"seamless robe" view of, 120
See also conversion; divorce
Judaism, language of:
conceptual ambiguity of, 10, 15, 191
Orthodoxy as language of faith, 106–107, 112, 131–132, 134–135, 248–249
rhetoric of conflict, 242, 243
imperative of moderation, 217
and language of discourse, 251–252

kabalat hamitzvot (acceptance of commands), 210
Kahana, Rabbi, 117
Kalischer, Rabbi Zvi Hirsch, 5, 57–58, 87
Kant, Immanuel, 61, 179
Kantian ethics, 2, 115, 178, 180
Kaplan, Mordecai, 34, 81, 172n33, 197
Karaites:
exclusivist view of, 162
in Jewish schools, 258

Maimonides on, 247, 258
schism with Rabbanites, 45, 104, 194
uncertain status of, 220
Karelitz, Rabbi Abraham (Chazon Ish),
126, 138, 144, 145, 146–147, 247, 250
kashrut (dietary laws), 126
Katz, Jacob, 61
Katz, Steven, 10
Kaufmann, Yechezkel, 242
kehillah (community), 31, 78, 95, 117,
199, 246
Kellner, Menachem, 17
keneset Yisrael (totality of Jews):
as bearer of covenant, 21, 75
Buber on, 241
as "church," 37, 103
as community of birth, 140, 153–154
and *da'at torah*, 121
Soloveitchik on, 89–90
See also covenant
Klatzkin, Jacob, 158
Koestler, Arthur, 227, 244
kohen, sanctity of, 178
Kook, Rabbi Avraham Hacohen:
ambiguity of writing, 16
death of, 89
on heresy, 138, 139–143
on his unique generation, 222–223
as inclusivist, 162, 247–248
and Jewish unity, 84
on "light of prophecy", 208, 208n33,
254
mysticism of, 84, 85, 106, 152
on *nefesh* and *ruach* ("soul" and
"spirit"), 152
as peacemaker, 94
and pluralism, 164, 166
on *teshuvah*, 84–85, 200
on Torah and secular culture, 71
on Zionism, 59, 87, 254, 257

Krochmal, Nachman, 190

Lamm, Rabbi Norman, 72n53, 258
Langer, Jiri, 151
Law of Return, xviii, 214, 219, 221, 222.
See also diaspora; "Who is a Jew?"
leadership, 116, 117, 206
East European Torah, 87
Halakhic, 208
lay, 41
Orthodox rabbinic, 93
prophetic, 127
religious, 28
Leibowitz, Yeshayahu, 203, 204, 205, 226,
261n99
Levy, Marion J., 72–73
Liberal Judaism. *See* Britain, Jews of
liberal Judaism (general term):
and autonomous self, 180–181
conflicting tendencies, 256
and halakhic argument, 148–151
inclusivist approach to, 252–261
and integrity, 183–184, 188–191
pluralism vs. inclusivism, 173–175
positive consequences of, 254–255
and role of choice, 178–179
Liberles, Robert, 79, 91n40
Lichtenstein, Rabbi Aharon, 46, 128n79
Liebman, Charles, 15, 39, 65, 127, 129–130
lifnim mishurat hadin ("beyond the
letter of the law"), 105, 130, 131
Lithuanian yeshivot, 70, 96
liturgical innovation, 201
The Lonely Man of Faith
(Soloveitchik), 16, 71, 96–97
Lubavitch movement. *See* Chabad
Luria, Rabbi Shlomo, 113

Maccabean revolt, xvi, 23, 225, 236
Maccoby, Hyam, 109n17, 237n20
MacIntyre, Alasdair, 1, 2, 15, 19, 177, 251

Maimon, Rabbi Judah Leib, 205

Maimonides:

on aim of rabbinic legislation, 122

on apostasy, 148–149

on *chakham* and *chasid*, 127–129

on charity, 254

on Christianity and Islam, 164, 254

on conversion and heresy, 141–143, 162, 220, 239–240, 253

disputes involving, 104, 131, 193

on divorce, 38, 147

"four cubits of halakhah", 72

on Karaites, 247, 258

on law of the rebel, 185

"Laws of Kings", 204

on legal interpretation, 108–109

legal perspectives in, 201–202

letter to Shmuel ibn Tibbon, 116

on prophets and sages, 119

on rabbinic authority, 252

on reproof and coercion, 38–39, 88, 249–250

on Sabbath desecration, 142–143

to sages of Marseilles, 55

on a Sanhedrin, 205

Mainz, Moses, 92

mamzerut (illegitimate descent in Jewish law), 213, 213n46, 214

Manasseh (King), 24

marranos, 38–141. See also *conversos*

marriage, eligibility for, 213. *See also* conversion; divorce; intermarriage

Marx, Karl, 58, 61, 241

Maskilim. See Enlightenment

Mauthner, Fritz, 241

Meir, Rabbi, 110, 143, 239

Mekhilta (early rabbinic commentary on the book of Exodus), 22, 22n1

Mekhilta Derabbi Shimon bar Yochai, 24, 238

Menasseh ben Israel, 31

Mendelssohn, Moses, 31, 94

messianic age, 6, 9, 18, 25, 33n23, 56, 58, 59, 83, 107, 111, 139, 135, 152, 164, 183, 194, 227, 237, 248, 250, 254

metahalakhic principles in Talmud, 252

Meyer, Michael A., 32–33n23

midrash (inner biblical exegesis), 24, 108n13, 196, 234, 235, 246

migrations, mass Jewish, xiv, 125

mikveh (ritual bath), 13, 92, 211

milah (circumcision), xvii,

minhag avoteihem beyadeihem (following ancestors' customs), 136, 137, 153

Mishnah:

and "argument for the sake of heaven", 73, 166

and concept of Orthodoxy, 166

and "fence for the Torah", 68

and Jewish-Gentile relationships, 67

mitzvah. See commandment

mixed marriages. *See* intermarriage

Mizrachi movement, 90, 91, 93

Mizrachi, Rabbi Elijah, 258

moderation as religious norm, 127–131

modernity, the Jewish experience of, 29–31

Modern Orthodoxy, 66, 71, 96, 102, 248

modern self, 175–178. *See also* autonomous self

Moses, 44–45, 52–53, 215, 231, 233, 249

musar (ethical discipline), 70

Nachmanides, 55, 107–108, 159, 170n24, 185, 234–235, 254

and Disputation of Barcelona, 107, 109n17

Napoleon Bonaparte, 31, 78

Nathan, Rabbi, 187

Nathansohn, Rabbi Joseph Saul, 137–138, 247

Neo-Orthodoxy, 16, 66, 79, 96

Neology (early Reform movement), 91

Neusner, Jacob, 10, 157, 227

Nineteen Letters (Hirsch), 94, 55–56, 250n68

"non-denominational non-Orthodoxy", 194

Nordau, Max, 30–31

"not-yet-Orthodoxy", 199, 200

Oakeshott, Michael, 176

optimism and pessimism, regarding unity, xii,

Orthodox Judaism in the United States: divisions within, xv, 46–47
    growing influence of, xv
    and growth of yeshivot, 125
    and Modern Orthodoxy, 66, 71–72, 102, 248
    secessionist pattern in, 97

Orthodoxy:
    adjectival, 48, 73, 104
    boundary principles of, 52
    conversion within, 13, 134, 149, 213, 218, 221
    characterized, 51, 73, 163
    divorce within, 134, 210, 213, 215, 216–217, 218
    fragmentation within, 46–47, 73, 151–152, 243
    Gemeinde, 93, 102
    history, culture, and, 51–73
    "intermediate structures" of, 97
    and inclusivism, 96–97
    and integrity, 182–184
    and Jewish peoplehood, 75–99
    and Jewish unity, 44–47
    as a language, 106–108, 134–135

Modern, 66, 71, 96–97, 102, 248, 257–258
    mutual misunderstanding with Reform, 36–40
    nineteenth-century rhetoric of, 15–16
    and "not-yet-Orthodoxy", 199, 200
    "Orthodox" as term, 31–32, 36
    and pluralism, 35–36
    and secession, 90–94, 102, 116–117, 154
    separatism as a survival strategy, 65, 97, 105
    survival and growth, xvi–xvii, 13, 158, 210, 260
    See also halakhah; schism; sects

patrilineal principle, xvii, 13, 212, 217, 220, 256

Paul of Tarsus, 237

peoplehood:
    am Yisrael (as key term), 3
    beyond parameters of halakhah, 51, 118
    concept of, 11–15
    Holocaust and Israel, 167–168
    moral-mystical dimension, 24
    and Orthodox dialectic, 152
    and Orthodoxy, 75–99
    and sanctity of Jewish people, 257, 259
    See also unity

pessimism and optimism regarding unity, 18–19

Petuchowski, Jakob, 256

Pharisees, 45, 104, 237

Pinsker, Leon, 81

pluralism, 245–248
    aggadic, 106–112, 114, 120, 121, 131
    cognitive, 165
    and concept of unity, 193

and denomination, 28–29
and divorce, 214–217
and exclusivism, 245–248
and inclusivism, 173–175, 245–248
and other faiths, in Genesis, 231
and paradox of integrity, 188–191
and post-Holocaust theology,
    as a religious term, 161
and secessionist Orthodoxy, 97
social context of, 166–169
and tradition, 164–166
Podhoretz, Norman, 11
positivism, 170n24
premarital sex, 256
Pressburg, Slovakia, 69, 70, 71, 95
Protestrabbiner, 58

rabbinic Judaism:
    and aggadah, 108–112
    and apostasy, 33
    and chosen remnant, 234, 235,
        238–241
    and concept of integrity, apostasy,
        184–188
    and *derekh eretz*, 66–70
    "dina demalkhuta dina", 33
    emergence of, 2–3
    Greenberg on, 43
    and idea of unity, 21–25, 48–49, 249
    midrash, 24, 108, 234–235, 246
    pluralism within, 164–166
    and language of respect, 248–249
    See also Maimonides
Rabinovitch, Rabbi Nachum, 139,
    148n42, 219, 250, 258n96
Rapoport, Rabbi Solomon Judah, 190
Rashbam, 108, 108n13
Rashi, 22, 108, 148–149, 198, 218, 239
Rathenau, Walter, 241
Rava, 184, 184n54

rebellious elder, case of the, 171n24, 184–
    185, 188
Reconstructionist Judaism, xvii, 3, 25, 36,
    39, 51, 133, 172n33, 193
redemption. See *ge'ulah*
Reform Judaism:
    and "not-yet-Orthodoxy", 199, 200
    and pluralism, 245, 246
    as counter-assimilatory force, 33–34,
        150
    characterized, 33n27, 163
    contemporary tendencies, 256–257
    differences with Orthodoxy, 53–54,
        174
    emergence of, 2–3, 28–29, 31–33
    and heresy, 39–40
    Hirsch and Chajes on, 190–191
    in Britain, xvii-xviii
    in Eastern Europe (historical),
        80–81
    in England and France (historical)
        76–79
    in Germany and Hungary
        (historical), 78–82
    misunderstanding of and by
        Orthodoxy, 36–40
    rhetoric in the nineteenth century,
        16, 167
    unexpected persistence of, 209
    See also Conservative
        Judaism; Liberal Judaism;
        Reconstructionist Judaism
Reform Judaism in the United States,
    xvii–xviii
    divorce and conversion, 209–214
    growth, 60
    institutional change, 201
    integrity and function, 183
    patrilineal principle, xvii, 13, 212, 217,
        220, 256

search for coexistence with, 134

Reines, Rabbi Isaac, 59, 82–84, 85, 87, 90, 151

"rejection of rejection", 229–233

religious elitism. *See* sects and religious elitism

remnant of Israel:
    accidental or chosen, 234–236, 155–156
    after the Holocaust, 7, 155
    attitudes to in nineteenth century, 250–251
    "faithful", 124
    saved and the condemned, 236–237, 240, 243
    and sectarian dualism, 240, 243
    she'erit hapeleitah, 124, 240
    she'erit Yisrael, 234

Resh Lakish, 238

revelation:
    and *berit ye'ud*, 89
    denial of, 104
    and historical progress, 54
    law as primary content of, 131
    Rosenzweig and Fackenheim on, 194–201
    and study, 251

Ritva, 145n35

Robertson, Roland, 103

Roman oppression, 110, 158–159

Rome and Jerusalem (Hess), 58, 84–85

Rosenheim, Jacob, 65

Rosenzweig, Franz, 151, 194–201, 205, 209, 222

Russian Jewry, 81, 82, 106, 221, 228, 242. *See also* Soviet Jewry

Sa'adia Gaon, 24–25, 40–41, 104

Sabbath, 6, 33, 92
    desecration of, 135–136, 138, 143, 147, 12–153, 173, 258

laws of, 46, 136, 201, 217n50, 226
    sages and saints, 127–129

Salanter, Rabbi Israel, 70

Samaritans, 45, 135, 174, 190, 220

sanctity, of Jewish people, 43, 157, 257, 259

Sanhedrin, 31, 32, 119, 171, 205
    in France (1807), 78

Sartre, Jean-Paul, 176

Satmar Hasidim, 7, 69, 87

Schick, Moses, 69

Schiffman, Prof. Lawrence, 213

schisms:
    collision of consciousness, 161–191
    divided unity", 222–223
    in the Jewish past, 45, 104
    inclusivist recommendations, 248–261
    incompatible concepts, 194
    neutralizing device, 153
    non-Orthodox attempts to avoid, 194–201
    Orthodox attempts to avoid, 201–208
    outstanding problems, 209–214
    and pluralism, 167, 169, 174, 191
    potential between Orthodoxy and Reform, 133–134, 193–223
    resolution of outstanding problems, 214–222
    within Orthodoxy, 48–49, 73, 131–132, 243
    See also excommunication; Jewry, fragmentation of; heresy

Schneersohn, Rabbi Shalom Baer, 87

Schneerson, Rabbi Menachem Mendel, 86, 257

Scholem, Gershom, 68, 151, 244

Schwab, Rabbi Simon, 113

Schweid, Eliezer, 9, 173n35, 256

"Science of Judaism", 151, 255

Secession. *See* Orthodoxy
sects and religious elitism:
    beyond sectarianism, 131–132
    characteristics of sects, 29, 95
    consequences of secession, 94–98
    elite piety, 105
    halakhah applied to aggadah, 113–
        114, 131–132
    in Israel, 207
    and religiosity, 126
    the sages on, 239
    search for stringency, 124–126
    voluntary stringency, 131–132
secular culture and secularization:
    and emancipation, 30–31
    and persistence of religion, 26–28
    as fact not value, 99
    as religious strategy, 29–30, 95
    deepening impact of, 168
    in England and France, 62, 77–79
    of halakhah, 173–174
    in Israel, 135n45, 206–207, 226, 242–
        243, 256
    post-Holocaust, 97
    resistance as a religious strategy,
        28–29
    and Orthodox strategies, 52
secular Jewish identities, 3
    of unity, 40–44
    See also *derekh eretz*; Hirsch,
        Samson Raphael
secular Judaism, contemporary:
    conflicting tendencies in, 256
    inclusivist approach to, 252–256
    positive consequences of, 254–256
selfhood. *See* autonomous self; modern
    self; Jewish self, traditional
Sephardim, 25, 107, 193
    Syrian, 218
    See also Ashkenazim

Shabbatai Zvi, 194
Shammai. *See* Hillel and Shammai
Shaw, Bernard, 6
shekhinah (divine presence), 259
Shimon bar Yochai, Rabbi, 110, 111n28,
    113, 249
Shimon ben Adret, Rabbi, 113
Shimon ben Zemach Duran, Rabbi, 113
Shulchan Arukh, 91, 125
Sifra, 238, 239
Silberman, Charles, 14
Sittlichkeit (education in respectability),
    61
Six-Day War (1967), 8, 89
social change, cognitive impact of,
    143–147
sociology of religion, terminology of, 203
Sofer, Rabbi Abraham, 69, 71, 92, 93
Sofer, Rabbi Moses (Chatam Sofer),
    54–56, 57, 58–59, 70, 72, 73, 76, 93,
    94–95, 144, 202, 222
    and secession, 76, 92–93, 94–95,
        202, 222
    and secular culture, 69, 72–73, 125
    and Zionism, 56–57
Soloveichik, Rabbi Chayyim, 71, 89
Soloveitchik, Rabbi Joseph:
    on *berit goral*, 7, 89–90
    on *berit ye'ud*, 89
    on conversion and Jewish identity,
        221
    on Israel's independence, 7
    and Mizrachi, 90
    on *teshuvah*, 200
Soviet Jewry, 12, 244. *See also* Russian
    Jewry
Spain, Jews of, xvi, 103–104, 104n3, 141,
    245
Spektor, Rabbi Yitzchak Elchanan, 130

Spinoza, Baruch, 4–5, 6, 32, 33, 40, 158,
    256
status, Jewish:
    ambiguities of, in past, 220
    basic halakhic determinants of, 134
    See also conversion; divorce
Steinsaltz, Rabbi Adin, 257
Steinschneider, Moritz, 151
Strawson, Peter, 112, 131, 181
subjectivism, compared with pluralism,
    163
Sulamith (periodical), 61
survival, Jewish, 12, 13, 15, 32, 155, 157, 158,
    159, 227
synagogues:
    choirs in, 77
    decorum in, 62, 68
Syrkin, Nachman, 5

Teitelbaum, Rabbi Joel,
Temple, second, times of, x,
teshuvah (return),
tevilah (ritual immersion), xi,
theology, Jewish:
    post-Holocaust, 153–160
    and State of Israel, 10
tinok shenishbah:
    and apostasy, 38
    generalization of concept, 144
    as halakhic strategy, 137, 153–154,
        247–248
    and language of respect, 249
    and Reform, 39–40, 256–257
Torah:
    as code or culture, 60–63
    as constitution of a people, 22, 25,
        172, 238,
    "fence around", 68, 69, 145n35
    "not in heaven", 119, 187
    as "portable fatherland", 252
    as revealed legislation, 179

Sa'adia Gaon on, 104
    and unity, 23, 47–48
Torah im derekh eretz, 62, 62n25, 63,
    64n35, 66, 67, 78, 69, 71, 72, 83, 93, 95,
    97, 102, 113–114, 120
Torah Vada'at yeshiva, 83
Tosafists, 144, 218
Tower of Babel, 26, 230
tradition and diversity, 101–132
Twersky, Isidore, 240

Ullman, Salomon (*grand rabbin de
    France*), 78–79
United States, Jews of (general):
    civil Judaism, 10, 12, 17–18
    community trends, 14–15
    unnecessary conflict, 243
    emergence of denominations,
        193–194
    intermarriage and divorce, 13–14,
        183–184, 209–214, 217–218
    See also Conservative Judaism
        in United States; Orthodox
        Judaism in United States;
        Reconstructionist Judaism;
        Reform Judaism in United
        States
unity, Jewish:
    desire for, 23, 41, 190, 263
    "divided unity" paradox, 222–223
    Greenberg on, 42–44
    incompatible conceptions of,
    Orthodoxy and, 44–47
    pessimism and optimism regarding,
        xii,
    as religious concept, xii,
    secularization of, 40–44
    See also peoplehood
Uziel, Rabbi Ben-Zion, 130

virtues of modernity, 175

Vital, David, xviii, 10, 228
Volozhiner, Rabbi Chayyim, 70
Volozhyn yeshiva, 70, 71, 82

Warsaw Ghetto uprising, 9n16
Wasserman, Rabbi Elchanan, 253n81
Weber, Max, 26, 29
Weinberg, Rabbi Yechiel, 130, 258
Wessely, Naftali Herz, 62n25
West London Synagogue (Reform), 77
"Who is a Jew?" controversy, xviii, 13,
    134, 210, 219, 220. *See also* Law of
    Return
Williams, Bernard, 180n47
Wilson, Bryan, 29, 168
women, 212
    American Reform and British
        Liberal Judaism on, 201
    distinctive roles within religious life,
        178, 204–205
    participation in elected government,
        203
    sensitivity of Jewish law to, 252
    social situation of, 46
    See also conversion; divorce;
        intermarriage
Woocher, Jonathan, 12, 17
Wuerzburger Rav, the. *See* Bamberger
Wyschogrod, Michael, 140, 188n68, 241

yeshivot, 70, 106, 123, 125, 226

Yiddish, 60, 68, 125, 242
yoredim, 12

Zalman, Rabbi Shneur, 86, 116n39
zealots, 45, 94. *See also* Hellenizers
Zera, Rabbi, 239
Zionism:
    conflicting expectations of, 226
    and diaspora, 227, 241–245
    and dissension, 91
    in Eastern Europe, 80–85
    emergence of, 3
    First Congress, 30, 58
    Hamburg temple, 54
    Hasidic attitudes (contemporary),
        85–89
    and Holocaust interpretation, 7–8
    Kook's vision, 70–71, 83–84
    Orthodox attitudes (historical), 51,
        55–57
    polemics, 16
    positive and negative stances in,
        95–96
    religious, 97, 102, 207
    secular, 58, 59, 81, 84, 85, 91, 93, 96,
        101–102, 150, 151, 167, 247, 255
    split between faith and action in,
        5–6
    Tenth Congress, 90
    theological neglect of, 10

About the Author

Rabbi Lord Jonathan Sacks (1948–2020) was a global religious leader, philosopher, award-winning author, and respected moral voice. He was the laureate of the 2016 Templeton Prize in recognition of his "exceptional contributions to affirming life's spiritual dimension." Described by HM King Charles III as "a light unto this nation" and by former British Prime Minister Sir Tony Blair as "an intellectual giant," Rabbi Sacks was a frequent and sought-after contributor to radio, television, and the press, both in Britain and around the world.

After achieving first-class honours in philosophy at Gonville and Caius College, Cambridge, he pursued post-graduate studies in Oxford and London, gaining his doctorate in 1981 and receiving rabbinic ordination from Jews' College and Yeshivat Etz Chaim. He served as the rabbi for Golders Green Synagogue and Marble Arch Synagogue in London before becoming principal of Jews' College (now the London School of Jewish Studies).

He served as Chief Rabbi of the United Hebrew Congregations of the Commonwealth for twenty-two years, between 1991 and 2013. He held seventeen honorary degrees, including a Doctor of Divinity conferred to mark his first ten years in office as Chief Rabbi, by the then Archbishop of Canterbury, Lord Carey.

In recognition of his work, Rabbi Sacks won several international awards, including the Jerusalem Prize in 1995 for his contribution to Diaspora Jewish life, the Ladislaus Laszt Ecumenical and Social Concern Award from Ben-Gurion University in Israel in 2011, the Guardian of Zion Award from the Ingeborg Rennert Center for Jerusalem Studies at Bar-Ilan University, and the Katz Award in recognition of his contribution to the practical analysis and application of halakha in modern life in Israel in 2014. He was knighted by Her Majesty the Queen in 2005 and made a Life Peer, taking his seat in the House of Lords in October 2009.

The author of more than forty books, Rabbi Sacks published a new English translation and commentary for the *Koren Sacks Siddur*, the first new Orthodox siddur in a generation, as well as powerful commentaries for the *Rosh HaShana, Yom Kippur, Pesaḥ, Shavuot, and Sukkot Maḥzorim*. A number of his books have won literary awards. *Not in God's Name*, was awarded a 2015 National Jewish Book Award in America and was a top ten Sunday Times bestseller in the UK. Others include *The Dignity of Difference*, winner of the Grawemeyer Award in Religion in 2004 for its success in defining a framework for interfaith dialogue between people of all faiths and of none, and National Jewish Book Awards for *A Letter in the Scroll* in 2000, *Covenant & Conversation: Genesis* in 2009, and the *Koren Sacks Pesaḥ Maḥzor* in 2013. His Covenant & Conversation commentaries on the weekly Torah portion, which are translated into numerous languages, including Hebrew, Spanish, Portuguese, and Turkish, are read in Jewish communities around the world.

Rabbi Sacks was married to Elaine for fifty years. They have three children and several grandchildren.

www.rabbisacks.org / @RabbiSacks